the cinema of ROBERT ALTMAN

DIRECTORS' CUTS

the cinema of
ROBERT ALTMAN

hollywood maverick

Robert Niemi

 **WALLFLOWER PRESS** LONDON & NEW YORK

A Wallflower Press Book
Published by
Columbia University Press
Publishers Since 1893
New York • Chichester, West Sussex
cup.columbia.edu

Wallflower Press® is a registered trademark of Columbia University Press

A complete CIP record is available from the Library of Congress

ISBN 978-0-231-17626-2 (cloth : alk. paper)
ISBN 978-0-231-17627-9 (pbk. : alk. paper)
ISBN 978-0-231-85086-5 (e-book)

Series design by Rob Bowden Design

Cover image of Robert Altman courtesy of Kobal Collection

Columbia University Press books are printed on permanent
and durable acid-free paper.
This book is printed on paper with recycled content.
Printed in the United States of America

c 10 9 8 7 6 5 4 3 2 1
p 10 9 8 7 6 5 4 3 2 1

CONTENTS

For Keechie (Connie), she of infinite patience and good cheer

ACKNOWLEDGEMENTS

I offer thanks to Kate Hutchins and Peggy Daub of the Special Collections Library, University of Michigan at Ann Arbor, where the Robert Altman Archive is housed. They and other archivists were most helpful in accommodating my research visit to the Altman Archive in the summer of 2013. A hearty thanks to St. Michael's College, for generously subsidizing that important and inspiring trip through a faculty development grant – and for faithfully supporting my research and writing endeavours over the last twenty-five years through numerous other grants and three sabbaticals. I am blessed to work at such a place. Thanks also to the folks at St. Michael's Durick Library, who were quick and efficient in fulfilling inter-library loan requests and purchasing Altman DVDs. I also want to acknowledge Ron Jacobs for being a friend, colleague, stimulating conversationalist and kindred spirit. His passionate, encyclopedic knowledge of counterculture history and radical politics far exceeds my own. Special thanks to Lorrie Smith, who has been a supportive and emotionally generous SMC colleague and the kindest of friends. Thanks, also, to Bill Grover, Jeff Ayres, Richard Kujawa, Joan Wry, Toni Messuri, Bill Ellis, Herb Kessel, George Dameron, Katie Kirby, Phil Yates and Joel Dando for sharing stories about life in the (teaching) trenches and reflections on film, music, pop culture and politics. Their friendly collegiality is much appreciated. On the editorial front I owe a huge debt of gratitude to Yoram Allon, Commissioning Editor at Wallflower Press. This book would never have come to fruition if it were not for his patient commitment, a commitment which never wavered – even when mine did. Thanks, Yoram, for believing in me. You are a scholar and a gentleman. Finally, my warmest thanks go to my wife, Connie Dufour, who put up with this long ordeal, watched a lot of Altman movies with me, listen to me drone on, and came to share my passion for his work. You're simply the best.

Writing a book on Robert Altman can be a daunting, even scary undertaking. Ever since he started attracting notice in the late 1960s, up until his death in 2006 and beyond, some twenty books and hundreds of articles and reviews have been published on Altman and his uneven but magnificent body of work. What would justify another book on Altman? What can one say about this legendary American film director that has not already been said, and said well, by so many others? That question dogged me during the early, tentative stages of this project. Gradually, after a lot of thought and research and a number of false starts and conceptual dead-ends, a realisation began to take shape. It occurred to me that there has been altogether too much emphasis placed on the two most obvious aspects of Altman's career: as an innovative cinematic artist and as Hollywood's *enfant terrible*, an untamed and unrepentant rebel against film industry business practices and aesthetic conventions. Both these perspectives have great merit, of course, but it seems to me neither is sufficiently *political* in the deepest and most integrative sense of the term. Focusing on Altman's artistic wizardry or his life-long battle against purely commercial filmmaking imperatives tends to obscure another and arguably more trenchant point of view, the one that considers Robert Altman as a social critic; or, to put it in more specific terms, a relentless debunker and demystifier of America's dominant ideology, the winner-takes-all ideology of patriarchal capitalism. Though putatively meritocratic and fair-minded, our long-reigning American Dream ethos has always been something of a hypocritical farce. Beneath all the carefully contrived and cheerful advertising that bombards the citizenry every day, cynicism, ruthlessness and a hyper-individualistic code of Social Darwinism prevails, one that fetishises personal wealth, success and fame without too many qualms about their manner of attainment or any other considerations, e.g. community, democracy, compassionate other-directedness or the cultivation of a genuinely creative inner life that stands apart from the single-minded pursuit of money. Unbridled artistic freedom and restless experimentation were Altman's hallmarks but, as I will argue here, his motivating passion was to comment on the state of modern American society and the thinking individual's relation to that society.

Of the many books written on Altman, four of them subject varying parts of his body of work to penetrating ideological critique: Helen Keyssar's *Robert Altman's America* (1991), Robert T. Self's *Robert Altman's Subliminal Reality* (2002), Robert Kolker's *A Cinema of Loneliness* (2011), and *A Companion to Robert Altman* (2015), edited by Adrian Danks. Keyssar's monograph offers many valuable insights but is somewhat prolix, and is now dated as it does not include coverage of Altman's last dozen films. Self's impressive study manifests a remarkable mastery of postmodern critical discourse but covers only twenty-one of Altman's three dozen films in depth, and tends to concentrate on formal and aesthetic concerns related to 'art cinema', i.e. filmmaking that defies Hollywood's classicist norms. Kolker's excellent book, updated over four editions between 1980 and 2011, does cover Altman's entire oeuvre and is easily the best written, but does not have quite the necessary depth and detail insofar as his discussion of Altman constitutes just one chapter of a book that also deals with a half dozen other film major American directors. *A Companion to Robert Altman* is a superb compilation of twenty-three critical essays by various film theorists and critics, largely from historicist and ideological perspectives, but it concentrates on about fifteen of the most celebrated Altman films (and other topic areas as well, e.g. his early television career and the critical reception to his work).

All of these works are of estimable value but there is, I think, still room for the book before you: a fairly comprehensive ideological survey of Altman's work, rendered more or less chronologically, academically rigorous but also aimed toward a more general audience, and one that delves into Altman's work, not merely as a series of filmic 'texts' to be dissected in the abstract but as experiments in filmmaking conducted in the real world, against generally hostile market forces. Accordingly, this book examines how Altman chose projects; how he adapted them from source material; how, when and where he developed, financed and shot them; how they were received and to what effect, given the politico-cultural context that prevailed at the time. Robert Altman was a naturalistic filmmaker avid to get his art as close to life as possible. He was, moreover, an intellectual without intellectualist pretensions, a misanthrope who was, paradoxically, also a compassionate student of the human condition, and very much an artist in search of creative magic and a genuine sense of community. The present study tries to do justice to these sorts of qualities and concerns.

INTRODUCTION

Well, I don't have any goals. I consider myself an artist, and I don't have anything to say. I just show what I see. This is the way it looks to me.

           – Robert Altman

Andrew Sarris, the leading proponent of auteur theory, famously averred that 'the strong director imposes his own personality on a film; the weak director allows the personalities of others to run rampant' (1996: 31). Sarris, writing just before Robert Altman emerged on the scene, did not foresee a third, counterintuitive possibility: that the strong director might allow the personalities of others healthy amounts of creative freedom and still be a 'strong' director, perhaps all the stronger for it. Over the course of a career that spanned nearly four decades, Robert Altman departed from Hollywood's quasi-autocratic directorial tradition by regularly inviting talented actors and crafts-people to make meaningful, even crucial, contributions to his films. He also deconstructed or satirised Hollywood genre conventions and cookie-cutter narrative formulae in favour of heterogeneous structures, codes and languages: a style of film-making that, in the words of Robert T. Self, tended to 'threaten, delimit, and define the apparent unity sought by dominant strains of auteur criticism' (2002: xiii). Accordingly, in his book, *Robert Altman's Subliminal Reality*, Self eschewed an auteur-centred approach to Altman in favour of a structuralist examination of Altman's major films in order to show how they 'both adhere to and embody characteristics of art-cinema narration' (ibid.).

While acknowledging that Self's approach to Altman and his films makes good sense – and that the auteur concept is problematic because filmmaking is a highly collaborative enterprise – I would argue that Altman's rejection of Hollywood's cherished narrative classicism in favour of a destabilising multifariousness of form and content still constitutes a distinctive directorial style, albeit a style that suggests the need for a subversive revision of auteur theory, at least in Altman's case.[1] What follows, then, is an auteur-centred, historicist approach to Altman that draws on psychoana-lytic, Marxist, feminist and structuralist theory, and acknowledges the special challenges Altman's case poses to the director-as-author paradigm.

Altman's Background

Robert Altman was born on 20 February 1925 in Kansas City, Missouri, which he later described as 'a rather uneventful, American middle-class community' (in Zuckoff 2009: 11). Altman had, by his own account, an 'ordinary, untraumatic' childhood.[2] His father, Bernard Clement ('B.C.') Altman (1901–1978), was a highly successful insurance salesman but also a womaniser, a compulsive gambler and something of a con man (see Zuckoff 2009: 19). According to his third wife, Kathryn, Altman was 'influenced a lot by his dad and his dad's behavior' (in Zuckoff 2009: 24). As Altman told interviewer Aljean Harmetz, 'I learned a lot about losing from him: that losing is an identity; that you can be a good loser and a bad winner; that none of it – gambling, money, winning or losing – has any real value; that the value you thought came with winning $10,000 simply isn't there; that it's simply a way of killing time, like cross-word puzzles' (in Sterritt 2000: 15). Patrick McGilligan asserts that Altman 'came to emulate his father. Like B.C., he became the outgoing con salesman and the mischie-vous charmer, the incessant gambler, and the scandalous womaniser. But at the same time – unhappily – Altman grew remote from his father' (1989: 32). Robert T. Self and Terry F. Robinson argue that the 'biography of Altman's professional career indicates that Altman's antipathy to producers, writers, and stars derives from his never-resolved feelings of inferiority and insecurity around the imposing and threatening figure of his father, "B.C."' (2000: 54). Self and Robinson go on to observe that Altman's films are rife with images of dominating or absent fathers. On the other hand, his mother, Helen (née Matthews) Altman, a Mayflower descendant from Nebraska was, according to Altman's high school girlfriend, Jerre Steenhof, 'the sweetest, most considerate, charming lady' (in Zuckoff 2009: 19). She and Altman's two younger sisters, Joan and Barbara, evidently provided feminine nurturance and gentility to counter B.C.'s brash, self-centred ways. Another major influence was Glendora ('Glen') Majors, a wise, tough-minded but kind African-American maid who served as confidante and intermediary between young Bobby and his parents. According to Altman's friend, Harry Belafonte, Glen also 'opened him up on race. He'd see through her eyes. She played an important part in his growing up, maturing, and in that maturity, found his centre' (in Zuckoff 2009: 28). Majors also introduced Altman to jazz music (a legacy he would showcase in *Kansas City* (1996)).

In sum, unusually comfortable circumstances and female love and stability leav-ened male adventurousness to produce the more or less confident, assertive, risk-tol-erant extrovert that was Robert Altman. But these two ingrained polarities – empathy and other-directedness on the one hand, and an inveterate gambling instinct on the other – were in tenuous balance and made for a complex, conflicted personality, at once intensely amicable but also restless, proud, sensation-seeking and highly individ-ualistic. As McGilligan notes, Altman's self-image was 'as a lone wolf and an outsider

... a maverick, a gadfly, a posturer above the fray' (1989: 40). Self and Robinson note that Altman's films tend to 'explore a troubled masculinity, perceived as a refusal, a fear, a lack, a breakdown, a violation of authority. Together with the exploration of the displacement of women from roles of social power and control, these films develop a subjectivity of the guilty male, insecure and defensive, in retreat from the very phallic authority to which by his gender and the tradition of modernism he is naturally heir' (2000: 54). The troubled masculinity – and empathy for women – that runs through much of Altman's work obviously emanated from Altman's vexed relationship with his father.

Another key formative element in Altman's upbringing was his Catholicism. His parents, both staunch Catholics, enrolled him at St. Peter's School, a Catholic parochial school in Kansas City, which he attended from 1931 to 1938 (ages six to thirteen). Altman also briefly attended Rockhurst High School (a Jesuit institution), before transferring to Southwest High School (a public school), and then attending Wentworth Military Academy in Lexington, Missouri, from which he graduated in 1943. Though Altman often denied the Catholic influence, his years at St. Peter's and Rockhurst were undoubtedly crucial to the formation of his personality. Catholic schools not only provided a solid educational foundation but also instilled in him self-discipline, a strong work ethic and an elevated moral awareness: attributes that would serve him well for the rest of his life. As he matured, Altman rejected the Church's social and sexual conservatism and would later ridicule religion in some of his films (e.g., *M*A*S*H* (1970), *McCabe & Mrs. Miller* (1971), *A Wedding* (1978)). Though he renounced Catholicism, Altman remained a nominal Catholic – he had his children baptised – and appears to have struggled all his life with the nagging, nebulous sense of guilt that most Catholics, lapsed or not, tend to experience. His biographer, Patrick McGilligan, reports that Altman's friend, John Stephens 'believed Altman to be very conflicted about his Catholic upbringing, and guilty, still, for having torn himself away from it. "He was fighting against it... Anyone with a strong Catholic upbringing who breaks away from it will always have those guilt feelings as to whether or not you're really doing the right thing. Once you're exposed, once you're taught, you can say anything you want to say about what you don't believe – but what is it you don't believe?"' (1989: 146). Paul Giles argues that a 'residual element of cultural Catholicism is imbedded in the formalistic patterns of Altman's movies' (1991: 156), as evidenced by the preponderance of ritual moments in Altman's films (e.g., weddings and funerals). Giles also notes that the Catholic imagination tends to be analogical, a mode of thinking that stresses 'the interpenetration of unity and multiplicity, sameness and difference'. For example, *A Wedding*, 'formalistically and thematically emphasizes analogies and resemblances among heterogeneous groups of people'; furthermore 'the central theme of *Brewster McCloud* (1970) is the communal nature of social life, the necessary sharing and indeed interchangeability of human characteristics' (1991: 147). In sum, Giles sees Altman and America's other great Catholic film director, John Ford, as rejecting 'the dialectic of good and evil, opting instead for an all-embracing universalism. Their styles of filmmaking, with a heavy emphasis on ritual and a consequent tendency to disrupt and dislocate the solipsistic vision of any one individual character, function as a corollary to this thematic impulse' (1991: 163). Indeed, it takes no great leap of imagination to see that Altman's fondness for ensemble work and his affinity for de-centred, multi-protagonist films that downplay the role of the individual hero derive from the communitarian ethos that Catholicism imbued within him.

Still more critical than his parents' influence and Catholic upbringing to Altman's mature sense of self was his service in World War II. After graduating from Wentworth Academy, Altman joined the United States Army Air Forces at the age of nineteen. During the war, Altman flew an astonishing forty-five bombing missions as the co-pilot of a B-24 Liberator with the 307th Bomb Group, 13th Air Force, in Borneo and the Dutch East Indies. His friend, Frank W. Barhydt later observed, 'all that he saw and all that he experienced, and how long past the longevity of an average pilot he lived, all that had an effect on him. It had a lot to do with how he lived his life' (in Zuckoff 2009: 53). Altman's friend, Garrison Keillor, put it more forcefully: 'When you have done that at the age of nineteen or twenty you really have crossed a bridge ... left your youth in Kansas City behind you. And that's how you get the chance to die old and beloved and distinguished in California, by being extremely lucky when you are nineteen or twenty. He really was a man who believed in his luck. When you've flown fifty missions in a B-24 Liberator bomber over the Pacific, what's the worst they can do to you in the movie business? Nothing. Nothing whatsoever' (in Zuckoff 2009: 52).

Also crucial to Altman's formation as a filmmaker and unique to him among his peers was his long and deep apprenticeship in industrial filmmaking and television work in the 1950s and 1960s. Many of Altman's younger contemporaries in New American Cinema (Martin Scorsese, Francis Ford Coppola, George Lucas, Steven Spielberg, Paul Schrader and Terrence Malick) were the products of graduate film programmes. Altman's training was strictly on-the-job. Following unsuccessful post-war stints in Hollywood and New York City, Altman moved back to Kansas City in 1949 and worked as a writer-director for the Calvin Company, an educational and industrial film production outfit that was the largest and most successful film producer of its type in the United States. Over the next eight years Altman wrote and directed some sixty-five 16mm industrial training films and documentaries for the Calvin Company and learned every imaginable aspect of the filmmaking process from the ground up. In 1957 he released his first full-length fiction film, *The Delinquents*, a Kansas City-based teen exploitation opus purchased for distribution by United Artists that resulted in a tidy profit for Altman and a return to Hollywood, where he co-directed *The James Dean Story* (1957), a feature-length documentary put out to capitalise on the burgeoning James Dean youth cult that emerged after Dean's death in a car crash in September 1955. Altman subsequently spent the next decade as a TV director, directing more than 120 half-hour episodes of some two dozen network television series, most notably *The Millionaire, Whirlybirds, Troubleshooters, U.S. Marshal, Bonanza, Bus Stop* and *Combat*. After what could be termed a twenty-year 'apprenticeship', Altman's career as a Hollywood film director began in 1967, when Warner Bros./Seven Arts hired him to direct *Countdown* (1968), a low-budget space-flight drama starring James Caan and Robert Duvall – a project from which he was ultimately fired by Jack Warner for allowing overlapping dialogue.

Larger cultural changes he lived through also shaped Altman in profound ways. Raised in affluent circumstances in heartland America in a relatively innocent time, Altman was thrust into postmodernity by World War II and then sexually and emotionally liberated by the postwar cultural thaw that soon followed. Though orderly and driven in his work habits, Altman was a hedonist by disposition. He lived large, worked compulsively and played hard. He was a heavy drinker and a marijuana enthusiast throughout his adult life: manifestations, perhaps, of a naturally ebullient personality but perhaps more likely indicative of a man struggling to escape or insulate himself from insoluble inner contradictions.

All of the factors just alluded to – Altman's innate temperament, his family background, his Catholic schooling, his war service, his protracted apprenticeship – made him a disciplined, resourceful and technically proficient filmmaker. The banality of so many of the film projects that were thrust his way in the early years also made him a restless innovator. To allay boredom and dress up otherwise hackneyed material, Altman experimented with visually exotic location shooting, inventive sound techniques, unorthodox camera work and other tactics used to suppress artifice and heighten a sense of spontaneous reality. As Altman progressed in his career, he honed these techniques and also came to understand that his preference for exploring human character and relationships over linear, plot-driven scripts depended upon an abiding trust in the creativity of his actors. As he told an interviewer,

> When I cast a film, most of my creative work is done. I have to be there to turn the switch on and give [the actors] encouragement as a father figure, but they do all the work… All I'm trying to do is make it easy on the actor, because once you start to shoot, the actor is the artist… I have to give them confidence and see that they have a certain amount of protection so they can be creative… I let them do what they became actors for in the first place: to create. (Stevens Jr. 2012: 7–8)

Regarding the Altmanesque

What is stylistically characteristic about Robert Altman's films? By and large, Altman was what might be termed a naturalistic filmmaker. Mostly character-driven and open-ended, Altman's films aspire to be plausible renditions of life's unfolding chaos while undermining film genre clichés. Hence, storytelling is de-emphasised. The use of multiple plots, loose plots or virtually no plots at all, subverts conventional Hollywood narrative mechanics in favour of a focus on evolving human behaviour and relationships that elude definitive closure. Accordingly, Altman films typically feature 'natural' (i.e. desultory, sometimes actor-improvised) dialogue and richly textured visual content (i.e. wide-screen compositions and mobile, fluid camera work; e.g. a profusion of long shots, telephoto shots, arcing crane shots, slow tracking shots, zooms, etc. in lieu of more stable/stabilising deep focus shots, close-ups and shot/reverse-shot sequences). Altman films are also famous for being aurally dense and realistic (i.e. lots of overlapping, even simultaneous, dialogue and ambient sound). Taken together, these formal practices make for a busy, diffuse *mise-en-scène* that problematises point of view or disperses it to the periphery, necessitating heightened attention and greater viewer involvement.

In terms of character depiction, Altman's films are consistently anti-heroic; they tend to feature deluded, passive, manipulative or marginalised protagonists. For example, in Altman's women-centred films – *That Cold Day in the Park* (1969), *Images* (1972), *3 Women* (1977) and *Come Back to the Five and Dime, Jimmy Dean, Jimmy Dean* (1982) – his oppressed and neurotic female protagonists undergo catastrophic personality implosions. In more ironic and less emphatic ways, most Altman films echo some of the salient features of a different genre: American literary Naturalism, a deterministic subset of the Realism tradition, insofar as he depicts the typical American individual as orthodox and lacking in self-awareness, i.e. always-already interpellated by, and therefore at the ultimate mercy of, a venal and cynically manipulative social order.[3] Altman also subverts the bourgeois subject structurally, by deemphasising its centrality to the cinematic narrative. Quite a number of Altman's films – *Nashville* (1975), *A Wedding, HealtH* (1980), *Short Cuts* (1993), *Prêt-à-Porter* (1994), *Gosford Park* (2001), *A Prairie Home Companion* (2006) – employ large ensemble casts in multi-plotted carnivalesque fashion, rather than the traditional hero-protagonist (or two), around which the standard Hollywood storyline revolves: a formal tendency that carries strong ideological implications. Altman further destabilises character representation through casting choices. His films usually feature celebrity actors but often in roles that use their established star personae in ironic or subversive ways. He also puts major stars in minor roles or has them play themselves in cameo, or turns musicians into actors (e.g. Lyle Lovett, Tom Waits, Huey Lewis), or actors into musicians (e.g. *Nashville*). Such Brechtian stratagems combine with the typically decentred and multivalent Altman *mise-en-scène* to undermine representations of the stable subject while also deflating the dominant American ideology of heroic hyper-individualism: characteristics that militate against easy viewer identification and are therefore guaranteed to baffle viewers accustomed to more familiar fare.

As for Altman's recurrent themes – isolation, loneliness, madness, betrayal, deception, theatricality, deal-making, social climbing, gambling, delusion, failure, death – these rather grim motifs add up to a vision of America as an atomised society of driven, often desperate hustlers, a vision that runs counter to the dominant 'American Dream' ideology that simplistically equates individualism with 'freedom' and autonomy. In terms of narrative pedigree, Altman's perennial themes exemplify what Northrop Frye dubbed the 'archetype of autumn: tragedy' but are more thoroughly evident in Frye's 'archetype of winter: irony and satire', which are the forms that dominate Altman's oeuvre. Indeed, most of Altman's films are satiric on three broad, interlocking levels: (i) they deconstruct the bourgeois myth of the stable self and satirise its vacuity; (ii) they dramatise the exploitation and duplicity that marks interpersonal and larger social relationships in capitalist patriarchy; (iii) they expose and satirise Hollywood genre conventions as absurd clichés emblematic of an infantilising culture industry. All the devices noted above, and the characteristic Altmanesque themes and concerns they enact and support, might best be described as existentialist. *Contra* dominant pieties that extol the stable bourgeois subject moving confidently through an essentially just and well-ordered world, Altman's movies typically depict fragile and confused human beings often living in 'bad faith' (passivity, denial, self-deception) but nonetheless 'condemned to be free', as Sartre puts it, by the boundless, protean nature of the Real, whose centrifugal force insistently supersedes individual schemes and societal constructs.[4]

Still, a formal analysis of the films as finished products is incomplete and somewhat misleading. For Altman, the filmmaking *process* was as important and gratifying as the finished film itself – perhaps even more so. In a 1977 interview, when publicist Jack Hirschberg asked what really drove him the most, Altman replied, 'Well, I don't know. I call it the sand castle syndrome. I like to play. And I know that the joy or fun of it is in the doing – not in the result. Once it's finished it's in the can in a closet somewhere. Or the ocean comes and takes it away.'[5] While Altman satirised the American hustler mentality, he was himself a compulsive gambler and hustler, always working or scheming to finance new work. What separated him from the object of his derision was that his primary purpose was to make art, not money. Accordingly, Altman assumed the role of a Prospero-like *paterfamilias* on set, working with a changing but 'dependable community of production people and players, a mini-studio in which the logistics and complexities of his films were worked out among individuals familiar and comfortable with his methods and approach' (Kolker 2011: 305). As McGilligan nicely put it, 'It [was] as if his collaborators [were] a bridge to the self for Altman, as well as to the audience' (1989: 329). In a way, Altman was a throwback to the pre-modern artist. Encouraging collaboration, improvisation and company solidarity – creative suggestions were welcome (though not always implemented), attendance at nightly rushes was strongly encouraged and socialising was routine – Altman created and orchestrated a series of small societies of creative fellowship, something like latter-day crafts guilds for each of his film projects. Consciously or not, Altman was trying to replicate what German sociologist Ferdinand Tönnies idealised as 'Gemeinschaft' (Community): a cohesive congregation marked by informal, cooperative relations based on cultural homogeneity and imbued with a sense of loyalty and moral obligation to the group, i.e. the kinds of relationships found in hunter-gatherer, horticultural and other small-scale societies before the development of industrial capitalism. Not surprisingly, Altman's films often satirise Gemeinschaft's polar opposite, 'Gesellschaft' (Society), i.e. the sort of rationalized, impersonal, large-scale social order that is epitomised by the modern, technocratic-corporate state and characterised by centralized bureaucracy, wholesale corruption, class stratification, division of labour, political disenfranchisement, and the lonely and alienated pursuit of individual self-interest. It must be noted, though, that Tönnies' categories – Gemeinschaft and Gesellschaft – are ideals that have never existed in pure form. While Altman sought to make unconventional movies in unconventional ways, he was still beholden to the powers that be for financial backing. That he made as many films as he did for so little money while so many of them were unprofitable was a miracle of ingenuity on Altman's part that will never be repeated.

To sum up, stylistic and thematic features common to Altman's films and filmmaking process suggest a homologous series of binary oppositions. Helene Keyssar identified these 'points of tension and conflicts of values' as 'community and indi-vidualism, mediation and realism, reproduction and production [as] the primary oppositions in the stories Altman tells' (1991: 16). I would add others: plot and char-acter, authority and subversion, stasis and fluidity, univocality and multifariousness, commercialism and aestheticism, Gesellschaft and Gemeinschaft. All these related dichotomies, ultimately weighted toward the second term, point to an artist in search of authentic community but knowing full well that, in modern business civilisation, the search is likely to find its object only intermittently, if at all. At the same time, Altman's iconoclastic investigation of social structures and mores, combined with his compulsive work habits and restless experimentalism, indicates an outer-directed flight from self-consciousness, a perennial escape from inwardness. Altman admitted as much in his interview with Jack Hirschberg:

> I really try not to look upon myself because the minute I – I mean even this conversation I consider as dangerous. I mean I really think it's dangerous. I really think that the minute I start to lose my naïveté – the minute I lose an honest enthusiasm – the minute I have to say 'oh, I wonder what so and so is going to think about that when I say it' – then I decide not to say it. There's value gone. Then I'm only saying the safe things… And if you start thinking about yourself or how you look or about how you're going to appear – and it's impossible… You're limiting you're creativity, your ability to do what you want to do. That's why I drink a lot. I like to get stoned or whatever. And just somehow keep my attention away from my own thoughts…[6]

Altman's ostensible rationale for avoiding introspection as 'dangerous' because it stifles the spontaneous creative impulse is plausible enough on its own terms, and certainly a staple axiom of romantic aestheticism (i.e. the 'anti-self-consciousness theory' that dates back to Thomas Carlyle and the British Romantic poets). At the same time, Altman's flight from self-reflexivity and inwardness might be seen as an instinctive evasion of core feelings that could only foster aesthetic paralysis, probably feelings of self-loathing and self-doubt. For Altman, obsessively making films was his best means of constructing a heroic self-concept, keeping a step or two ahead of his demons, main-taining a sense of community, amusing himself and contributing something mean-ingful to the world. Many artists are similarly motivated; what makes Altman rather unique, especially in the world of cinema, is the relentless intensity he brought to his life's mission. For him, filmmaking wasn't just a profession; it was a deeply personal struggle against his own alienation, the alienation that pervades everyday life in the modern world. Not to say that Altman was a Marxist; he was a liberal democrat. Nor was he consciously pursuing a sophisticated ideological agenda – very few filmmakers do – but his films were political in the sense that all films are ineluctably 'political'; that they cannot help but bear some definite relation to the dominant ideology, a relation that is conformist, ambiguous or oppositional. Altman's films tend toward the latter two categories, hence their limited popular appeal but their enduring fascination for film scholars and critics.

In 'Cinema/Ideology/Criticism' (1969), a groundbreaking *Cahiers du cinéma* essay on the ideological analysis of movies, Jean-Luc Comolli and Paul Narboni assert that 'film is ideology presenting itself to itself, talking to itself, learning about itself. Once we realize that it is the nature of the system to turn the cinema into an instrument of ideology, we can see that the filmmaker's first task is to show up the cinema's so-called "depiction of reality". If he can do so, there is a chance that he will be able to disrupt or possibly even sever the connection between the cinema and its ideological function' (1976: 25). Comolli and Narboni go on to divide all movies into six general categories ('a' – 'f') that cover, in descending order, the spectrum from strict conformity to strident opposition to the dominant, capitalist ideology. Of particular interest is category 'e' because it's the one that best defines Altman's work:

> Films which seem at first sight to belong firmly within the ideology and to be completely under its sway, but which turn out to be so only in an ambiguous manner. For though they start from a non-progressive standpoint, ranging from the frankly reactionary through the conciliatory to the mildly critical, they have been worked upon, and work, in such a real way that there is a noticeable gap, a dislocation, between the starting point and the finished product... The films we are talking about throw up obstacles in the way of the ideology, causing it to swerve off course. The cinematic framework lets us see it, but also shows it up and denounces it. Looking at the framework one can see two moments in it: one holding it back within certain limits, one transgressing them. An internal criticism is taking place that cracks the film apart at the seams. If one reads the film obliquely, looking for symptoms; if one looks beyond its apparent formal coherence, one can see that it is riddled with cracks; it is splitting under an internal tension which is simply not there in an ideologically innocuous film. (1976: 27)

Though recognisably 'Hollywood', Altman's films are filled with the 'internal tension' that Comolli and Narboni describe: self-deconstructive fissures that induce viewers to glimpse the artifice beneath the movies' putative 'depiction of reality' and perhaps begin to recognise that artifice is ideology (and vice versa): a political construct, not 'the way things are' and, as such, worthy of interrogation and rethinking.

***

As noted above, Robert Altman was, by and large, a satirist whose interrelated target areas were conventional ideologies of self, society and the filmmaking industry. His best films managed to attack all three areas with nearly equal efficacy. More often, though, Altman went through phases that concentrated on one of these areas or oscillated between them. Accordingly, this book's structure represents a slight compromise between chronological and thematic arrangements, to highlight those shifts in approach and emphasis. Chapter one, 'Three Dream Films: Explorations of Female Identity', deals with those of Altman's films that deconstruct the myth of the stable bourgeois subject under patriarchy: *That Cold Day in the Park* (1969), *Images* (1972) and *3 Women* (1977). Chapter two, 'Experiments in Genre Revision', surveys the many films that deconstruct the conventions governing various Hollywood film genres: *M*A*S*H* (1970), *Brewster McCloud* (1970), *McCabe & Mrs. Miller* (1971), *The Long Goodbye* (1973), *Thieves Like Us* (1974), *California Split* (1974) and *Buffalo Bill and the Indians, or Sitting Bull's History Lesson* (1976). Chapter three, 'Large Canvases', focuses on Altman's early multi-protagonist satires of modern American business civilisation as dehumanising Gesellschaft: *Nashville* (1975) and *A Wedding* (1978). Chapter four, 'Falling from Grace', examines the string of artistic misfires that marked the end of Altman's most fecund filmmaking period: *Quintet* (1979), *A Perfect Couple* (1979), *HealtH* and *Popeye* (1980). Chapter five, 'In the Wilderness', covers Altman's exile from Hollywood in the 1980s, when he directed theatre, dabbled in opera and filmed a series of stage plays: *Come Back to the Five and Dime, Jimmy Dean, Jimmy Dean* (1982), *Streamers* (1983), *Secret Honor* (1984) and *Fool for Love* (1985) and other works. Chapter six, 'Return to Form', covers the projects that returned him to prominence: *Tanner '88* (1988), *Vincent & Theo* (1990), *The Player* (1992) and *Short Cuts* (1993). Chapter seven, 'Final Phase: More Large Canvases and Minor Works', deals with the large-ensemble films that dominate the last phase of Altman's career: *Prêt-à-Porter* (1994), *Kansas City*, (1996), *Gosford Park* (2001), *The Company* (2003) and *A Prairie Home Companion* (2006). As for an overall pattern to Altman's career, one can see that early explorations of individual identity give way to genre deconstructions, which give way in turn to big cast mosaics, then play adaptations, and then another and final raft of big cast mosaics and minor works. The movement is from self, to craft, to larger society in ever widening arcs and with a growing sense of empathy; Altman's last film – *A Prairie Home Companion* – shows none of the bitterness that permeates earlier 'large canvas' projects. It seems that Robert Altman made peace with his world in the end.

Notes

1   As applied to himself, Altman thought that 'auteur theory is wrong. I mean I think I work in a much more collaborative way. It depends on your description of auteur'. From the transcript of an unpublished Altman interview with Jack Hirschberg that took place in Waukegan, Illinois on 4 June 1977, p. 34; Altman Archives, University of Michigan, Ann Arbor.

2   From Hirschberg's interview, Waukegan, Illinois, 4 June 1977, p. 1.

3   Eric Sundquist's definition of American Naturalism: 'Reveling in the extraordinary, the excessive, and the grotesque in order to reveal the immutable bestiality of Man in Nature, naturalism dramatises the loss of individuality at a physiological level by making a Calvinism without God its determining order and violent death its utopia' (1982: 13).

4   Critics have complained that Altman's work is cynical if not misanthropic and criticise him for wallowing in the epiphenomena of capitalist modernity without discovering and critiquing root causes. Yet as Robert Kolker points out, 'Altman,

finally, cannot be singled out for a failure to deal directly with the abhorrent situations he perceives or to seek more deeply for causes. No other American filmmaker does, and Altman is the only filmmaker who has sought as much and as consistently' (2011: 380).

5   From Hirschberg's interview, Waukegan, Illinois, 4 June 1977, p. 25; Altman named his production company 'Sandcastle 5'.

6   Ibid., 57–8.

CHAPTER ONE

Three Dream Films: Explorations of Female Identity

I think I've supported the feminists. I'm not showing you the way I think things should be, but the way things are. That is the way women are treated. I got a lot of flak after *M*A*S*H* in 1970, they said, oh, it's terrible the way you treat... I say, it isn't the way I treat women, that's the way I see them treated. So I'm making my point for you.

– Robert Altman

From its inception to the present day, the Hollywood film industry has been remorselessly male-oriented in its hiring practices, ideology, subject matter and visual strategies. Though innovative in other ways, the New American Cinema did not depart from, or repudiate, phallocentricism. If anything, American films of the 1960s and 1970s were some of the most sexist and misogynist in the industry's history. In this context it is rather remarkable that Robert Altman made a number of films that actually focus on women: their desires, vulnerabilities and sexual, psychological and emotional problems, most of which arguably stem from a traditionally subordinate position *vis-à-vis* men. This does not make Altman a 'feminist' but it does manifest an easy confidence in his own masculinity and a commendable willingness to step outside the strict confines of the Hollywood code of phony machismo that is in keeping with his generally iconoclastic tendencies.

Persona / Personae

Certainly two but arguably three of Altman's early films dealing with women – *That Cold Day in the Park, Images* and *3 Women* – have their creative genesis and inspiration in Ingmar Bergman's enigmatic masterpiece, *Persona* (1966; released in the US in 1967). In an interview with David Thompson, Altman admitted that *Persona* 'impressed me a lot. I'm sure that film was largely responsible for *Images* and *3 Women*. There was a power in *Persona*, and I think that came from the fact that one woman talked and the other didn't, more than anything else. We know the situation, and if we know all these situations, then we have a certain expectation of what these situations are going to bring. The trick, to me, is not to bring [about] that expectation' (2006: 71).

Though largely unknown by American audiences outside of graduate film courses and art-house revivals, Bergman's *Persona* remains a key film in European avant-garde cinema. Indeed, its powerful influence on Altman also makes it an important precursor of the New American Cinema as well. Bergman's scenario is virtually without plot. Elisabeth Vogler (Liv Ullmann), a prominent Swedish actress, goes mute during a stage performance of Aeschylus's *Electra* – presumably because she is depressed by the state of the world and has had her fill of empty roles, whether on stage, as a wife, a mother, or in any other capacity. Her doctor (Margarethe Krook) suggests a long convalescence at the doctor's summer cottage on the tiny, remote island of Fårö, Northern Gotland. Looking after her is Sister Alma (Bibi Andersson), a naïve young nurse who carries on a nonstop monologue, partly to escape solipsism, partly to try and remedy her patient's silence. Once Elisabeth seems to shows some signs of attentive engagement, Alma becomes infatuated with her patient and begins to pour her heart out, confessing infidelities, a secret abortion and an unwanted pregnancy. Particularly engrossing is Alma's vivid description of a sexual encounter with two teenaged boys while she was sunbathing in the nude. The relationship is transformed, though, when Alma discovers an unsealed letter by Elisabeth, which reveals that she has been using Alma as a char-acter 'study'. At first enraged by the betrayal, Alma soon asks forgiveness. From that point on the two women seem to exchange identities and then, ultimately, merge into a single individual. Nonlinear, surreal, rife with visually and symbolically ambiguous scenes and images, *Persona* confounds easy interpretation and understanding. Instead the viewer is left with a host of vexing epistemological questions. Is Alma (Spanish for 'soul') Elisabeth's *doppelgänger*, or vice versa? Or, to put it another way, are they the inner and outer aspects of the same person? Do they embody something like Ego and Superego? Likewise, the term 'persona' (Latin for 'mask') is pregnant with meaning. In theatrical terms it of course refers to the masks that actors wore in classical drama. In Jungian terms the persona 'is a complicated system of relations between individual consciousness and society, fittingly enough a kind of mask, designed on the one hand to make a definite impression upon others, and, on the other, to conceal the true nature of the individual' (Jung 1953: 192). Clearly, as an actress, Elisabeth specialises in the conscious cultivation of personae but then, according to Jung, everyone is an actor presenting a plausible façade to the outer world. Perhaps Elisabeth has confused persona for self, hence the recourse to muteness – but then other permutations slide into view. Of the two women, which one functions as persona or outward mask of the other? Or do both simultaneously? Is the convergence and ultimate merger of the two identities a kind of salvation or a spiritual death? Are we dealing with psychological realism or a kind of spiritual or philosophical allegory? All sorts of hermeneutic avenues remain open and interpretive possibilities multiply uncontrollably.

For a daring, iconoclastic American director like Altman, long schooled in the mechanics of plot-driven cinematic narratives but hungry for new ideas and approaches, Bergman's *Persona* hit like a bombshell. Here was film as postmodern dreamscape; one that vigorously refused closure or resolution or interpretative certainties of any kind – on the visual level, on the aural level, on the level of spoken (and written) discourse. Here, also, was a film that constantly risked absurdity and pretentiousness to tackle the most profound and unanswerable questions regarding human identity, social roles, relationships, communication of meaning and the potentialities of the cinema for exploring these kinds of psycho-existential concerns. For Altman, after *Persona*, recourse to conventional, plot-driven Hollywood cinema was no longer an option.

That Cold Day in the Park (1969)

Significant as being the first film over which Altman had complete artistic control, *That Cold Day in the Park* performed poorly at the box office and was generally dismissed by critics. Many Altman scholars dutifully continue to discount the film as an early misstep. Altman himself felt differently. In a 1978 interview with Charles Michener he declared the film 'one hell of a movie!' (in Sterritt 2000: 94). Though not without its flaws the film is, indeed, much more accomplished and intriguing than the critical consensus would indicate, and is well worth careful consideration.

In 1967 Altman purchased the rights to *That Cold Day in the Park* (Delacorte, 1965), a decidedly offbeat novel by child actor-turned-writer Richard (aka Peter) Miles (pseudonym of Gerald Perreau Saussine, 1930–1991). Miles' novel deals with a wealthy Parisian spinster who holds a seemingly mute homosexual 16-year-old street waif captive in her apartment for companionship and sexual favours. Intrigued by striking thematic similarities to the *Persona* scenario – muteness and *folie à deux* – Altman managed to secure $500,000 in funding from his friend, the cosmetics heir, Donald Factor, and $700,000 from the Canadian production company, Commonwealth United. He then hired novelist-screenwriter Gillian Freeman (*The Leather Boys*) to adapt Miles' novel to the screen. From the outset, Altman's interest in *That Cold Day in the Park* revolved around the fraught and mysterious relationship between the woman and the boy. He instructed Freeman to delete the book's copious homosexual content, cut ancillary characters and incidents, and just focus on the bare bones of the story (see McGilligan 1989: 281). Altman wanted to shoot the film in London, possibly with Elizabeth Taylor or Ingrid Bergman in the lead, but ultimately opted to shoot the film in Vancouver, British Columbia, with Academy Award-winner Sandy Dennis in the starring role.[1]

In Freeman's adaptation, Miles' Parisian old maid – a shadowy, underdeveloped character known only as 'Madame' – is fully fleshed out as Frances Austen (Dennis), a prim and proper single woman who, by coif, clothing and manner appears to be well ensconced in middle age (though Dennis was only thirty-one at the time). Evidently quiet affluent, Frances lives alone in a large, nicely appointed Vancouver apartment inherited from her deceased parents: an apartment beautifully rendered in shadowy earth tones on a sound stage at Panorama Studios in West Vancouver by set designer Leon Ericksen. Also inherited from her parents are Frances's housekeeper and 'friends': a deadly dull set of bourgeois fogies at least a generation older than she is. During a boring dinner party for these people, Frances observes outside her window a handsome, blonde young man (played by Michael Burns, twenty-one years old at the time) huddled on a bench in an adjacent public park. After her guests leave, Frances brings the young man back to her place, ostensibly to get him out of the cold and the rain, but it soon becomes evident that strong unconscious motivations are at work. Because he is too lightly attired for the weather and does not speak, Frances quite naturally assumes that he is nothing more or less than a post-adolescent mute street urchin, as does the viewing audience. The young man's youth, good looks, stony silence and apparent vulnerability make him pitiable, safe and therefore desirable to the obviously lonely older woman. She invites him to bathe, dry his clothes, have dinner and even stay the night in his own bedroom, all the while chattering at him incessantly to fill the conversational vacuum created by his muteness. On a deeper level, the young man's silence makes his personality opaque and cryptic: an empty vessel that Frances proceeds to fill with projected fantasies and desires.[2] Frances buys her acquaintance new clothes, invites him to stay as long as he wants, and begins, rather ominously, to lock him in at night. Unfazed, the young man makes the first of many nocturnal flights via the bedroom window and fire escape and goes to visit his sister, Nina (Susanne Benton), and her American draft-dodger boyfriend, Nick (John Garfield Jr.). Though they are making love when the waif happens onto the scene, he happily observes until his sister warns him away (a later scene between brother and sister, in Frances's bathroom, is plainly incestuous). Also revealed in this scene, some forty minutes into the film, is the fact that the supposedly dumb boy can speak. Nina tells Nick that her brother has occasionally feigned muteness, sometimes 'for days', since childhood.

Somewhat surprisingly, the young man returns to Frances's apartment and continues his mute charade, probably because he revels in the elaborate game, likes Frances in a way, enjoys the plush accommodations and perks – he proudly tells his sister, 'I have my own room and my own bed' – and is flattered by her attentions. Frances, in turn, becomes more obsessively infatuated. After rejecting the gauche advances of Dr. Stevenson (Edward Greenhalgh), a cloying, desiccated member of her mother's social set, she visits a gynecologist's office to be fitted for a diaphragm in eager anticipation of consummating her relationship with her protégé. During this four-and-a-half-minute sequence, Frances is often filmed in long shots and through glass partitions and windows, while most of the dialogue is supplied by three other young women in the waiting room chatting about sex and contraception. The net effect is to accentuate Frances's discomfort and isolation – and generate similar feelings for viewers. What follows are crosscut scenes of the boy incestuously bathing with his sister and Frances attending a boring bocce match (and being pestered by Stevenson), a juxtaposition meant to underline the extreme sexual divide that separates Frances from her love object. The divide reaches its climax that night, when Frances enters the boy's darkened room, lies down on his bed and in the film's most powerful and poignant scene pours out her heart to him, expressing her sexual disgust for Stevenson and offering herself to him. To her shock, Frances discovers that she's been confessing to an inert form on the bed fashioned from blankets and a pillow that the boy has put together to conceal his absence. Early the next morning, when he sneaks back in, he notices that his bed is remade but shrugs off this new development as of no consequence: unwise complacency, because Frances has nailed the windows shut and the boy's final imprisonment has already begun. The film draws to a close after Frances flies into a jealous rage and fatally stabs Silvia (Luana Anders), a prostitute she has brought home to service the young man's sexual needs. In the final scene he stands petrified against a hallway wall while she strokes his face and coos reassuringly; she is in complete control of the situation and now utterly out of her mind.

The facile critical interpretation of *That Cold Day in the Park* labels the film as an overwrought, misogynistic exercise in Gothic horror featuring the stock homicidal *vieille fille* in the Bertha Mason tradition. Altman scholar Helene Keyssar takes a far more perceptive tack in arguing that the hippie youth played by Michael Burns is every bit as crazy as Frances Austen, perhaps more so (1991: 201–3). His passive-aggressive bid to control the relationship by feigning muteness is morally untenable and smacks of psychic regression. In a larger sense the young man's instinctive recourse to manipulative farce bespeaks a dark strain in the 1960s youth counterculture: its knee-jerk contempt for 'straight' society, which it views as clinging to old-fashioned, repressive social proprieties and conventions versus the existential freedom, spontaneity, sexual license and playfulness prized by the younger generation. In sum, *That Cold Day in the Park* is several things: a film about loneliness, a duel character study, a cultural allegory dramatising the endemic generational schism that erupted in the 1960s. Wisely, Altman refuses to validate either side of the cultural-generational divide. Frances Austen's bourgeois existence is safe and respectable but also bereft of love, joy and emotional intensity. The hippie youth's life, though freewheeling and fun loving, is ultimately vapid and amoral. Both cultures, Apollonian and Dionysian, dead end in spiritual vacuity because neither one by itself is able to do justice to the complex, multifarious totality of the human experience that requires a delicate balance between freedom and restraint. When these two stubbornly habituated worldviews collide, as they do in *That Cold Day in the Park*, calamity is the predictable result.

That Altman was not to have good luck with his first film as auteur was augured by what happened at the 1969 Cannes Film Festival. Screened out of competition, *That Cold Day in the Park* was not seen in its entirety because the projector room caught fire (see Cagin and Dray 1994: 115). A short theatrical run generated anemic ticket sales and critical reviews were harsh – for what turned out to be a watered-down version of Altman's original vision. As Justin Wyatt notes, 'Against [Altman's] will, the film was edited by producer Donald Factor to obtain an R, rather than an X, rating. As Factor (or the Max Factor family) was the financier of the picture and Altman had little experience with moviemaking, cuts were made to assure the commercially more acceptable R rating. Distributor Commonwealth United was able to muster little interest for the film, even with the less restrictive rating' (1996: 54). *That Cold Day in the Park* probably met with tepid reviews and poor box office because it lacked sympathetic characters while presenting a weirdly sombre tone and a markedly sinister ending. No doubt the film's mordant perspective on alienation and the wages of sexual repression were out of sync with the weltanschauung of the late 1960s. As Michael Turner notes, 'Although set in 1968, *Cold Day* is really about the stodgy 1950s, as personified by the uptight spinster and the world that keeps her chained' (2006: n.p.).

Images (1972)

While *Images* was Altman's fourth film as auteur, conceptually it was his first. It supposedly had its genesis in London in 1967, when Altman had a dream about a woman whose perception of reality begins to warp and fragment as she succumbs to schizophrenia. Some months later, back in Santa Barbara, Altman took up the idea again and soon completed an eighty-page treatment that set the story on the coastline of either California or Maine. As Gerard Plecki points out, 'most of the ideas and actions of *Images*' are there 'in their barest form', albeit with different character names (1985: 52). Altman approached every major studio but no one in Hollywood was interested in producing a cryptic, downbeat psychological thriller so Altman had to shelve the project for four years, until the immense success of *M*A*S*H* suddenly made him a hot property. In the interim Altman rewrote *Images* at least eight times, making the script the most carefully wrought of his career.

Originally Altman wanted to shoot *Images* in Vancouver with Sandy Dennis in the lead role but *That Cold Day in the Park* took its place. He later considered casting Julie Christie as Cathryn and, later still, pondered Sophia Loren in the lead role with the film set in Milan. When these options evaporated, he set out to scour Europe for a lead actress and a suitable location. The first problem was quickly solved when Altman happened to watch Susannah York portray the title role in Delbert Mann's *Jane Eyre* (1970), an in-flight movie he watched on Aer Lingus (see McGilligan 1989: 351). The film was mediocre but something about York's ethereal beauty convinced Altman that she was right for the part. He immediately sent the script to York on the Greek island of Corfu where she was vacationing with her husband, Michael Wells. Bewildered by what she read, York telephoned Altman to turn down the role. Unfazed, Altman insisted on flying the 7,000 miles from Los Angeles to Corfu for further negotiations: an extravagant gesture that made him hard to refuse a second time. York almost dropped out of the picture during pre-production in London when she discovered she was pregnant but Altman convinced her to play the movie pregnant (see Thompson 2006: 72). With York signed up, Altman scouted a number of locations on the continent before settling on Ardmore Studios and environs in County Wicklow, Ireland, just south of Dublin. The rugged, beautifully desolate landscape of coastal Ireland proved a richly evocative setting for Cathryn's psychological disintegration. As for the rest of the cast, Altman regular Rene Auberjonois plays Cathryn's caring but somewhat petulant husband, Hugh. Marcel Bozzuffi – (in)famous as the villain in William Friedkin's *The French Connection* (1971) – plays Cathryn's spectral lover, Rene (dead three years). Hugh Millais – the grandson of Pre-Raphaelite painter John Everett Millais, who played hired assassin Dog Butler in Altman's previous picture, *McCabe & Mrs. Miller* – plays Marcel, friend of Cathryn and Hugh, and Cathryn's former and would-be lover. Cathryn Harrison plays Marcel's twelve-year-old daughter, Susannah.

Having secured a topflight cast, Altman – though hamstrung by a modest production budget of $800,000 – was able to create astonishingly good production values. Superb art design by Leon Ericksen finds perfect complement in the sombre-toned cinematography of the great Vilmos Zsigmond and a moody, Academy Award-nominated score by John Williams, punctuated by Stomu Yamashta's tinkling, crackling 'sound sculptures'. The net impact of a weird script, offbeat musical score, autumnal country scenes and moody interiors shot in stark, naturalistic fashion, is to establish and sustain a lonely, brooding aura of mystery and melancholy that haunts the viewer like the vague emotional after-effects of a troubling dream.

Clearly inspired by one aspect of *Persona*, i.e. Bergman's deliberate refusal to distinguish between reality, dream and fantasy in the way he shoots certain scenes, Altman explores the imploding psyche of a hypersensitive, over-imaginative woman whose inability to have a child leads to guilt-inducing affairs, which precipitate a mental breakdown.[3] Cathryn begins to have hallucinations of lurid telephone calls, glimpses of herself from a distance and former lovers sometimes when she is alone, sometimes in the presence or in place of her husband, Hugh. Hoping to rid herself of these frightening visions, Cathryn ultimately hits upon the simple expedient of killing them off in various ways (by shotgun, knife and automobile). The nerve-wracking problem for Cathryn and the viewer – who is always and only privy to her highly solipsistic point of view – is that it is impossible to distinguish hallucination from reality; both are equally 'real' visually. In the film's closing scene Cathryn disposes of what she thinks is another hallucination by running it off a steep cliff with her car. The final shot pans down the cliff, through a cascading waterfall, to reveal that the figure was not a figment of Cathryn's imagination but was, in fact, her husband, Hugh.

The final shot provides catharsis and resolution by distancing the viewer from Cathryn's mad visions but cannot retroactively resolve the many oscillations between hallucination and reality that come before. And therein lays the rub. As Plecki points out, 'the analysis of self-image and self-perception in *Images* ... is quite confusing [because the] already-complicated personality of Cathryn is hidden with obscure visual riddles, enigmas, conflicts, and subplots. Cathryn remains virtually unknowable' (1985: 49). Perhaps it would be more accurate to say that the forces that precipitate Cathryn's schizophrenia are never adequately established or explained. She is young, intelligent, beautiful and affluent and no debilitating trauma seems to have befallen her. It would also be accurate to say that the film's final settling on a realistic point of view does not adequately mitigate all the epistemological confusions that precede it. We awaken to reality but a reality that will never quite regain its former stability.

3 Women (1977)

As had been the case with *Images*, *3 Women* literally had its basis in a dream. In the latter months of 1976 things were going badly for Altman. His revisionist western,

Buffalo Bill and the Indians, had flopped – effectively ending Atman's six-year run as a more-or-less bankable director. After the commercial failure of *Buffalo Bill and the Indians,* producer Dino de Laurentiis fired Altman as director of *Ragtime* and replaced him with Milos Forman. Altman voluntarily withdrew from another project, a comedy entitled *The Yig Epoxy* with Peter Falk. Nor could he obtain the rights to Kurt Vonnegut's novel from 1973, *Breakfast of Champions,* which he was extremely keen to film (see Kass 1978: 36). To make matters worse, Altman's wife, Kathryn, suddenly took ill and had to be rushed to the hospital in the middle of the night.[4] At his home in Malibu during his wife's hospitalisation, Altman had a dream about making a movie in a desert setting entitled '3 Women' that would star Shelley Duvall and Sissy Spacek as two of the three women. The plot was murky but centred on what Altman calls 'personality theft', a central theme of Bergman's *Persona*: 'Two young girls from Texas, dreaming of the good life, meet in a desert community, come to terms with the undercurrents in their lives and undergo a metamorphosis.'[5] After scribbling down some notes, Altman developed a fifty-page treatment with a young writer named Patricia Resnick (a former American Film Institute intern who had worked as a PR assistant on *Buffalo Bill and the Indians*) and convinced 20th Century Fox's Alan Ladd Jr. to green-light the project, budgeted at a modest $1.5 million, without a finished screenplay. Indeed, Altman decided, much to Resnick's chagrin, that he did not want a finished screenplay. Instead he decided as he so often did, to embrace his instincts and mostly improvise the movie as he went along, with the actors (especially Shelley Duvall) contributing much of their own dialogue. In his director's commentary to the 2004 Criterion DVD edition of *3 Women*, Altman said 'too much emphasis is placed on scripts'. He deliberately avoided careful scripting in order to make a 'very organic' and 'impressionistic' film about 'the ambiguity of lost souls'.

What ultimately emerged was an extraordinary film, weirdly cryptic and ambiguous but also strangely fascinating. Off the bus from Quitman, Texas (a real city, east of Dallas), a naïve young waif named Mildred 'Pinky' Rose (Spacek) obtains a job as an orderly at Desert Springs Rehabilitation and Geriatric Center, a facility in the desert a hundred miles or so east of Los Angeles, nicely described by Scott Von Doviak as 'a ghastly mausoleum of decrepitude overseen by penny-pinching misanthropes'.[6] Mildred 'Millie' Lammoreaux (Duvall), also young but a veteran employee, is assigned the task of showing Pinky the ropes. The two soon become friends of a sort, and roommates. Both are lost souls, with Pinky essentially a woman without selfhood, a *tabula rasa* seeking inscription from something or someone. In his commentary for the 2004 Criterion DVD edition, Altman aptly describes her as 'like a soul that appeared on the planet and said, "How do I make myself [into] a person?"' Almost equally vapid, the male-centred Millie is an ungainly narcissist filled with justified anxiety about her attractiveness who pretends to a worldly sophistication that is far beyond her grasp. A fatuous pseudo-individual who derives her identity from women's magazines and mail order catalogues, Millie is the pure product of America's degraded popular culture.[7] She tries to flirt with men and chat up women acquaintances but no one will give her the time of day – except Pinky, who mistakes Millie's obliviousness to social rejection

Under the sign of patriarchy: an emboldened Pinky Rose (Sissy Spacek) tries target shooting as Edgar Hart (Robert Fortier) looks on.

as cool self-assurance. Indeed, Pinky comes to idolise and emulate Millie, believing her to be 'the most perfect person' she has ever known: a funny but also poignant case of the blind following the blind. Millie soon takes Pinky to her favourite leisure destination, 'Dodge City'; a bar and social club on the outskirts of town aptly described by Ron Peterson as 'a poor man's western backlot where "cowboys" try their marksmanship and ride motorcycles bronco-style over the dunes'.[8] Edgar Hart (Robert Fortier) owns Dodge City and also owns the Purple Sage, the apartment complex where Millie and Pinky share a small unit. A swaggering, alcoholic middle-aged faux gunslinger in dark shades and an Australian bush hat, Edgar is a living caricature of the macho western hero, the embodiment of all that is false, preening and self-deluded about the masculine world. Unsurprisingly, Edgar is a philanderer, despite the fact that his wife, Willie (Janice Rule) – a mostly mute painter of lurid, cryptic swimming pool frescoes – is expecting a child.[9] Appalled and undone when Edgar and Millie have a sexual assignation at the apartment, Pinky attempts suicide by jumping into the swimming pool at the Purple Sage from a second-floor balcony. After being rescued from drowning by Willie and other residents, a badly injured Pinky falls into a coma. Once she awakens, Pinky's elderly parents (played by actor-director John Cromwell and his real-life wife, Ruth Nelson) visit her in the hospital but she angrily claims not to know them (either because she is suffering from temporary amnesia or has undergone a radical personality change). Pinky's misrecognition scene is juxtaposed by an odd, disconcerting revelation scene in which Millie accidentally intrudes on the Roses as they are making love. Upon recovery, Pinky is mysteriously transformed into a Millie clone with a more sexualised appearance, brighter clothing and a decidedly more confident affect. Guilt-stricken by Pinky's near demise and shaken by her startling encounter with the reality of geriatric sex, Millie gravitates towards Pinky's timid and restrained former self; her new identity is as Pinky's caring, loyal friend. Ironically, in her new incarnation, Pinky (who now insists on being called by her real name, Mildred) is the toast of the Purple Sage, attaining the attentions of Edgar and popularity with the other young singles to which Millie had always aspired. But this role reversal is short-lived. Mildred undergoes psychic regression after she has a terrible nightmare (visualised in a dream sequence featuring Willie's ominous murals). Demoralised and deeply shaken, Mildred reverts to 'Pinky' and climbs into bed with Millie for solace. At that moment a drunken Edgar lets himself into their apartment and announces that his wife, Willie is in labour. The two women rush to Willie's aid at her house behind Dodge City. Millie takes over as midwife and orders Pinky to summon an ambulance but to no avail; emotionally paralysed, Pinky remains a helpless bystander while Willie gives birth to a stillborn baby. The closing scenes reveal that Edgar has succumbed to a gunshot wound but whether it was suicide, an accident or murder is left to conjecture. In the end, the three women are shown living together in Willie's house behind Dodge City with Willie assuming a grandmother role, Millie – now dressed in Willie's attire – the role of a carping mother and Pinky, the role of a young, submissive daughter. A final, lingering shot of a pile of discarded tires near the house seems to serve no other purpose than to suggest that Edgar's corpse might lie beneath. In his Criterion commentary Altman said 'that's really what the film is about – what happens when the last male dies'.

Robert T. Self argues, from a structuralist perspective, that *3 Women* is a textbook art-cinema film that subverts classical narrative protocols by attempting 'to liberate spatial, temporal, graphic, and rhythmic dimensions from narrative altogether' and accentuate 'the process of signification itself' (2002: 63). From a Marxist-feminist perspective, Michael Ryan and Douglas Kellner credit *3 Women* with threatening the 'dominant system of gender construction' by depicting women 'who undergo or undertake changes in socialized gender position'; they go on to note, however, that *3 Women* 'tends to recuperate this potentially radical insight into the [socially] constructed nature of such positions by ontologizing an ideal of feminine nature' (1988: 147). Film critic Stuart Byron offers a different assessment. In an unpublished review, he describes Altman as two filmmakers: the 'Marxian Altman and Freudian Altman'.[10] The former Altman is 'obsessed with Marx's concept of alienation as it applies to the relationship of the individual to mass culture': an approach that has resulted in 'some of the deepest, more reverberative films of our times'. For Byron, the Freudian Altman is 'simplistic, applying textbook psychoanalysis in a sophomoric manner'. Byron sees *3 Women* as brilliant Marxian Altman through three quarters of its length – until the final sequence: 'a reductionist tract' in which 'very particular people in a very particular set of circumstances suddenly become symbols of the id [Pinky], ego [Millie], and superego [Willie]'. Film critic Stephen Farber sees the film's ending not as too reductive but as too enigmatic: 'The problem is that this ending is so opaque and impenetrable; that virtually any interpretation is possible. Altman closes us out of the puzzle' (1977: 84). Whatever one makes of its ending, *3 Women* clearly bifurcates into two almost unrelated films: a trenchant satire of American cultural vacuity that ultimately devolves into the cryptic and arguably meaningless Freudian tableau derived from Altman's *Persona*-inspired dream. Too beholden to his original concept, Altman obviously felt he had to end up there. Had he allowed for an ending that organically developed from his satiric storyline, *3 Women* might have been a masterpiece instead of the near miss that it ultimately is.

Notes

1   Elizabeth Taylor was not considered 'bankable' and Ingrid Bergman found the script 'disgusting'.

2   From a Lacanian point of view, the young stranger is physically mature and post-'mirror-stage', i.e. has a sense of self as a discreet individual, but because he is seemingly pre-verbal, he remains within the Imaginary order that precedes the Symbolic. To Frances, he seems to remain free of all the baggage of social conditioning that comes with the acquisition of language and therefore represents a kind of regressive wish-fulfillment fantasy of escape from adulthood.

3   Roman Polanski's eerie psychological thriller, *Repulsion* (1965) is another likely inspiration.

4   The malady turned out to be a deep-seated peptic ulcer.

5   *3 Women*, 20th Century Fox Film Co. Production Notes, p. 1.

6   Scott Von Doviak, 'Weird Altman': http://www.thehighhat.com/Potlatch/007/BShelf_vondoviak.html.

7   To develop her character, Shelley Duvall created a diary for Millie Lammoreaux.

8   Ron Peterson, 'Discovering the Perils of SHE in Altman's '3 Women' (unpublished).

9   Willie's symbolic-visionary frescoes, depicting threatening reptilian male figures, were painted by artist Bodhi Wind (real name: Charles Kuklis, 1950–1991).

10 From the Altman Archives, University of Michigan, Ann Arbor.

CHAPTER TWO

Experiments in Genre Revision

Apparently [genre debunking] is something that attracts me. But I see it only after the fact, and then I say to myself, there I go again. I think what happens is that I research these subjects and discover so much bullshit that [my movie] just comes out that way [i.e. revisionist].

— Robert Altman

Through the beneficence of the celluloid gods, synchronicity or just sheer luck, Robert Altman – who was already forty-three – finally broke into Hollywood at just the right historical moment: when industry conditions happened to align perfectly with his maverick sensibilities. By the late 1960s the old studio system was collapsing, as were its tired genre formulae. After having ruled production standards for almost forty years, the Hays Code finally disintegrated in 1968 and was replaced by the more liberal MPAA rating system. At the same time, auteurist film theory was affirming the director (often, also, the writer and producer) as the chief creative force behind a film, while the disruptive features of French New Wave cinema – improvised dialogue, long tracking shots, jump cuts, violations of the 180° rule, etc – were exerting powerful influences on Hollywood filmmaking. On a wider front, the Civil Rights struggle melded into an increasingly passionate anti-Vietnam War movement that polarised the country and politicised a large swathe of American youth: a rebellious counterculture demanding more iconoclastic fare that confronted and challenged the old, shopworn verities. The commercial success of youth-oriented films like *Bonnie and Clyde* (1967), *The Graduate* (1967), *Easy Rider* (1969) and *Midnight Cowboy* (1969) prompted the old studio moguls to reluctantly hand the reins over to a new generation of directors, ushering in a brief period of intense creative freedom that has since been dubbed the

'Hollywood Renaissance' or 'New American Cinema'. Though hardly a Young Turk, Altman was at the vanguard of this new movement and one of its chief practitioners, especially in regard to the making of films that revised, ironised or otherwise demolished Hollywood genre conventions.

M*A*S*H (1970)

Heister Richard 'Dick' Hornberger, M.D. (1924–1997), a thoracic surgeon who practiced medicine in Waterville, Maine unwittingly transformed Altman's career as a filmmaker when, under the pseudonym Richard Hooker, he finally published *MASH: A Novel About Three Army Doctors* (Crown, 1968), after scores of publisher rejections. A former army surgeon with the 8055th Mobile Army Surgical Hospital (MASH) who treated combat casualties during the Korean War, Hornberger (with the crucial assistance of freelance sportswriter W. C. Heinz) turned his war experiences into a comic romp. Asked to write a promotional dust-jacket blurb, the once-blacklisted screenwriter Ring Lardner Jr. read the book in galley form and thought it would make a great movie.[1] Producer Ingo Preminger (Otto's brother) agreed, and hired Lardner to write a screen adaptation. Altman was only offered the job of directing the film after some sixteen other directors – among them George Roy Hill, Stanley Kubrick and Sidney Lumet – turned it down or were otherwise unavailable. Despite the fact that his stingy contract with 20th Century Fox called for modest pay ($75,000) and no profit-sharing 'points', *M*A*S*H* would prove to be Altman's most commercially successful film and a tremendous boon to his career.

Though reluctant at first to take on the project, Altman soon warmed to the material. Lardner's adaptation of Hornberger's novel was anti-authoritarian, called for a large ensemble cast and was highly episodic – really just a disjointed series of comic vignettes: a film project uniquely suited to Altman's talents and predilections. He immediately put his stamp on the movie by casting mostly no-name actors so as to keep the scenario realistic and off-beat. After securing his three main co-stars – Donald Sutherland as Benjamin Franklin 'Hawkeye' Pierce, Elliott Gould as John Francis Xavier 'Trapper John' McIntyre and Tom Skerritt as Augustus Bedford 'Duke' Forrest – Altman recruited most of his cast of extras from the American Conservatory Theater in San Francisco with the help of theatre impresario Bill Bushnell. Sutherland and Gould were beginning to attract notice but were hardly household names; Skerritt had done lots of television but this was his first film. Amongst the rest of the principle cast – Sally Kellerman as Margaret 'Hot Lips' Houlihan, Robert Duvall as Major Frank Burns, Roger Bowen as Colonel Henry Blake, Rene Auberjonois as Father John 'Dago Red' Mulcahy, John Schuck as Captain Walter 'Painless Pole' Waldowski and Gary Burghoff as Corporal 'Radar' O'Reilly – Kellerman and Duvall had extensive television resumes but had not done much film work while all the others had almost no television or film credits. Budgeted at a modest $3.5 million, *M*A*S*H* was mostly shot at a sprawling outdoor set near Malibu Creek State Park in the Santa Monica Mountains twenty miles north of Los Angeles: a site meant to approximate a MASH camp in the barren hill country of South Korea. The cast and crew lived in tents during principal photography and Altman characteristically encouraged a collaborative sense of community (though Gould and Sutherland, unnerved by Altman's free-wheeling directorial style, spent much of the time trying to get him fired).

Whether pro-war or anti-war, war movies tend to take their subject matter very seriously. There have been comedies in war settings (e.g., *No Time for Sergeants* (1958), *Mr. Roberts* (1955), *Kelly's Heroes* (1970)) and Stanley Kubrick's *Dr. Strangelove* (1964) parodied the Cold War but, before *M*A*S*H*, war film spoofs were quite rare. However, the intense controversy and divisiveness aroused by the Vietnam War, which was at its height when *M*A*S*H* was being made, rendered the time auspicious for a movie that would bring some comic relief to an ongoing national nightmare, while spoofing the war film genre and the underlying ideology the genre affirms. Though it is set during the Korean War, everyone understood that the implicit subject of *M*A*S*H* was Vietnam. The conflation of past and present US military adventures in Asia might also seem to suggest that the object of the film's satire was not any particular war but all war. Yet a careful analysis shows that *M*A*S*H* is only tangentially an anti-war film; the principal object of its satire is not war but the authoritarian mindset that supports the dominant order and makes wars possible.

M*A*S*H's anti-genre bent is immediately evident from its setting: an army field hospital near the front lines, where the torn and bloody casualties of war are treated. There are no stirring and heroic combat sequences. Only the grisly aftermath of the fighting is shown, as helicopters fly in the wounded during the opening credit sequence, to the tune of 'Suicide is Painless', a distinctly anti-genre theme song that is no paean to patriotic exploits but a strange, ironic anthem to the depredations of time, chance and life's futility (music by Johnny Mandel, lyrics by Altman's then fourteen-year-old son, Michael).[2] The film's three protagonists – 'Hawkeye' Pierce, 'Trapper John' McIntyre and 'Duke' Forrest – likewise confound genre expectations. Physicians who are only nominal military officers, the trio are hearty drinkers, carousers and scoffers at all aspects of military discipline and bureaucracy that infringe upon their individual freedoms. But these three also happen to be highly skilled surgeons who routinely save lives, thus positing the notion that competence on the job is easily compatible with anarchic rebelliousness off duty (indeed, Hawkeye and Duke arrive at the 4077th in a stolen jeep).

In marked contrast to our hip and genial anti-heroes are the film's villains: Major Frank Burns and Major Margaret 'Hot Lips' Houlihan. Both characters, at least initially, are sanctimonious hypocrites who avidly support Christian piety, war and the military establishment – perfect exemplars of what Theodor W. Adorno *et al* defined as the 'authoritarian personality'.[3] Essentially fascist martinets, Burns and Houlihan are belligerent conformists who instinctively affirm Gesellschaft authority over individual autonomy. At base, this makes them proponents of the established military order that the war film genre usually idealises.[4] While the genre generally supports the traits they exhibit – discipline, patriotism, piety – it insists that such traits be made manifest in moderation, so as to conceal their authoritarian underpinnings. As *reductio ad absurdum* caricatures of 'good soldiers', Burns and Houlihan show that militarism ultimately amounts to Gesellschaft dehumanisation at its worst.

Accordingly, *M*A*S*H* is structured to vilify and ridicule Burns and Houlihan or to more broadly satirise the authoritarian-corporatist values they and the war film genre embody – though it should be noted that the film ultimately recuperates Houlihan's character (probably because she's a beautiful woman: an identity that trumps her backward ideas and unctuous careerism). When Burns tries to teach a Korean messboy English by reading the Bible, Duke and Hawkeye offer the boy pornography as a more engaging text. When Burns tries to discourage his tent-mates, Duke and Hawkeye, from drinking alcohol by kneeling and reciting the Lord's Prayer, they turn the tables on him by hoisting rakes and marching as they mockingly sing 'Onward Christian Soldiers'. Other vignettes, not involving Burns or Houlihan, also mock F-scale values (e.g. religious superstitions, sexual prudishness). An early scene, set in a surgical tent, drives home the contrast between religiosity and reality. Father Mulcahy, who is giving a dead soldier the last rites, is interrupted by Duke, who is operating on a live one and needs the chaplain to stanch the patient's bleeding: 'I'm sorry, Dago, but this man is still alive and that other man is dead and that's a fact. Will you hold it with two fingers, please?' In another early scene, while Hawkeye is seducing WAC lieutenant 'Dish' (Jo Ann Pflug), she guiltily informs him that she is married. He replies that he is too, that he loves his wife, and 'if she was here I would be with her'. In yet another brief vignette, Burns falsely accuses Boone (Bud Cort), an orderly, of killing a patient: an act of emotional sadism that infuriates Trapper John, causing him to knock Burns to the floor with a fist to his face – but only after enquiring if he's finished his shift in the operating room. John's assault on Burns binds him to Hawkeye and Duke, who heartily approve.

The film's deployment of sex as an anti-genre device finds its most intense expression in a key sequence that depicts the outwardly chaste Burns and Houlihan hypocritically having an extramarital affair with each other. When commanding officer Henry Blake (Roger Bowen) is called away, the MASH camp devolves into bacchanalian decadence. Burns and Houlihan, drawn together in their abhorrence of the camp's 'unwholesomeness', make love, only to discover that the amplified sounds of their lovemaking are being broadcast all over the camp via a PA microphone surreptitiously placed under Burns' cot by Radar. The couple are further humiliated and taunted the next morning at breakfast; so much so, that Burns loses his mental equilibrium and ends up being shipped back home in a straightjacket.

Norman Kagan points out that the Burns-Houlihan sex sequence can be seen as a satiric inversion of a key war film genre motif: the testing of one's manhood in combat. Here, the primal moment, usually rendered in war films as a public rite of passage involving killing and survival, is reconfigured as the sex act, normally private but mockingly made public, so as to nullify its masculinity-affirming potential (1982: 34–5). Conventional aspirant to military honour, Burns is emasculated and defeated by prankster-nihilists, thus showing, as Kagan puts it, that war's 'survivors are those canny outsiders who can maintain their own style and savvy' (1982: 35).

After Major Burns is dispatched, *M*A*S*H* loses much of its steam. Another setpiece evidently designed to attack the war film genre's masculinist ideology features 'Painless Pole' Waldowski, aka the 'Dental Don Juan of Detroit' (John Schuck), the

Mocking ritual: the 'last supper' of Capt. Walter 'Painless Pole' Waldowski (John Schuck).

unit's dentist and oral surgeon, who experiences a single incidence of impotence, convinces himself that he's a latent homosexual and (ridiculously) opts for suicide. What follows is a tableau that mocks Da Vinci's Last Supper, followed by a scene featuring Waldowski lying in a coffin awaiting a poison pill his friends will supply to usher him into the afterlife. The pill is a fake. The real remedy is Lt. Dish, who obligingly has sex with the Painless Pole, thus remasculinising him. Kagan reads the scene as a spoof of the 'mad warrior'; a 'tragic and romantic' (1982: 36) staple of the war film genre, the mad warrior usually dies in a sacrificial, suicidal act of incredible bravery that saves the lives of many of his comrades. Here the mad warrior is reduced to a narcissistic buffoon while the communal rite of sacrifice is reprised as sexist farce. Unfortunately the skit doesn't work because it is too contrived and absurd to have any satiric bite, the relevance of the Last Supper is tenuous at best, and the mocking allusion to a stock figure from the war film genre is too obscure to really resonate with viewers.

The film's next set piece, which involves the second sexual humiliation of Major Houlihan, is more successful cinematically but also more ideologically suspect than the 'suicide' scene. Curious as to whether Houlihan is a 'true blonde' or not, Hawkeye, Trapper John and Duke contrive to pull away the canvas tarp that encloses her shower stall while she's taking a shower. Revealed naked to the entire camp, which has gathered to watch the prank (perverse theatre), Hot Lips is suitably startled and mortified – but does win the sympathy of her fellow nurses. To add insult to injury, when she goes to Col. Blake right after the incident and threatens to resign her commission if he doesn't have the perpetrators arrested by MPs, he casually rebuffs her. If the shower scene and aftermath were supposed to reinforce the film's construction of Major Houlihan as a moralistic crank, the sequence fails. The shower stunt is self-deconstructing insofar as it comes off as vicious fraternity hazing – not righteous or funny but mean-spirited and misogynistic. Conversely, Hot Lips Houlihan is transformed into a sympathetic victim who is then denied just recourse by a sexist boss. Feminist critics can justifiably cite lots of elements in *M*A*S*H* as evidence of Altman's unexamined misogyny but the shower scene, though clearly voyeuristic, ends up humanising Houlihan by show-casing her vulnerable humanity.

The film's third major set piece features Hawkeye and Trapper John venturing to Japan to operate on a wounded Congressman's son in a Tokyo Army hospital: a junket they naturally turn into a short vacation, featuring lots of irreverent banter, golf and whorehouse carousing. The shower incident redeemed Hot Lips Houlihan through victimhood and put the movie's protagonist trio (and all the men of the MASH unit) in a less than flattering light. The Tokyo sequence seems designed to morally recuperate Hawkeye and Trapper John by showcasing their humanitarian instincts while reinforcing their identities as talented surgeons and fun-loving, anarchic individualists. It also gently spoofs the class privilege that prompted their mission in the first place. Upon their return to the 4077th, Hawkeye and Trapper John enter the tent they share with Duke just after Duke and Hot Lips have evidently concluded a sexual encounter – a scene that completes the trio's moral rehabilitation by suggesting that Duke has made it up to Houlihan for everyone who conspired to humiliate her and that Hot Lips has forgiven her tormentors and is now fully integrated into the MASH community.

The film's final set piece revolves around an amateur football game arranged as a betting opportunity between Col. Blake and visiting General Hammond (G. Wood) (with lots of side bets by Hawkeye *et al*) that pits members of Blake's unit against Hammond's team. Though it starts out as an apparently fair contest, the game soon devolves into a chaotic farce, rife with blatant cheating (e.g. the clandestine use of pro players and an illegal play that 'wins' the game for the 4077th), bumptious cheerleading, bureaucratic rivalry and a raucous carnival atmosphere obviously meant to mock war as the most corrupt 'game' of all and lampoon the earnestness of the war film genre that almost always features unalloyed heroism, grit and a culminating victory. Satirised on the gridiron, martial glory is further blunted by an anti-climactic ending, with Duke and Hawkeye returning to surgery after the game, only to learn that their tour of duty has expired and they can unceremoniously go home. Altman further deflates the contrived 'realism' of the genre by self-reflexively using PA announcements as a means to introduce both cast members and the film itself as it closes.

Though it has not aged well, *M*A*S*H* was a huge hit in 1970, making nearly $92 million in box office proceeds against a $3.5 million budget, winning rave reviews, and a raft of prestigious awards (including five Academy Award nominations and a Best Screenplay Academy Award for Lardner). His miserly contract denied Altman a big payday but *M*A*S*H* did propel him into the ranks of bankable directors, at least for a few years. Taking advantage of the film's success, Altman formed Lion's Gate Films, a mini-studio in Los Angeles (named after the suspension bridge that connects Vancouver to West Vancouver) that would be his business bulwark until he was forced to sell it in 1981. In the final analysis, though, *M*A*S*H* was very much a matter of timing and novelty. A sloppy, episodic comedy whose humour now seems jejune and overwrought, *M*A*S*H* was greeted in its day as an exhilarating departure from standard war film fare. Here was something new, or so it seemed: a supposedly brash counterculture retort to the musty patriotic propaganda served up by the likes of John Wayne, with his abysmally clichéd and justly reviled Vietnam War film, *The Green Berets* (1968). Still, the intervening years allow us to see that *M*A*S*H* is neither a very good film *qua* film, nor politically courageous. Though it pretends to a certain radical subversiveness, *M*A*S*H* never explicitly criticises the Korean War or the Vietnam War for the geopolitical and military debacles they were. And while the film features extravagantly bloody surgical operations as a supposedly grim, anti-war counterpoint to its comic antics, it never quite manages to make the connection between combat and physical injury *feel* direct and inevitable, probably because the casualties remain nameless cyphers: a mere backdrop for wisecracks. The film's main selling point – providing a crowd-pleasing wish-fulfillment fantasy of 'sticking it to the man' – is also its most problematic feature. Hawkeye, Trapper John and Duke get away with all manner of hi-jinx because, as physicians and commissioned officers, they're older, vastly more educated, and far more valued than the average G.I., who was and is most decidedly expendable. Paradoxically the special class position they enjoy in the military hierarchy allows the film's heroes the rare luxury of non-conformity without penalty (and without altering the hierarchy): an elitist, meritocratic exceptionalism about which the film is too blithe. Robert Kolker puts it well: 'There is a smugness not merely in the characters but in the way the narrative allows them to prevail without forcing them to confront anything – such as the notion of why they are where they are' (2011: 325). The complacency that Kolker detects was already in Lardner's reductively partisan script but Altman did nothing to counter its manipulative premises. Two-and-a-half years after Altman's movie, Larry Gelbart launched *M*A*S*H*, an extremely popular television series based on the film that ran for eleven seasons (256 half-hour episodes), a spin-off that Altman hated. As he told David Thompson, 'Every Sunday night an Asian war was in our living rooms, and no matter what platitudes they came out with, still the bad guys were the dark-skinned, yellow-eyed people. I just thought that was obscene at the time, when we were still in Vietnam [until April 1975]. It was the opposite message to what we felt we were making in the film' (2006: 55).

Brewster McCloud (1970)

Altman's next film, *Brewster McCloud*, can be interpreted as a deeper probing of themes treated by *M*A*S*H*. On the surface the two movies have little in common; one is a comedy about army doctors in Korea, the other is a fantasy film about a strange young man obsessed with self-powered human flight. Yet both films address the central counterculture preoccupation of their day: how to achieve personal liberation from the prevailing social order, which is judged as corrupt and repressive. The solution adopted by *M*A*S*H*'s heroes is stylistic and therefore superficial; while quite literally oper-ating within the System, they feign rebellion and achieve emotional release through hedonism, stunts and wisecracks. Brewster McCloud's solution is even more puerile and regressive; he aspires simply to fly away from it all. Like the mythical Icarus, Brewster fashions wings that will carry him aloft, above society's imprisoning laby-rinth and, like Icarus, he falls to his death. Brewster's fate is, therefore, a repudiation of the monomyth central to the fantasy genre and a prescient swipe at the politically bankrupt hippie ideology of social disengagement in pursuit of one's personal Utopia – Aquarian Age narcissism that would unfortunately become a cultural mainstay of the 1970s and beyond.[5] At the same time, Altman is equally unsparing in his depiction of mainstream American society as degraded Gesellschaft populated by arrogant dowagers, greedy capitalists, sleazy politicians, craven flunkies, crooked and/or dumb cops, dimwitted opportunists and violent rednecks. *That Cold Day in the Park* pitted the bourgeoisie against the youth counterculture and found both wanting; *Brewster McCloud* is broader in scope but reaches similar conclusions.

The source for *Brewster McCloud* was 'Brewster McCloud's Flying Machine', an original screenplay written in 1967 by Doran William 'Billy' Cannon (1937–2005), purchased by record producer Lou Adler, and brought to Altman by agent-producer George Litto (see McGilligan 1989: 331). Altman thought the script was 'just a dreadful piece [but] it was a kid flying, a gem of an idea I could work off [of]' (in Zuckoff 2009: 202). The screenplay was set in New York City but, at the suggestion of MGM vice president Herb Solon, Altman relocated the setting to Houston so that he could utilise the Houston Astrodome: a gigantic domed stadium completed in 1965 and billed as the 'eighth wonder of the world', enclosing the world's largest indoor space, and equipped with the 'Astrolite', an immense, four-story electronic scoreboard, the world's first animated one. An imposing venue for sports contests, concerts, political rallies and other orchestrated spectacles of nationalistic self-congratulation and amusement, the stadium is Altman's perfect metaphor for America's all-encompassing politico-cultural reality. *Spectacle* is the key term here. As Guy Debord argues, 'The spectacle manifests itself as an enormous positivity, out of reach and beyond dispute. All it says is "Everything that appears is good; whatever is good will appear." The attitude that it demands in principle is the same passive acceptance that it has already secured by means of its seeming incontrovertibility and indeed by its monopolization of the realm of appearances' (2000: 7).

As aspiring counterculture rebel, Brewster McCloud covertly occupies a fallout shelter in the bowels of the Astrodome (i.e. society) like Ralph Ellison's Invisible Man, while he fashions his wings of transcendence. Brewster hopes to depart from the 'passive acceptance' of his fellow citizens but Altman's setting suggests from the outset that Brewster's quest is doomed; 'fantasy' in the worse sense of the term. When he tries to fly away from it all, he will fly in an enormous room that affords no exit to the open skies and real freedom. Thus Altman retains the Icarus theme from Cannon's script but reconfigures the image to much greater symbolic effect. In the Greek myth, Icarus, guilty of hubris, flies too close to the sun; his wax wings melt, and he falls to his death into the sea. Brewster's fate is not the result of some innate character flaw; it is dictated by ironclad societal parameters that he refuses to acknowledge – another Altman protagonist blinded by ideology.

Altman veers from his source material in other ways as well. He softens Brewster's character by casting the physically slight, soft-spoken and boyish-looking actor Bud Cort, then aged twenty-two, in the title role and costuming him in wide-striped jerseys and large round eyeglasses that quite appropriately give him a childlike, owlish appearance. The original screenplay was, in Lou Adler's words, 'much more of a sexcapade', but Altman makes Brewster a virgin until near the end of the picture. (Brewster has a young admirer named Hope, played by Jennifer Salt, but he will not sleep with her so she masturbates under a blanket when Brewster does bodybuilding pull-ups in his underwear.) Billy Cannon's script was also more violent – in addition to being an aspiring flyer, Brewster McCloud is, paradoxically, a serial killer – but Altman has all half dozen murders occur off-screen to blunt their impact and even hints that they may somehow be the work of Brewster's mysterious guardian angel, Louise (Sally Kellerman), who is always accompanied by a raven, the black bird of death or fate (see McGilligan 1989: 333).

Largely improvising scenes as he went along, Altman also adds a number of satiric, anti-genre elements.[6] The movie opens with a lecture on birds and flight delivered by 'The Lecturer' (René Auberjonois), who is first heard in voice-over at the appearance of the MGM lion during the title sequence saying, 'I forgot my lines': an early warning that the film is likely to depart from convention all over the place. Intermittent clips of his bird lecture in the course of the film show the eccentric, beak-nosed professor gradually morphing into a squawking, flapping, feathered bird himself. A caricature of the stereotypical 'egghead' identifying too closely with the object of his passion, the lecture also functions as a derisive judgement on Brewster's quest as it dramatises the absurdity of human beings aspiring to be birds.

Altman adds other characters to serve as satiric targets. One of these is Miss Daphne Heap, a wealthy, petulant old maid depicted in an early scene at the Astrodome, singing off-key as she rehearses the national anthem and terrorises her African-American back-up orchestra. The embodiment of old-fashioned patriotism bound up with smug class and race privilege, Daphne Heap is tellingly played by Margaret Hamilton, the actress famous for playing the Wicked Witch of the West in Victor Fleming's *The Wizard of Oz* (1939). Arguably the best loved American fantasy film of all time, *The Wizard of Oz* reprises the hero's journey of successful self-transformation to which *Brewster McCloud* stands in ironic counterpoise. When Miss Heap is discovered dead and covered with bird droppings – Brewster's first murder victim – she is wearing Dorothy's red ruby slippers: a visual joke that undermines the Utopian premises of the fantasy genre by collapsing the hero and villain into a single figure.

Another object of satire is Abraham Wright (Stacey Keach), supposedly the surviving brother of Orville and Wilbur Wright.[7] Meant to evoke the human attainment of flight by association but also to suggest an ugly falling away from the heroic inventiveness his brothers embodied, Abraham Wright is superannuated and wheelchair bound, a nasty-tempered, greedy and lecherous miser: Altman's type for the American rentier-capitalist at his most rapacious and inhuman. For a time, Brewster is Wright's chauffeur, driving him around town in a 1963 Rolls Royce Phantom V limousine to collect rents, while being constantly subjected to the old man's verbal abuse (sometimes, to Wright's annoyance, Brewster pushes a button and raises the glass partition that separates the car's driver and passenger compartments to tune out his boss). In the end, Abraham Wright's depredations earn him the same fate as Miss Heap; he is found strangled and covered in bird faeces.

While it takes potshots at jingoism, greed and other societal foibles, *Brewster McCloud* basically reduces to an intriguing blend of two anti-genre films: anti-fantasy and anti-cop movie. Altman utilises Cannon's murder subplot to spoof the police procedural-thriller genre, specifically Peter Yates' popular *Bullitt* (1968), starring Steve McQueen as the title character: a handsome but taciturn maverick super-cop from San Francisco who wears his shoulder holster over sporty turtleneck sweaters and has to fight meddling bureaucrats to get his job done, a stock cliché of the genre. *Bullitt* also features a protracted and frantic car chase sequence over San Francisco's steep streets often regarded as the greatest car chase scene in American cinema.

Brewster McCloud has its own Steve McQueen figure: the priapically-named Frank Shaft (Michael Murphy), a vain San Francisco super-cop in turtlenecks and blue-eyed contact lenses brought in by a high-placed Houston official named Weeks (William Windom) to solve the murders proliferating across the city, with the victims always absurdly bespattered by bird shit. A car chase sequence further mocks *Bullitt* by becoming a Keystone Cops farce. Instead of just one car chasing another, as is *de rigeur*, Brewster's car – a stolen, souped-up Plymouth Road Runner driven with gleeful abandon by a new acquaintance of Brewster named Suzanne (Shelley Duvall) – ends up being chased by Shaft in a fast Camaro, closely followed by a Plymouth Fury prowl car driven by a traffic cop named Johnson (John Schuck), which is closely followed by Brewster's guardian angel, Louise, bringing up the rear in a red AMC Gremlin hatchback. The chase is chaotic, vaguely circular, and at one point involves all four cars comically bumping up and down over railroad ties on a train trestle, to banjo music reminiscent of the sort used to accompany the car chase scenes in Arthur Penn's *Bonnie and Clyde*. In the end, contrary to genre expectations, Brewster's vehicle escapes after Shaft crashes his Camaro into a pond. Badly injured and trapped in his sinking car, Shaft decides to blow his brains out with his own pistol – a stunning rejoinder to the cop-worshipping, right-wing ideology implicit in conventional thrillers like *Bullitt*.

Indeed, *Brewster McCloud* manifests a disdain for cops and cop culture that is bitter and thoroughgoing: an ideological slant unthinkable at almost any other moment in recent American history. One of the film's running gags involves Officer Eugene Ledbetter (Dean Goss), the epitome of officious incompetence. Ledbetter is a 450-pound Astrodome security guard in dark sunglasses and pith helmet who waddles hurriedly in pursuit of Brewster as he leaves or returns to his fallout shelter hideout, but can never catch him. The other cops who appear in *Brewster McCloud* are equally silly or reprehensible. Houston's Detective Captain Crandall (G. Wood) is a bad-tempered boor. Shaft's assigned sidekick, Johnson, is a dim-witted stooge. Worst of all is narcotics officer Douglas Breen (Bert Remsen), a venal, homophobic, family-abusing shake-down artist who tries to frame Brewster for drug possession in order to steal his expensive (already stolen) Nikon camera, and winds up murdered with bird shit on his face.[8] To further mock and disparage Breen after his demise, Altman stages his funeral as a maudlin affair on a rainy afternoon, with the police chaplain (W. E. Terry Jr.) reading Elizabeth Barrett Browning's 'How Do I Love Thee?' poem – an absurdly romantic elegy for a vile wretch like Breen – while his widow (Angelin Johnson), who is not exactly heartbroken, covertly makes eyes at her longtime lover, Officer Hines (Corey Fischer), who is always misidentified as 'Haynes' by his oblivious boss, Crandall.

After Brewster and Suzanne evade capture, they repair to Suzanne's apartment and have sex – Brewster's first time and evidently a fatal mistake, as it constitutes a falling

Icarus faltering: the law of gravity begins to overtake Brewster McCloud (Bud Cort).

away from the preternatural innocence needed to attain his ideal, at least according to Louise, who expresses her disappointment with Brewster in a crosscut scene. Thinking he's in love, Brewster naively discloses his scheme of self-powered flight. Suzanne's reaction is to imagine extravagant material rewards ('Brewster, you could be a million-aire! ... You could get a limousine ... a house on River Oaks Boulevard!'). Her crass opportunism deflates popular romance ideology and disappoints Brewster but doesn't prevent him from revealing a much darker secret: that he's somehow 'responsible' for 'all the people who died'. As soon as they part, Suzanne phones Bernard (William Baldwin), her former boyfriend (now Weeks' personal assistant) and betrays Brewster, precipitating a stream of police cars rushing to the Astrodome to apprehend him while Louise, his supernatural protector, quietly departs the scene. On his own now and trying to evade the cops, Brewster dons his mechanical wings and jumps off a high balcony inside the stadium. Predictably, he stays aloft for a few moments of strenuous flapping but soon tires and plummets to his death. In a rather bizarre coda evidently meant to underscore the theatricality of it all, Altman has his cast parade into the Astrodome dressed as circus performers and introduce themselves.

A quirky cinematic experiment, poorly marketed by MGM, *Brewster McCloud* earned less than a million dollars at the box office – even in an era unusually tolerant of movie weirdness. It was, in the words of Michael Murphy, 'a huge flop' (in Zuckoff 2009: 205). As Justin Wyatt puts it, 'Commercially, the project illustrates many of the economic pitfalls which Altman films would experience later: the difficulty of selling movies without any allegiance to genre or stars, the lack of communication between Altman and the distributor, and the public's growing aversion for films which experi-ment with narrative and cinematic codes' (1996: 54). The film's only real claim to notoriety is that it enjoyed the largest premier in Hollywood history on 5 December 1970, when it was shown at the Houston Astrodome to an audience estimated at almost 24,000 people on a 156' x 60' screen. Unfortunately, the audio that night was all but indecipherable, rendering the event a fiasco. In its afterlife, the film has become something of a minor cult classic.

McCabe & Mrs. Miller (1971)

Robert Altman's next project, *McCabe & Mrs. Miller*, came to him through fortuitous coincidence. David Foster, Steve McQueen's former publicist turned fledgling film producer, had been approached by agent Ellen Wright (widow of writer Richard Wright) with a western novel entitled *McCabe* (Macmillan, 1959) by one of her Paris clients, Edmund Naughton, an American expatriate newspaperman turned novelist. Foster liked the book, bought the rights in 1968, and tried unsuccessfully to interest John Huston and then Roman Polanski into making a film version before being approached in 1969 by Altman's agent, George Litto, who conveyed Altman's desire to make a revisionist western. For his part, Altman saw that *McCabe* would provide the stable basis he needed to 'mess around in the corners and details and tell the story in a different way', as he put it in the director's commentary to the DVD edition. Foster wanted Altman to direct the film but had to wait until *M*A*S*H* came out in January 1970. Once it broke big all the major studios clamoured for Altman's services; Foster and co-producer Mitchell Brower knew then that they could secure a production deal. With Altman officially hired, Warren Beatty and his then-girlfriend Julie Christie were secured for the lead roles, and a deal was signed with Warner Bros. in May 1970.

Naughton's novel takes place in Presbyterian Church, a small zinc-mining settlement situated somewhere in the Pacific Northwest. The book does not mention a specific year or period during which the action is set but when Altman and his friend and occasional collaborator Brian McKay co-wrote a screen adaptation (originally titled 'The Presbyterian Church Wager'), they evidently did their homework.[9] A reference in the novel to Snake River prompted Altman and McKay to set the action in Washington State, possibly in the Metaline Mining District, Pend Oreille County, in the northeast corner of the state, where lead and zinc mining began in the late 1890s. Accordingly, they set the time frame for 1895–97.[10]

For Altman's revisionist purposes, a new approach to setting and milieu was crucial. Over the course of many decades the western film genre had spawned a stable of endlessly repeated visual and thematic clichés that have reduced the enormously complex history of the Old West to stock cowboys, Indians, sheriffs, cattlemen and gunfighters battling it out in some dusty town near Monument Valley under the eternal summer sun. Naughton's *McCabe* suggested an unconventional western setting – densely forested mountains in the rainy Northwest – that Altman adopts to give the film a bracing and sombre atmosphere 'a long way from the dry, dusty, sunlit deserts so long ridden by John Wayne'.[11] To further defamiliarise the western genre, Altman sets his movie in autumn and winter and allows the often miserable weather its full due. Overwhelmingly white and male-oriented in keeping with their conservative bias, traditional westerns tend to repress America's ethnic and cultural diversity, but as Altman would later note, 'There wasn't anybody who spoke Texas: "Howdy, pardner." That didn't exist' (in Zuckoff 2009: 209). Instead of the stereotypical drawling Scots-Irish Texas cowboys in Stetsons and chaps, Altman populates Presbyterian Church with a varied array of first-generation European immigrants, Chinese labourers, even a middle-class African-American couple: a far more realistic representation of late nineteenth-century American demographics. Against genre convention, Altman also insists that the mostly working-class inhabitants of Presbyterian Church actually look like the part; the 'costuming for the picture was mostly a matter of keeping the clothes heavy, well-worn, dirty, with plenty of suspenders, furs, hats, flannel shirts, and muddy boots'.[12]

The same painstaking quest for realism extended to the on-location set. Altman decided to shoot the film on a mountainside site above Upper Levels Highway in West Vancouver, British Columbia: terrain that was similar in appearance to the rugged terrain of northeast Washington State but more congenial to filmmaking and close to the familiar and amicable city where he made *That Cold Day in the Park* two years earlier. In the fall of 1970 a crew supervised by Leon Ericksen cleared several acres of forest leased from Cypress Park Estates, a planned real estate development, and commenced building an authentic *fin de siècle* mining hamlet that eschewed the symmetry of the traditional Hollywood western town, i.e. buildings with wooden sidewalks and hitching posts in front, neatly lined up on both sides of a wide, flat tumbleweed-strewn main street. In marked contrast to the genre cliché, Presbyterian Church is laid out scattershot fashion, in keeping with the uneven terrain and the haphazard growth of a mining settlement.[13] Furthermore, the structures were not stage façades but real buildings, roofed and fully enclosed. Vancouver historian Michael Turner: 'Set carpenters doubled as extras, and many of the cast and crew took up lodgings in the fictive village. Even more remarkable was that some of these carpenters came from the Maplewood Mudflat squat, just east of the Second Narrows Bridge, an alternative community made up of artists, environmental activists, and American draft resisters.'[14] Altman even had ore tailings dumped on the ground, as would be expected in a mining community. More than just a movie set, Presbyterian Church also became a kind of living history museum and an impromptu counterculture commune: a short-lived example of Altmanesque Gemeinschaft at its most earnest.

Altman also bucked genre conventions as to the look of the film. During pre-production, his cinematographer, Vilmos Zsigmond, read an article in *American Cine-matographer* about flashing, i.e. a method of contrast control that utilises the physical properties of chemical-emulsion film stock to bring out detail in darker areas of the print.[15] Zsigmond made tests before he got to Vancouver and described the effect as 'sort of grayish, very grainy, especially if you underexpose it and push the film you are going to get this old look' (in Zuckoff 2009: 215). With Altman's enthusiastic approval, Zsigmond shot the film slightly dark, used lens filters, and then had most of the negative footage flashed (i.e. exposed to light before developing) fifteen per cent during lab processing. Altman loved the slightly grainy look but Warner Bros. execu-tives hated it, thinking it was merely the result of incompetence. Zsigmond recalls that Altman calmed the nervous suits by blaming the unusual effect 'on a new lab here in Vancouver' and assuring them that proper processing in Hollywood would solve the alleged problem. According to Zsigmond, 'He was conning them. He didn't want interference from anybody' (ibid.).

Another key element in Altman's revisionist strategy was his innovative use of sound and music. As he had done with previous films, Altman allowed for overlapping dialogue, ambient noise and lots of people talking at the same time – as they tend to do in real life. To get 'the feeling of reality [rather than] that clear, perfect, beautiful sound recorded on a soundstage', sound was recorded on sixteen tracks and one voice would be brought forward during the mixing phase for intelligibility's sake: a realistically noisy aural milieu (see Zuckoff 2009: 219). As for music, Altman avoided the lush orchestral score associated with western epics in favour of diegetic music provided by a fiddler (Brantley Kearns) in certain scenes. Non-diegetic music in a few other scenes consists of three songs by Canadian poet and folk-rock singer-composer Leonard Cohen: 'The Stranger Song', 'Sisters of Mercy' and 'Winter Lady'. Altman was already familiar with Cohen's debut album from 1967, *Songs of Leonard Cohen*, on which these songs appear; he had played the album constantly in off hours while making *That Cold Day in the Park*. After hearing the record again at a party in Paris a few days after the *McCabe & Mrs. Miller* shooting wrapped, it occurred to him that Cohen's 'songs of romantic despair' uncannily fit the tone and mood of the film and could be used as a connective thread in the storyline 'like the loudspeaker announcements in *M*A*S*H* or the ornithological digressions in *Brewster*' (McGilligan 1989: 347). Warner Bros. executives balked at the expense of obtaining the Cohen songs so Altman traced Cohen's whereabouts to Nashville, phoned him directly, and asked for his help. A huge admirer of *Brewster McCloud*, Cohen was more than happy to permit Altman to use his songs.

Shooting took place in 'dead sequence' – a rather rare approach to principal photography – between October 1970 and January 1971, while the town was still under construction. The screenplay called for an opening shot of 'the blackened ruins' of Presbyterian Church in the present day, to establish that the town 'has died and time has all but buried it': an image suggesting that the American experiment in nation-building has ended in abject failure.[16] The next four shots were to be glimpses of Presbyterian Church in 1901 just prior to John McCabe's arrival. Never a slave to the script, which he considered just a 'selling tool', Altman opted to discard all these shots and start the film *in media res*, on a windy, rainy late fall day, with following shots, left to right, of a hunched-over McCabe in fur coat and derby, approaching the town on horseback, and serenaded by Cohen's 'The Stranger Song' playing on the soundtrack: an exquisitely evocative opening that establishes a lonely, autumnal mood.[17]

Just before entering town, McCabe takes off his big fur coat to reveal a dark wool suit, high collar, tie, gold watch chain, a gold tooth and gold tie pin: the theatrical costuming of a well-heeled 'dude' aiming to impress the local rubes with his prowess as cardsharp and 'businessman'. Posturing aside, John Quincy McCabe is actually a dull-witted penny-ante hustler: a dubious 'hero' markedly at odds with the strong, silent protagonist of the traditional western. McCabe enters Sheehan's, the town's only saloon, which looks like a dark and rustic Breughel painting come to life. He organises a poker game to establish a persona as a wheeler-dealer but cards will no longer be McCabe's principal stock in trade; he has come to Presbyterian Church to open his own saloon/casino/whorehouse. Accordingly, in the next sequence, McCabe rides to the nearby town of Bear Paw to purchase three 'chippies' for $200. When he returns to Presbyterian Church with his trio of homely, bedraggled prostitutes in tow, McCabe passes by the newly built church that is the young town's namesake at the exact moment that Rev. Elliot (Corey Fischer), silhouetted against a rising (or setting?) sun, is placing a cross atop its steeple. The shot is stunningly beautiful and brimming with ironic symbolism.[18] Officially, the town (allegorically, the nation) is being founded on pious Christian virtues. In reality, it is being created to serve commerce and hedonism. Temporal ambiguity – is it the dawning of a new day or sunset? – contributes to the scene's suggestive power. McCabe's second arrival thus signals the real beginning of the transformation of Presbyterian Church from mining camp to town. It also identifies the first part of *McCabe & Mrs. Miller* as the type of western that Frank Gruber calls 'the empire story', with a plotline that involves building up a ranch or oil empire from scratch, a classic rags-to-riches saga that reaffirms American Dream ideology (Howard Hawks' *Red River* (1948) is a prime example). Going against genre conventions, McCabe seeks to establish an 'empire', but one based on booze, gambling and prostitution – vital parts of the real frontier infrastructure, not the colourful accents that more generic westerns would have us believe.

A few weeks after McCabe's arrival, Sheehan (René Auberjonois), an obtuse but typically greedy and hard-nosed capitalist operator, tries to interest him in a partnership that would keep out would-be competitors or take a 'cut' from them, if they're allowed in. McCabe demurs, saying 'Partners is what I come up here to get away from'. But McCabe's individualistic resolve is immediately ironised by an emergency that disrupts his meeting with Sheehan. One of his prostitutes suddenly goes berserk on a customer and begins stabbing him with a large hunting knife as they both tumble out of her tent. McCabe has to hurriedly intervene and disarm the hysterical woman before she commits murder. The scene shows that McCabe is woefully out of his depth as aspiring pimp and whoremaster. It also provides a fitting segue for the arrival of Mrs. Constance Miller (Julie Christie), an English madam, who comes to the rescue from Bear Paw on a wagon pulled by a large, loud steam tractor in the very next scene.

Allegorically, Mrs. Miller's circus-like arrival, not by horse but by a smoke-belching, whistle-blowing mechanical conveyance, signals the arrival of the twentieth century: a bigger and bolder new era marked by newfangled technologies and sharper business strategies that will also provide unprecedented opportunities for capable women. A smart, no-nonsense businesswoman, Constance Miller easily overmatches the bluffing dimwit McCabe – and provides a pointed repudiation of the western genre's routine subordination of women as decorative love objects or helpless victims and bystanders. Where Edmund Naughton titled his book *McCabe*, Altman calls his film *McCabe & Mrs. Miller*: a designation that not only brings her into the picture but gives her equal billing, while the ampersand nicely connotes a business partnership and nothing more.

Following hasty introductions McCabe escorts Mrs. Miller to Sheehan's, where she immediately puts McCabe in his place ('If you want to make out you're such a fancy dude you ought to wear something beside that cheap Jockey Club cologne'). After devouring a huge meal in decidedly unladylike fashion, Mrs. Miller strikes a blow for gender equality *avant le lettre* by presenting McCabe with a '50/50' partnership deal. She persuasively argues that she will more than make up for his lack of experience in the prostitution business: 'I haven't got time to talk to a man who's too dumb to see a good proposition. Do we make a deal or don't we?' Contrary to his individualistic creed, an emasculated McCabe sheepishly acquiesces. The victim of an unexpected gender role reversal, McCabe is already smitten with the beautiful and commanding Mrs. Miller – an unrequited infatuation that will only grow and gnaw at his self-esteem, drive him to drink and eventually cost him his life. No generic western would ever allow its male hero such emotional vulnerability at the hands of a supposedly lowly female.[19] During the scene the town's resident fiddler plays the popular Stephen Foster parlour song, 'Beautiful Dreamer'. As Helene Keyssar points out, 'McCabe, not Mrs. Miller, is the beautiful dreamer of this movie, and Mrs. Miller wishes neither to be the object nor the perpetrator of anyone's dreams' (1991: 183).

The following scenes establish that some months have elapsed, winter has descended on Presbyterian Church and McCabe's 'House of Fortune', whorehouse and adjacent bathhouse – Mrs. Miller insists on 'proper hygiene' to prevent venereal disease – have all been completed and are now money-making enterprises. The fraught relationship between McCabe and Mrs. Miller is further developed; he continues to secretly desire her but, like the stereotypical henpecked husband, expresses his frustration by fretting about business expenses associated with their joint enterprises. She insists that he's not spending enough ('You have to spend money to make money'). There is also a harbinger of the bloodshed that will mark the picture's second half. Bart Coyle (Bert Remsen) brawls with a man who mistakes his mail-order bride Ida (Shelley Duvall) for one of Mrs. Miller's prostitutes and gets his head 'all busted open', an act of frontier mayhem witnessed by a terrified Ida, an uneasy Sumner Washington (Rodney Gage), the town's black barber, and his wife (Lili Francks), a characteristically indifferent Reverend Elliot, and two newly arrived strangers in town: Eugene Sears (Michael Murphy) and Ernie Hollander (Antony Holland).

Sears and Hollander are emissaries from the M. H. Harrison Shaughnessy Mining Company and their mandate is not only to purchase the local zinc deposits but to buy up all the other suitably profitable businesses, including Sheehan's and all of McCabe's holdings. Their arrival on the scene signals the film's transition from empire building to a middle-phase western movie subgenre that focuses on conflicts threatening the stability of the new community (a typical battle: ranchers versus 'sod-busters' over land use). *McCabe & Mrs. Miller* revises the defining conflict as fundamentally between small business and big business; Presbyterian Church has reached a growth stage that has attracted the attention of a mining conglomerate epitomising all the large, soulless corporations that have come to dominate life in modern America.[20] Unfortunately for McCabe, his judgement is impaired by egotism and alcohol when Sears and Hollander approach him with an offer. He refuses their bid of $5,500 and treats the pair in a cavalier manner; his first mistake. Later that night, having taken the requisite bath – house rules – a still intoxicated McCabe visits Mrs. Miller for paid sexual services. When he boasts about his prowess as a negotiator – 'I played it smart as a possum. Just turned them down flat as a pancake!' – she cuts through his cliché-ridden brag-gadocio with a dose of reality about corporate America: 'You turned down Harrison Shaughnessy. Do you know who they are? ... You just better hope they come back.

They'd soon as put a bullet in your back as look at you.' For a moment Mrs. Miller's fears seem to be unfounded when Sears and Hollander show up at the whorehouse and up their offer to $6,250. But, incredibly, McCabe turns them down again.[21] While McCabe is risking his fortune and life, Altman crosscuts to Mrs. Miller in her upstairs bedroom, smoking opium: a secret addiction that allows her to cope with the Darwinian nastiness of her world. Crosscut back to Sears and Hollander. Annoyed by McCabe's truculence, they utter vaguely worded threats. McCabe, persistent in his cluelessness, proposes an absurdly extravagant counter-offer ('$14,000, $15,000') and invites Sears and Hollander to breakfast the next morning to 'talk about it'. Little does he know that he has already signed his own death warrant. When McCabe returns to Mrs. Miller's room again, he labours under two romantic delusions: that he's about to reach a lucrative deal with Harrison Shaughnessy (actually, the deal is as good as dead) and that Mrs. Miller's beatific smile is proof of her genuine love for him (actually, she's high on opium). Before she allows McCabe to sleep with her, Mrs. Miller coyly reminds him that he has to pay first. He counts out five dollars – a princely sum in 1902 – and tucks them into a heart-shaped wooden box on her bureau before climbing into bed.[22] Altman ends the scene by zooming in for a close-up of the box: a shot that debunks love and romance mythology and quietly reminds the audience that human interactions in capitalist America almost always reduce to monetary transactions or 'deals'. Crosscut to a brief scene that ends the sequence, showing Sears and Hollander discussing the state of their negotiations with McCabe over dinner. Sears, the younger man, is optimistic that a deal can be struck. Hollander, jaded and dyspeptic, has reached the end of his patience. He tells Sears, 'After seventeen years [with the company] I deserve something better than a goddamn snipe hunt like this.' Sears agrees and they depart.

The next morning, amid news that Bart Coyle is in 'horrible' condition from his injury, McCabe makes hurried preparations for his important breakfast meeting with Sears and Hollander – until he's informed that they have already left. Smalley (John Schuck) rubs it in: 'You handled them beautifully. They knew they weren't dealing with no tinhorn.' The next scene adjusts the film's mood downward and quotes western lore ironically, by presenting a living tableau of some of the townspeople at Bart Coyle's funeral. They listen to Mister Elliot, in voiceover, unctuously delivering a grotesque hellfire and brimstone prayer for the dead, followed by mournful fiddle music and a maudlin hymn, sung off-key by Mrs. Miller's prostitutes. If religious rituals are supposed to be comforting, these awkward rites ring a little hollow.

In the midst of Coyle's funeral a mysterious cowboy (Keith Carradine) suddenly appears nearby and McCabe, Mrs. Miller and Smalley all assume that the man on horseback is a hired gun for Harrison Shaughnessy sent in to kill McCabe. McCabe adopts his best gunfighter's stance as he strides up to confront the stranger. Meanwhile, in the background of this deep focus shot, a frightened Mrs. Miller scurries away (her likely destination: the town's Chinese opium den), a foreshadowing of things to come. McCabe is relieved to discover that the cowboy is merely in town to enjoy 'the fanciest whorehouse in the whole territory'. The scene references the classic western gunfight scenario, only to dismiss it as an unrealistic cliché. Yet the very next scene contradicts

McCabe's relief: Harrison Shaughnessy's real enforcers – not one rider, but three – are shown on the trail, making their way to Presbyterian Church.

What follows is a sequence of whorehouse scenes that further develop the movie's quasi-feminist subtext and provide a calm interlude before the film's final, violent phase. One scene shows the randy cowboy expressing his desire to have sex with every available whore in Mrs. Miller's establishment. His virility is, however, undercut by one of the women he's already slept with. She whispers into the ear of a co-worker and poses her index finger an inch or so away from her thumb, obviously indicating that the man has an unusually small penis: a gesture that takes the self-congratulatory smile off the face of the cowboy – a scene unimaginable in a conventionally phal-locentric western. Another scene shows McCabe wanting to see Mrs. Miller on the pretext of delivering a package but he glumly desists after being informed that 'she's with someone'. Yet another scene depicts Mrs. Miller breaking in Bart Coyle's widow, Ida, who must now work as a prostitute because her sole former means of support has ceased to exist – deeply ironic because Coyle died defending Ida's honour after she was mistaken as a whore. When Ida expresses trepidation about her new profession, Mrs. Miller encourages her to think in terms of economic pragmatism: 'See, the thing is, it don't mean nothing. You never know. You might even get to like it. You managed it with Bart, didn't you?' When Ida protests that it was her duty as a wife, Mrs. Miller delivers a blunt critique of capitalist patriarchy by demolishing the romantic myth behind the marriage institution: 'It weren't your "duty", Ida. You did it to pay for your bed and board. And you do this to pay for your bed and board, too. You get to keep a little extra for yourself and you don't have to ask nobody for nothing; just honest in my mind.'

McCabe & Mrs. Miller is structured concatentively, by a series of arrivals. The arrival of the three hired killers – Butler (Hugh Millais), Breed (Jace Van Der Veen) and the Kid (Manfred Schultz) – signals the film's transition into its third and final phase: a revisionist version of the End-of-the-West western, a subgenre that typically depicts the closing of the frontier and the cessation of the rugged individualism and lawlessness that made the West 'wild' (examples include *True Grit* (1969 and 2010), *The Wild Bunch* (1969) and *Butch Cassidy and the Sundance Kid* (1969)). The sudden and ominous appearance of the hired killers on horseback breaks up nocturnal fiddling and dancing festivities on the iced-over pond in front of Sheehan's and sends the reve-lers packing; they instinctively know what these strangers are bringing to town. Mrs. Miller does too; she tries to convince McCabe to flee in a covered wagon but he refuses, even after learning from Smalley that making some sort of deal with these men is highly unlikely ('They said there was nothing to talk about'). Ever the foolish optimist, McCabe grabs some cigars as intended gifts and proceeds to Sheehan's to try to parlay with Butler, the leader of the killer trio. A huge bear of a man in dirty goat fleece, wide-brimmed black hat and drooping Fu Manchu moustache, Butler is a charming psychopath whose size, appearance and Marlin octagonal-barrel long rifle mark him as a truly menacing figure. He keeps McCabe waiting while he regales Shee-han's other patrons with a racist anecdote about using 'Chinamen' to cheaply detonate dynamite in mining operations and blow them up in the process ('You know what the fine is for killing a Chinaman? $50, maximum'). To punctuate his story Butler loudly drops a breakfast tray to simulate an explosion at the rock face of a mine: a stunt reminiscent of an incident in John Ford's *The Man Who Shot Liberty Valance* (1962), when Valance (Lee Marvin) trips Ranse Stoddard (Jimmy Stewart), sending a steak dinner plate crashing to the floor and precipitating a confrontation between Valance and Tom Doniphon (John Wayne), the steak's intended recipient. The difference here is that, unlike Stoddard, McCabe does not have John Wayne to come to his defence; he must face Butler and his henchmen alone. McCabe tries to offer the big man a conciliatory cigar but, in true Freudian fashion, Butler counters with a much larger one of his one. McCabe also tries to get Butler to talk in private. Butler politely refuses, preferring instead to play an elaborate verbal game of cat and mouse. He pretends for a while to entertain McCabe's more moderate offer of $6,500 before finally admitting, 'I don't make deals.' For a moment Butler even denies that he's in the employ of Harrison Shaughnessy. He then goads McCabe into a fight by asking if he shot 'his best friend's best friend', a man named Bill Roundtree (a rumour learned from Sheehan); but, in the end, he tires of the game and tells McCabe he's going to count to ten and 'if you're not on the bridge when I finish, I'm going to get very cross with you'.

Anxious to avoid the wrath of Butler and his compatriots, McCabe ventures to the Harrison Shaughnessy office in Bear Paw to see if he can intercept Sears and Hollander before they leave the territory but is told by a glum clerk (played by screenwriter Joan Tewkesbury) that they've left already. He then meets with a lawyer named Clement Samuels (William Devane) to seek some sort of legal redress.[23] Tellingly, a framed portrait of President William McKinley adorns Samuels' office wall. In 1902 the president is actually Teddy Roosevelt, McKinley's successor after McKinley was assassinated by an anarchist named Leon Czolgosz in Buffalo, New York in September 1901.[24] The image of a recently slain president does not bode well for the efficacy of the rule of law versus the law of the jungle, which the film implicitly submits is the real ethos that governs American life. Nonetheless, Samuels, a glib opportunist with political ambitions blathers on about the glories of 'free enterprise' and the need to protect the entrepreneurial spirit from the 'sons of bitches' out to crush the 'little guy'. Samuels wants to use McCabe to bust 'these trusts and monopolies' that are 'at the very root of the problem of creating a just society'. He proclaims (somewhat illogically): 'Until people start dying for freedom they ain't gonna be free.' McCabe is less ambitious; he just doesn't 'want to get killed'. Samuels assures McCabe that a court case and the attendant publicity will bring him national notoriety on a par with William Jennings Bryan, thereby protecting him from harm.[25] The gaping flaw in the lawyer's logic is that the process he describes will take a good deal of time to develop, time McCabe doesn't have.[26]

That night, back in Presbyterian Church, when McCabe parrots Samuels' lofty trust-busting ideals to Mrs. Miller, she passionately rejects his talk as boastful nonsense and renews her plea for him to leave town: 'They'll get you, McCabe. They'll get you and do something awful to you!' McCabe sees that Mrs. Miller's emotional intensity betrays real affection for him. He tries to comfort her but that makes her all the more defensive and angry ('Don't give me that "little lady" shit!') and protests that her concern is solely motivated by economic self-interest. The scene makes it clear that McCabe and Mrs. Miller care about each other but lack the emotional capacity to be fully human; both are the outcast products of a harsh, Darwinian universe that has rendered them mere survivalists incapable of real love and trust.

The next scene does not advance the main storyline but does further Altman's critique of western genre clichés and establishes a moral framework through which to 'read' the violence that will punctuate the film's final, twenty-minute sequence. It is also profoundly affecting in its own right. Having had his run of the whorehouse, the cowboy prepares to leave Presbyterian Church but not before stopping over to the general store inside Sheehan's to buy some socks for his journey. Standing on the porch at Sheehan's, the Kid – a puggish, blond teenager with a Dutch boy haircut – is target shooting while Breed and Butler look on. Embarrassed by missing a shot at a clay jug he's slid over the ice, the Kid is spoiling to prove his shooting prowess and, by extension, his manhood. When the cowboy attempts to cross the rope bridge over the pond to Sheehan's the Kid taunts him, tricks him into drawing his gun, and then blasts the cowboy off the bridge in a cold-blooded mockery of the traditional western gunfight. In the aftermath, Sheehan and a few other bystanders stare in uncomprehending horror at the corpse of the cowboy bobbing in a patch of icy, open water under the bridge: a shot rendered in slow motion to maximise its tragic effect. The scene stands as a resounding repudiation of one of the pillars of the western genre (and of American phallocentric ideology in general): the notion that gun violence is somehow redemptive, a decisive and manly act that solves otherwise intractable social problems and moves the world in a positive direction.[27] The murder of the cowboy, a character well established as harmless and amicable, is depicted as a senseless atrocity, sickeningly craven and sadistic. Westerns and other action genre films typically present instances of lethal gunplay as entertaining spectacles that are ethically neutral, or, more often, cathartic and exhilarating demonstrations of heroism and righteousness. Here, to haunting effect, Altman refuses to grant the gun its traditional, phony mystique.

In the long sequence that brings the film to closure, McCabe and his three would-be assassins stalk each other, guerilla fashion, through the deserted streets of town in the early daylight hours during a snowstorm: a far more evocative and realistic scenario than the generic western showdown on main street, and one that both references and contradicts Fred Zinnemann's *High Noon* (1952).[28] In that picture, Will Kane (Gary Cooper), a retired Hadleyville, New Mexico Marshal, is stalked by Frank Miller (Ian Macdonald), a paroled criminal seeking vengeance on Kane for putting him in prison years earlier. Miller is in league with three other gang members but Kane is pretty much on his own despite his strenuous efforts to recruit townsfolk to his cause. In the end Kane's young bride, Amy Fowler (Grace Kelly), a Quaker, renounces her pacifism to assist in her husband's defence. In marked contrast to Amy Fowler, Constance Miller is nowhere to be seen in McCabe's hour of need. Nor is McCabe anything like Will Kane; he already knows that no one will risk their life to assist him so he doesn't bother to ask for help.

At the start of the final sequence McCabe climbs the church steeple to reconnoiter and spies Butler and his two sidekicks leaving McCabe's casino and splitting up to look for him. On his descent, he finds that Mister Elliot has confiscated the double-barreled shotgun he left at the foot of the ladder. When McCabe asks for it back, Elliot speaks on screen for the first time: 'This is a house of God.' Elliot's righteous assertion is, however, contradicted by the church's interior, which is not a functioning presbytery but rather a chaotic jumble of discarded wagon wheels and building materials: the tangible sign that his church (literally and figuratively) is nothing but an empty shell.[29] McCabe presses his case ('Them men out there are trying to kill me') but Elliot cocks both triggers, levels the gun at him, and forces him out of the building – hardly an example of Christian compassion, especially inasmuch as churches are supposed to provide sanctuary and right of asylum for people in trouble. Elliot's inhospitable manners soon rebound on him however. Moments later, after McCabe has stumbled away, Butler kicks in the door, fires on Elliot with his long rifle, and blows him apart. The shooting also shatters an oil lamp Elliot is holding, starting a fire that will nearly consume the church.

Hiding in the bathhouse, McCabe (unheroically) shoots the Kid in the back when he enters. The Kid manages to get off two shots, wounding McCabe in the leg and stomach, before reeling dead into one of the baths: a karmic, watery fate similar to the one he inflicted upon the cowboy – though, with symbolic appropriateness, the Kid dies in *hot* water. Immediately thereafter one of the townspeople notices the fire in the church and rallies the town to fight it. The remainder of the sequence crosscuts between McCabe's struggle to stay alive and the town's concerted efforts to fight the fire. Repairing to his casino, where the trio has already looked for him, McCabe (again, unheroically but pragmatically) shoots Breed in the back as the man passes by his window. While on his way out of town to hide in a nearby mine, McCabe is shot from some distance behind by Butler's 'blunderbuss', as Mrs. Miller calls it. When Butler approaches McCabe to make sure he's dead, McCabe puts a bullet through Butler's forehead with a Derringer, like David slaying Goliath. At that moment the fire is put out and the townsfolk rejoice at the success of their collective effort.

As David Foster notes in his voiceover commentary to the DVD edition, Altman could have contrived a happy ending by having Mrs. Miller rescue McCabe, who would survive his wounds; such an ending would have undoubtedly generated much better box office receipts. But Altman stays true to Naughton's novel and his own artistic vision. McCabe tries to make it back into town but is too badly wounded; he collapses and dies alone in a blowing snowdrift. A crosscut to Mrs. Miller shows her reclining in an opium den in the town's Chinese quarter, stoned and dreaming an escapist dream. Juxtaposed but in deep visual contrast, these culminating images suggest the depth of the gulf between McCabe and Mrs. Miller (and, more generally, between men and women in patriarchal society), while neatly allegorising the death of the American Dream and the degraded nature of American society. McCabe's frozen demise also suggests that America's vaunted entrepreneurial spirit is a fragile construct, useful perhaps in the early stages of nation building, but always eventually overcome and destroyed by corporatist imperatives.[30] Founded on coarse and selfish Gesellschaft values, McCabe's individualism is, moreover, a cold existential dead-end. Mrs. Miller's is a figurative and spiritual death, marginalisation and self-exile that speak to

Stoned alone: Mrs. Miller (Julie Christie) lost in an opium reverie while McCabe dies in the snow outside.

the suffocating oppressiveness of the patriarchal order. Her opium addiction figures for America's descent into drugs and political passivity in the post-Vietnam era. Or as Michael Turner puts it, *McCabe & Mrs. Miller* 'is really about the collapse of 1960s idealism, the belief that you could forge an alternative reality, and occupy it, like the town of Presbyterian Church' (2006: n.p.). As for the naïve citizens of Presbyterian Church, they have the saddle on the wrong horse, as McCabe would say, rallying to save a meaningless symbol while their leading citizen is being hunted and killed by corporate thugs. As Robert Kolker rightly notes, *McCabe & Mrs. Miller* 'denies absolutely the possibility of an individual triumphing, in fact or in spirit' (2011: 383), a denial that strikes at the heart of business civilisation ideology, which officially champions individual agency while its corporate structures actually undermine and nullify such agency at every turn.

Yet Kolker detects redemptive possibilities in the movie's 'lyricism and gentleness'. Somewhere 'between the adolescent romanticism of McCabe and the hardness of Mrs. Miller, love might possibly exist on terms other than the raucous sentimentality American film depends upon. There is the suggestion too that a community might cohere on terms other than self-interest and a brutality that arises from greed' (2011: 332). Indeed, something like real Gemeinschaft can be found is Mrs. Miller's bordello, where the whores, lowest of the low in conventional society, live and work together and are shown to have fashioned a genuinely caring and close-knit community. While dependent upon the larger economic order, the communal female subculture they inhabit is quite distinct from it in more profound, even revolutionary, ways: Altman's suggestion that if genuine community is going to be found in modern America, it's going to be found in its marginalised countercultures.

McCabe & Mrs. Miller is a technically flawed film. Some of the opening shots in Sheehan's tavern are too dark, visually almost indecipherable, and the overall soundtrack is far less than optimal. In the words of Altman's editor, Lou Lombardo, 'The sound was fucked but he never changed it … a dirty [sound]track, a muddy track. It was like trying to get an out of focus picture in focus (in McGilligan 1989: 344). Though well-reviewed, *McCabe & Mrs. Miller* was not particularly successful when it was released in the summer of 1971; it earned just $4 million at the box office – not much more than it cost to make. Nonetheless, the film is now widely recognised as Altman's masterpiece and one of greatest westerns ever made. Often erroneously termed an 'anti-western', the movie is more properly understood as a *corrected* western. Altman's method is 'not an avoidance of convention, but a reworking of it', in the judicious words of Dan Menaker (1971: D12). More than a western, *McCabe & Mrs. Miller* is perhaps the definitive filmic allegory about the rise and fall of capitalist America: a sobering political statement and a stunning aesthetic achievement. Indeed, the usually circumspect Roger Ebert went so far as to call *McCabe & Mrs. Miller* 'a perfect film' (1971: n.p).

The Long Goodbye (1973)

Critics are divided as to its merits, but Raymond Chandler considered *The Long Goodbye* (Hamish Hamilton, 1953) his best novel. Four other Chandler novels featuring his iconic private detective, Philip Marlowe – *Farewell, My Lovely, Murder My Sweet, The Big Sleep* and *The Lady in the Lake* – had been made into films in the 1940s, so a movie version of *The Long Goodbye* was long overdue when Elliott Kastner and Jerry Bick commissioned Leigh Brackett (co-screenwriter with William Faulkner of *The Big Sleep* (1946)) to write a screenplay. Howard Hawks and Peter Bogdanovich had already passed on the project when George Litto sent Brackett's script to Altman in Ireland, where he was working on *Images*. Altman initially didn't want to do it either but liked Brackett's ending, which had Marlowe killing his friend, Terry Lennox: an ending he found 'so out of character' and 'very surprising'. He agreed to direct, but only if his contract stipulated that Brackett's ending survived intact (see Thompson 2006: 77). Kastner wanted Robert Mitchum to play Marlowe but David Picker, head of United Artists, disagreed. Lee Marvin and Walter Matthau were offered the part but turned it down. Picker then suggested Elliott Gould, Altman's *M*A*S*H* co-star and friend. Altman concurred, called Gould, and signed him on (see McGilligan 1989: 360).

To a great extent, casting Elliott Gould as Philip Marlowe set the anti-genre tone for the movie. Gould's quirky screen persona was that of a slightly effeminate, compulsively talkative counterculture schlemiel: worlds away from earlier portrayals of Marlowe as a taciturn, world-weary tough guy – though, as Bill Oliver points out, Altman and Gould's Marlowe 'leaves about the character some of those qualities which appealed to audiences most – his uncompromising moral code, his doggedness in finding out the truth, his honesty and disdain for privilege. The difference is, the private eye's code is no longer armor and his honesty and quest for the truth are no longer sufficient for dealing with corruption in the seventies' (1975: 243). Altman's other casting choices were equally inspired: Sterling Hayden as Roger Wade, a troubled alcoholic writer (as was Hayden was in real life); Nina van Pallandt (Swedish mistress of Howard Hughes 'autobiography' forger Clifford Irving) as Wade's trophy wife, Eileen; Mark Rydell (film director) as crime boss Marty Augustine; Henry Gibson (diminutive comic actor from the TV show, *Laugh-In*) as Verringer, Wade's sinister and corrupt detox doctor; and Jim Bouton (former major league baseball pitcher and bestselling memoirist) as

Marlowe's friend, Terry Lennox.[34] Van Pallandt and Bouton had never acted before. A non-speaking role, as one of Augustine's flunkies, went to a young bodybuilder from Austria named Arnold Schwarzenegger.

Leigh Brackett made significant changes to Chandler's novel, streamlining a complicated storyline by eliminating a number of characters, adding a few (racketeer Marty Augustine and his gang), changing the circumstances of Roger Wade's death (from being murdered to committing suicide), relieving Eileen Wade of all crimes except adultery, and allowing Marlowe to kill his double-crossing 'friend', Terry Lennox (see Dunkle 1987: 127). Altman liked Brackett's screenplay and adhered to it quite closely but as always the story wasn't important; it was style, tone and mood that would make the movie 'Altmanesque'. Casting Gould was a crucial anti-genre gambit but equally important was the decision to set the film in the present (c.1972) rather than the 1949–50 timeframe of the novel – and to make Gould's Marlowe into a walking anachronism. As Altman told an interviewer, 'I decided we were going to call him Rip Van Marlowe, as if he'd been asleep for twenty years, had woken up and was wandering through this landscape of the early 1970s but trying to invoke the morals of a previous era. I put him in that dark suit, white shirt and tie, while everyone was smelling incense and smoking pot and going topless; everything was health food and exercise and cool. So we just satirised that whole [earlier] time' (in Thompson 2006: 76). Altman added and subtracted some scenes, afforded Gould space for improvisation, and allowed the always inebriated Sterling Hayden to ad lib his own dialogue – to great effect, as it turned out.

Some of the cinematographic techniques that Altman and Vilmos Zsigmond employ for *The Long Goodbye* follow established noir stylistics as delineated by Paul Schrader in his well-known essay, 'Notes on Film Noir', but most do not. Schrader notes that, in classic noir, there 'seems to be an almost Freudian attachment to water'. Altman follows tradition by shooting a number of scenes at the Wade's waterfront Malibu house (actually Altman's rented home at the time) and two main characters – Roger Wade and Terry Lennox – die in water (as did the cowboy and the Kid in *McCabe & Mrs. Miller*). Schrader notes the 'majority of [noir] scenes are lit for night'. There are a number of key night scenes (e.g. Wade's death) in *The Long Goodbye* but most of Altman's movie is shot in broad daylight and, as they had done with *McCabe & Mrs. Miller*, Altman had Zsigmond post-flash the film, to give it 'the soft pastel look you see on old postcards from the 1940s' (in Thompson 2006: 77): a look quite unlike the low-key chiaroscuro lighting of classic noir films. 'The effect,' notes Richard K. Ferncase, 'rather than one of inscrutable darkness and menace, is more like the insidious glare of a smoggy Los Angeles afternoon' (1991: 88). In noir, says Schrader, 'oblique and vertical lines are preferred to horizontal' lines and light enters dingy rooms in odd shapes – 'jagged trapezoids, obtuse triangles, vertical slits' (1972: 11) – but Zsigmond's loosely framed, light-flooded compositions, often in long shot, tend to avoid these visual patterns; if anything, they are decidedly horizontal, to emphasise the impersonal vastness of contemporary Los Angeles. Schrader also argues that classic noir favours tableau-like 'compositional tension' created by a static camera rather than physical action. Altman shuns compositional tension altogether: 'I decided that the camera should never stop moving. It was arbitrary. We just kept the camera on a dolly and everything would move or pan but it didn't match the action; usually it was counter to it' (in Thompson 2006: 77). Classic noir often employs voiceover narration to create 'an irretrievable past, a predetermined fate and an all-enveloping hopelessness' and typically adopts a 'complex chronological order' that reinforces 'feelings of hopelessness and lost time' (Schrader 1972: 11). No fan of fatalistic storylines, Altman follows Brackett by eschewing both of these devices in favour of a broadly linear but still meandering narrative structure in keeping with the bewilderingly decentred nature of life in LA's postmodern landscape and culture. As Kolker notes, 'Rather than being witness to a dark and doomed world, as in classic film noir … the viewer shares the point of view of a Marlowe so completely out of control of his world that there is no possibility of detection, but only, perhaps, of accidental discovery' (2011: 341).

For sound, Altman employed his trademark ambient sound atmospherics and overlapping dialogue and, for music, he used just two songs. One of these was 'The Long Goodbye', the film's title theme by John Williams and Johnny Mercer that appears diegetically throughout the movie in different arrangements and by different artists (the Dave Grusin Trio, Jack Sheldon, Clydie King, Jack Riley, Morgan Ames' Aluminum Band and the Tepoztlan Municipal Band). As Altman told an interviewer, 'I've always said at the beginning of conceiving a film, "I'd love the music to be indigenous, so that there's not going to be any violins you can't see, that it won't come from nowhere". I've never completely achieved that, though in *The Long Goodbye* the music became a character in itself' (in Thompson 2006: 80). To emphasise the inherent artificiality of noir as a genre, the film begins and ends with 'Hooray for Hollywood', a well-known paean to the movie industry that calls attention to itself and to the film as artifice by being so obviously out of place in a noir film.[35]

The first sequence in Brackett's screenplay calls for Marlowe to be importuned in the middle of the night by his friend Terry Lennox, who vaguely alludes to trouble with his wife, Sylvia, that necessitates immediate transport to Mexico in an inconspicuous automobile not his own (in keeping with his anachronistic ways, Marlowe drives a 1948 Lincoln convertible). Marlowe dutifully takes Lennox to the border but upon his return to his apartment several hours later, he is intercepted by two LA detectives who have located Lennox's car parked nearby and have found Marlowe's name in an address book Lennox left behind. The cops inform Marlowe that Sylvia has been found beaten to death. They want to know where Lennox is and how Marlowe is connected to the murder and his friend's disappearance. When Marlowe refuses to cooperate, the cops bring Marlowe 'downtown' for interrogation. After still refusing to cooperate, Marlowe is jailed for three days before he is suddenly released on news from Mexico that Lennox has confessed to the murder of his wife and has committed suicide.

To establish *The Long Goodbye* as genre parody, at least in part, Altman embellishes the opening sequence by inserting some mildly absurdist material before Lennox's arrival that does not advance the plot but does develop Marlowe's character while suggesting certain themes. In Altman's version Marlowe is not awoken by Lennox but by his hungry cat. Out of cat food, Marlowe tries to feed the finicky feline cottage cheese. After the cat paws the dish to the floor, Marlowe is forced to go to an all-night store for his cat's favourite brand, Coury Cat Food, but not before putting on his

Not Bogart: Philip Marlowe (Elliott Gould) tries to fool his cat – and fails.

suit and tie. On his way to the store, the 1940s clash with the 1970s when Marlowe passes by his attractive, semi-nude hippie girl neighbours, who ask him to buy brownie mix so they can make pot brownies. At the store, Marlowe discovers that the brand of cat food he seeks is not available. He buys an alternate brand and tries to fool his cat by putting some of the substitute food into an empty Coury can but the cat sees through his ploy and flees the apartment in evident disgust, never to return. Unthinkable in classic noir – Humphrey Bogart's Marlowe didn't have a pet and never would – the droll cat routine establishes Altman's Marlowe as a lonely, vulnerable eccentric manipulated and abandoned by his cat when its needs are not met: an example of friendship betrayed that turns out to be the film's main theme.[33] William Van Vert argues that the 'cat sequence also establishes sexuality patterns in the film, and all sexuality patterns are in some way or another deviant, perverse, off-colour, or so Altman seems to be telling us. The cat is Marlowe's sexuality. He is impervious to the nudity of his neighbors, equally oblivious to the come-on of Eileen Wade [in later scenes]. Marlowe only jumps for his cat' (1974: 12). In the police station scene Gould further develops Marlowe's clownishness with some improvisation. Inked for fingerprinting, Marlowe rubs the ink on his face while being interrogated and imitates Al Jolson in blackface singing 'Swanee' from *The Jazz Singer* (1927), an allusion to the first 'talkie' and another Brechtian reminder to viewers they're watching a film.

The screenplay has Marlowe traveling to Mexico immediately after his release from jail, to confirm Lennox's death. Altman defers this scene in favour of introducing the seemingly unrelated story of Roger Wade's disappearance. Hired by Eileen Wade to locate her wayward husband, Marlowe quite efficiently finds Wade at Dr. Verringer's psychiatric hospital and returns him home. As in the screenplay, the third strand of the narrative begins when Marty Augustine and his henchman call on Marlowe at his apartment to determine his connection to Lennox (as reported in the newspapers) and to hopefully retrieve a large sum of Augustine's money in Lennox's possession that has gone missing (a motive made clear in the movie but not in the script). In Brackett's screenplay Augustine's underlings follow standard operating procedure for noir gangsters by beating and pistol-whipping Marlowe and ransacking his apartment.

To defamiliarise a genre set piece and bring it to life, Altman concocts a startling bit of sociopathic cruelty instead. Suddenly and without warning, Augustine smashes a Coke bottle across the face of his mistress (Jo Ann Brody) just to show Marlowe how ruthless he can be ('Now that's someone I love. And you I don't even like'). The attack is so unexpected and violent that even Augustine's hoodlums are confounded, to say nothing of viewers' reactions.[37] Coming at almost the half-way point of the movie, the Coke bottle incident works as a sobering rebuke to viewers who think they have *The Long Goodbye* figured out as an unrealistic travesty of noir.

Unfazed by Augustine's chilling object lesson, Marlowe surreptitiously tails the gangster when he drives away and is surprised to observe him arriving at Wade's house in Malibu and conferring with Eileen, thereby somehow tying together two of the movie's narrative strands. In the screenplay Marlowe calls on Roger Wade the next day, to interview him about Terry Lennox. In the movie Altman defers the interview; when Marlowe arrives, a jealous Wade asks him to wait on the beach while he has a few words with his wife, whom he suspects of being attracted to Marlowe. The inserted scene is one of the film's most emotionally wrenching. Hopelessly afflicted by writer's block undoubtedly exacerbated by alcoholism, a blustering Wade tries to preserve his crumbling ego and save his faltering marriage by appealing to his wife's sympathies but, having heard and seen it all before, she remains distant and unaffected – and then finally turns cruel, reminding Wade of his impotence. A large, bearded man (6'5' and 230 pounds), Hayden evokes the iconic mid-century masculinity style of Ernest Hemingway in clothing, appearance and general bearing and also displays Hemingway's (and Raymond Chandler's) suicidal tendencies in his ensuing conversation with Marlowe ('Ever think about suicide, Marlboro?').[38] If Marlowe's peculiar brand of masculinity seems suspect, Wade's more grandiose version of manliness is in critical condition.

In the next scene Marlowe is riding the elevator to his apartment after collecting his mail when he opens a letter from Lennox ('Good Bye, Phil. I'm sorry. Terry') accompanied by a $5,000 bill as evident payoff for the ride to Mexico. The timing, the terse wording of the note, and the exorbitant compensation make Marlowe suspicious. We next see him arriving in Mexico, to verify Lennox's death (the scene that Brackett put near the beginning of the movie, more appropriately placed and better motivated here). Mexican officials show Marlowe the dossier on Lennox's death, including alleged photos of the corpse, but Marlowe remains suspicious, wondering how Lennox managed to get to such a remote location and why he would do so, just to take his own life.

Marlowe calls on the Wades again in the middle of a lively afternoon social gathering and is menaced by their dog: a repeat of earlier occurrences that marks him as the perennial outsider to the bourgeois decadence of 1970s California. A moment later Dr. Verringer also crashes the party, to collect $4,400 owed him for Roger Wade's recent stay at Verringer's clinic.[36] As written, the scene is crisp and succinct. As realised on film, the scene is far more operatic. A very drunken Wade calls Verringer 'Minnie Mouse' and 'the albino turd' and tries to publicly humiliate him by insightfully declaring to his guests that Verringer is 'the epitome of all that's wrong with this world' because 'he pretends to cure people'. Unfazed, the steely-eyed Verringer savagely slaps Roger in the face (echoing Augustine's attack on his mistress) while sternly and repeatedly demanding payment. Suddenly brought to momentary sobriety, a thoroughly humiliated Wade retreats to his study with Verringer, writes a check for the money owed – the only 'writing' the once-great author can now manage – and then collapses into a drunken stupor. A fading relic of an archaic he-man ethos, Roger Wade is brought low by a 'liberated' trophy wife he cannot satisfy or control and by Verringer, the avatar of a dawning postmodern order whose distinguishing features are rabid greed and psychological manipulation masked as 'therapy'. Wade's writer's block is the sign of a larger existential paralysis; his 1940s sensibility cannot limn or narrate the reality of a contemporary culture vastly more cold-blooded, narcissistic and treacherous than former times.

That night, in a scene appropriately switched from an earlier moment in the screenplay, Roger Wade sleeps off his inebriation while a flirtatious Eileen makes a sumptuous dinner for Marlowe, who has chosen to stay for support – but also to interrogate her about Augustine's mysterious visit. After dinner, in a well-conceived deep focus shot, Marlowe quizzes an increasingly distraught and defensive Eileen while they stand opposite each other in front of a large picture window overlooking the ocean, a window through which viewers observe Roger Wade leisurely making his way to the waterline.[40] A reverse shot, from the beach up to the window, shows Eileen finally looking out toward the ocean and another reverse shot shows Wade falling into the pounding surf. A reaction shot registers the alarm of both Eileen and Marlowe and they run into the surf to try and save Wade's life, the chaos and pathos of the scene emphasised by Wade's barking dog who runs back and forth on the shoreline. It soon becomes clear that their efforts are in vain; Wade is swallowed by the sea and the darkness, a perfect metaphor for the psyche drowning in the depths of the Unconscious.

In the aftermath, with police and neighbors swarming the scene, Eileen tearfully tells a drunken and half-hysterical Marlowe that her husband was having an affair with Sylvia Lennox and she thinks her husband killed Sylvia in a fit of jealousy after Terry found out, despite Terry's confession that *he* killed his wife. A gullible Marlowe buys Eileen's story (perhaps she believes it herself) and immediately confronts LAPD Detective Farmer (Stephen Coit), demanding that the Sylvia Lennox case be reopened. Farmer informs Marlowe that Roger Wade left the Lennox home well before the murder and checked into Verringer's clinic and that his alibi has been verified. Frustrated once again, Marlowe departs the scene spouting obscenities at the police.

Summoned to Marty Augustine's LA penthouse office to produce the missing $360,000, Marlowe faces dire prospects. In Brackett's screenplay, Augustine's thugs give Marlowe another severe beating: *de rigeur* in classic noir. Altman, however, opts for an absurdist take on the clichéd gangster shakedown. In his version as filmed, Augustine tells Marlowe he stripped naked to apologize to Jo Ann for bashing her face and then suggests that he, his men, and Marlowe all take their clothes off to somehow get to the truth about the missing money. A wry parody of 1970s encounter group sessions, the scene marks Augustine and his gang as anachronistic as Marlowe and Roger Wade and even more ridiculous in their awkward efforts to appear hip and trendy. Luckily, Marlowe's 'fairy godmother' Eileen Wade, saves him from nudity and much worse by delivering the missing cash to Augustine: a *Deus ex machina* gambit that reveals her likely involvement with Terry Lennox. Marlowe spots her as she departs the scene in her Mercedes convertible and runs after her but is hit by a car and hospitalised. In a surreal and dreamlike scene, Marlowe awakens relatively unscathed in a hospital room he shares with a person completely bandaged, like an Egyptian mummy (Marlowe quips, 'You're gonna be okay. I've seen all your pictures too'). For some obscure reason, the mumbling, mummy-like figure gives Marlowe a miniature harmonica. A 2,000-year-old corpse reanimated, the atavistic mummy is the ultimate anachronism; thus, an extreme version of Marlowe.

Another visit to the Wade's residence reveals that it is already up for sale and Eileen is nowhere to be seen. Surmising that she is probably joining Terry Lennox in Mexico, Marlowe returns there and uses the $5,000 bill Lennox sent him to bribe Mexican police into revealing his whereabouts.[32] Finding Lennox very much alive (his suicide elaborately faked), Marlowe confronts him about murdering his wife. In the manner of a smug sociopath, Lennox rationalises the killing as an 'accident' and mocks Marlowe for his exaggerated concern about the whole affair, 'What the hell? Nobody cares.' Marlowe replies, 'Yeah, nobody cares but me.' Lennox: 'That's you, Marlowe. You never learn. You're a born loser.' Replying, 'Yeah, I even lost my cat', Marlowe quickly pulls out his .38 and shoots Lennox in the heart: the perfect murder because Lennox is already officially 'dead'. Lennox falls into a pond, another death in water that echoes Roger Wade's demise (and the watery deaths in *McCabe & Mrs. Miller*). Having achieved his vengeance, Marlowe spits on the ground to punctuate his bitterness, and then saunters down a dusty, tree-lined Mexican road. A jeep driven by Eileen passes by in the opposite direction. She recognises him and stops for a moment, then drives on, unaware that her lover is now dead. Marlowe continues to walk away from the camera, kicking up his heels and tootling on his miniature harmonica, and the strains of 'Hooray for Hollywood' take over as the closing credits roll.

Though the narrative's logical ending, and emotionally satisfying in a perverse way, Marlowe's killing of his friend remains shocking, given Marlowe's heretofore laidback manner and general characterisation as a somewhat befuddled bystander always a step or two behind the real action. The killing is also anti-genre, as Kolker points out: 'The fact that neither Chandler's Marlowe, nor any of his forties film incarnations, could kill a friend coldly and unflinchingly is a convention of Hollywood morality that Altman cannot abide, and he [reveals] the weakness and falseness of it' (2011: 349–50). Kolker goes on to note that 'Altman is one of the few American filmmakers who examines the results of the violent act, which more often than not only reaffirms the state that existed previous to it. The act of violence alters nothing. After the killing, Marlowe is still a jerk, still unconnected to his world' (2011: 351). Altman himself saw Marlowe's murder of Lennox in more sympathetic terms: 'My intention [was to show that] the greatest crime that could be committed against Philip Marlowe, who was a romantic, is that his friend broke faith with him. So he killed him' (in Sterritt 2000: 111). For Jonathan Kirshner, the killing is 'the only act of moral enforcement that occurs in the movie' (2012: 171). Perhaps, but murder seems an overreaction to a friendship betrayed, making Kolker's interpretation the more valid one. Less convincing is the notion that Marlowe remains 'unconnected from his world'. One could argue the opposite; when Marlowe kills Lennox he finally catches up to the historical moment he's actually living in. It's true that his violent act alters nothing in the world – Lennox was already 'dead' to the world anyway – but the killing rectifies Marlowe's injured vanity more than it rights a wrong. Having had his loyalty betrayed, he abandons it in favour of solipsistic egotism. Throughout most of the film Marlowe is a man caught between two historical epochs. In the end, he becomes an emphatically self-absorbed denizen of the 1970s, just like most of his contemporaries. But Philip Marlowe also becomes Altman's ideological surrogate; his killing of Lennox breaches noir's chivalric code of individual agency predicated on a stable sense of self: an identity paradigm that no longer applies in a profoundly decentred and amoral postmodern era. Perhaps because it so obviously denigrates the masculinist-individualist genre code that governs film noir, *The Long Goodbye* performed poorly at the box office, even after the release of a revised movie poster by cartoonist Jack Davis that made the movie's satiric intent abundantly clear. Critical response was likewise mixed.

Thieves Like Us (1974)

While he was making *McCabe & Mrs. Miller* Altman was given a copy of Edward Anderson's 1937 crime novel, *Thieves Like Us*, another property owned by Elliott Kastner and Jerry Bick. Altman loved the book. Unaware that Nicolas Ray had already made a film version (*They Live by Night* (1948)), Altman resolved to make his own. He hired his *McCabe & Mrs. Miller* script supervisor, Joan Tewkesbury, to write a screen adaptation that stayed close to the novel; an earlier screenplay by Calder Willingham was discarded as being too much focused 'on the mechanics of the robberies and the chase scenes' (Plecki 1985: 66). Altman told Tewkesbury, 'Don't help it. Just translate it' (in Thompson 2006: 81). Anderson's harsh and fatalistic saga follows the exploits of three Depression-era crooks – Elmo 'Chicamaw' Mobley, T. W. 'T-Dub' Masefield and Bowie Bowers – who escape from an Alcatona, Oklahoma prison in 1935 and go back to the only profession they know: robbing banks. Inevitably they all come to grief. T-Dub is killed trying to rob a bank. Bowie rescues Chicamaw from a prison farm but soon abandons him on a country road. Bowie and his girlfriend, Keechie, are ultimately gunned down in a police ambush, as were Bonnie and Clyde, the notorious outlaw couple on which they are obviously modeled.

As was her mandate, Tewkesbury's screenplay stays close to the letter and spirit of Anderson's novel. The only major change from novel to screenplay is the survival of Bowie's girlfriend, Keechie; Altman and Jerry Bick wanted to avoid an ending too closely resembling Arthur Penn's *Bonnie and Clyde* (see Plecki 1985: 66–7; McGilligan 1989: 369–70). Despite some streamlining, Altman adheres to the script more closely than any other movie he ever made. As always, he manipulates tone through casting, setting and cinematographic choices. Unglamorous Altman regulars John Schuck and Bert Remsen play a psychopathic Chicamaw and somewhat simpleminded T-Dub, respectively. Keith Carradine, the ill-fated cowboy in *McCabe & Mrs. Miller*, plays Bowie, the lead male role, and Shelley Duvall, Suzanne in *Brewster McCloud* and Ida in

McCabe & Mrs. Miller, plays Keechie, the female lead. Both actors were young, gangly and immensely talented: well-equipped to convey the naiveté and ordinariness of poor, uneducated Southern whites. Rounding out the cast: *M*A*S*H* star Tom Skerritt as Chicamaw's cousin, Dee Mobley; Jerry Bick's wife, Louise Fletcher, as T-Dub's sister-in-law, Mattie; and Ann Latham as Lula, T-Dub's wife.

The film's setting was switched from Oklahoma to Mississippi; presumably because the Dust Bowl of the 1930s was no longer a Dust Bowl in the 1970s, but perhaps also to avoid the kind of landscape already made so familiar by John Ford's *Grapes of Wrath* (1940). At any rate, rural Mississippi was a worthy candidate for a low-cost period film; not much had changed since the Great Depression, so suitably rustic locations were not hard to come by (see McGilligan 1989: 370). Altman, Tewkesbury and co-producers Jerry Bick, George Litto, Robert Eggenweiler and Thomas Hal Phillips found most of their shooting locations in the area between Hermanville and Jackson, in the west-central part of the state. Unusually heavy rains and flooding during the 43-day shoot in the summer of 1973 necessitated some site changes but Altman was able to stay on time and within the movie's very modest $1.125 million budget (thanks in part to the use of the 'cinemobile', a fully-equipped mobile movie studio invented by director Fouad Said). Unable to avail himself of the services of Vilmos Zsigmond a fourth time, allegedly because of the high fees that Zsigmond could now command, Altman hired French cinematographer Jean Boffety, who had worked with Robert Enrico, Vittorio De Sica and Alain Resnais but never worked in the United States.[39] As Altman later told an interviewer, 'I wanted a European cameraman who would not have a prejudice when I said "Mississippi" and would look at it and shoot it for what it is' (in Thompson 2006: 84). Though the region is the poorest and most backward in the country, its verdant fields and thick forests lend it a pastoral beauty that Boffety's unjaundiced eye was able to capture with great efficacy. Green is the colour that predominates in *Thieves Like Us*, not shades of Dust Bowl grey associated with the sombre black and white photographs of Walker Evans, Dorothea Lange, Ben Shahn and many other FSA photographers who commemorated the poverty and devastation of the era, thus creating its enduring visual iconography.[31] Working in colour and anxious to avoid pictorial clichés, Altman sought to recreate the texture of American life in the 1930s by concentrating on an often overlooked aspect of that period's culture: the persistent power of consumerism and advertising, even in a time of prolonged economic catastrophe. Accordingly, the movie's *mise-en-scène* is strewn with newspapers, cigarettes, liquor, popular and detective magazines, comic books, sheet music (used as wallpaper), car and home radios, endless bottles of Coca-Coca and found footage of Coca-Cola signs. As ubiquitous as Coke is the radio, chief purveyor of popular culture and advertising before the advent of television a generation later. In a phone interview after the film's release, Altman told film critic Ted Mahar that adapting Anderson's novel 'hit me as a simple way of showing the era in our history when we were just beginning to feel the influence of mass communications. The radio was everywhere but there was nothing good coming out of it. It was being used to sell Coke and toothpaste. Right from the start it was being used as an opiate rather than an incentive' (1974: 83). Radio broadcasts, diegetically featured throughout the film, convey period atmosphere or comment ironically on the action. There are snippets of speeches by FDR and his right-wing nemesis, Fr. Charles E. Coughlin, music broadcasts and advertisements. There are also bits and pieces of radio melodramas, like *The Shadow* and *Gang Busters* (which dramatised actual FBI cases), that underscore the extent to which sensationalised treatments of crime fired the imagination of the populace. An audio snippet from a corny radio dramatisation of *Romeo and Juliet* – 'Thus did Romeo and Juliet consummate their first interview by falling madly in love with each other' – is thrice-repeated while Bowie and Keechie first make love. Norman Kagan sees this odd device as 'a momentary anti-genre expression of healthy love' (1982: 110). A more plausible interpretation is that Altman meant the repeated radio snippet to be as annoying as it sounds, thus functioning as a cynical mockery of naïve romantic excess.

To complement the film's welter of realistic period detail, Altman opts to unfold his narrative at a snail's pace and to keep most of the bank heists and murders off-screen: seemingly perverse anti-genre choices that serve to conjure the essential quiescence of the Depression-era heartland: those backwater expanses largely unaffected by that era's radical politics and labour strife but still very much a part of a mass consumer society stuck in neutral and only capable of offering cheap blandishments and empty distractions to its passive, impoverished citizenry.

Arthur Penn's aforementioned *Bonnie and Clyde* was wildly successful because it portrayed the infamous outlaw couple as glamorous counterculture rebels who had the verve to take what they wanted in an otherwise demoralised world – and achieve heroic martyrdom in the process. It didn't matter that the real Bonnie Parker and Clyde Barrow were psychopathic serial killers spewed forth from lumpen misery outside Dallas, Texas who looked and acted nothing like sexy Warren Beatty and Faye Dunaway. The point of *Bonnie and Clyde* was to tailor an old folk myth of outlaw romance to the 1960s youth *zeitgeist*, a moment of rising affluence and dissident energy fundamentally different in kind from the dogged proletarianism of the 1930s. Whether or not it was specifically meant as a rejoinder to the rank mendacity of *Bonnie and Clyde*, *Thieves Like Us* manages to present a far more authentic rendering of the Depression as a dispiriting slough of widespread desolation suffused with inchoate class resentment at odds with standard American success ideology. As LeRoy Panek notes, 'Anderson's novel gets its title from the gang's repeated comparisons of themselves to other professions: politicians, bankers, policemen, druggists, lawyers, and so on, are "thieves like us"' (1990: 143).

In terms of setting and plot trajectories, *Bonnie and Clyde* and *Thieves Like Us* have a good deal in common but the two movies reach fundamentally different conclusions about individual agency, society, heroism and violence – thus providing an illuminating comparison. As for *Bonnie and Clyde*, Arthur Penn's *faux*-'true crime' biopic is symptomatic of a certain kind of nihilistic romanticism characteristic of the 1960s counterculture. The forces of law and order ultimately overcome and destroy Bonnie and Clyde (i.e. an expression of nihilistic defeatism) but the outlaw pair and associates manage to run wild for a time and offer viewers all sorts of vicarious thrills (i.e. a romantic affirmation of criminal rebelliousness). Robbing banks all over the South and Midwest, the Barrow gang displays a knack for audacious crime and hair-raising escapes that make them well-publicised folk heroes. (The exuberant energy the gang generates is epitomised by 'Foggy Mountain Breakdown', an exhilarating Flatt and Scruggs banjo tune that plays on the soundtrack during getaway sequences.)

The real Bonnie and Clyde were vicious murderers but Hollywood's Bonnie and Clyde only resort to violence in self-defence or in order to evade capture: a cynical falsification of history that elicits viewer sympathy and mitigates violence as merely a necessary tool to maintain freedom. In a similarly manipulative fashion the downfall of Bonnie and Clyde is attributed to the hypocrisy and mean-spiritedness of older, more conventional men. Seeking a lighter prison sentence for his son, C. W. Moss (Michael J. Pollard), a Barrow gang member, the outwardly obsequious Ivan Moss (Dub Taylor) betrays Bonnie and Clyde's whereabouts to a vengeful Frank Hamer (Denver Pyle), a Texas Ranger once captured and humiliated by the Barrow gang. Hamer sets up an ambush and, in the film's apocalyptic climax, he and a sizeable posse concealed behind bushes riddle Bonnie and Clyde with bullets on a country road in Louisiana, rendered in slow motion for maximum shock effect. Thus perpetrators become victims and suicidal nihilism is glorified as tragic martyrdom. Though they know their crime spree will result in doom, Bonnie and Clyde persist anyway. Brief empowerment and lasting notoriety are preferred to grinding poverty, boredom and eternal obscurity.

Thieves Like Us implicitly rejects the notion of heroic individual agency embraced by *Bonnie and Clyde*. It does so by offering soberingly realistic characterisations of its protagonists and of the social forces arrayed against them. It also depicts the use of violence in an entirely different light. Warren Beatty's Clyde, though sexually malad-justed, is handsome, daring, charismatic and full of libidinal energy sublimated to criminal aims. Beautiful and restless, Faye Dunaway's Bonnie is more than willing to be swept off her feet by Clyde, who promises excitement and danger even though he is not able to immediately consummate their relationship. By contrast, Keith Carradine's boyish Bowie has a high-pitched voice, is slight of build, immature and obviously an inexperienced lover. Unlike Bonnie, Shelley Duvall's distinctly odd-looking and world-weary Keechie is initially resistant to her would-be lover's attentions; romance ignites only after she is called upon to nurse Bowie after he is badly injured in a car wreck. While it's true that Bonnie eventually tires of her career as a gun moll and wants to settle into an improbable life of domestic tranquility, Keechie (who becomes preg-nant by Bowie) never displays any real enthusiasm for a life of crime. Other movies of the period – Terrence Malick's *Badlands* (1973) and Steven Spielberg's *The Sugar-land Express* (1974) – glorify outlaw couples on the run as quirky, free-spirited rebels, but Altman refuses the temptation, recognising commercial pablum masquerading as counterculture fantasy when he sees it. As Kolker puts it, 'Bonnie and Clyde transcend for a moment the emptiness and banality of their culture; Bowie and Keechie merely sink beneath it' (2011: 336). Bowie and Keechie sink beneath their culture because they are too much a part of it; its crushing injustices and brainless trivialities keep them emotionally blunted and mentally impoverished. They simply lack the wisdom and imagination to be true rebels.

Beyond his characterisations of Bowie and Keechie as the anti-Bonnie and Clyde, Altman categorically refuses to validate or mythologise crime, criminals and violence.

Bonnie and Clyde's scruffy fellow gang members look almost gallant next to Bowie's lowlife compatriots. T-Dub is a lame, lecherous braggart who keeps on inflating the number of banks he's knocked over. He dies off-screen. Chicamaw is even more detestable – a sullen and solitary misanthrope who becomes a full-blown psychopath after T-Dub and Bowie partner off with women. When Bowie is injured in a car accident, his partners fatally shoot two police officers who arrive on the scene to investigate: a cold-blooded murder at the midpoint of the film that darkens the mood considerably. During a subsequent bank robbery in Canton, Mississippi the trio matter-of-factly shoot a bank clerk who attempts to activate an alarm. Altman films the scene from a camera above and behind, a perspective that distances viewers from the action and diminishes its value as sensationalistic entertainment. Later, when Bowie impersonates a sheriff to spring Chicamaw from a prison farm, they take the warden, Capt. Stammers (Al Scott), captive in Bowie's car. Bowie stops on a lonely country road and Chicamaw takes Stammers into the woods, supposedly to tie him up and leave him there, but Chicamaw shoots the man instead. Though the killing happens off-screen, the gunshot we hear is chilling evidence of Chicamaw's sadism. When he returns to the car Chicamaw is so obnoxious that Bowie orders him out at gunpoint and drives away, leaving his still prison-striped associate to a well-deserved fate. In the movie's final violent set piece, Bowie returns to a motor court owned by the late T-Dub, where he and Keechie are staying, unaware that T-Dub's sister-in-law Mattie has betrayed them to the authorities. As soon as Bowie enters his cabin (the unlucky no. 13) law officers emerge from hiding and perforate the building with a fusillade of bullets and buckshot while Keechie, who is next door at the office to get a Coke, screams in inconsolable horror as Mattie restrains her. Moments later the men enter the cabin and emerge with Bowie's thin corpse, wrapped in a blood-soaked quilt, and lay it on the muddy ground: a killing utterly devoid of the sympathetic shock effect that marks the brutal assassination of Bonnie and Clyde in Arthur Penn's movie.

Ignominious end: the bullet-riddled corpse of Bowie (Keith Carradine) is laid in the mud.

The film could well have ended with Bowie's death but Altman adds a scene in order to end on an ambiguously positive note – and to generate a subtle sense of historical perspective. Keechie is shown at Jackson's Union Station, waiting for a train that will take her on a long journey west, to Fort Worth, Texas and a new start. Drinking her beloved Coca-Cola and chatting with another woman (screenwriter Joan Tewkesbury) in the waiting room, Keechie says she's expecting, thinks it will be a boy, and declares that 'he will not be named after his daddy, rest his soul. He crossed me up once too often; he don't deserve to have no baby named after him.' When she lies about the manner of his death ('consumption'), she speaks a metaphoric truth and makes it abundantly clear that Bowie and his partners in crime will not live on in myth, like Bonnie and Clyde. The last, slow motion shot is of Keechie submerged in a crowd of people climbing the stairs to the waiting train: an image of the masses passing through history toward an unknowable future.

Released domestically on 11 February 1974 and screened at Cannes in May, *Thieves Like Us* did negligible box office and garnered mix reviews. Altman was lauded on his visual style but criticised for an allegedly underdeveloped narrative and too much objectivity and distance applied to his characters. Pauline Kael praised Altman for finding 'a sure, soft tone in this movie' and never losing it; she termed the film 'sensuous right from the first pearly green shot, and it seems to achieve beauty without artifice' (1982: 757). Roger Ebert's review was more ambivalent: 'The movie's fault is that Altman, having found the perfect means for realizing his story visually, did not spend enough thought, perhaps, on the story itself' (1974: n.p). Molly Haskell panned the film altogether, observing that its characters 'go through elaborate motions bereft of meaning, with the momentary fascination and ultimate senselessness of chickens with their heads cut off' (1974: 63). Gary Arnold called *Thieves Like Us* 'inert' (1974: C13). It's clear from these reviews that Altman's studied quest to debunk the romantic myth of the outlaw as tragic rebel was often misconstrued as merely inept character development.

California Split (1974)

The driving force behind Altman's next film, *California Split*, was Joseph 'Joey' Walsh, a former child star, sporadically employed actor and longtime gambling addict. In a recent interview, Walsh recalled meeting with director Peter Bogdanovich, who was more interested in reading a newspaper than listening to Walsh's pitch: 'I'm about to punch a hole right through the newspaper and end my career in Hollywood. Instead I just walked out the door, sat down and asked myself what I knew better than anyone. And I knew so much about gambling. And nobody writes gambling well' (Haney 2008: n.p.) Walsh and his friend, the promising young director Steven Spielberg, collaborated on a gambling movie script tentatively entitled 'Slide' for nine months in 1971 and soon secured a production deal with MGM head James T. Aubrey, with Spielberg as director, Walsh as producer and Steve McQueen cast in the starring role. Unfortunately, the studio started making unreasonable demands, such as requiring that the screenplay come in at an exact number of pages and demanding the movie be set at MGM's Circus Circus casino in Las Vegas for the purposes of cross-promotion. A month before the scheduled start of shooting, newly appointed executives at MGM upped the ante by removing Walsh as producer and demanding that Spielberg transform the film into a mafia-related 'sting' picture with Dean Martin as one of the two main characters – presumably to try to emulate the immense success of Universal's *The Sting* (1973). A disgusted Walsh and Spielberg quit MGM and took the script to Universal Pictures where they made a deal with co-producers Darryl Zanuck and David Brown; but then Spielberg dropped out, eventually opting to work on another project with Zanuck and Brown (*The Sugarland Express*). Having had two production deals fall through, Walsh directed his agent, Guy McElwaine, to contact Altman's agent, George Litto, who sent the script to fellow gambler Robert Altman, who loved it. Altman and Walsh secured a deal with David Begelman, the new studio chief of Columbia Pictures (coincidentally also a gambling addict) that contracted Walsh as producer and guaranteed that his screenplay would not be tampered with.[41]

Unfamiliar with Altman's reputation as an improvisatory director who always played fast and loose with screenplays, Joseph Walsh had to get used to Altman's free-wheeling style. There were arguments and confrontations but writer and director soon came to agreement about the film's direction and meaning. Casting was another issue. George Segal was hired early on to play Bill Denny, an otherwise respectable magazine editor whose gambling addiction is threatening to upend his life. Peter Falk and Robert De Niro were considered for the other lead role, Denny's friend, Charlie Waters, an even more inveterate gambler, but the part finally went to Altman stalwart Elliott Gould, who happened to be a longtime friend of Joseph Walsh and a serious gambler himself. As Walsh recalled, Gould's intensity unnerved the more sedate Segal: 'Elliott lived his gambling; he came out of the box just like in a horse race when a great horse comes out of the box. The first day of shooting, he was there as that character. He floated through that picture. After seven days, George Segal came to me and said, "This guy's unbelievable. He's an octopus. He is absolutely strangling me to death. I don't even know what to do." The man was pleading for his life.' Walsh told Segal that Gould 'lived this [gambling] life … don't try to act with him … be off-base – just what you're feeling – and it's all working' (in McGilligan 1989: 377, 378). As Altman later remarked, 'George [Segal] brought a tension into it, because in a funny way he was in over his head' (in Thompson 2006: 86).

Always keen to avoid that highly polished and predictable Hollywood patina, Altman considered hiring the great Haskell Wexler as his cinematographer but finally went with a younger and more malleable cameraman: Paul Lohmann, a former documentary filmmaker with just one movie to his credit, a Pam Grier blaxploitation film titled *Coffey* (1973). As regards sound, *California Split* was the first Altman film to use Lion's Gate 8-Tracks, an experimental eight-track sound system developed by Jim Webb that allowed eight separate audio channels to be simultaneously recorded through eight microphones (two or three on the main actors in a scene, the rest on various extras): a technology particularly well-suited to noisy gambling rooms. As Jonathan Rosenbaum explains:

Plant enough microphones around the set … and one could always adjust the volume later, when the separate channels were being mixed together and one could decide which channels should predominate, and in which proportion. In other words, assuming that you had a certain amount of scripted dialogue and a certain amount of 'background' improvs being delivered at the same time – the *modus operandi* of many Altman movies, especially this one – trusting to luck was a matter of recording all this dialogue on eight separate tracks. And listening to voices was what you did afterward – shoot first and ask questions later, working out a hierarchy of what should have the most clarity after the fact. If an improv was funnier or more relevant than a scripted line delivered at the same moment, allow the former to overtake the latter. (N.d.: n.p.)

Among a number of professional poker players and gamblers who appear in the film as extras was Thomas Austin Preston Jr. (1928–2012), aka 'Amarillo Slim', winner of the 1972 World Series of Poker. Many of the other extras were members of Synanon, a well-known Santa Monica-based drug rehabilitation programme. The first half of the film takes place at various locations around Los Angeles (i.e. a dancehall dressed to look like a poker den, a private home, a bar, the Santa Anita racetrack and various street scenes). The second half is centred at the Mapes Hotel and casino, a historic but fading venue in Reno, Nevada that served as setting, cast and crew accommodations and all-around leisure site for the filmmaking company in off-hours.[42] As Altman said in an interview, 'Everybody was involved in that atmosphere, and there was a sense of reality because one minute you were downstairs in the Mapes casino losing money and winning money, and then a minute later you were upstairs on the set filming a crap game' (in Reid 1974: 26).

Like most films, Altman's do not fall neatly within one genre classification. *California Split* is essentially two genre films: the gambling movie and the buddy film. The gambling movie genre is complex and often melds with gangster-crime films (some alleged gambling movies are better categorised as criminal caper films, e.g., *Oceans 11* (1960) or *The Sting*). Most true gambling movies might be termed 'big score' movies: phallocentric wish-fulfillment fantasies that have many variations but often feature an ambitious young hustler competing against an old and jaded master, ultimately winning big and proving his manhood, but learning valuable life lessons in the process (e.g. *The Hustler* (1961) or *The Cincinnati Kid* (1965)). In some versions the gambler may end up broke or in serious trouble but gambling is generally depicted as a glamorous and exciting means of self-expression. As gambling psychology expert Mark Griffiths notes, 'many of these film representations tend to cast gambling in an innocuous light, and often portray gamblers, largely male, as hero[ic] figures' (n.d.: n.p.). In reality, gambling is a devastating addiction. Summarising Edmund Bergler's psychodynamic account, Griffiths explains the underlying motivation: 'Gambling is a rebellious act, an aggression against logic, intelligence, moderation and morality… According to Bergler, the unconscious desire to lose arises when gambling activates forbidden unconscious desires (e.g. parricidal feelings). The financial loss provides the punishment to maintain the gambler's psychological equilibrium. According to this view, gambling is, in essence, masochistic' (ibid.).

Underneath the obvious thrill seeking, unconscious masochism does seem to play a major role in the first half of *California Split*. As gamblers, Bill Denny and Charlie Waters seek to win but continually subject themselves to danger and physical punishment. In the opening scene, in a squalid LA poker club where the two men first meet, Charlie goes out of his way to verbally bait a hulking sore loser named Lew (played by Joseph Walsh's brother, Ed). Predictably, Lew physically assaults Charlie and has to be restrained by security. Later that night, after Bill and Charlie bond over drinks at a nearby bar, both are beaten, kicked and robbed by Lew and compatriots who were obviously lying in wait. Strangely, neither Bill nor Charlie displays any remorse or self-pity, as if these beatings were a routine price to pay for the kind of life they're living, perhaps even a badge of honour. On the bus to Santa Anita the next day to bet on horses, Charlie once again sets himself up for trouble by warning a fellow gambler off a horse called Egyptian Femme. Charlie bets on the horse, it wins, and the irate woman he discouraged from betting on it rails and throws objects from her purse at him on the racetrack escalator. Charlie then spots his nemesis, Lew, at the track and follows him into a rest room to retrieve his money. Charlie wins the ensuing fistfight and recovers his money but not before being sucker-punched and floored: a blow that Charlie masochistically applauds as masterful ('Oh my God, that was the greatest punch!'). The more than subliminal equation made between gambling and physical punishment is reinforced when Bill and Charlie attend a brutal Mexican boxing match that evening. The boxers pummel each other but so do some of the spectators, as fights break out in the stands. After the bout, the two are robbed for the second time in two days, on this occasion at gunpoint by a jittery black man in the street. Angered at being robbed again, Charlie tempts fate by insisting that the bandit take just half their money: a bit of reckless insouciance that could have gotten both of them killed. As the more cautious and conservative Bill is drawn deeper into Charlie's world, his life comes under greater jeopardy. This is dramatised by a scene at the midpoint of the film that depicts Bill meeting with his bookie, Sparkie (played by screenwriter Joseph Walsh), who proffers ominous threats about money owed him: a crisis that compels Bill to pawn his car, typewriter and other possessions in order to finance a desperate gambling trip to Reno with Charlie, to recoup his fortunes.

The second half of the film is marked by a number of changes: a shift from varied settings in LA to a unified setting (the Mapes) in Reno; a shift in focus from Charlie to Bill; a concomitant shift in theme, from gambling as masochism, to winning as an oddly disenchanting experience. The movie also becomes more obviously anti-genre as Bill and Charlie combine their scant monies so that Bill can buy into a high stakes poker game in a private room at the casino, equipped with bar, buffet and the requisite grizzled, impassive card sharps. A conventional gambling genre movie would concentrate on the big game and ramp up dramatic tension with lots of harsh lighting, tight framing, close-ups, reaction shots and psychological cat-and-mouse action. As Walsh later observed, if Spielberg had directed the picture as originally planned, he 'would have built up that last scene, that gambling scene, into one gigantic orgasm, climaxing the last forty pages of script until you were on the edge of your seat' (in McGilligan 1989: 381). Altman characteristically chooses to buck genre requisites and actually dissipate tension by having Bill ban Charlie from the big game because his presence is too distracting. Then, as Norman Kagan puts it, instead of a suspenseful focus on the climatic game, we mostly get to 'watch Charlie's comic-pathetic efforts to gamble with a tiny stake, the streetwise manager archetype wheedling for change or mugging like a brainless tourist on his first casino visit' (1982: 121). Indeed, the big poker game isn't even climatic; Bill wins $18,000 but doesn't quit. Convinced he is on a phenomenal lucky streak, he goes on to play blackjack, roulette and craps, winning at everything and eventually cashing out with $82,000. Charlie is naturally ecstatic but an exhausted Bill finds himself strangely disappointed: 'Charlie, there was no special feeling. Everybody said there was.' Commenting on that line, Altman said, 'He never felt it, because he has nothing to feel' (in Thompson 2006: 87). As originally written, the film's ending had Bill and Charlie departing the Mapes and entering a cab but, at the last second, Charlie changes his mind and heads back into the casino to do his own high stakes gambling. Bill rolls down the window and asks Charlie what he's going to do with his life. Charlie replies: 'I'm gonna take the best price I can.' He holds up his hand and flashes the two-fingered v-for-victory sign. The last shot was to be a freeze-frame of Charlie's radiant smile. The ending that actually got on film was decidedly more downbeat. After the big win, Bill says to Charlie, 'I gotta go home.' Charlie replies, 'Yeah, where do you live?' Bill stares at him then says again, 'I gotta go home, Charlie.' Bill walks out and Charlie spins the wheel of fortune. The credits roll. Joseph Walsh's upbeat ending tended to mitigate Bill's unwelcome insight; that gambling is ultimately a pointless endeavour that takes too high a toll on the psyche and the wallet. Altman's ending (based on improv by Gould) underscores Bill's insight and completes the movie's larger thematic premise; that gambling, for all its risk-taking, adrenalin-filled highs and masochistic lows, is a nihilistic, self-destructive addiction. Joseph Walsh became convinced that Altman's 'strange' ending 'cost the picture $10 million… You don't pull the rug from under an audience's feet … audiences didn't know what to feel when they walked out of the theater after those two guys broke off like that. If they would have [gone] out the other way, it would've been tragic-sweet: They're leaving each other, but because one guy's smiling, you know they're gonna get back together again' (2008: n.p.).

As Walsh's remarks suggest, Altman's ending negates gambling movie triumphalism. It also alters the character of *California Split* as a buddy movie. Buddy movies of the 1960s and 1970s – e.g. *Butch Cassidy and the Sundance Kid* (1969), *Easy Rider* (1969), *Midnight Cowboy* (1969), *Scarecrow* (1973), *Thunderbolt and Lightfoot* (1974), *Dog Day Afternoon* (1975) – obviously constituted a thinly-veiled backlash against an emerging feminist movement. As Philippa Gates observes: 'To punish women for their desire for equality, the buddy film pushes them out of the centre of the narrative … By making both protagonists men, the central issue of the film becomes the growth and development of their friendship. Women as potential love interests are thus eliminated from the narrative space' (2004: 21). *California Split* is certainly guilty of pushing women out of the centre of the narrative. In the movie's first half Bill and Charlie consort with prostitutes Barbara Miller (Ann Prentiss) and Susan Peters (Gwen Welles) but these relationships are depicted as superficial. Indeed, the women simply disappear once Bill and Charlie travel to Reno. As the misogynist buddy movie warrants, the focus remains almost entirely on the development of the collusive friendship between the two male protagonists. But the abrupt parting of Bill and Charlie at film's end violates buddy genre conventions. In other buddy movies, though one or both buddies might die or fall by the wayside, the friendship is not voluntarily broken as it is in *California Split* (a fate ironically referenced by the film's title). Equally significant is the reason for the breakup; Bill plumbs the depths of his gambling addiction, discovers its essential emptiness, and walks away. Charlie, unenlightened, will remain within the shadow of the gambling pathology, probably for life. No longer on the same wavelength the two men are unlikely to ever see each other again: a lonely resolution that also points up the intensely self-centred and solipsistic nature of the gambling addiction, a disease that allows for no real friendships because it's all about self-gratification.

Buffalo Bill and the Indians, or Sitting Bull's History Lesson (1976)

After *California Split*, Altman made *Nashville* (discussed in the next chapter) before trying his hand at a second revisionist western some five years after *McCabe & Mrs. Miller*: *Buffalo Bill and the Indians, or Sitting Bull's History Lesson*, a film 'suggested by' (i.e. very loosely based upon) an absurdist one-act play by Arthur Lee Kopit entitled *Indians* (1968). Paul Newman and television talk show host/producer David Susskind had purchased the film rights to Kopit's play in 1969 for $500,000. A film adaptation to be directed by George Roy Hill and starring Newman was planned but failed to materialize, probably because Newman's hectic schedule couldn't accommodate it for years on end. In the wake of *Nashville*'s success Susskind and movie mogul Dino de Laurentiis approached Altman to direct the Kopit property, which was budgeted at $6.5 million – Altman's most expensive film to date. Altman initially passed on the assignment but finally decided to take it on in 1975 when other projects had to be postponed or cancelled altogether. Kopit's Buffalo Bill play was about the power of show business celebrity so it was essential that a big name movie star be hired for the lead role. Altman considered Marlon Brando and Jack Nicholson but ultimately went with Paul Newman, mostly because he had been associated with the project since its inception and was anxious not only to deflate Buffalo Bill but his own outsized image as a movie star (see Sterritt 2000: 38–39).

Arthur Kopit's *Indians* was actually a product of the anti-Vietnam War movement of a decade earlier. On 25 August 1966 Kopit was listening to Charles Ives's Fourth Symphony and reading a news story in the *New York Times* that reported General William Westmoreland, commander of US forces in Vietnam, as being regretful about civilian casualties inflicted by Allied forces, which he disingenuously termed 'a great problem' that must be solved. Kopit later recalled: 'In [Ives's symphony] two orchestras play against each other. One plays chamber music, the other, distorting band music. The idea and form for the play seemed to come to me in a flash' (Funke 1969: 37). *Indians* isn't about Vietnam directly but about 'what happens when a social and political power imposes itself on a lesser power and creates a mythology to justify it, as we did with the Indians, as we have tried to do in Vietnam… And, in the manner of the symphony, it would be a counterpoint of memory and reality' (ibid.). As Michael C. O'Neill notes, counterpoint does indeed constitute the play's structuring device:

> The thirteen scenes of Indians … constitute a memory play in which [Gilded Era Western showman] Buffalo Bill [Cody] … recalls his past. These scenes are divided into three distinct lines of action, or, to use the musical term, melodies. The play begins and ends with Buffalo Bill, alone, a man who has created for himself a heroic posture and, in so doing, realizes how unheroic his position finally has become. Scenes three, seven, ten, and twelve show both Cody's development into a fabricated hero and his attempts to aid the Indians. Scenes one, five, and nine are the Wild West Show, and scenes two, four, six, eight, and eleven constitute what is in fact the continuous action of a single meeting based on the 1886 United States Commission to investigate Indian grievances held at Standing Rock Reservation. The three lines, or melodies, converge in scene thirteen, the aftermath of Wounded Knee, in which Cody, confronted by Sitting Bull's ghost, tries to defend United States Indian policy in a long, ironic speech, and finally mounts his horse to ride in the gaudy pageantry of his Wild West Show. (1982: 496)

Directed by Gene Frankel and with a cast of forty-six actors headed by Stacy Keach as Buffalo Bill, Manu Tupou as Sitting Bull, Charles Durning as Ned Buntline and Sam Waterston as John Grass, *Indians* enjoyed a respectable 96-performance run at the Brooks Atkinson Theatre in New York City over the closing months of 1969 – at the height of American involvement in Vietnam. Critically acclaimed, Kopit's play earned three 1970 Tony nominations: Best Play, Best Actor in Play (Stacy Keach) and Best Lighting Design (Thomas Skelton).

It's easy to see why *Indians* would appeal to Altman's sensibilities. Here was a large-cast mosaic about American history, show business and image-making that was stylistically unconventional and politically provocative. A revisionist product of 1960s radicalism, *Indians* re-presents Buffalo Bill Cody as a self-promoting imperialist ideologue who considered himself a well-meaning liberal. Moreover, Kopit's play debunks 'Buffalo Bill's Wild West' show as a jingoistic theatre of lies that transformed the genocidal Indian Wars into Gilded Era triumphalist mythology, laying the groundwork for myriad western novels, films and TV shows that would follow. In dialectical fashion, Kopit's play counterpoises Buffalo Bill's pageantry with sombre scenes dramatising the government's indifference toward the plight of Native Americans, who were driven off their land, starved, massacred and finally consigned to barren reservations: internal colonialism that formed the basis for more recent colonialist adventures overseas.

The historical Buffalo Bill Cody (1846–1917) was a rather paradoxical figure. Though a proud hunter and killer of buffalo and Indians who made a fortune romanticising his own exploits – his show toured North America and Europe from 1872 to 1906 – Cody professed to respect Native Americans and to support their rights.

Besides Sitting Bull, he employed lots of other Indians and paid them a living wage. Calling them 'the former foe, present friend, the American', Cody acknowledged: 'Every Indian outbreak that I have ever known has resulted from broken promises and broken treaties by the government' (in Wilson 1998: 316). He also supported women's rights and conservation. In short, William F. Cody's views were quite progressive for his day but as a firm believer in Manifest Destiny he was not inclined to do too much soul-searching about the political implications or deeper ethics of his role in 'the taming of the West'.

To counter hegemonic ideology, Arnold Kopit presents his own rendition of Buffalo Bill, not as the energetic showman he was, but as a man haunted by guilty ruminations that are assailing his complacent sense of self as western hero. Accordingly, toward the end of the play, Buffalo Bill has a conversation (either supernatural or hallucinated) with the ghost of Sitting Bull, the great Lakota Sioux chieftain who presided over Custer's annihilation at the Little Bighorn in 1876, briefly joined Buffalo Bill's Wild West Show in 1885, and was assassinated at Standing Rock Indian Reservation, South Dakota, in 1890. Functioning as Buffalo Bill's guilty conscience, Sitting Bull's spirit calmly berates Cody for professing to 'love' the Indians while being complicit in their destruction – and then proceeding to dishonor them at his Wild West Show: 'You came and allowed us to imitate our glory... It was humiliating!' Though remorseful about Sitting Bull's demise, Kopit's Buffalo Bill goes to considerable rhetorical lengths to rationalise the genocidal wages of westward expansion: 'Reports that the Cherokees were unhappy at their removal are decidedly untrue. And though many, naturally, died while marching from Georgia to the Mojave Desert, the ones who did, I'm told, were rather ill already, and nothing short of medication could have saved them. Indeed, in all ways, our vast country is speedily being opened for settlement.' The play ends with all the great Indian chiefs – Sitting Bull, Black Hawk, Tecumseh, Crazy Horse, Red Cloud, Geronimo – dying off. A shaken Buffalo Bill tries to assuage his guilt with feeble appeasement: 'Moccasins. Beads. Feathered head-dresses for you children... Pretty picture postcards. Tiny Navajo dolls. The money from the sale of these few trifling trinkets will go to help them help themselves. Encourage them a bit. You know, raise their spirits... Ah! Wait. No, sorry, that's a-uh-buffalo skin.'

When Altman and co-writer Alan Rudolph adapted *Indians* to the screen, they discarded most of its actual content; only a few lines from the play make it into the film. They also abandoned Kopit's elaborate contrapuntal structure by taking out all the US Commission scenes at Standing Rock and most of the material related to Buffalo Bill's self-mythologising. Kopit set only three brief scenes at Buffalo Bill's Wild West Show but Altman and Rudolph set all the action there, so as to emphasise Altman's basic premise: that American civilisation is a gargantuan show business spectacle. Altman and Rudolph retain Kopit's large cast of characters but opt to foreground the relationship between Buffalo Bill and Sitting Bull while altering Kopit's characterisations to suit their own purposes. In the film version, Buffalo Bill (Paul Newman) is an alcoholic, philandering narcissist enraptured by his own star power and jealously competitive with Sitting Bull (Frank Kaquitts), who is mute and mostly poker-faced throughout the picture – except for a few lines spoken in Lakota that no one can understand. Kopit's Vietnam-era Buffalo Bill is a tragic figure, a tired salesman for imperialist conquest who cannot outrun his guilt. Altman's post-Vietnam Buffalo Bill is a fatuous loudmouth because Altman wants to focus on a different theme at America's Bicentennial; not the wages of imperialist war, but the mythologising of the nation's real history that is a crucial but largely veiled ideological function of its culture industry. As Robert Kolker puts it, 'the film is about the generation of ideology itself' (2011: 359). Arthur Kopit gives Sitting Bull an eloquent voice. Altman's silencing his version of Sitting Bull looks like a reiteration of the hegemonic effacement of Native Americans that Altman wants to critique. Yet the contrast between Sitting Bull's stoical demeanor and Buffalo Bill's raucous egotism achieves Altman's purpose not through dialogue but visually and dramatically. It is made abundantly clear that the Lakota chief is a true and tragic hero and that Buffalo Bill, whatever his real accomplishments, is a glib bullshit artist. Indeed, the film is structured like *M*A*S*H* and *Brewster McCloud*, as a series of comic vignettes designed to point up the essential difference between two opposing ideologies and the people who subscribe to them. In scene after scene, a cynical and maladroit Buffalo Bill tries to maintain his bloated self-image and manage his lucrative circus of make-believe while Sitting Bull's arrivals and disappearances, impassive silence and general truculence mark him as more commanding and principled – an adversary who can be hired, fired, disrespected and denounced but will not be broken because his ultimate loyalty is not to money or himself but to his people, a communitarian ethos that William T. Cody will never understand.

Buffalo Bill's trademark – the substitution of artifice for reality – is dramatised by the opening title sequence. What looks like an Indian raid on a frontier homestead is soon revealed to be a rehearsal of a skit from Buffalo Bill's Wild West Show at its 'Mayflower' campus, a fictional location where all of the movie's subsequent action will take place. As is always true in Altman's films, setting carries abundant meaning. The historical reality is that there was no company encampment; Buffalo Bill's Wild West was a traveling show that seldom stayed in one location for more than a day. Setting the show at a static site was not just a pragmatic bid to keep down the movie's production costs; it was also a means to produce allegorical resonance not unlike Altman's deployment of the Houston Astrodome for *Brewster McCloud*. As Kolker states, 'America and its history is [put] in an enclosed compound of actors and producers who keep sucking the past into the arena and re-creating it into a banal and simple present' (ibid.).

If the Mayflower campus is best understood as an ideological echo chamber where history is homogenised into pop culture clichés, Robert T. Self astutely argues that Altman's movie portrays Buffalo Bill at the moment in his long career when William T. Cody is being swallowed alive by 'Buffalo Bill', the burgeoning myth (2002: 110–11). A pioneer of modern celebrity culture, Cody cannot help but be interpellated by its discourse. The perverse dynamism of hero-worship, fuelled by endlessly reiterated publicity, infantilises its followers and is apt, in the long run, to turn its luminaries into egotistical monsters hypocritically spouting pseudo-populist ideology. But the idol cannot invent himself singlehanded; star- and myth-making is a complicated corporate enterprise involving continual refinements in technology and labour utilization. Accordingly, Altman peoples his movie with all of the progenitors and custodians of the Buffalo Bill myth machine, a forerunner of the film industry. As Altman said in an interview soon after the film's release: 'We were making comparisons to show business as it is today. That was the beginning of show business. Buffalo Bill had the producer, the publicist, the hangers-on, the star, the semi-star, and the extras' (Olderman 1976: 36).

The *éminence grise* of these figures is Ned Buntline, 'The Legend Maker' (Burt Lancaster). Buntline (real name: Edward Zane Carroll Judson Sr.) was a publicist and dime novelist who published a serial novel about Cody entitled *Buffalo Bill, the King of the Border Men* (1869–70), a book used by New York playwright Frank Meader as the basis of a play about Cody's life in 1872. In December of that year, Buntline wrote *Scouts of the Prairie*, a Buffalo Bill play of his own, starring Cody himself. Buntline's popular play ran for ten years and brought Cody fame as a western hero, which he parlayed into his own Wild West Show in 1883. In real life, Buffalo Bill never forgot his debt to Buntline; they remained friends until Buntline's death in 1886. In the movie, Buntline's presence at the Mayflower campus is unwelcome. Nate Salsbury (Joel Grey), Buffalo Bill's slick producer, and Major John Burke (Kevin McCarthy), the show's florid-tongued publicist, see Buntline and fellow hack writer Prentiss Ingraham (Allan Nicholls) as practitioners of an obsolete mythification technology (the dime novel) superseded by the live, large-scale and lucrative Buffalo Bill Wild West productions presented to mass audiences. For his part, Buffalo Bill sees Buntline as an embarrassing reminder that his fame was not some natural outgrowth of his greatness but a carefully contrived publicity event. Buntline also serves as a kind of Greek chorus, making occasional pronouncements on the proceedings.

Taking advantage of Sitting Bull's notoriety after Custer's Last Stand in 1876, Buffalo Bill hires him as a star attraction for the 1885 season ('foe in '76, friend in '85') but soon comes to rue his decision. At their first meeting, which Bill arranges with band music, pomp and circumstance, Sitting Bull's Indian interpreter, William Halsey (Will Sampson) stonily refuses to laugh at Bill's jibes and a silent Sitting Bull yawns. Shortly thereafter, Sitting Bull and the Indians who have accompanied him astonish Cody and his management team by crossing an adjacent river thought to be 'impossible' to cross, in order to set up their own camp on the facing heights – a sign of Sitting Bull's preternatural abilities, also of his refusal to be contained by the White Man. At their next encounter, Sitting Bull demands blankets for his people, a demand that angers Cody until he's informed by Halsey that 'there are only 106 Hunkpapa Sioux left at Grand River'. After declaring that there were '10,000 braves alone' counted there just five years before, Cody uncharacteristically falls into shocked silence. Refusing to be a passive addition to Buffalo Bill's show, Sitting Bull goes on to demand six weeks pre-payment (to send to his people) and ownership rights over photographs taken of him (to guard the integrity of his identity), demands that cause Cody to storm out of the meeting in a rage. When Salsbury tries to offer the chief a six-month contract, Halsey (speaking for Sitting Bull) declines, telling Salsbury that Sitting Bull will leave the show after he's seen 'the Great Father' (US President Grover Cleveland), a meeting he's envisioned in his dreams. Contrasting Sitting Bull's integrity, the next scene dramatises Cody's lack of it. While Buffalo Bill practices his target shooting, his nephew, Ed Goodman (Harvey Keitel) reads him a letter from his wife

Louisa, who calls him an adulterer, 'the cheapest man who ever lived and a profane drunkard as well', and asks for a divorce. From Bill's bored reaction, we surmise that these letters are a regular occurrence.

In the next scene, Buffalo Bill invites Halsey and Sitting Bull to observe a rehearsal of a reenactment of the Battle of Little Bighorn with 'a coloured' (Robert DoQui) standing in for Sitting Bull because 'he's the closest thing on our staff to a real injun'. In the reenactment, 'Sitting Bull' tricks 'General Custer' into a fake duel and then has his warriors shoot Custer in the back. The ersatz chief climbs on a fake rock and holds Custer's 'scalp' aloft but his head-dress keeps on falling over his face, rendering the moment unintentionally comical. Offering an unsolicited critique, the real Sitting Bull (speaking through Halsey, as always) debunks this rendition as inaccurate, noting that he wasn't even present on the battlefield that day.

In a related scene that follows, Halsey and Sitting Bull suddenly appear at Buffalo Bill's quarters at midnight for an unplanned meeting with Bill and his lieutenants. Speaking through Halsey, Sitting Bull demands that Cody revise another Wild West Show reenactment, of the Battle of Killdeer Mountain (28 July 1864). In Cody's version the battle will be depicted as a fair fight won by US government troops against Sioux warriors. Sitting Bull, who was there but managed to escape, knows the real history. Col. Robert McLaren and his commander, Gen. Alfred Sully, were war criminals 'who murdered women, old men, children', even dogs, without provocation. Buffalo Bill will hear none of it; he flies into a rage and fires Sitting Bull on the spot. The next morning, though, Bill is forced to relent when another star attraction, the famous sharpshooter Annie Oakley (Geraldine Chaplin) threatens to quit the show unless Sitting Bull is reinstated. She admonishes Cody, 'Why can't you tell the truth, just once?' He angrily replies, 'Because I have a better [i.e., more show business-suitable] sense of history than that.' Once he realises Annie will stick to her guns, he angrily capitulates: 'The little bastard can stay.'

Cody's decision is rendered ironic shortly thereafter, when Sitting Bull and his company are observed riding away from the area, Buffalo Bill forms a posse of his subordinates and rides out in pursuit of the wayward 'injun' (an ironic reference to John Ford's *The Searchers*) but comes back empty-handed and humiliated: another indignity at the hands of Sitting Bull that Cody compensates for by blasting away at the caged bird of his mistress, the Mezzo-Contralto, Margaret (Bonnie Leaders) with six-shooters in each hand. As is typical of Altman's dialectical method of scene juxtaposition, Sitting Bull and Halsey unexpectedly return to camp a bit later and Halsey informs Bill that the chief wasn't running away or hiding but had gone to the mountains for religious reasons.

His ego now seriously eroded by Sitting Bull's unpredictable antics, Buffalo Bill refuses to let the chief stand next to Annie Oakley for a group photograph. Encountering the usual resistance, Cody relents, reasoning that the photograph can be doctored later anyway – another ironic comment on the malleability of historical representation. As the photograph is being staged, a telegraph message comes in informing the company that President Grover Cleveland (Pat McCormick) and his newly-wedded First Lady (Shelley Duvall) will be visiting the Mayflower campus on their honeymoon for a nighttime command performance of the Wild West Show. Overcome with excitement, everyone abandons their positions in front of the camera – except for Sitting Bull and Halsey, who get their picture taken, thereby amusingly defying historical erasure (and confounding the cliché that Indians are superstitious about being photographed).

During the performance for the President, an understandably nervous Annie Oakley accidentally wings her comically gun-shy husband-manager, Frank Butler (John Considine) in the shoulder. They both conceal the illusion-breaking wounding with a hurried exit: threadbare showbiz improvisation covering up a darker reality. Next to perform is Sitting Bull, who circles the arena on his horse in front of President Cleveland, stops, then utters something in the Lakota language. Asked if he knows what the chief said, an advisor (played, uncredited, by the historical novelist E. L. Doctorow) sardonically replies, 'No, but I can guess.' Then, to everyone's horror, Sitting Bull draws his pistol and levels it at the President but pulls it up and fires into the air at the last second. Cleveland, much relieved, interprets the incident as a joke and admires Sitting Bull as a great comedian. But the chief isn't done with the President. He and Halsey show up uninvited to Buffalo Bill's presidential banquet that night – much like the unsettling appearance of Banquo's ghost at Macbeth's banquet. Halsey declares that Sitting Bull has a 'simple request' but the President summarily preempts the request before it is even specified and the Indians leave. Buffalo Bill, who mistakenly admires the President's dismissiveness as a sign of strength rather than the cowardly evasion it is, declares: 'The difference between a president and a chief in this situation is that the president always knows enough to retaliate before it's his turn!'

Flash forward to 1890. The beginning of the last act of the movie is marked by the startling news that Sitting Bull has been assassinated, breaking Annie Oakley's heart. In general terms but in an altered context, the film's closing moments parallel the Return of the Repressed depicted in the closing moments of Arthur Kopit's play. Erupting from the (historical) unconscious, the ghost of Sitting Bull in full headdress silently appears, disappears and reappears repeatedly to Buffalo Bill in his private quarters on a stormy night. An agitated and defensive Bill Cody protests his racial superiority as a white man and his show business superiority as a star, but he doth protest too much; the daunting reality of Sitting Bull's life and death and all that he represents cannot be refuted.

Nonetheless, in the film's final scene, Buffalo Bill characteristically attempts to exorcise the chief's ghost through theatrical means; by staging a 'duel to the death' skit for his Wild West Show that reiterates the Custer death and scalping scene but inverts it as a vengeful wish-fulfillment fantasy in service to white triumphalist ideology and Cody's ego. Upon his entrance into the arena, Chief Sitting Bull (now played by Halsey) is mendaciously described by the show's master of ceremonies (allegorically, the victors' history) as a 'warrior of the western plains who has murdered more white men [and] spoiled more white women than any other redskin'. Buffalo Bill and Sitting Bull dismount their horses and playact wrestle for a knife. Naturally, Buffalo Bill overcomes his adversary, 'kills' him and then 'scalps' the chief's headdress, to ritualistically establish that he, the white man, is the greater warrior and the perennial champion.

Prisoner of myth: Buffalo Bill Cody (Paul Newman) succumbs to megalomania.

A final close-up of Buffalo Bill's smiling face shows his eyes flashing in maniacal self-delusion; like Frances at the end of *That Cold Day in the Park*, the film's protagonist has gone stark, raving mad.

A different kind of revisionist western than *McCabe & Mrs. Miller, Buffalo Bill and the Indians, or Sitting Bull's History Lesson* is far more radical as ideological critique but far less successful as filmmaking. The former film corrects and revitalises stock genre devices by investing them with palpably authentic historical content. The latter film deconstructs the mythmaking process itself, as regards individual celebrity and historical discourse. A postmodern parody of the 'let's-put-on-a-show' musical, *Buffalo Bill and the Indians...* attempts to achieve its purpose by inventing behind-the-scenes vignettes that continually demonstrate the contrived and misleading nature of the proceedings. At the same time, the movie builds a characterisation of 'Buffalo Bill' Cody as a megalomaniac trapped by the increasingly oppressive demands of his own public persona – in stark contrast to the taciturn figure of Sitting Bull. Frederic and Mary Ann Brussat rightly note that the 'depiction of the Indians is too idealised and the slam on Cody, too overdrawn' (Brussat and Brussat n.d.: n.p.). Furthermore, as Gerald Plecki observes, 'The problem with *Buffalo Bill and the Indians* is that it presumes more knowledge of history than most viewers could bring to the theater' (1985: 91). Viewers might recognise that the film is full of satiric invention but they have no way of knowing which parts, if any, are real and true to history. Ned Buntline says at one point, 'History, real history is hard [to] come [by].' Though not originally intended as a Bicentennial movie, *Buffalo Bill and the Indians* was released on the Fourth of July, 1976. More filmic essay than conventional western, it garnered mixed reviews from uncomprehending critics and performed dismally at the box office, grossing just $869,569 against a production budget of $6.5 million – a net loss of $5.6 million.

Notes

1   Ring Lardner Jr. was one of the 'Hollywood Ten' who refused to cooperate with the HUAC anti-communist witch-hunt in 1947. Convicted of contempt of Congress, Lardner served a year in Danbury Prison, was fined $1,000, fired from his job at Fox and ultimately banished from the film industry for eighteen years.

2   Ironically, Mike Altman made a great deal more money on song royalties than his
     father did directing the film.

3   In the late 1940s Adorno and his colleagues developed an 'F-scale' (F for fascist)
     and enumerated a cluster of associated traits: Conventionalism (rigid adherence
     to conventional, middle-class values); Authoritarian Submission (submissive,
     uncritical attitude toward idealised moral authorities of the in-group); Authori-
     tarian Aggression (tendency to be on the lookout for, and to condemn, reject and
     punish people who violate conventional values); Anti-intraception (opposition to
     the subjective, the imaginative, the tender-minded); Superstition and Stereotypy
     (a belief in mystical determinants of the individual's fate; the disposition to think
     in rigid categories); Power and 'Toughness' (preoccupation with the dominance-
     submission, strong-weak, leader-follower dimension; identification with power
     figures; overemphasis upon the conventionalized attributes of the ego; exaggerated
     assertion of strength and toughness); Destructiveness and Cynicism (generalised
     hostility, vilification of the human); Projectivity (the disposition to believe that
     wild and dangerous things go on in the world; the projection outwards of uncon-
     scious emotional impulses); Sex (exaggerated concern with sexual 'goings-on'); see
     T. W. Adorno, E. Frenkel-Brunswik, D. J. Levinson and R. N. Sanford (1950) *The
     Authoritarian Personality*. New York: Harper & Row.

4   One of the staple features of the war film genre is that collective imperatives must
     take precedence over individual goals.

5   The monomyth, as summarised by Joseph Campbell: 'A hero ventures forth from
     the world of common day into a region of supernatural wonder: fabulous forces
     are there encountered and a decisive victory is won: the hero comes back from
     this mysterious adventure with the power to bestow boons on his fellow man.'
     Joseph Campbell (1968) *The Hero with a Thousand Faces*. Princeton, NJ: Princ-
     eton University Press, 30.

6   C. Kirk McClelland's book, *On Making a Movie: 'Brewster McCloud'*, documents
     Altman's freewheeling experimental methods, which were at their most intense on
     this film.

7   The Wright brothers' only other sibling who survived to adulthood was a sister,
     Katharine, who died in 1928.

8   Altman's use of the surname Breen is an in-joke reference to Joseph Ignatius Breen
     (1890–1965), the film censor with the Motion Picture Producers and Distribu-
     tors of America (MPPDA) who applied the Hays Code to film production.

9   The screenplay was completed on 27 June 1970.

10   After production designer Leon Ericksen purchased a working 1899 Case steam
     tractor (and other props) at a Canadiana Museum auction in Fort MacLeod,
     Alberta, which ended up being prominently featured in the film, Altman set the
     action forward a bit, to 1901–02.

11   From *McCabe & Mrs. Miller* Warner Bros. Press Kit, Altman Archives, University
     of Michigan, Ann Arbor.

12   Ibid.

13 As David Foster noted in the film's press kit: 'The way a [frontier] town grew... was that the first guy would pitch a tent under a tree for protection, say, and the next guy would settle down some place near the water. Or maybe two or three of them would make camp near the entrance of a mine, and so on, as little groups scattered about and formed a community.'

14 Turner goes on to note 'many of these carpenter/extras could relate to the film's subplot: a small community being threatened by larger market forces (what Altman has referred to as the "corporate settling of the West"). The Mudflatters were under constant harassment. Not by business interests (at least not directly), but by the District of North Vancouver, who eventually evicted the squatters and burned down their houses shortly after *McCabe and Mrs. Miller's* release.'

15 'Flashing (cinematography)', http://en.wikipedia.org/wiki/Flashing_(cinematography).

16 *McCabe & Mrs. Miller* screenplay, on-line at: http://www.awesomefilm.com/script/mccabeandmrsmiller.pdf.

17 Altman frequently departed from his screenplay, mostly cutting scenes and streamlining dialogue to keep the film uncluttered and coming in at two hours. Warren Beatty also rewrote most of his lines.

18 Fischer plays the Rev. Elliot but the man on the steeple is actually a stunt double.

19 McCabe's inferior position *vis-à-vis* Mrs. Miller is further dramatised in the next scene. A drunken and depressed McCabe pays a visit to Mrs. Miller, ostensibly to discuss expenses associated with bringing in five new whores from San Francisco, but she refuses to see him.

20 The film's anti-corporate bias is also abundantly evident in Naughton's novel.

21 Mrs. Miller's commonsensical involvement might have saved the day but societal dictates keep women frozen out of the business world.

22 As Robert Kolker points out, her cashbox is Mrs. Miller's 'very literal ... heart of Gold' (2011: 330).

23 Clement Samuels is, of course, an ironic inversion of Samuel Clemens (aka Mark Twain, 1835–1910), a trenchant and vocal critic of American imperialism and monopoly-style capitalism in the waning years of his life.

24 The year the action occurs in the second half of the film is established by the death date clearly visible on Bart Coyle's grave marker in the funeral scene.

25 As a populist reformer, prohibitionist, anti-Darwin crusader and repeatedly failed Democratic presidential candidate, Bryan embodies the shortcomings of turn-of-the-century bourgeois liberalism.

26 What ended up on film was radically different than the screenplay version of McCabe's visit to the lawyer. The screenplay followed Naughton's novel quite closely by depicting the lawyer (named Clark Tucker) as a dour, circumspect older man with a hatred of corporatism but a decidedly fatalistic view of McCabe's chances.

27 See Richard Slotkin's indispensable studies of American gun culture and violence, listed in the bibliography.

28 To contrast this final sequence with the rest of the picture, Altman opted not to flash it.

29 In a deleted line from earlier in the screenplay, McCabe tells Elliot, 'God is dead, you prick.'

30 As the lawyer says in Naughton's novel, 'Company is like any animal, organism; second it stops growing, it starts dying. Grows by corruption and fear…' (p. 57).

31 Altman's original choice for Roger Wade was his friend Dan Blocker of *Bonanza* fame but Blocker died of a pulmonary embolism in May 1972, just a month before shooting began.

32 The anti-genre theme is further sounded by a recurrent shtick: a gatekeeper (Ken Sansom) at the Wade's Malibu community does corny imitations of old Hollywood stars (e.g. Barbara Stanwyck, Walter Brennan, Cary Grant).

33 'Friendship is always a difficult subject for Altman, and his films constantly probe the proximity of friendship to betrayal' (Kolker 2011: 343).

34 The coke bottle scene is not unlike the brutal killing of the cowboy in *McCabe & Mrs. Miller* for shock value.

35 Despondent over the death of his wife, Raymond Chandler attempted suicide in 1955. Suffering from clinical depression and no longer able to write, Ernest Hemingway committed suicide in 1960.

36 The original debt was $5,000 – the same amount Lennox sends Marlowe as a payoff.

37 As Robert Kolker notes (p. 437), in Altman's films 'a window is used as a barrier to direct emotional contact'.

38 Even the $5,000 bill is symbolic; it features a portrait of Alexander Hamilton, who was shot to death (in a duel by Aaron Burr in 1804), i.e. a harbinger of Terry Lennox's fate.

39 Director Mark Rydell (Marty Augustine in *The Long Goodbye*) had wooed away Zsigmond and art designer Leon Ericksen to work on his film, *Cinderella Liberty*.

40 Arthur Penn's *Bonnie and Clyde* invokes this work with simulated FSA stills during its opening credit sequence.

41 Caught forging checks and embezzling money, David Begelman was fired from Columbia Pictures in 1977. He committed suicide in 1995.

42 The Mapes Hotel (built 1947; abandoned 1982; demolished 2000) was the first skyscraper built in the western United States since the start of World War II. An Art Deco style twelve-story, 300-room high-rise built to combine a hotel and casino, the Mapes was the prototype for all modern hotel-casinos.

CHAPTER THREE

Large Canvases

Many people, I guess, want to know exactly what it is they're supposed to think. They want to know what your message is. Well, my message is that I am not going to do their work for them.

– Robert Altman

Nashville (1975)

As was usually the case with his film projects, Robert Altman did not initiate *Nashville*. In 1972 United Artists approached him with a script for a movie about the Nashville music scene entitled 'The Great Southern Amusement Company', a star vehicle concocted for the Welsh pop singer Tom Jones who was signed to the studio's record division. Altman, who had never been to Nashville and detested country music, hated the script. He made a counteroffer; if UA would finance *Thieves Like Us*, he would make his own Nashville movie for them – though he didn't tell studio execs that *his* Nashville movie would satirise the misogynistic, flag-waving, right-wing politics of the country music scene that epitomised Richard Nixon's 'silent majority'. The studio gave Altman the green light and he then hired screenwriter Joan Tewkesbury to write a Nashville script that would, in her words, 'make a statement about American politics and politicians like [Richard Nixon]' (in McGilligan 1989: 400). Tewkesbury's first research visit to the country music mecca was a three-day guided tour in the fall of 1972 that yielded little of value. While he was shooting *Thieves Like Us* in Jackson, Mississippi in the spring of 1973, Altman sent Tewkesbury back to Nashville again. On her own this time for a five-day visit, she arranged to attend recording sessions, one of which featured the Jubilee Singers, an African-American gospel group. At another session she watched Loretta Lynn perform a duet with Conway Twitty and marvelled at Lynn's intense work ethic. Tewksbury also interviewed music engineers on every facet of the business and spent time at the Exit/In, a small but important music venue on Elliston Place near Centennial Park and Vanderbilt University, opened in 1971 that hosted (and continues to host) a wide array of talent (see Stuart 2000: 45–58). Upon leaving the Exit/In one night, Tewksbury suddenly realised she had her organising principle:

> There were several people I had seen throughout the day. The city is built in a circle, so if I saw you in the morning and didn't know who you were, I'd see you at least two times before the end of the day ... I said, 'Shit, everything runs in circles in this town.' I said, 'Fuck, this is it. It's all about overlaps and connective tissue.' (In Zuckoff 2009: 275)

Tewksbury soon turned the journal she kept of her Nashville visits into the first draft of a screenplay but Altman sensed that there was something missing. With the mounting Watergate crisis occupying the national consciousness, he felt that a movie only about the Nashville music scene lacked gravitas: 'I think there's got to be a political umbrella on this, otherwise it's just gossip' (in Thompson 2006: 93). To give the movie proper heft, Altman suggested that it end with an assassination – not of a political figure (the too-obvious choice) but of one of the music celebrities, a fictive country singer named Barbara Jean. Polly Platt, the ex-wife of director Peter Bogdanovich and Altman's art designer on the project, hated the idea, quit over it, and was replaced by Robert M. Anderson. Tewksbury also balked but had no choice; she either had to accept Altman's terms or remove herself from the project, a career-jeopardising manoeuvre she was not prepared to take. But Altman's instincts were both correct and prophetic; five years before John Lennon's murder the killing of Barbara Jean by a deranged 'fan' *was* the most incisive way to dramatise the widening schism in American life between the advertised ideal and the deeply flawed reality – a schism that has led in recent decades to rising levels of alienation and increasingly more frequent acts of mass gun violence. The final script, by Altman and Tewksbury, added Barbara Jean's killing, a third party presidential campaign and six more characters to the original eighteen, bringing the total to twenty-four. United Artists studio head David Picker judged the project 'unformed' and of doubtful commercial potential and ultimately refused to green-light it. Fortunately, through the auspices of music producer Jerry Weintraub, Altman managed to secure a $2.2 million deal with ABC.

Production funding obtained, Altman ran into the usual casting difficulties, all of which were resolved to satisfaction, if not brilliantly. The role of the runaway wife, Albuquerque, was first offered to Bette Midler and then Bernadette Peters but eventually went to Barbara Harris. Gary Busey was supposed to play Tom Frank, a womanising folksinger, but dropped out to take a TV series. He was replaced by Altman stalwart, Keith Carradine. Robert Duvall was supposed to play the country music star-impresario Haven Hamilton (perhaps a composite of Roy Acuff, Hank Snow and Porter Wagoner) but 'something didn't click' for him – probably the fact that Hamilton's character, a dictatorial wheeler-dealer, offended Duvall's conservative political sensibilities. He was fortuitously replaced by Henry Gibson (see Zuckoff 2009: 283). The role of gospel singer Linnea Reese was created for (and by) Louise Fletcher, who was the daughter of two deaf parents and knew sign language, but she dropped out to take the role of Nurse Ratched in Milos Forman's *One Flew Over the Cuckoo's Nest* (1975), for which she won an Academy Award. Fletcher was replaced by Lili Tomlin, who had ironically turned down the Nurse Ratched role. Finally, the crucial role of Barbara Jean (loosely based on Loretta Lynn and Tammy Wynette) was supposed to be played by Susan Anspach but she quit over a compensation dispute. Anspach was replaced by singer-songwriter Ronee Blakley: a fortuitous last-minute choice, as Blakley's poignant rendition of the doomed singer would win her Academy Award, BAFTA and Golden Globe nominations (and a spot on the roster of Bob Dylan's Rolling Thunder Review tour in the fall of 1975). The rest of the main cast includes Barbara Baxley as Lady Pearl, Haven Hamilton's alcoholic mistress; Ned Beatty as Delbert Reese, Linnea's scheming husband; Karen Black as Connie White, the vain but mediocre country singer (reputedly based on Lynn Anderson); Geraldine Chaplin as Opal, a clueless British journalist; Shelley Duvall as Martha, a vapid gamin who calls herself 'LA Joan'; Allen Garfield as Barnett, Barbara Jean's crusty husband-manager; Scott Glenn as Pfc. Glenn Kelly, an obsessed Barbara Jean fan; Jeff Goldblum as 'Tricycle Man', an eccentric motorcyclist; David Hayward as Kenny Fraiser, Barbara Jean's lonely assassin; Michael Murphy as John Triplette, a cynical front man for fictive presidential candidate Hal Phillip Walker; Dave Peel as Haven Hamilton's bland son, Bud; Bert Remsen as Albuquerque's jilted husband, Star; Robert DoQui as Wade Cooley, an airport restaurant cook; Gwen Welles as Sueleen Gay, an aspiring but awful singer; Keenan Wynn as Mr. Green, LA Jones's elderly uncle (whose wife, Esther, is dying in a Nashville hospital); Richard Baskin as Frog, a studio musician (also, in reality, the film's musical arranger); Allan Nicholls (Bill) and Cristina Raines (Mary) as a married couple who comprise a folk trio with Tom Frank called Bill, Mary and Tom – modelled on Fat Chance, a short-lived folk trio comprised of John Denver and Bill and Taffy Danoff that was modelled in turn on the popular folk trio, Peter, Paul and Mary (see Stuart 2000: 41).

Though it's not thought of as such, *Nashville* is essentially a musical, so Altman's early decision to have his actors write and perform their own songs (live, in concert settings) was as crucial as any casting choice. Altman's decision was mostly driven by financial exigencies; buying the rights to well-known country hits (and perhaps having the actual artists performing them) would have been prohibitively expensive; as Altman later told Jan Stuart: 'Everybody's going, oh, my songs will cost you this and this and I want so and so! I just didn't want to deal with any of that. I didn't want the agents walking around telling me what to do, mainly what the fucking songs would be' (in Stuart 2000: 79). Another consideration was aesthetic; Altman told an interviewer he wanted 'a cross-section of songs, good and bad… [the country and western people in Nashville] felt I should have used their stuff. But I was satirizing them. Their stuff would have been too on the nose' (in Thompson 2006: 92). As Stuart notes: 'One of the most significant impacts of Altman's decision is that it made the film less "about" Nashville, 1976, and more of an idea of America, 1976' (2000: 78). Actors and music secured and settings chosen, *Nashville* was shot on location in forty-three hectic days between 10 July and 31 August 1974 and released ten months later, on 11 June 1975.

In many ways *Nashville*'s overall meaning is neatly encapsulated in its ten-minute-long opening title sequence that was not in the screenplay. The inserted sequence opens with an imitation K-Tel ('As-Seen-On-TV') ad. A loud, frenetic hard-sell commercial (i.e. scrolling names and song titles, revolving artists' faces and song samples) for the record album that accompanies the film, showcasing the songs of 'twenty-four of your very favourite stars' – the ad is a parodic jab at hyped-up commodity fetishism and the ineluctably commercial nature of mass-marketed 'popular culture'. The film proper begins with a brief scene showing the Tennessee state campaign office of 'Replacement Party' ('New Roots for the Nation') presidential candidate, Hal Phillip Walker. A campaign poster-festooned garage door ascends, unleashing a white Econoline van with campaign markings and four loudspeakers mounted on its roof. As the van moves through Nashville's city streets, its speakers blare a pre-recorded speech by candidate Walker that deplores the high cost of living and argues the need for widespread, populist engagement in the political affairs of the nation. The remaining seven-and-a-half minutes of the title sequence crosscut between two scenes that take place in adjacent Nashville recording studios. In Studio 'A' Haven Hamilton is recording '200 Years', a mawkish and militaristic paean to America for its upcoming Bicentennial. The camera pans the low-lit but spacious studio full of musicians and the glass-partitioned control room full of family members and technicians before it settles onto Hamilton singing into a microphone in a glass-windowed isolation booth while four backup singers croon in another booth behind him. Short, short-tempered and absurdly accoutered in toupée, sideburns, white scarf and an ostentatious white and green rhinestone outfit, vainglorious Hamilton is obviously a reigning king of the Nashville country music scene. The aural and visual effect of the scene is to emphasise hierarchy, tight control, exclusivity and fragmented spaces: fitting images of the white, Christian, sanctimonious Republicanism that Haven Hamilton embodies. After a run-through of his jingoistic anthem, Hamilton is upset by the presence of an unauthorised person in the control room: Opal, a hippie-attired (perhaps *faux*) journalist from the UK armed with a tape-recorder and microphone, allegedly making a documentary about the Nashville music scene.[1] Hamilton instructs his son, Buddy, to remove Opal from Studio 'A' and accompany her to Studio 'B' until the session is concluded. In the much smaller but more brightly lit Studio 'B', white gospel singer Linnea Reese is leading the Fisk Jubilee Singers, a black gospel choir, in 'Yes, I Do', a rousing, up-tempo gospel number short on propagandistic lyrics but filled instead with hand-clapping, gyrating bodies and a general sense of joyous exuberance – in marked contrast to the grim undertaking in the studio next door. Indeed, crosscuts back to Studio 'A' show Haven Hamilton losing his temper with Frog, a bored studio musician not playing to Hamilton's satisfaction. Ultimately an exasperated Hamilton storms out of the studio but not before firing Frog and insulting him for good measure ('You get your hair cut! You don't belong in Nashville!'). In sum, the failure of '200 years' (i.e. the hegemonic American narrative) to coalesce is a failure of Gesellschaft, an authoritarian corporate structure that functions through top-down discipline and money incentives, not through any shared vision of community or higher purpose. Conversely, the celebratory gospel hymn, 'Yes, I Do' coheres because it freely affirms life and faith as ends in themselves: Gemeinschaft values opposed to the cash/power nexus and all its machinery.

Seemingly unrelated vignettes, the three parts of the title sequence form a dialectical suite that introduces the film's overarching conceit; that, in America, politics and show biz are in many ways one and the same.[2] Or, to put it another way, politics is best understood in broader terms as ideology, and ideology in modern capitalist America equates to a fame/money/success ethos mostly conveyed through mass celebrity culture. The first part of the title sequence satirises the breathless inanities of capitalist hucksterism. The second part derides conventional electoral politics as another sort of hustle, less compelling and technologically anachronistic to boot. Hal Phillip Walker's stately rhetoric notwithstanding, it's never clear that anyone is actually listening (or even could listen) to the words emitted from Walker's constantly roving 1930s-style sound truck. In a radically depoliticised polity dedicated to the vicarious pleasures of consumerism and pop idol worship, the persuasive efficacy of briefly heard snatches of political sloganeering is dubious at best. If the first two parts of the title sequence contrast two types of politico-cultural dissemination and consumption, one emergent, the other residual, the longer third part offers glimpses of two contrasting styles of cultural production. Here, commerce and politics (ideology) are performatively reified into the gestalt of everyday life in modern America but to very different purposes. Allegorically, Studio 'A' and Studio 'B' neatly encapsulate the two Americas, what Calvinist/Puritan doctrine terms the Elect (the chosen) and the Preterite (the damned), side by side but walled-off and sound-proofed from each other. The hegemonic culture is moneyed, male-dominated, white, irascible and politically conservative while its subaltern cultures, mostly nonwhite and far less affluent, are demonstrably more human and decidedly more egalitarian in their politics. Admittedly, Linnea Reese's starring role in the choir affirms white privilege but it also challenges patriarchy and she and the Fisk Jubilee Choir transgress Southern racist-segregationist taboos by singing side by side in exuberant harmony.

Class and race segregation normally ensure that the two societies exemplified by the two recording sessions are kept separate and unequal but, in the diegetic world of the film, Opal's interloping ruptures the frame and leads viewers from the idealised version of American society in Studio 'A' to the repressed but more real version in Studio 'B'. In this regard one could say that Opal is a stand-in for Altman himself, i.e. an outside observer with recording equipment who manages to catalyse highly revealing representations of contemporary society. The crucial difference, though, between Opal and Altman is Opal's resounding ignorance of American folkways, especially her condescending, essentialising naiveté about blacks and black music. She marvels to Bud: 'Look at that rhythm, it's fantastic! You know it's funny, you can tell it's come down in the genes through ages and ages and hundreds of years but it's there. Take off those robes and one is in darkest Africa. I can just see their naked, frenzied bodies dancing! Do they carry on like that in church?' Bud's unknowingly sagacious reply – 'It depends on which church you go to' – neatly summarises the fundamental spiritual and cultural differences that divide black, poor America from white, rich America but his words are lost on a dimwitted foreigner blinded by romantic notions of black authenticity that are devoid of historical context.

Having staked out, in introductory set pieces, a constellation of thematic param- eters – commercialism, politics and pop culture as the battleground of competing but ultimately complementary ideologies – *Nashville* presents a series of converging storylines that dramatise how these forces interpellate celebrities, hangers-on, celeb- rity wannabes and ordinary citizens, and motivate their lives over a five-day period in Nashville (America, writ small). As Robert Kolker aptly observes: 'The frame narrative – the organizing of a rally for candidate Hal Phillip Walker – easily holds the parts together, and the controlling thematic of celebrity, power, their illusions and abuses, is addressed in each sub-narrative and through each character' (2011: 355). Accordingly, the characters that populate the movie occupy positions along an elaborate pecking order, (over)determined by monetary, political, racial and sexual capital. The (white) rich, famous, and well-connected occupy one end of the spectrum, the poor and anon- ymous the opposite end and various aspirants jostle for better position somewhere in the thick of the predatory melée.[3]

At the summit of (potential) power is Hal Phillip Walker, the mysterious third party presidential candidate who has already won three primaries and promises to set America right. A spectral transcendental signified, Walker looms over the proceedings; his presence is felt and his words constantly heard, but he is ultimately never seen. When Barbara Jean is fatally shot during the rally at Nashville's Parthenon, Walk- er's security detail abruptly cancels his scheduled appearance and speeds him away from the scene in a black Cadillac limo with dark-tinted windows – a saviour whose coming, like Godot, is yearned for but always deferred, suggesting the chimerical nature of utopian dreams proffered by run-of-the-mill politicians. Walker's true nature and motivations are also called into question by the character of his advance man, John Triplette, a glib Machiavellian operative who views the Nashville locals as ignorant rubes to be manipulated for publicity purposes favourable to the Walker campaign. Triplette is Altman's synecdochical figure for the professional-managerial class, whose job is to serve the ruling elites by keeping the rabble in line and productive.

A more tangible pseudo-father-figure than Walker is Haven Hamilton, the pint- sized Nashville mogul with a Napoleon complex who bullies his son, studio musicians and anyone else who gets in his way, but knows how and when to charm the public or curry favour with elite personages. His name functions as a symbolic statement that equates the homeland to Alexander Hamilton (1755–1804), the Federalist first Secre- tary of the Treasury, who distrusted democracy and advocated for a quasi-monarchical executive that made American Gesellschaft possible. Hence, 'Haven Hamilton' desig- nates Henry Gibson's character as the heir and epitome of a monetarist elitism that can be traced back to the nation's founding. Ruthless careerist and social climber, Haven Hamilton hopes to parlay his show business celebrity into political power, some years before the practice became commonplace in American politics. John Triplette promises Hamilton Walker's backing should he (Hamilton) choose to run for governor, so long as there is evident *quid pro quo*. As Hamilton's mistress, Nashville nightclub owner Lady Pearl ranks high in the city's social hierarchy but her overlapping identities as (the other) woman, alcoholic, Catholic and liberal Democrat remove her from its power centres. In a poignant monologue (written by Barbara Baxley and edited by Baxley and Tewkesbury three days before the scene was shot) a drunken and maudlin Lady Pearl provides dramatic counterpoint to Hamilton's scheming by mournfully remembering the murdered Kennedy brothers: whatever their actual faults, they were politicians who seemed to embody hope for progressive social change now extinguished in the more nakedly cynical and sociopathic era of Richard Nixon.[4]

If Haven Hamilton is the titular king of the Nashville music scene, Barbara Jean is queen, but an anguished one. After receiving treatment for burns suffered in a 'flaming baton' accident, Barbara Jean is the subject of a garish homecoming at Nashville's airport featuring a high school marching band, baton twirlers (an ironic touch), TV coverage, 3,000 unruly fans and Haven Hamilton's intrusive grandstanding. But the event proves too taxing. Emotionally and physically fragile, Barbara Jean faints from the heat and needs to be hospitalised, a happenstance that will keep her from making a scheduled appearance at Nashville's Grand Ole Opry. Once it's aborted, the saccharine spectacle of Barbara Jean's homecoming is then mocked by a sequence depicting a mad dash from the airport by the country star's fawning admirers who instantly transmogrify into selfish and impatient motorists. Ironically, their haste to depart the scene culminates in the protracted stasis of a massive traffic jam on the highway caused by a multi-car pile-up: Altman's synecdoche for a mechanised, competitive consumer Gesellschaft come a cropper through its heedless insistence on the atomising autonomy afforded by the automobile.

Barbara Jean also comes to grief, partly through her own flawed character but mostly through the workings of fate. While she might appear simply sweet and virginal to her adoring public, the real Barbara Jean is a narcissist who seems to suffer from a species of borderline personality disorder marked by moodiness, extreme sensitivity, a weak and wavering self-image and dependency issues. In her hospital bed the night of the Opry show, she hears her rival Connie White sing in her stead on the radio and flies into a puerile pique of jealousy and frustration that is quelled with difficulty by her hard-bitten husband-manager, Barnett, who has to resort to hectoring and flattery to keep his wife's fragile ego from imploding. The essential vacuity behind Barbara Jean's persona is further dramatised in a brilliant scene set two days later on an outdoor stage at the new Opryland USA theme park just outside Nashville. After successfully performing a couple of songs with her band, Barbara Jean lapses into a regressive fugue and begins to ramble on confusedly about her childhood instead of starting the next song – yet another Altman female protagonist stricken by psychosis.[5] To avoid scandal and mollify the restive crowd, Barnett hurriedly escorts her off stage and publicly promises that she will perform for free at the start of the Hal Phillip Walker rally to be held at the Parthenon the next day, something he was adamantly opposed to because he didn't want Barbara Jean's innocent (i.e. apolitical) image tarnished by politics. Thus Barbara Jean's psychological fragility puts her at the Walker rally where she will be assassinated.

Slightly further down the pecking order, just below Barbara Jean's rival, Connie White, is the folk trio, Bill, Mary and Tom, who are in Nashville to cut a record. Though last in billing, Tom Frank is first in stage charisma, sexiness and suave self-confidence: assets he leverages to bed as many woman as he can manage. In the five-day timeframe of the film his sexual conquests include his musical partner Mary (wife of Bill, his other partner in the trio), Opal, the inane journalist, LA Joan and Linnea Reese. Tom appears to love women but in reality he is indifferent to them as human beings. Indeed, at base, Tom is a predatory narcissist with a dread of intimacy who uses casual sex to maintain his self-preoccupation and grandiose sense of superiority – the antithesis of Alfred Adler's concept of *Gemeinschaftsgefuhl* ('community feeling' or 'social interest'; the term is used by Adlerian psychologists to describe the state of social connectedness and interest in the well-being of others that characterises psychological health). A sociopath normally able to affect the convincing façade of a sensitive artist, Tom allows his mask to slip just once. After sex with Linnea Reese in his hotel room, he has his vanity offended when she refuses to stay, citing family obligations. He retaliates by phoning another paramour while Linnea is still there, getting dressed. The scene is an especially meaningful one because Linnea, though admittedly cheating on her husband, still qualifies as the only good and admirable person in the film. A truly talented vocal artist (Tom's equal in that regard), a devoted mother to her two deaf children and an unjustly neglected wife, Linnea embodies the other-directedness and wounded compassion that Tom so convincingly feigns. He tries to humiliate her but she possesses too much self-awareness to be Tom's (or anyone's) victim. The same cannot be said of Bill's wife, Mary, whose love for Tom Frank reduces her to angry desperation. Tom's other conquests – Opal and LA Joan – are both sex- and celebrity-obsessed pseudo-individuals unworthy of a second thought.

If Tom Frank is the ultimate sexual victimiser, Sueleen Gay is his mirror opposite: the quintessential sexual victim, not of Tom – they don't cross paths – but of an array of misogynistic males, most notably Delbert Reese and John Triplette: *de facto* pimps who arrange to have her perform at an all-male fundraising smoker for Hal Phillip Walker. The talentless and dim-witted Sueleen is a waitress at the airport diner under the delusion that she can sing and that, allowed a foot in the door, she'll be able to emulate Barbara Jean and forge her own career in show business. Sueleen's brutal degradation at the smoker is another one of the film's most arresting set pieces. Initially booed off the stage for singing horribly – and not taking her clothes off, as was expected – Sueleen is ready to flee the building but is persuaded by Del Reese and Triplette to stay and strip on the promise that if she does so, they will let her sing the next day at the Parthenon with Barbara Jean. Deluded ambition easily trumps self-respect. Though visibly shaken, Sueleen proceeds to disrobe, to the delight of her audience: a horde of cat-calling, drunkenly slavering lechers. After Sueleen's public humiliation ritual, an inebriated Del Reese drives her home and then comes on to her, but Sueleen is rescued by Wade Cooley, who tries to make her realise that she cannot sing and pleads with her to go back to Detroit with him the next day. Sueleen refuses because she is determined to appear at the Parthenon with Barbara Jean. Thus, true to life, reason and love are rejected in favour of the illusory brass ring. Wade's marginal status as a working-class black man unjustly renders him inconsequential.

Joining Wade at the base of *Nashville*'s social pyramid is a motley collection of solitary, mostly deracinated men: Pfc. Glenn Kelly, a stalwart, lonely Vietnam War veteran in love from afar with Barbara Jean who has come to Nashville to see her perform; the 'Tricycle Man' who rides his long, low-slung three-wheel motorcycle everywhere, for no good reason (other than to serve as a connective device between disparate scenes); Mr. Green, the aging uncle of Martha, who tries but fails to get his selfish, empty-headed niece to visit his dying wife; Norman, the chauffeur hired to drive Bill, Mary and Tom during their stay in Nashville who deludingly believes himself to be their friend and confidante; Star, an irritable man chasing after his runaway wife, Winifred (Albuquerque); Frog, the disaffected session musician. At the very bottom of the heap is Kenny Frasier, an anonymous loner who 'looks like Howdy Doody', carries a violin case, and rents a room from Mr. Green. He ends up amid the crowd at the Parthenon for the Hal Phillip Walker rally, pulls a pistol out of his violin case, and abruptly shoots Barbara Jean as she performs on stage.

In Tewksbury's screenplay, Frasier is at least afforded some sort of paranoid political motivation. After shooting Barbara Jean he shouts: 'I could have got that Walker bastard before. I've been closer, closer than this, but my Nash broke down and somebody kept stealing my things. I wanted to get him the day before, and then Mr. Green's wife died, so this was the right time. I love the President of the United States. I love him.' When he actually shot the scene, Altman wisely chose to delete these lines, transforming the shooting into a violent act without rhyme or reason – perhaps an impulsive expression of alienated rage, or perhaps, in the manner of Lee Harvey Oswald or Arthur Bremer, a loser's desperate bid to finally be somebody, albeit forever despised and infamous. What is finally remarkable about the incident is its jarring absurdity. Connie Byrne and William O. Lopez rightly note that in *Nashville* 'the plot – the impulse toward suspense or resolution – is entirely subordinated to the moment. The story does not move toward any predictable *dénouement*, rather it just meanders along. *Nashville* doesn't really lead

Loser's revenge: Kenny Frasier (David Hayward) takes aim at the American Dream.

up to "the assassination", nor does it end with it. The murder simply happens and people are already singing again by the final backwards zoom' (in Sterritt 2000: 20). Tellingly, the refrain of the song they sing, led by Albuquerque, who is getting her big break in show business quite literally over Barbara Jean's dead body: 'You may say that I'm not free/ But it don't worry me.' The song affirms a dull, uncomprehending docility as the best way to cope with dangerous crises in the public sphere: the kind of bovine stupidity that would later be perversely celebrated by Robert Zemeckis's execrable but wildly popular and critically esteemed *Forrest Gump* (1994). But if the star-struck populace is reliably oblivious to reality, the always savvy Haven Hamilton is most assuredly not. Though wounded in the arm by one of Kenny Frasier's bullets, Hamilton makes the most of misfortune by going to the microphone and pleading for calm, commanding the singing to resume, and then helping to carry a moribund Barbara Jean off-stage: a quick-witted display of courage and leadership that will likely catapult him to the governor's mansion and perhaps to points beyond. While not specifically thinking of *Nashville*, social critic Henry Giroux offers illuminating words on the film's culminating scene when he observes that 'authoritarianism is often abetted by an inability of the public to grasp how questions of power, politics, history and public consciousness are mediated at the interface of private issues and public concerns' (2011: 86). In the final analysis, *Nashville* posits the depressing notion that once a sizeable portion of the citizenry has been led away from informed engagement in the civic affairs of the country by the vicarious thrills of celebrity culture and show business spectacle, democracy is in serious trouble, if not doomed altogether.

In a way, the film's box office performance proved its own thesis. While *Nashville* earned a respectable $9.9 million domestically, almost five times its modest budget, Steven Spielberg's monster-thriller *Jaws* (which was released ten days after *Nashville* in the summer of 1975), was a monster hit, earning an astonishing $100 million at the box office – the highest grossing movie up to that time. A carefully contrived, formulaic blockbuster, *Jaws* essentially signaled the end of the Hollywood Renaissance, the beginning of the Cineplex movie as sensation-saturated thrill ride for the widest and lowest demographic, and another step in the relentless homogenisation and dumbing down of American culture that *Nashville* satirises. J. Hoberman neatly summarizes the opposing ideological positions staked out by these two films:

> *Nashville* had offered a glibly pessimistic view of American life, predicting the rise of a politics as meretricious and authoritarian as the mass culture industry. *Jaws* was glibly optimistic in offering itself as a solution. Altman's complex interplay of sound and image – the overlapping mix of conversation, traffic noise, radios and soundtrack – was the precise inverse of Spielberg's total orchestration, the musical score (so close to the angst-producing theme from *The Twilight Zone*) functioning like an emotional rheostat, everything harmonized for maximum effect. (2004: 210–11)

In keeping with its vision of America as a radically fragmented and decentred Gesellschaft of self-interested individuals, *Nashville* employs a non-totalising, multi-perspectival aesthetic that allows for a range of interpretations and emotional responses. The film acknowledges the existential isolation imposed upon the individual by modern consumer-capitalism but nonetheless seeks to actualise an always latent potential for a nonconformist critical awareness. Slavoj Žižek argues that *Jaws* does much the opposite:

> Ordinary Americans, as ordinary people in all countries have a multitude of fears… We fear immigrants, maybe, or people we perceive as lower than ourselves, attacking us, robbing us. We fear people raping our children. We fear natural disasters… We fear corrupted politicians. We fear big companies which can do with us whatever they want. The function of the shark [in *Jaws*] is to unite all these fears so that we can, in a way, trade all these fears for one fear alone. In this way our experience of reality gets much simpler. Why am I mentioning this? Because… the most extreme case of ideology, maybe, in the history of humanity – Nazi-fascist anti-Semitism – worked precisely in the same way… You need to generate an ideological narrative which explains how things went wrong in a society, not as the result of the inherent tensions in the development of this society, but as the result of a foreign intruder… It's the same operation as with the shark in *Jaws*. (*The Pervert's Guide to Ideology*, 2012)

As Žižek astutely argues, Spielberg's *Jaws* expresses a crypto-fascist aesthetic in keeping with the totalising aims of a reemerging Hollywood corporatism that would find its apotheosis in the age of Reagan. *Jaws* tells us how to think and feel, just as it combines all fears into a neat package that can be literally detonated by a people's saviour, the cop-hero Martin Brody (Roy Scheider), and banished from consciousness in a filmic resolution that allows for no ambiguity or doubt – a deeply satisfying authoritarian wish-fulfillment fantasy that *Nashville* repudiates.

A Wedding (1978)

Work on two films – *Buffalo Bill and the Indians* and *3 Women* – intervened before Altman was ready to try his hand at a second large-canvas satire of the contemporary scene: *A Wedding*. The movie started out as a joke. On the set of *3 Women* in Palm Springs, Karen Stabiner, then film critic for *Mother Jones* magazine, asked Altman what his next film would be about. In the midst of shooting a difficult scene in 107 degree heat he peevishly retorted that he was going to film weddings. The more he thought about it, though, the more Altman was intrigued by the idea (see McGilligan 1989: 457–8). He told Charles Michener in a 1978 interview: 'A wedding would provide a device to explore the foibles of a society. After all, people behave differently when they're placed in formal situations. At a wedding or a funeral … you follow the amenities of the culture. You don't act the way you normally act; you're putting on a front… So we had the arena for a multicast, cultural, comedy situation' (in Sterritt 2000: 85). Though Altman would never have stated it thus, he was, in effect, saying that he wanted to explore how Gesellschaft prerogatives – status seeking and individual self-interest – infiltrate and reshape the kinship culture of the extended family, once Gemeinschaft in character but now an institution thoroughly degraded by the pervasive commodification processes of business civilisation. As Kolker puts it, 'Altman sees the family as a barren place, as barren as the ideology it reproduces and which reproduces it' (2011: 378). Indeed, Kolker deems *A Wedding* Altman's 'most vicious attack on domestic institutions … a film which offers a climax to Altman's explorations and revelations of hypocrisy, duplicity, manipulation, and humiliation' (ibid.).

As was often the case, Altman's choice of topic seemed to reflect salient currents in the American *zeitgeist*. After the seismic political upheavals of the 1960s, Americans increasingly turned to personal and domestic concerns in the 1970s – a trend signaled by Craig Gilbert's *An American Family*, a surprisingly popular documentary series focusing on an affluent Santa Barbara family that aired in 1973 and is now considered the first 'reality' television series. Another *zeitgeist* barometer was Christopher Lasch's *Haven in a Heartless World: The Family Besieged* (1977), a bestselling scholarly assessment of the state of the family that lamented the fact the 'same historical developments that have made it necessary to set up private life – the family in particular – as a refuge from the cruel world of politics and work, an emotional sanctuary, have invaded this sanctuary and subjected it to outside control. A retreat into "privatism" no longer serves to shore up values elsewhere threatened with extinction' (1977: xviii). While acknowledging that societal imperatives have badly damaged the autonomy of family life – arguably once an incubator for healthy egos – Lasch called for a recuperation of the family as the haven it once was. Yet, for all his erudition, Lasch was strangely non-specific about *social class*, as if American families of every stratum were basically in the same boat.

Having to film a specific set of people in specific circumstances, Altman had to choose a specific class context. So when he opted to focus on the matrimonial joining of two wealthy families, he deliberately chose a setting that moved the family away from Lasch's notion of extrinsic victimisation by invasive, authoritarian bureaucratic structures. Set amongst the rich, *A Wedding* is not about disempowerment. Instead, it portrays a rather rarified sort of class conflict. As Altman told Charles Michener: 'I wanted to deal with rich people: *very* rich, very conservative, very old, deep money – so old and deep that hardly anybody can remember where it originally came from. A matriarchy… We wanted to play the border southern *nouveau riche* family against the decadence of this matriarchy, a family that had almost no connections to the outside world' (in Sterritt 2000: 85). Juxtaposing a residual social formation to an emergent order that will soon absorb and supplant it, *A Wedding* finds comedy and drama in the clash between snobbery and social climbing – but also finds larger commonalties: indiscriminate lusts, duplicity and the compulsive worship of money and status, all wrapped up in an unthinking reliance on threadbare ritual. As the film's pompous wedding director, Rita Billingsley (Geraldine Chaplin), proclaims just before the cutting of the cake, 'Now there are certain, accepted customs which one must observe, some because they involve social and economic factors…' Mention of the other factors, whatever they might be, is tellingly rendered inaudible by the Altmanesque intrusion of another, louder conversation.

After settling on a general schema, Altman turned to John Considine, a trusted Lion's Gate associate, to develop a script for his wedding movie.[6] Considine recalls that Altman 'wanted a big wedding because he wanted the story to have to do with the wedding business and what it meant in our lives. He told me a lot of key things: he outlined the two families and made them disparate in every conceivable way, religious background, educational, old money, new money' (in McGilligan 1989: 460). Altman also decided that he would arbitrarily double the number of characters featured in *Nashville*, from twenty-four to forty-eight, making for a much larger and more diffuse filmic canvas than he had ever attempted. But to give the picture focus, he set the action all in one location in one day (in Sterritt 2000: 85).

Considine and Altman developed ideas over a series of creative discussions, Considine took notes, fashioned a thirteen-page treatment to show to Fox for financing, and eventually wrote a 134-page script. At the start of principal photography (on location at the Lester Armour House in Lake Bluff, Illinois in June 1977), Altman brought in Patricia Resnick and Allan Nicholls to revise Considine's script – without first informing Considine that he was going to have co-writers. Surprised and humiliated, Considine nearly quit the picture but decided to stay on because he wanted to work for Altman again as an actor. Taking up an entire wing of the Armour mansion, Altman and his three writers concocted the family trees and back stories for all forty-eight characters, and then each writer took charge of a dozen or so characters and further polished characterisation. Patrick McGilligan recounts that Resnick took most of the young female characters, Nicholls took most of the young male characters, and Considine took the elders (1989: 463). In keeping with Altman's improvisatory-collaborative ethos, cast members were given outlines and brief descriptions of their characters *in lieu* of scripts and encouraged to 'bring their own ideas for specific scenes or dialogue changes to the writers' who would work with them 'in writing fresh material' (McGilligan 1989: 484). Margaret Ladd, a young actress with a small part in the film who kept a diary of her experiences during the shoot, wrote that Altman gathered the cast on 9 June and gave them a pep talk of sorts: 'I know all of you are very worried because no one really knows what's going on and you're all saying to yourselves, this picture could be the end of my career but I just want to reassure you that I've made a lot of bad pictures and I'm still working.' Ladd notes that Altman 'didn't really mean it to be funny but everyone got very giddy'.

Filmed by Charles Rosher Jr., Altman's cinematographer for *3 Women*, *A Wedding* was shot in sequence between 16 June and 9 August 1977. During the first three days of the shoot Altman filmed the elaborate wedding ceremony that opens the film at the Grace Episcopal Church in Oak Park, Illinois. The remaining forty-two days of shooting occurred in and around the Armour mansion thirty-six miles to the north and the cast was relocated to the Sheraton in Waukegan, about thirteen miles north of the mansion. With most of the filming taking place at one site and most of the film's personnel lodged together at another, Altman was able to create his customary artists' Gemeinschaft during principal photography. According to Gerard Plecki, 'Carol Burnett described the group experience as a wholesome, happy, "Saturday night matinee family atmosphere." Others agreed that warmth and friendship were shared in the undertaking, even under time and budget constraints' (1985: 106).

In the world of the film a very different sort of society prevails, one marked by sexual intrigue, faltering pretensions, comic pratfalls and suppressed secrets, gradually revealed. In short, nothing goes as planned and nothing is what it appears to be. Pomp and circumstance seem to abound when Muffin Brenner (Amy Stryker) is married to Dino Corelli (Desi Arnaz Jr.) in an ornate church ceremony. The dignity of the proceedings is undercut, however, by a close-up of the bride smiling, revealing a mouth full of braces, and by the confused ministrations of Bishop Martin (John Cromwell), a senile octogenarian who cannot remember (or perhaps believe) the bride's name. A sumptuous reception awaits the wedding party at the Corelli family mansion but once again things quickly go awry when the Corelli family matriarch, Nettie Sloan (Lillian Gish), succumbs to old age in her upstairs bedroom just before the guests arrive. Dr. Jules Meecham (Howard Duff), the family's hard-drinking physician, keeps Netti's demise quiet for a while, so as not to disrupt the wedding reception: a denial of death that makes a larger statement about the human avoidance of mortality and ironises all the nuptial festivities that follow in its wake.[7] The temporarily concealed death of Nettie Sloan also allegorises the attenuated end of WASP social hegemony, 'old money' superseded by the rise of new mercantile wealth from formerly ostracised ethnic groups. Indicative of changing times and mores, Nettie's daughter, Regina (Nina van Pallandt) has indeed 'married down'. Her husband is Luigi Corelli (Vittorio Gassman), an Italian waiter she met on vacation, a marriage that Nettie Sloan only agreed to sanction on the condition that Luigi conceal his lowly origins by keeping his relatives away from the Sloan (now Corelli) mansion. As Helen Keyssar notes, the secret pact between Nettie and Luigi 'suggests a class consciousness that underlies the American melting pot but also points to the many covenants made possible in a country where past histories and cultural differences can be obliterated with relative ease and within the national code of ethics' (1991: 286). That the reception takes place at the family home of the groom shows status prerogatives trumping the requisites of ritual. Custom normally dictates that the wedding reception be planned and held by the bride's family but the father of the bride, Liam 'Snooks' Brenner (Paul Dooley) has to defer to the Corelli-Sloans as to setting even though he gets to pay for the reception to the tune of $20,000. The millionaire founder of a successful trucking business, Snooks (a nickname that evokes street-tough commonness) is actually wealthier than the Corellis but he must bow to an unwritten rule governing elite social class relations, i.e. that vintage money, even in lesser quantities, translates into cultural capital superior to the kind produced by newly minted wealth.

Behind the stale respectability that comes with old money, the Sloan-Corellis have fallen into discord, decadence and hypocrisy. Nettie's sister, Aunt Beatrice Sloan Cory (Ruth Nelson), is, to her family's considerable annoyance, a left-wing bohemian of long standing. Intentionally or otherwise, Aunt Beatrice scandalises everyone at the reception when her gift to the newlyweds is unveiled: a shockingly realistic nude portrait of Muffin Brenner painted by a socialist artist that conjures the free thinking days of Louise Bryant's Greenwich Village. As Keyssar puts it, the incident 'has a kind of historical accuracy in reminding us of the conjoining of aesthetic, sexual, and political battles in the struggles of an earlier generation of liberated women' (1991: 288). The sins of the other Sloans are more characteristically bourgeois in that they involve covert drugs and sex. Regina, mother of the groom, is a closet heroin addict (and the alcoholic Dr. Meecham is her pusher). Another daughter, Clarice (Virginia Westhoff) is transgressing class and race lines by carrying on a secret affair with Randolph (Cedric Scott), Nettie Sloan's dapper African-American factotum. Mackenzie Goddard (Pat McCormick), the husband of a third daughter, Antoinette Sloan Goddard (Dina Merrill), betrays his wife by falling head-over-heels in love with the mother of the bride, Tulip Brenner (Carol Burnett), during the wedding reception. In the course of the afternoon Muffin's mostly mute sister Buffy (Mia Farrow) reveals that she is pregnant and that Dino Corelli, the groom, is the culprit. Called on the carpet by an angry Snooks, Dino disingenuously avers that most of his military school classmates have also slept with Buffy, who is evidently something of a nymphomaniac. The ensuing rancour devolves into full-blown chaos when news arrives at the mansion that the newlyweds fled the reception unnoticed in their wedding-gift sports car and were killed nearby in a fiery highway crash with a gasoline tanker truck. The two families show their true colours by turning on each other, hurling bitter recriminations, only to discover that Muffin and Dino are alive and well and that the people killed in the accident were Muffin's former boyfriend, Wilson Briggs (Gavan O'Herlihy) and Dino's former girlfriend, Tracy Farrell (Pam Dawber). Amid all the relief and joy at this revelation, Luigi Corelli observes that no one gives a damn about the deaths of Briggs and Tracy. Disgusted by such a shameful lack of empathy – indifference to others' suffering emanating from deep, selfish class insularity – Corelli decides to quit the Sloans and relinquish the riches he's just inherited as Nettie's heir. After paying his final respects to Nettie, he departs the mansion for his real family in Italy. In so doing Corelli repudiates Gesellschaft America and reaffirms the more genuine Old World Gemeinschaft values that make him the film's most sympathetic character.

Coming just two years after *Nashville*, *A Wedding* represents a considerable falling away from the earlier film's level of achievement. Robert Kolker rightly observes that almost 'every cut, every zoom [of *A Wedding*] reveals another bit of banal or embarrassing behavior without seeking to reveal the root causes of the banalities or to explain why they are so ridiculous' (2011: 379). Whereas at least some of the characters that populate *Nashville* have a modicum of depth and complexity, *A Wedding* is almost entirely comprised of caricatures set up to be, in Kolker's words, 'laughed at and degraded'. He further notes that the 'emotional contours of *Nashville* and the intellectual engagement that informs *Buffalo Bill* and *3 Women* are not much in evidence' (ibid.). Part of the problem is the sheer size of the cast, which inevitably results in a thinning out of individual characters. Equally problematic is the film's comic aspirations. Unlike *Nashville* – a satiric drama wedded to a musical – *A Wedding* is basically a comedy of manners that tries to combine broad humour ridiculing individual foibles and satire critiquing social mores. These aims are somewhat at cross purposes and result in tonal ambiguity and an aura of contrivance. For Robin Wood, *A Wedding* is, 'in its smug superiority to and contempt for its characters and in its unquestioning assumption of the audience's complicity, one of Altman's most unwatchable and embarrassing films' (1986: 43). Wood's judgement is harsh but not far off the mark; *A Wedding* lacks *Nashville*'s poignancy, moral seriousness and political incisiveness. Patrick McGilligan rather astutely characterises the film as an 'inconsequential' comedy of manners 'a tad on the overlong side … ultimately not so much a congealed story as a kind of orgasm of characterization' (1989: 465).

Notes

1   Film critic Roger Ebert suggests that she may not even be a filmmaker but just a groupie.

2   In an early scene, folksinger Bill (Allan F. Nicholls) notices a poster of Connie White at the Nashville airport gift shop that sports a Hal Phillip Walker bumper sticker and quips, 'Wait a minute! Wait a minute! Hal Phillip Walker looks exactly like Connie White!' – which is to say that politics looks exactly like pop culture celebrity.

3   Citing the large cast of characters and the limited time to properly develop them all, Neil Feineman finds most of the characters in *Nashville* 'caricatures, stereotypes, and simplifications' (1978: 172) but one could argue that the stunted personalities on display is precisely Altman's point.

4   Nixon resigned the presidency on 5 August 1974 while the *Nashville* shoot was at its midpoint.

5   Tammy Wynette had several notorious breakdowns on stage in the course of her ill-fated career.

6   Considine played a small part in *California Split* and portrayed Annie Oakley's manager-husband, Frank Butler in *Buffalo Bill and the Indians*.

7   See Ernst Becker's *Denial of Death* (Free Press, 1973).

CHAPTER FOUR

Falling from Grace

In order to attain power, every nation, group, large culture or what-have-you has to have a slave class. And the slave class of America is the middle class.
— Robert Altman

Though it was not readily apparent at the time, *A Wedding* marked the beginning of the end of Robert Altman's most fertile filmmaking period. His sinking fortunes coincided with the waning days of the Hollywood Renaissance, already effectively done in by 'high concept' blockbusters (e.g. Spielberg's *Jaws* and George Lucas's *Star Wars* (1977)), right-wing, crypto-racist feel-good movies (e.g. John G. Avildsen's Sylvester Stallone vehicle, *Rocky* (1976)), and the rise of the new studio movie mogul (e.g. Paramount's Barry Diller, Jeffrey Katzenberg and Michael Eisner). The twilight of the New American Cinema was also coincident with the dissolution of the American counterculture from which it derived its iconoclastic energy and artistic verve. Trends in the filmmaking industry reflected larger socio-economic shifts emerging in the late 1970s. By this point the politico-cultural progressivism of the 1960s was already a distant memory, nullified by post-Vietnam disillusionment, protracted economic doldrums, deindustrialisation, the concomitant decline of the labour movement and the faltering presidency of Jimmy Carter – all of which were setting the stage for a reactionary-corporatist Thermidor fronted by former B-movie actor and GE pitchman Ronald Reagan in 1980. Reagan's ascendancy would steer the country hard-a-starboard politically and render the cultural climate increasingly inimical to subversive, visionary filmmakers like Altman who refused to make formulaic genre pictures.

Quintet (1979)

As the country quietly but inexorably moved to the Right at the end of the 1970s Altman spent the last years of the pre-Reagan era digging himself deeper into a hole, career-wise. Always an embattled figure within his industry, and increasingly disenchanted with mainstream America, Altman was in a decidedly sombre mood in the early months of 1978, as his 77-year-old father, B.C., lay dying of cancer (Altman's mother had died in 1976).[1] It was in these circumstances that Altman hatched his next film after *A Wedding*: in his words, 'a grim Grimm's fairy tale' (in Sterritt 2000: 90) entitled *Quintet*. The idea for the movie came to Altman in a hotel room in Rome. He later told Richard Combs and Tom Milne that he overheard an indistinct conversation in the suite next door while peering out on a distant courtyard where two men were conversing: 'So I was watching one thing and hearing something else; and the idea came that if these people were plotting an assassination, and those I was watching were its victims ... where did that put me?' (in Sterritt 2000: 102). Altman initially envisioned *Quintet* as 'a kind of surrealistic thriller' set in 'the underbelly of Chicago, looking kind of like *Odd Man Out* or *The Third Man*' (ibid.). He wanted Walter Hill to write and direct but, as he told Charles Michener, 'it became more about life and death, and how you can't have one without the other. *It deals with the death of a culture*' (emphasis added) (in Sterritt 2000: 90).

As was by now his customary *modus operandi*, Altman sold the film to 20th Century Fox based on nothing more than a short treatment which would soon be rendered unrecognisable or, more likely, discarded altogether. He then had his new agent, Sam Cohn, hire a writer to develop his rather nebulous conceit into a script. Accordingly, Lionel Chetwynd, a British-Canadian screenwriter best known for his adaptation of *The Apprenticeship of Duddy Kravitz* (1974), was contracted to pen a novella on which a screenplay could be based. Altman hated Chetwynd's work, castigated and fired him, replacing him with *A Wedding* co-writer Patricia Resnick, who found herself baffled by murky subject matter that no one could quite understand. Altman also rejected Resnick's version as unsatisfactory. Ultimately, the script was overhauled and finished by Frank Barhydt, the son of an old Calvin Films associate from Kansas City. What finally emerged from such a tortuous and confused gestation process can best be described a post-apocalyptic-existentialist sci-fi fable set in a new Ice Age that may or may not be happening on planet Earth. As John Kenneth Muir notes:

> The underlying idea for *Quintet's* post-apocalyptic world arises out of the scientific and media history of the 1970s. In the early years of the disco decade, scientists began to become aware of a cooling trend on Earth, one that existed between the years 1945 and 1975, roughly. Popular news outlets jumped on the idea that a new ice age could be dawning, replete with a re-glaciation of the planet. In summer of 1974, *Time* magazine featured an article called 'Another Ice Age,' and worried about a 'global climactic upheaval' as the 'interglacial period' that had nurtured and nourished mankind for all his history came to an abrupt end. In 1975, *Newsweek* followed-up with an equally alarming article called 'The Cooling World.' A hot seller at book-vendors in the same era was called *The Weather Conspiracy: The Coming of a New Ice Age* [Ballantine Books, 1977]. (N.d.: n.p.)

As *Quintet* evolved into a kind of futuristic-primeval science fiction opus, Chicago ceased to be a suitable shooting location. Associate producer Allan Nicholls, a Montreal native, suggested his hometown in the dead of winter as a setting more amenable to the dystopic vision Altman was seeking. Locations were scouted there and Altman finally opted to shoot most of the film in and around the crumbling remains of the 'Man and His World' pavilions of the 1967 Montréal World's Exposition (aka 'Expo '67').[2] Under the supervision of Altman's trusted production designer Leon Erikson, crews were able to transform the dilapidated Expo structures into a convincingly bleak cityscape in its snowy death throes. To further enhance the sense of a world long submersed in deep cold, streams of water were continually sprayed on the buildings in sub-freezing temperatures to keep the ominous set draped in thick layers of ice (making for an usually dangerous set). To accentuate the desolate mood supplied by the setting, Altman and his French New Wave cinematographer, Jean Boffety (who shot *Thieves Like Us*) avoided an anamorphic format in favour of a 1.85:1 aspect ratio. They used diffusion filters and specially made filters (dubbed 'O' filters) on zoom lenses in order to create a circular deep-focus area in the centre of the lens while the periphery remained blurred: an iris effect 'to keep you in a kind of interior claustrophobia', as Altman put it (in Delson 1979: 35). The film's opening and concluding scenes were shot in thirty-degrees-below-zero weather amidst the Arctic wastes near Frobisher Bay in the Northwest Territories now known as Nunavut (see Delson 1979: 24).

While creating a convincing and deeply evocative *mise-en-scène*, Altman was able to assemble a first-rate international cast: Paul Newman, Vittorio Gassman, Fernando Rey, Bibi Andersson, Brigitte Fossey and Nina Van Pallandt. Unfortunately these formidable resources are placed at the service of a largely incomprehensible storyline based on a board game invented by Altman. Paul Newman plays Essex, a seal-hunter returning to his icebound home city after an absence of twelve years with his pregnant companion, Vivia (Brigitte Fossey) in order to reunite with his brother, Francha (Thomas Hill). The reunion proves to be short-lived, however. A gambler named Redstone (Craig Richard Nelson) throws a bomb into Francha's apartment, killing Francha, his family and Vivia. Redstone is, in turn, killed by another gambler named St. Christopher (Vittorio Gassman): a murder witnessed by Essex, who then assumes Redstone's identity and ventures into the Hotel Electra, a gambling resort in another sector of the city, to try and discover why Vivia and Francha were murdered. Thereafter Essex is caught up in Quintet, a complicated pentagonal board game for six players that is the culture's central pastime and fixation – evidently the way that inhabitants of a dying society generate some semblance of existential purpose and urgency in an otherwise spiritually annihilating landscape. But Quintet is more than just a game. Essex soon discovers that moves on the board dictate parallel moves in the real world and that the object of the game is to kill or be killed; the last player left alive 'wins'. After a bewildering series of complex cat-and-mouse manoeuvrings that take up most of the picture, the stalwart (and largely affectless) Essex does indeed emerge alive and victorious. A far more desolate version of Luigi Corelli at the end of *A Wedding*, Essex opts to leave the dying and death-obsessed Gesellschaft of the frozen city and venture back out into the open tundra from which he emerged. Grigor (Fernando Rey), Quintet's chief referee, warns Essex, 'You'll freeze to death.' Essex replies, 'You may know that. I don't.'

Though it sounds intriguing in the abstract, *Quintet* makes for an excruciatingly dull viewing experience – so visually and emotionally austere, so dreary, uninvolving and glacially paced that it is virtually unwatchable. Few critics could find anything good to say about it. Pauline Kael (hitherto an Altman fan) characterised *Quintet* as unintentional self-parody, 'like a Monty Python show played at the wrong speed' (1979: 100). David Denby deemed the film 'awesomely bad ... a muffled, private, proudly inexpressive movie, with monochromatic acting, a grating musical score, and metallic-and-gray sets, all dripping wet, as if the entire movie had been staged in a sewer that was being defrosted' (1979: 82). Stanley Kauffman pronounced the movie 'paralyzing stupid' (1979: 24). Critically, *Quintet* fared better abroad. French film critic Alain Masson was respectful in his assessment, terming the film 'a philosophical fable which reminds us of *Babylon Lottery* by [Jorge Luis] Borges and also confirms the judgment of St. Thomas Aquinas: "If the game were an aim in itself, we would have to play ceaselessly, which is impossible"' (1979: 2). Likewise, Brazilian film theorist Marcos Soares chose to ignore the film's abject failure as dramaturgy and take it seriously 'as an allegory of the system of Hollywood filmmaking (a theme which, understandably became an obsession with Altman), but it can also, of course, be more widely seen as an allegory of the market and the contemporary regime of the global division of labor; in this dystopian world, the forces of production are frozen (literally, in this case), immobilized, driven by invisible and irrational forces which can, indeed, lead to the death of those involved' (2007: 74–5).

Soares' interpretation is not without merit; *Quintet* conjures the twilight of capitalism as postmodern hell, perhaps post-nuclear, but presumably after the military-industrial-consumerist complex has metastasised over the entire planet, resulting in

Bleak future: postmodern civilization goes to the dogs in *Quintet*.

ecological Armageddon, catastrophic species population decline and a new Ice Age. At the end-game stage of civilisation depicted in the film, after all production and reproduction has ceased, the pathocratic political machinations that inexorably led to disaster are now pursued in their purest and most thanatoid form. Why not? At this point 'there's nothing left but the game' as Francha puts it. Robert Kolker rightly sees *Quintet* as 'the pessimistic, indeed nihilistic extension of *McCabe & Mrs. Miller*', i.e. a vision of the ultimate Hobbesian Gesellschaft: a desperately atomized pseudo-society literally and figuratively devoid of warmth that perversely affirms life by affirming death through the lethal gambling obsession at its centre (thus also evoking and extending the nihilistic compulsiveness that also animates *California Split*) (2011: 333). Kolker's interpretation is confirmed by Altman's own explanation: 'We're showing the destruction of what I consider human, when everything gets down to the smallest set of rules and emotions disappear' (in Sterritt 2000: 101).

Philosophical conceits notwithstanding, *Quintet* is indisputably Altman's least entertaining film, probably one of the least entertaining films ever made. Obsessed with creating a visually stunning world, Altman failed to develop a story commensurate with the setting. In the words of film critic Robert C. Combow, the film takes 'an unoriginal, lumberingly obvious, altogether hokey script' and couples it 'with a visual and audial atmosphere so overpowering that one wishes to forgive the film its lack of narrative integrity out of respect for what it does to the perception and the nerves' (1979: 47). For Patrick McGilligan, Altman was 'his usual magnetic self on the set' but nonetheless displayed 'vindictiveness … in pushing this film past the money people and his own cast and crew … egomania that that was also self-destructive' (1989: 470). A less judgemental interpretation: in making *Quintet* Altman lost control over his creative obsessions or was perhaps offering an unwitting disclosure of his own personal anguish and alienation. The movie exceeded its original budget by almost $1 million for a final production cost of $7.6 million – all a dead loss, as the film made next to nothing at the box office (see Wyatt 1996: 56).

A Perfect Couple (1979)

Making a fiercely pretentious and solipsistic movie that turned out to be as bad as *Quintet* probably would have resulted in permanent banishment from the film industry for a less esteemed director. But Altman still had two movies left in his five-picture deal with 20th Century Fox and a modicum of credibility at his disposal; he was able to soldier on with several more offbeat movies before Hollywood stopped returning his calls. The first of these projects, a romantic comedy/musical entitled *A Perfect Couple*, would thankfully be a far cry from *Quintet* in mood, setting and theme. It had to be; as a resolutely uncommercial work of abstract postmodern negation, *Quintet* marked an aesthetic terminus. Altman's only choice was to move back toward something resembling commercial filmmaking. Usually he started with an idea; this time Altman began with actors and built an idea around them. While he was making *A Wedding* Altman was struck by the refreshing contrast between Paul Dooley's hangdog face and his considerable acting talent and decided that he would create a starring vehicle for him.

Initially Sandy Dennis was envisioned as the female lead – the part was written for her – but she had to drop out after it was discovered that Dooley was severely allergic to the dander of Dennis's many cats. The role was offered to Shelley Duvall but she declined, so it ultimately went to Marta Heflin, who had a small role in *A Wedding*. As Dooley explains: 'Altman wanted to do a film about people who weren't conventionally pretty people or the right age or just the way Hollywood would do it. He does most of what he did to say "Fuck you" to Hollywood. He didn't like conventional, formulaic movies [and] was cynical about the idea he was supposed to do things a certain way. It might be anti-authoritarianism or something' (in Zuckoff 2009: 333, 334). The film's musical orientation reiterates *Nashville* but actually derives from the involvement of Allan Nicholls, a longtime Lion's Gate stalwart who had organised Keepin' 'Em off the Streets, an amateur soft-rock band (six musicians and nine singers) comprised of former cast members of the musicals *Hair, Godspell* and *Jesus Christ, Superstar*. Altman filmed performances of the band in Los Angeles just before shooting *A Wedding* and decided that he would use a fictive version of the band's communal life to counterpoint the Dooley/Heflin romance. Accordingly, he and Nicholls developed a story idea 'about two people meeting from different walks of life. And yet two people firmly involved in family. [For] one of them, the family was a band. For the other, the family was their heritage' (in Zuckoff 2009: 333). While Altman set out to fashion a more realistic romance that would circumvent Hollywood romantic comedy genre clichés, he also sought to create a variation on *A Wedding* by exploring the dramatic possibilities (and ideological implications) in the collision of another two kinds of Gemeinschaft, from different social classes and cultural coordinates. In this case, the communities at odds are a tradition-bound patriarchal Old World family and a counterculture musical commune, i.e. a 'family' of unrelated persons who coalesce around a common passion and purpose. These two cultures exert opposing pressures that keep the lovers at bay *à la Romeo and Juliet* and present another version of the Apollonian/Dionysian conflict previously explored in *That Cold Day in the Park*.

Alex Theodopoulos (Dooley) meets Sheila Shea (Heflin) through a computer video dating service called 'Great Expectations': a plot device that points up modern society's increasing commodification of romance (while allowing for a punning allusion to Dickens, suggesting 'Dickensian' cultural impoverishment).[3] A lonely, fiftyish antiques dealer, Alex still lives at home in protracted pre-Oedipal thrall to his autocratic father, Panos Theodopoulos (Titos Vandis) and to the rigidly Puritanical codes of conduct that govern his aristocratic Greek family. Sheila is a pop singer. Far younger (early thirties) and poorer than Alex, she hails from a seemingly very different world: a raucous musical commune of young performers living together and practicing their music in the loft of a former industrial building in the Little Tokyo district of Los Angeles. But there are overarching commonalties. Ostensibly free-spirited, Sheila's band has its own despotic patriarch, Teddy (Ted Neeley), an egotistical taskmaster who rules over his troupe by dispensing a steady stream of orders and insults. The Theodopoulos clan also revolves around music – but of a very different sort; Panos is passionate about the classical variety and Alex's younger semi-invalid sister, Eleasua (Belito Mereno), is a cellist with the Los Angeles Philharmonic.

Alex and Sheila quickly fall in love but, in keeping with ineluctable romance genre imperatives, they separate and reunite a number of times before the film's *dénouement*. As one would expect, Alex finds it difficult to adjust to Sheila's allegedly plebeian musical tastes and hippie lifestyle while she finds Alex's timorous and stodgy conservatism tiresome. Alex's father's stern disapproval of Sheila makes matters worse. In the end, though, Alex is liberated from his father's repressive clutches by the sudden death of his sister, Eleasua, evidently from a heart ailment. He quits the family mansion (shades of Luigi Corelli in *A Wedding*) and the film comes full circle as Alex and Sheila reunite at a Philharmonic concert: site of their first date.

The central conceit of the romantic comedy is, of course, the notion that love conquers all. This is especially true as regards differences in social class, which are supposedly nullified when lovers from disparate backgrounds unite, e.g. *It Happened One Night* (1934) or more recently, *Saturday Night Fever* (1977), *Overboard* (1987), *Working Girl* (1988), *Pretty Woman* (1990) and *Maid in Manhattan* (2002). Hollywood wants audiences to have their cake and eat it too; typically the poorer but usually wiser and more virtuous member of the couple surmounts the snobbery and class prejudice of his/her lover (and/or rivals and would-be in-laws) and is ultimately assimilated into the romantic partner's wealthy world: a wish-fulfillment fantasy of circumventing the class structure by marrying into money that bears almost no relation to reality. In uniting people from markedly different class origins, the inter-class romantic comedy also attempts to nullify a host of tensions associated with those differing class positions (e.g. stark inequalities in autonomy, dignity, comfort, health, schooling, etc.): a move that serves the dominant American ideology of class denial by effacing the reality of class altogether. To Altman's credit, *A Perfect Couple* repudiates the utopian ideology of the inter-class romance genre by reversing the standard assimilation motif. In the end, Alex forsakes his wealthy family to join Sheila's bohemian counterculture; both can have love but neither can have love *and* money. *A Perfect Couple* also refuses to nullify the cultural differences embodied by Alex and Sheila's respective 'families'; in contradistinction to hegemonic 'melting pot' mythology, those differences remain intact, abrasive and seemingly impervious to change.

As Gayle Sherwood Magee points out, *A Perfect Couple* was one of a spate of films developed to cash in on the popularity of quasi-disco-style musicals in the late 1970s after *Saturday Night Fever* and *Grease* (1978) scored huge box office successes and their soundtrack albums went platinum (2014: 134). But like those other films – *The Wiz* (1978), *Thank God It's Friday* (1978), *Sgt. Pepper* (1978) – *A Perfect Couple* garnered tepid reviews and did poor box office. Though interesting as an anti-genre exercise, the movie fails to cohere, mostly because the relationship between Paul Dooley and Marta Heflin lacks the necessary chemistry to bring the story alive; as more than one critic noted, Heflin's performance was decidedly lacklustre. Furthermore, Altman and Allan Nicholls constantly interrupt the flow of the romance narrative with too many musical numbers that are merely innocuous at best. In the final analysis, *A Perfect Couple* remains a minor film in Altman's oeuvre – mildly amusing but not distinctive or distinctively Altmanesque.

HealtH (1980)

Having ventured into science fiction and revisionist romantic comedy Altman made *HealtH*, his fifteenth feature project, and after *Nashville* and *A Wedding*, his third stab at a large-ensemble satire of the contemporary American scene. *Quintet*'s script doctor, Frank Barhydt, who also worked as a freelance journalist, developed the idea while working for a health magazine. Written with help from actor Paul Dooley, *HealtH* is allegedly about the election for the president of a health food convention but is really a filmic allegory about American electoral politics. With the 1980 presidential election looming when it was made, the film parodies its own historical moment but also references the 1952 and 1956 elections that pitted conservative Republican Dwight D. Eisenhower against liberal Democratic candidate Adlai Stevenson (Eisenhower trounced Stevenson in '52 and won by an even larger popular vote and electoral margin in '56). The scion of an aristocratic Illinois family, Stevenson was a Princeton-educated lawyer, an articulate intellectual offering lofty ideas for progressive social change, but the American people much preferred Ike's unassailable war record and plain-speaking, folksy pragmatism. A liberal Democrat who subscribed to Stevensonian ideals, Altman saw Stevenson's electoral defeats as evidence of deep-seated American anti-intellectualism – the triumph of shallow charm over substantive policy positions – and an early sign that American politics was being inexorably fused with, and degraded by, the phony populism of show business spectacle, a process that would accelerate with the full emergence of television in the 1960s. By early 1979 Altman could see that history was likely to serve up a dichotomy similar to the Eisenhower/Stevenson rivalry, with the somewhat remote and cerebral Jimmy Carter, a liberal Democrat, likely to run for re-election against an allegedly charismatic Republican candidate, Ronald Reagan, the former Hollywood B-movie actor well-schooled in media-constructed populism camouflaging an elitist and pro-corporate agenda.

Nashville had already dramatised Altman's politics-as-theatre conceit, so Altman needed a different setting to revisit the issue. Barhydt's health food convention was deemed as good as any and more topical than most, as the country was in the midst of a health food fad. As he had done for the second half of *California Split*, Altman confined all the action to a grand hotel – the traditional site for large conventions – in this case, the Don CeSar Beach Hotel at St. Pete Beach on Florida's Gulf Coast: a palatial 40,000-square-foot edifice in Mediterranean and Moorish styles opened in 1928 and dubbed 'the Pink Palace' or 'Pink Lady'. Converted into a VA hospital during World War II, the Don CeSar was a vacant and graffiti-strewn derelict by 1969 but was saved from demolition and rehabilitated to its former splendor in the early 1970s. As had been the case with the Houston Astrodome, the 'Mayflower Campus', the Mapes Hotel, the Armour Mansion, etc., the Don CeSar Hotel functioned as a gigantic, self-contained theatre space that was also another kind of synecdoche for America. As critic Jim Ridley has noted, 'Altman didn't tell stories so much as he built ecosystems on film' (2015: n.p.).

Despite the unflagging support of studio head Alan Ladd Jr., Altman was in trouble with 20th Century Fox over the commercial failure of his last three pictures. He therefore rushed *HealtH* into production as quickly as possible, fearing that the studio would soon pull the plug on his financing. Nonetheless, care was taken to accurately replicate the feel of a real health food convention in the movie; co-writer Barhydt and art director Bob Quinn visited a health food conference in Boston before shooting began and over one hundred health food companies were afforded free product placement to contribute to the authenticity of the *mise-en-scène*. Principal photography began on 20 February 1979 and continued until late May.

As one would expect in a large-cast Altman mosaic, a carnivalesque atmosphere, constantly roving camera eye, overlapping dialogue and episodic structure are much in evidence. To accentuate the centrality of television exposure to the political process, the film starts poolside at the Don CeSar Beach Hotel with talk show host Dick Cavett (playing himself) doing a TV interview with two women who are vying to be elected president of an organisation called HealtH (an unctuously self-reflexive acronym for 'Happiness, Energy and Longevity through Health') at its Florida convention. The underdog candidate is Isabella Garnell (Glenda Jackson), a serious and self-righteous health advocate who inveighs against commercialism and materialism in the manner of Jimmy Carter and Adlai Stevenson. Indeed, she actually quotes Stevenson in her speeches. The front-running candidate is Esther Brill (Lauren Bacall), an 83-year-old virgin afflicted with narcolepsy who nonetheless calls herself 'the first lady of health'. Smug but intellectually vapid, seemingly robust but actually in dubious health, Brill evokes an aging and tired Dwight Eisenhower (who had a heart attack during his first term) while also suggesting the obtuse but supremely self-assured Ronald Reagan, who would become the oldest president in U.S. history (almost seventy when he took office). During her interview Brill suddenly raises her arm in an involuntary salute and falls into a narcoleptic torpor. Brill's infirmity, which portends a fundamental detachment from reality, forces Cavett to suspend his show.[4] Also running for president of HealtH 'on the independent ticket' is Gil Gainey (Paul Dooley). Gainey represents those occasional third party aspirants who mount a merely symbolic challenge to two-party hegemony (and may also be a specific reference to John B. Anderson, a former Republican who ran as an Independent in 1980 but didn't win a single precinct in the election). Frozen out of official media coverage, Gainey tries to remedy his status as a nonentity by feigning drowning in the hotel pool – twice. Observing the election process is Gloria Burbank (Carol Burnett), a high-minded and highly-strung White House deputy health advisor acting as the President's liaison to the convention. Burbank tries to maintain a neutral stance toward the candidates but leans toward the obviously more articulate and principled Isabella Garnell. Gloria Burbank's foil is Harry Wolff (i.e. 'hairy wolf', played by James Garner), Esther Brill's campaign manager and Gloria's philandering ex-husband. In a comic-romantic subplot, the lecherous Wolff is always available to come on to his ex-wife at her most vulnerable moments (Gloria suffers from an odd affliction: anxiety causes her to be sexually aroused).

On the evening of the second day of the convention, Colonel Cody (Donald Moffat), a cynical, bombastic right-wing businessman who claims to 'own' the entire organisation, arrives at the Hotel to size up Isabella Garnell. The two smoke cigars in Garnell's suite and engage in a heated partisan debate about political principles (or, in

Cody's case, lack thereof).[5] In the end, Cody concludes that Garnell is rigidly sincere in her left-wing beliefs and therefore hopelessly ill-equipped to engage in the sort of amoral flim-flam indispensable to political success in America: 'Lady, you have just told me exactly what I want to hear. You are for real. That means you're no threat to anyone.' To hedge his bets, though, Cody has hired political dirty tricks specialist Bobby Hammer (Henry Gibson) to deprive Garnell of governmental support. Knowing that sexual scandal is always the *bête noir* of liberals, Hammer, masquerading as a transsexual, tries to convince Gloria Burbank that Garnell is also a woman who was born male.

Not content to vet and dismiss Isabella Garnell and to engage in dirty tricks, Cody also mounts a frontal assault on the psyche of Gloria Burbank. On the evening of the third day of the convention, Cody channels business mogul Arthur Jensen (Ned Beatty) from Sidney Lumet's *Network* (1976) when he meets privately with Burbank and schools her on the true state of things, i.e. that government is the handmaiden of American business interests, not vice versa: 'You got no goddamn idea what you're dealing with… I make policy. I swing elections. You think you got the vote. I control what goes in the ballot boxes… Your work is meaningless. You're not going to change a thing.' Cody also implies that he had Dr. Guffy, the most recent president of HealtH, assassinated and issues a thinly veiled threat to Burbank in the same vein. Deeply distraught, Gloria rushes to Harry Woolf's room for solace and Harry takes full sexual advantage of her disillusionment and terror.

On the morning of the fourth and last day of the convention, Dick Cavett reconvenes his show poolside to televise the announcement of the election results. To no one's surprise Esther Brill is elected in a landslide. Gloria Burbank and Harry Wolff watch from the balcony of the hotel room where they have just shared the night. Gloria wonders aloud why no one believed (in) Isabella Garnell and Harry sagely replies that 'no one understood her'. The couple then observe Colonel Cody speaking with Bobby Hammer, who is still in drag. When Cody tries to pay off Hammer for his services with a stock certificate rather than money, as promised, a scuffle ensues. Cody punches Hammer and knocks him into the pool. Harry Wolff identifies Hammer, now *sans* wig, as a political operative and explains to Gloria that 'Colonel Cody' is actually Esther's crazy but harmless younger brother, Lester Brill. Incensed that Harry didn't disclose these facts earlier, Gloria curses him and storms off. With their business concluded, the HealtH convention participants disperse while Isabella Garnell makes an unctuous concession speech to which no one pays any attention. A symbolically appropriate hypnotists' convention (hosted by TV personality Dinah Shore, playing herself) supplants the HealtH convention and the farcical parade that is America's socio-political culture continues.

Lester Brill's shrill imitation of William F. Cody mocks right-wing nostalgia for America's 'golden age' of misogynistic individualism and roughshod entrepreneurial agency. It also obviously references *Buffalo Bill and the Indians*, to update to the contemporary scene that film's condemnation of America as the pure show business of empty spectacle, always and only advertising itself as the best of all possible worlds. Robert Kolker observes that the 'great liar and owner of all things historical proves, in his reincarnation in *HealtH*, to be still a fraud. He is not the right-wing lunatic he sounds like, but rather Esther Brill's crazy brother pretending to be a right-wing lunatic. Everything, finally, is … a perfect illusion, a manipulation of words, images, and individuals in a great, silly game' (2011: 365). In its sweeping depiction of American politics and culture as now a holographic network of artifices, *HealtH* anticipates Jean Baudrillard's notion of simulacra and simulation: a hyperreal world of signs and images beyond the merely fake to the point of being untethered from reality altogether, whereby the simulacrum precedes the original and the distinction between reality and representation vanishes. There is only the simulacrum, and authenticity becomes a totally meaningless concept. But therein lies the problem; *HealtH* relentlessly deconstructs and nullifies itself by featuring a bevy of cartoonish characters behaving foolishly and chewing the scenery – with the notable exception of Sally Benbow (Alfre Woodard), the hotel's African-American public relations director who observes the convention participants' antics with the kind of equanimity can only come from long experience with such narcissistic buffoonery. At any rate, Bertolt Brecht's *Verfremdungseffekt* (estrangement effect) is too much in evidence here; the willing suspension of disbelief that would foster viewer engagement is insistently undermined by the film's garish, carnivalesque content. Furthermore, an election campaign for a health food convention president at a posh Florida hotel is too localised, static and trivial an affair to convincingly figure for a modern US presidential election campaign which requires prodigious fund-raising, organisation building and endless publicity events all over the country.

Obviously intending the film as a political intervention, Altman wanted to have *HealtH* in wide release before the 1980 presidential campaign but Alan Ladd Jr., his champion at 20th Century Fox, left the company in a management shake-up and the film was initially shelved. Test screenings in April 1980 in San Francisco, Sacramento, Houston and Boston yielded audience-comment cards that Fox's new studio head, Norman Levy, characterised as 'the poorest I've ever seen' (Anon. 1980: 84). After a brief, unsuccessful run in Los Angeles, Fox deemed the film hopelessly uncommercial and opted against any further exhibitions. Incensed at Levy and the new management at Fox (except for Sherry Lansing, who loved the film), Altman took it upon himself to exhibit *HealtH* at a number of film festivals: exposure that prompted the studio to reconsider and hold another round of preview screenings at the UA Theater in Westwood, Los Angeles in September, 1980. Sparse attendance and negative reviews decisively precluded national release and Altman finally conceded that the film was a lost cause. Though occasionally shown on television and later released on DVD, Altman's most topical and timely film forfeited its *raison d'être* because almost no one saw it when it was meant to be seen. *HealtH* was the last of Altman's five contracted films for 20th Century Fox: a disappointing association for both parties. Altman's reputation suffered badly and Fox probably lost at least $10 million on what turned out to be a string of flops – not inconsiderable losses but sustainable in the wake of *Star Wars*, which eventually earned over $775 million. The studio could withstand a few minor setbacks but was no doubt relieved to have Altman leave the stable.

Popeye (1980)

Popeye the movie had its genesis on 13 May 1977 when Robert Evans, head of production at Paramount Pictures, attended a performance of the hit Broadway musical *Annie* at the Alvin Theatre on W. 52nd Street in New York City. Enthralled by what he experienced, Evans immediately called his studio in Hollywood to start bidding on the film rights. Columbia Pictures, equally avid to bring *Annie* to the screen, eventually won a bidding war with Paramount to the tune of $10 million. Disappointed, but undaunted in his desire to make a live-action musical based on comic book characters, Evans learned that Paramount still held all theatrical rights to the Popeye character because the studio had released Popeye cartoons produced by Fleischer Studios (and later Famous Studios) from 1932 to 1957. Evans promptly hired cartoonist-screenwriter Jules Feiffer to write a script but the choice of lead actors and a director would prove more elusive quarry. Evans' original plan was to have Dustin Hoffman play Popeye opposite Lily Tomlin as Olive Oyl, with John Schlesinger of *Midnight Cowboy* fame directing. Soon Hal Ashby replaced Schlesinger, Hoffman and Tomlin dropped out, and then Ashby left the project. To replace Hoffman, Evans secured Robin Williams, a young stand-up comedian enjoying phenomenal popularity playing a fast-talking, impish alien on *Mork & Mindy*, an ABC-TV sitcom that premiered in the fall of 1978. The Olive Oyl role was offered to Gilda Radner of *Saturday Night Live* fame. As for directors, Paramount wanted Evans to hire a 'box office director' – Arthur Penn and Mike Nichols were considered – but, through the auspices of Sam Cohn, Altman's name was put forward, Evans concurred, and Altman signed on as director in mid-April 1979 (see McGilligan 1989: 491–7).

Altman wasted no time in making *Popeye* an Altman film. Of the more than fifty characters that populate Popeye's adopted village, Sweethaven, eleven were played by performers that Altman had worked with before, most prominent of which were Shelley Duvall, who supplanted Gilda Radner as Olive Oyl, Paul Dooley as Popeye's hamburger-loving friend, Wimpy, and Donald Moffat as the Taxman (a figure invented by Jules Feiffer – not one of E. C. Segar's original comic strip characters). Altman stalwarts Allan Nicholls, Robert Fortier, Dennis Franz and David Arkin had smaller roles while Julia Janney, Patty Katz, Diane Shaffer and Nathalie Blossom, i.e. the Steinettes, an *a capella* doo-wop quartet featured in *HealtH* in vegetable outfits, appear as the baleful Walfleur sisters: Mena, Mina, Mona and Blossom respectively. Altman even pressed his own infant grandson Wesley Ivan Hurt into service, to 'play' the foundling baby, Swee'pea. Ray Walston (best known for the TV series *My Favourite Martian*) was cast as Popeye's father, Poopdeck Pappy/the Commodore, and Paul L. Smith, who played the vicious prison warden in *Midnight Express* (1978), was cast as Popeye's brawny nemesis, Bluto. Altman also utilised members of San Francisco's Pickle Family Circus (founded in 1974): Bill Irwin (playing Ham Gravy), Larry Pisoni (Chico), Geoff Hoyle (Scoop) and Peggy Snider (playing Pickelina and credited as Peggy Pisoni). Linda Hunt makes her film debut as Mrs. Oxheart, the 'mudder' of Oxblood Oxheart, the fighter (Peter Bray). As for the crucial appointment of musical composer, various composers were considered – Randy Newman, Leonard Cohen,

Paul McCartney, John Lennon – before Altman heeded the urging of Robin Williams and settled on Harry Nilsson, a kindred spirit who was also in a career slump and with a similar reputation for hedonistic excess that had rendered him dubiously employable in Hollywood (see McGilligan, 497–8).

Sweethaven could have been built on a sound stage at Paramount studios in Hollywood but Altman opted for a remote location shoot, this time on the Mediterranean island of Malta, a popular site for movie-making some 6,700 miles from Los Angeles, chosen for a huge salt water tank built there for a prior production, its climate, and sheer distance from meddling studio executives.[6] Working from June to December 1979, an international construction crew of 165 workers supervised by Robert 'Egg' Eggenweiler, C. O. 'Doc' Erickson and Wolf Kroeger built the seaside village of Sweethaven: nineteen fully enclosed and slightly surreal wooden buildings including a hotel, a schoolhouse, a store, a post office, a church, a sawmill, a tavern and a casino. Attendant structures included sheds, gangways, boardwalks and timber chutes (see McGilligan 1989: 501). Because there is no indigenous lumber on the island, hundreds of logs and several thousand wooden planks had to be trucked across Europe from the Netherlands and then shipped to Malta from Italy. Wooden shingles used in roof construction were brought in from Canada. Eight tons of nails and two thousand gallons of paint were used in the construction process. To protect the set from high seas, a 250-foot breakwater was built around the mouth of Anchor Bay while set dressing involved sinking a number of actually seaworthy vessels to festoon the harbor (see Plecki 1985: 118–20). A new road had to be built to the location. On the bluff above the village workmen constructed the film's production complex: a plaster shop, make-up and carpentry labs, a wardrobe unit, a rehearsal hall, an editing suite, a production office, a projection room for viewing dailies (flown in from a processing lab in Rome) and a state-of-the-art recording studio where Harry Nilsson and his musicians recorded the dozen songs he wrote that make up the film's musical score (see McGilligan 1989: 503).

Filming began on 23 January 1980 and wrapped twenty-two weeks later on 19 June (three weeks over schedule and $9 million over-budget, mostly due to construction overruns and delays caused by inclement weather). Cast and crew lived at the Mellieha Holiday Centre, a resort hotel in the nearby village of Mellieha, put in long hours on the set, and, as always, watched rushes and socialised together, seldom leaving the island during principal photography.[7] Robin Williams jokingly called it 'Stalag Altman', but among Altman productions, the *Popeye* shoot was probably Altman's most fully realised and intensive approximation of the artists' Gemeinschaft ideal, achieved extra-diegetically, and a sly realisation of oppressive, infantilising corporate Gesellschaft within the world of the movie. In an interview with Richard Combs and Tom Milne at the time of the film's release, Altman said that making *Popeye* was 'a chance to create my own environment, which I'd done with *Quintet* but that hadn't worked with audiences or critics', adding that the denizens of Sweethaven were like America's docile and bamboozled middle class, 'being exploited by a dictator [the Commodore] they've never seen' (in Sterritt 2000: 100, 103).

At first blush the small, quaint and otherworldly realm of Sweethaven bears the earmarks of a close-knit peasant community (Gemeinschaft) but signs that it is actually nearer on the societal spectrum to Gesellschaft are amply evident. The film begins with a doctored eighteen-second clip from Max Fleischer's old black and white cartoon in which Popeye protests that he's in 'the wrong movie': an admonition to viewers to jettison their cartoon genre-associated expectations. Likewise, the film proper (all live action) begins with a long shot of Popeye rowing an open dinghy in dangerously heavy seas and when the film's title appears on the screen, it is accompanied by lightning and thunder crashing – strangely ominous atmospherics for what is supposed to be innocuous children's fare. Self-reflexive allusions to two other Altman films provide further hints of a subtly subversive agenda. An initial pan of the village shows that the church perched above it bears more than a passing resemblance to the Presbyterian Church at the centre of its namesake hamlet in *McCabe & Mrs. Miller*. Indeed, Popeye arrives at Sweethaven as a seeker, alone and unknown, much like John Q. McCabe when he turns up at Presbyterian Church. As soon as Popeye docks his rowboat at the village pier, a garage door rattles up and the officious Taxman, riding a motorised tricycle (sporting a pennant that resembles the American flag), rolls out to accost the stranger with a long list of petty tariffs. The ascending garage door evokes a theatre curtain rising while quoting a similar image in the opening scene of *Nashville*, when a garage door rolls up and a loud-speaker truck for the Hal Phillip Walker campaign emerges to roam the streets. But between the two films, similarity and difference are rendered in equal measure. In *Nashville* the canned speech emanating from Walker's sound truck inveighs against government excess and lack of accountability. In *Popeye*, the Taxman on his tricycle is synecdochal for corrupt government bureaucracy in all its confiscatory rapaciousness.[8] Further establishing an image of Sweethaven as a polity closer to Gesellschaft is Nilsson's 'Sweethaven Anthem', which accompanies the opening scene and conveys the sense of an ocean-isolated populace rife with harebrained eccentrics who are happily oblivious to their own entrapment and oppression (i.e. America writ small). Sung by a solemn chorus, the anthem proudly intones that 'God must love us/ We the people/ Love Sweethaven/ Hurray hurray Sweethaven/ Flags are wavin'/ Swept people from the sea/ Safe from democracy…' Clearly referencing America with 'We the people', the 'Sweethaven Anthem' predictably posits religious faith as the ideological foundation for patriotic fervour. More obviously satiric is the bowdlerised catchphrase from Woodrow Wilson's 1917 war speech about making the world safe for democracy; Sweethaven prides itself on being 'safe *from* democracy'. Much like 'It don't worry me', the Alfred E. Neumanesque refrain at the conclusion of *Nashville*, 'safe from democracy' is really nothing to celebrate.

The sense that Sweethaven is an exclusionary society of childish and self-centred individuals plays out in Popeye's interactions with the locals. Numerous 'Keep Out' and 'No Trespassing' signs greet him at the dock, as does the aforementioned Taxman, and most of the townspeople either ignore him or are overtly hostile – at least during the first half of the movie. Olive Oyl initially treats Popeye with impatient gruffness when he rents a room at the Oyl residence; the Oyl family and their guest boarders (Wimpy and Geezil) gorge at the supper table while Popeye is ignored; a gang of toughs taunt and physically accost Popeye at breakfast at the town café the next morning; the celebrants at Olive Oyl's engagement party to Bluto that night shun Popeye as if he were an untouchable; later, an angry Bluto attacks and pummels Popeye after Olive Oyl breaks off her engagement with him.

Inasmuch as Sweethaven remains intractably indifferent to him, Popeye must take heroic measures to integrate into its world while also maintaining his own sense of identity and moral integrity. Popeye's assimilation into the Sweethaven community begins when he tentatively bonds with Olive Oyl over the foundling infant, Swee'pea, left in a wicker basket like some sort of cartoon Moses. This incident occurs right after Olive has rejected Bluto as her suitor, compromising her own heretofore favoured status in Sweethaven and bringing Bluto's wrath upon her family; he smashes up the Oyls' house and directs the Taxman to pauperise them. An opportunity for Popeye to publicly prove his worth presents itself soon thereafter when Olive's brother, Castor Oyl (Donovan Scott), steps into a boxing ring with a gigantic local heavyweight boxer, Oxblood Oxheart (Peter Bray), in a feeble attempt to win a hefty cash prize and redeem his family's fortunes. Oxheart easily knocks Castor out of the ring, prompting Popeye to take on and defeat the outsised boxer: a feat of athletic prowess and heroism that wins the respect of Sweethaven's citizens.

If the first half of the film depicts Popeye's pusillanimous efforts to merely fit into the society of Sweethaven, the second half deals with the growth of his private self, showing Popeye achieving self-integration and maturity by: (i) forging a family with Olive and Swee'pea; (ii) finding and reconciling with his long-lost father, Poopdeck Pappy (aka, the Commodore); (iii) and defeating his nemesis and Shadow Figure, Bluto, once and for all. Popeye's coming of age thus has psychological, moral and political dimensions.

Having defeated Oxheart, Popeye reprises his role as rescuer and further demonstrates his moral fibre by defending Swee'pea against exploitation. When it's discovered that Swee'pea can predict the future, Wimpy takes the infant to the 'horse races', a carnival game, and uses the baby's clairvoyance to win money – a selfish violation of childhood innocence that enrages Popeye, who rebukes Wimpy and the townsfolk with the manifesto-like song, 'I Yam What I Yam', which includes lines like 'I never hurts nobodys and I'll never tell a lie'. Popeye takes Swee'pea out of the Oyls' house and down to the docks so that he can better protect him there.[9] But Sweethaven isn't done with Swee'pea (the epitome of innocence) just yet; Bluto snatches the boy, takes him to the Poopdeck Pappy's ship, and presents him to the curmudgeonly Commodore, promising that he is worth a fortune. Touting his buried treasure as all the wealth he will ever need, the Commodore demurs, prompting the always irascible and now mutinous Bluto to tie him up, kidnap Olive Oyl along with Swee'pea, and set sail for Scab Island, site of the Commodore's coveted buried treasure. Enter Popeye, in pursuit of Bluto, who encounters the Commodore and realises that he has found his elusive father, Poopdeck Pappy. After initially denying paternity, Pappy effects an uneasy rapprochement with his son, thereby granting Popeye a tentative resolution to what has amounted to a protracted Oedipal crisis. Popeye, Pappy and the Oyl family board Pappy's ship and pursue Bluto to Scab Island, where a final showdown takes place. During Popeye's duel with Bluto, Pappy recovers his treasure chest to reveal not pirated gold and jewels, but a collection of sentimental objects from Popeye's infancy, including a few cans of spinach. At a crucial juncture in the fight with both Bluto and a giant octopus, Pappy supplies Popeye with spinach – a substance he has heretofore abhorred. This time it provides the Herculean strength he needs to vanquish Bluto and the octopus. In the end, Popeye is able to revel both in his victory and the reconstitution of his family, ultimately refusing the interpellation of others, to finally interpellate himself as 'Popeye the Sailorman'.

Abetted by Harry Nilsson's wry musical numbers – which are rife with double entendre and full of subversive political sentiments – Altman plays around the edges of the movie to lampoon the squeaky-clean pieties of the cartoon-based musical. He also sneaks in an artful critique of the ethical and political complacencies of Gesellschaft society by characterising Sweethaven's populace as ignorant, passive and only concerned with the rote satisfaction of daily appetites. Yet the film's dissident energies are ultimately contained and neutralised by Jules Feiffer's conservative script, which attributes any social malaise to individual corruption (e.g. a bad apple like Bluto) and recuperates the figure of the Commodore as another version of Daddy Warbucks, i.e. sequestered plutocrat to caring father, as if to suggest that within every rentier-oligarch there is always a rank sentimentalist clamoring to get out. But, of course, a safe and formulaic version of Joseph Campbell's 'hero's journey' is what Paramount Pictures and Walt Disney Productions demanded – and got. Altman was hired for his experience and technical expertise, not to make any sort of personal statement.

After four commercial failures in a row, Altman hoped that *Popeye* would be the kind of unequivocal success that would return him to favour with the major studios. The film grossed $6 million on its opening weekend in the United States (12–14 December 1980), made $32 million in thirty-two days, and eventually earned almost $50 million in domestic box office and $60 worldwide – more than double its budget but nowhere near the blockbuster numbers that Paramount and Disney had expected, so was therefore considered a 'flop'. Except for a friendly review from Roger Ebert, critical response ranged from tepid to hostile. In the immediate aftermath of *Popeye*, Altman's already shaky fortunes plummeted. MGM's new president, Norbert Auerbach, understandably skittish after the resounding box office fiasco that was Michael Cimino's *Heaven's Gate* (1980), cancelled Altman's next film project, an adaptation of an off-Broadway comedy by James McClure entitled *Lone Star* after he and Altman quarreled. Another Altman movie project, a woman-centred mystery entitled *An Easter Egg Hunt* (scripted by *That Cold Day in the Park* screenwriter Gillian Freeman) had to be abandoned when independent financing from Canada and the UK fell through. Summarily rejected by the major producers and studios as unbankable, Altman was forced to sell Lion's Gate Films (for $2.3 million) to a production group headed by Jonathan Taplin in July 1981. A few months later, to add injury to insult, Paramount filed a $250,000 lawsuit against Altman for breach of contract for going $9 million over *Popeye*'s $13 million production budget.

Notes

1   B.C. Altman died on 9 April 1978.

2   Expo '67 was where the film that ushered in the New American Cinema, Arthur Penn's *Bonnie and Clyde*, had its world premiere in August of 1967. It is ironic but also strangely fitting that *Quintet* was shot in the ruins of Expo '67 a decade later.

3   'Great Expectations' is an actual dating service that was started by Los Angeles businessman Jeffrey Ullman in 1976 and is still in operation.

4   Esther Brill's temporary lapse into a catatonic state also references an actual incident that occurred during the taping of a *Dick Cavett Show* episode on 8 June 1971. On that day, Cavett was interviewing journalist Pete Hamill when another guest he had just interviewed – J. I. Rodale, founder of the popular health magazine *Prevention* – died of a heart attack on set. The episode was never aired.

5   Isabella Garnell lights Colonel Cody's cigar and then proceeds to produce a much larger cigar for herself: an ironic and witty reference to a similar scene in *McCabe & Mrs. Miller* – when a conciliatory McCabe offers Butler a cigar, Butler refuses the offer and produces his own, much larger cigar.

6   Between 1925 and 2015 103 films have been shot on Malta.

7   Partying and drug use were reputed to be rampant on this shoot.

8   The motorised tricycle also evokes Jeff Goldblum's chopper-style tricycle motorcycle in *Nashville*.

9   In no mood for further harassment by the Taxman, Popeye throws the officious functionary down a chute and into the water – a public act of anti-government defiance that further enhances Popeye's public stature.

CHAPTER FIVE

In the Wilderness

> I don't know which comes first. Is it the political content that I'm interested in showing? Or is the political content simply the subject of the drama? So it's a little bit of both of those situations com[ing] together.
>
> – Robert Altman

At the nadir of his fortunes in the film industry, Altman took what he euphemistically characterised as 'a sabbatical' from Hollywood and returned to the theatre. He leased (and eventually sold) his home in Malibu and re-located to New York City, where he and his wife, Katherine, had been renting a *pied-à-terre* at 128 Central Park South as a second home since 1978. Altman's actual transition to the theatre came about when Leo Burmester, one of the actors involved with *Lone Star*, brought Altman *Rattlesnake in a Cooler*, a one-act play by a 32-year-old actor-playwright-performance artist named Frank South. Liking what he read, Altman met with South in New York City and then opted to direct two of his one-act plays – *Rattlesnake in a Cooler* and *Precious Blood* – at the Los Angeles Actors' Theater (now known as the Los Angeles Theater Center). Both plays were essentially slice-of-life monologues that explored American Dream aspirations and delusions and involved only four actors (Alfre Woodard, Guy Boyd, Leo Burmester and Danny Darst), a far cry from the massive and costly undertaking that was *Popeye*. Encouraged by strong reviews in LA, Altman opted to take '2 by South' back to New York as an off-Broadway production at a small venue, St. Clement's Theater, in the autumn of 1981. Once again the Frank South plays met with acclaim, prompting Altman to videotape them as *Two by South* for ABC's Cable Arts Network.

Come Back to the Five and Dime, Jimmy Dean, Jimmy Dean (1982)

Though he had a number of different plays under consideration, Altman's next theatre project was to stage *Come Back to the Five and Dime, Jimmy Dean, Jimmy Dean*, a 1976 woman-centred memory play by Ohio-based playwright Ed Graczyk that explores the emotional ravages wrought by patriarchy and the perennial human need to dwell in self-protective delusion. For his mostly female cast, Altman turned to several actors he had worked with before – Karen Black, Sandy Dennis and Marta Heflin – but also drew on fresh talent: Sudie Bond, Kathy Bates and the pop singer and TV star, Cher, who had never done any serious acting. After a dozen previews the play opened at the 1,400-seat Martin Beck Theater (now the Al Hirschfeld Theater) in New York City on 18 February 1982. Though he liked '2 by South', *New York Times* theatre critic Frank Rich (1982) judged *Come Back to the Five and Dime* 'gimmicky', confusing and poorly paced. Other notices were equally damning. Probably owing to Cher's star power, attendance started at about eighty per cent (1,100 per show) but soon dropped off to less than forty per cent (600 per show), forcing Altman to close down the play on 4 April, after just 52 performances. Despite waning attendance and critical savaging, Altman felt that Graczyk's drama would translate well to film. He had also invested $200,000 of his own funds in the play (25 per cent of the overall production budget) and was anxious to recoup his money. So while the play was still running, Altman made another $800,000 deal, this time with the play's production executive, Peter Newman, Mark Goodson Productions and Viacom Enterprises, to air *Come Back to the Five and Dime* on cable television's Showtime network.

Utilising the same cast as the stage play, the film was shot sequentially in Super 16mm (blown up to 35mm) in nineteen days in April 1982. As was always the case, Altman gave a lot of thought to the dramaturgical and symbolic implications of the *mise-en-scène*. He had production designer David Gropman construct two adjacent interior sets in a midtown Manhattan studio that were mirror images of the Woolworth's five and dime store in west Texas where all the action transpires. The moments that take place in the present are confined to one side, the past to the other side. What appears to be an ordinary mirror behind the store's soda fountain counter is actually a large Mylar window that both divides and links the two sets. When lit from just one side, the plastic sheet remains opaque and functions as a mirror. A pan to the mirror, fade-out, and cut to the other side, brightly or dimly lit, signals transitions back to the present or past.[1] At other times, though, the 'mirror' is lit from one side, then another, creating a superimposition effect, or both sides simultaneously, making it a transparent window between the sets. Both visual tropes link past and present in the same moment and suggest the enduring and powerful influence of past events.[2] As Robert Kolker has noted, 'often in Altman's films, a window is used as a barrier to direct emotional contact' (2011: 347). In *Come Back to the Five and Dime* the mirror that is sometimes a window is a more complex Lacanian device that seems to confirm the unambiguous solidity of the subject's identity but more often functions as a portal into backstories that complicate and contradict that identity.

Come Back to the Five and Dime is set in the mythical Texas town of McCarthy on 30 September 1975, the twentieth anniversary of the death of film star and youth idol James Dean in a car crash.[3] The Disciples of James Dean, a fan club formed in the spring of 1955 (not long before Dean made his third and last film, *Giant*, in nearby Marfa, Texas) are holding a reunion at the Woolworth's five and dime, where they held their meetings twenty years before. Sissy (Cher), a sexy, seemingly irreverent free spirit who still works at the store alongside Juanita (Sudie Bond), her sanctimonious, bible-thumping boss, welcomes the arrival of other fan club members: Edna Louise (Marta Heflin), somewhat dimwitted, poor and perpetually pregnant; Stella Mae (Kathy Bates), the bawdy, venal wife of an oil millionaire; Mona (Sandy Dennis), the fan club leader. Also a clerk at Woolworth's, Mona is the neurasthenic single mother of a mentally defective grown son – called Jimmy Dean, of course – that she keeps sequestered out of embarrassment. Later, a mysterious, elegant woman who identifies herself as Joanne (Karen Black) arrives from LA in a yellow Porsche. She soon reveals that she is a transsexual formerly known as Joe (Mark Patton), the effeminate boy who swept out the store but was fired by Juanita's bigoted husband, Sidney, and raped by the town bully, Lester T. Callaghan. As Robert T. Self observes, Joanne's sex change ('a dramatic retreat from the phallus') has afforded her special wisdom: 'Becoming female, she is not simply the castrato but the Tiresias, the truthsayer, the seer that has lived both lives' (2002: 164). Joanne's self-revealing becomes the catalyst for a series of revelations showing that her fellow 'Disciples' are not what they seem or who they think they are – but these moments of truth are imperfectly realised and won only after considerable resistance.

After Joanne reveals that she was once Joe, she tries to force pious Juanita to confront the fact that her late lamented husband, Sidney, was an alcoholic and a homophobe who fired Joe without just cause and cheered on Lester T. as he sodomised the boy. Juanita angrily denies that Sidney was a drunken lout. To admit otherwise would be tantamount to rejecting the rigidly partisan fundamentalist-heteronormative Christianity that forms her identity and to concede that her life has been a lie. Repulsed by Joanne's gender identity heresy, Juanita can easily dismiss her truth-telling as corrupted at the source, at least initially. But as the day wears on and alcohol loosens inhibitions, pretences begin to reel and fall like dominoes. (A further development: Mona's son, Jimmy Dean – who never appears on screen – absconds in Joanne's sports car; his flight out of town hangs over the second half of the work and lends the play its plaintive title.)

Unlike Juanita, Sissy is not beholden to a hypocritical religiosity that will admit no flaws. Furthermore, Joanne's disclosure of identity conversion based in bodily trans-formation inspires Sissy to make a surprising disclosure that concerns her own, altered body and sexuality. She admits that her prized 'bazooms' are fake; cancer has forced her to undergo a double mastectomy, a feminine catastrophe that caused her husband (and Joe's rapist) Lester T., to abandon her. Yet Sissy's ideological disinvestment is not total. Even after revealing her secret she still clings to the forlorn hope that Lester T. will one day return to her.

Sissy's honesty sets the stage for the play's most profound and shattering realisation, which belongs to Mona. For twenty years she has laboured under the near-psychotic delusion that her feeble-minded son was the product of sexual intercourse with James Dean when she was an extra on the set of *Giant* in the summer of 1955. Pursuing her self-appointed mission as truth-teller, Joanne forces Mona to confront the fact that it was he as Joe, not James Dean, who impregnated her and that (s)he is the father of Jimmy Dean, not the famous movie star. Rather surprisingly, Mona accepts the truth, professes mortification and explains that she 'just wanted to be noticed … chosen'. Joanne embraces Mona and assures her, '*I* chose you', a declaration of love tragic in its belatedness.

Still another domino falls when Mona's concession to reality compels Juanita to soften and admit that her own, self-abnegating investment in hegemonic ideology has been just as delusory: 'Believin' is so funny, isn't it? When what you believe in doesn't even know you exist.' Once again, though, ideological disinvestment has its limits, lest the interpellated subject implode altogether. Juanita admits she has been forsaken but cannot entertain an even more harrowing possibility: that the god of her ideology never existed in the first place.

As Robert Paul Holtzclaw notes, the two most conventional members of the 'Disciples', Edna Louise and Stella Mae, 'function as opposites, two extremes of behavior that bookend the range of recognizable and somewhat acceptable behavior' (1992: 37). Neither experiences an epiphany; having escaped McCarthy to marry, they adhere fully to the dominant ethos, which renders such moments of self-illumination impossible. Though alike in their conformism, these two women stake out destinies at opposite ends of the capitalist patriarchy, one precluding wealth and the other precluding family, suggesting that the attainment of both is a cherished cultural ideal heavily advertised but rarely achieved. As the simplest and least conflicted member of the group, Edna Louise has nothing to confess or reveal; inner self and persona are nearly identical. A loving woman of modest ego and intellect, she accepts Joanne's radical otherness just as she passively accepts her own meagre wages from the patriarchal order because she cherishes her role as a working-class wife and mother of a large brood (she's expecting her seventh child). Her life of maternal self-sacrifice and hardship is not to be despised but it nonetheless forecloses the possibility of attaining individual freedom and deeper self-realisation. Edna Louise's polar opposite, Stella Mae, might be considered the most tragic of the five women because she remains the most superficial and ideologically intractable. Though childless and in a loveless marriage, she clings to the pretence that she is happy; she *must* be happy because her husband is rich. When Edna Louise calls her bluff, Stella Mae angrily retorts, 'I'm happy, goddamit!' – thus inadvertently declaring the poignant truth of her situation without admitting it to herself.

Their secrets revealed and illusions shattered, the 'Disciples' disperse; but before they do Sissy, Mona and Joanne join together to reprise a favourite old routine; they sway and snap fingers in unison as they sing the 1955 McGuire sisters chart-topping hit, 'Sincerely'. A song about undying love for an unfaithful lover, 'Sincerely' functions as ironic commentary on the staying power of ideology. Even after it has been demystified and hollowed out, it retains its constitutive force; it can never be abandoned because there is nothing imaginable to take its place. While they sing, Pierre Mignot's camera pulls back from the mirror that frames them and the trio soon fades to black. As the song continues on the soundtrack, the camera roams the interior of the five and dime, now an abandoned and dusty ruin in some future moment that will never see another reunion of the Disciples of James Dean.

For the Disciples themselves, their reunion was supposed to be both a nostalgic commemoration and a ritualised conjuring of a kind of Second Coming of James Dean: sanctified pop cult icon as martyred Christ-figure who will bring renewed meaning to their banal lives. Intended as a gesture toward the apotheosis of their idol, the anniversary gathering unexpectedly becomes a long-overdue exorcism of Dean's musty ghost. In parallel terms *Jimmy Dean* functioned as a kind of cinematic exorcism for Altman, who was aware, no doubt, that his own James Dean documentary, *The James Dean Story* (1957), co-directed with George W. George, contributed to the self-pitying adolescent death-cult that sprung up around Dean, postmortem. Altman made *Jimmy Dean*, at least in part, as self-reflexive atonement for making the earlier film. He also understood that Graczyk's play constituted another exploration of the ravaged female psyche under patriarchy that would complement *That Cold Day in the Park, Images* and *3 Women*.

In a larger sense *Come Back to the Five and Dime* also serves to contrast the state of the American *zeitgeist* in the post-Vietnam era to what it had been in the mid-1950s. The epitome of an emotional vulnerability and romantic yearning that could only have flourished in the relatively innocent and depoliticiced era of Eisenhower, James Dean died just as an ebullient youth counterculture emanating from his own films, the Beat apostasy, and rock 'n' roll was being born. Subsequent events – the Civil Rights struggle and racial turmoil, the assassinations, the bitterly divisive war in Vietnam, the rise of a drug culture, Watergate, etc. – cast a disillusioning pall on American youth and fractured society as a whole, rendering it coarsened and cynical. The play/film does not need to cite or allude to the socio-political cataclysms that occurred between 1955 and 1975; their influence is everywhere implicit in a pervasive aura of spiritual desiccation and loss.

Usually discussed by film critics as an exploration of abnormal psychology, *Come Back to the Five and Dime* is ultimately more concerned with the influence of the corporate Gesellschaft, especially the modern culture industry, on the ideological shaping of the female self. Despite its melodramatic excesses, one of the signal strengths of the film is that it unmasks many of the key discourses of repressive patriarchy – homophobia, stereotypical gender roles, conventional religiosity, movie cult-hero worship, cloying top-forty romance songs, even 1950s nostalgia – as infantilising pablum for the consumerist denizens of Middle America that encourages bigotry, escapism and self-deception. Beholden to a disempowering imaginary, James Dean's self-appointed 'Disciples' cope poorly with the actual conditions under which they live and labour. As Kolker notes, *Come Back to the Five and Dime* 'deals with the crisis of women confronting the oppressions of patriarchy by dissolving them into neuroses. Unable to struggle, these figures first collapse within themselves and then extrapolate their delusions as protections against the world that surrounds them' (2011: 371). The spiritual sterility of the hegemon is figuratively borne out by the group's severely skewed record of reproduction. Edna Louise breeds like a rabbit but the rest of the group is barren – except for Mona and Joe/Joanne, who can only manage to sire an idiot son. A bad seed with a stunted mind and a tendency to steal cars as a means out of town, Jimmy Dean marks the chasm between Hollywood's meretricious dream of perfect romance and libidinal power and the pitifully quotidian reality of its deluded subscribers.

A sombre, claustrophobic actors' tour de force, *Come Back to the Five and Dime, Jimmy Dean, Jimmy Dean* was only intended for cable TV release but Altman persuaded Showtime to let him take it to a number of film festivals in 1982/83: Chicago (where it premiered on the 27th anniversary of James Dean's death and received a ten-minute standing ovation), Montreal, Knokke-Heist (Belgium), Venice, Deauville (France) and Toronto. Altman also arranged for limited theatrical distribution. Avoiding the major studios after the problems he had with 20th Century Fox over *HealtH*, Altman opted to let Cinecom, an independent distributor in New York City, exhibit the film at a few arthouse theaters (e.g. the Thalia in New York City) in November 1982. During its entire four-week run the movie grossed $841,000, essentially breaking even. Though Altman was no longer reaching wide audiences, he was at least proving that he could turn stage plays into absorbing movies for less than a million dollars each at a time when big-budget Cineplex blockbusters were all the rage.

Streamers (1983)

Having made a nearly all-female film, Altman experimented in the opposite direction with an all-male drama.[4] His next venture into theatre-to-film adaptation was *Streamers*, the last installment in Vietnam veteran David Rabe's so-called Vietnam Trilogy after *The Basic Training of Pavlo Hummel* and *Stick and Bones*. The title, *Streamers*, does not refer to patriotic banners; it is, in fact, a death term: military slang denoting parachutes that fail to open because their lines have become hopelessly tangled. After opening at the Long Wharf Theater in New Haven, Connecticut, *Streamers* enjoyed an almost year-long off-Broadway run in 1976/77 (478 performances). Directed by Mike Nichols, it won the 1976 Drama Desk Award for Outstanding Play, the 1976 New York Drama Critics' Circle Award for Best American Play, and was also nominated for a 1976 Tony Award for Best Play. Producers Robert Michael Geisler and John Roberdeau brought the play to Altman, who liked it because it was an anti-war drama that eschewed combat depictions altogether and approached military culture in psychological and emotional terms, especially regarding male psychosexual identity and the divisive politics of race and social class. Altman conducted casting in New York, hired an all-new troupe of actors and then had an authentic barracks cadre room, designed by *Popeye* set designer Wolf Kroeger, constructed on a sound stage at Los Colinas Studios in Irving, Texas (a Dallas suburb). Altman had already begun shooting scenes in July 1983 when he discovered that Geisler and Roberdeau did not have any money. Forced to buy the rights from them for $500,000 Altman quickly found a new financial backer in Nick J. Mileti, a successful lawyer, owner of the Cleveland Indians, and a founder of the Cleveland Cavaliers franchise, who had begun to dabble in motion picture production. Altman later admitted that Mileti 'saved my bananas' (in Thompson 2006: 131).

Always cognisant of the importance of establishing interpretive context, Altman employs an evocative framing device for *Streamers*. The film begins and ends with a crack drill team performing a complex series of precision manoeuvres involving close order marching and the synchronised twirling and exchange of rifles.[5] Shot in impressionistic fashion – shadowy helmeted figures silhouetted against a backdrop of hazy white light – the members of the drill team are rendered depersonalised automatons: the military ideal of perfect order and discipline.

Inside the dreary, claustrophobic confines of a barracks room at a Virginia army base in 1965 it is a very different story for Richie (Mitchell Lichtenstein, an openly gay actor playing a more-or-less openly gay character: a remarkably courageous casting choice in 1983), Billy (Matthew Modine), Roger (David Alan Grier) and Carlyle (Michael Wright): four young soldiers with the 83rd Airborne Division nervously awaiting deployment to Vietnam. African-American (Roger and Carlyle) and white/ college-educated (Richie and Billy), gay (Richie) and straight, upper-class (Richie), middle-class (Billy), working-class (Roger) and lumpen (Carlyle), the four men stake out a cross-section of the 1960s-era military and American society that upends one of the principal clichés of the World War II combat film: the ethnically diverse but always all-white, and always implicitly heterosexual squad of GIs that coalesces in combat to form an effective fighting unit representing the harmoniously unified nation for which it fights.

Rabe and Altman also problematise another traditional war film cliché: the gruff and battle-weary but kind-hearted non-com who mentors and protects his young charges (e.g. John Wayne's Sgt. John Stryker in Allan Dwan's *Sands of Iwo Jima* (1949)). *Streamers* features two staff sergeants haunting the barracks – Rooney (Guy Boyd) and Cokes (George Dzundza) – but far from being fatherly role models, both men are full-blown alcoholics prone to maudlin outbursts and childish horseplay who present an abysmally grim future in the military to their younger comrades, one filled with melancholy, inebriation and death.

Having yet to experience a tour of duty in Vietnam, Rooney is a loud, boastful cigar-chomping buffoon, also something of an emotional sadist who revels in hectoring the younger men: 'All you slap-happy motherfuckers are going [to Vietnam.] Gotta go kill some gooks!' Cokes, who has just returned from Vietnam, tries to match Rooney's bluster but comes off as a more doleful figure. He struggles with PTSD (termed 'gross stress reaction' at this time), guilt over killing a trapped enemy combatant with a hand grenade, and his own looming mortality in the aftermath of a leukemia diagnosis. Both men are lost souls, deeply dependent upon each other for companionship and emotional sustenance. The vain and rowdy Rooney displays all the earmarks of a narcissistic personality disorder, while Cokes, who oscillates between despair and rage, is clearly a broken man, a borderline personality who gains his sense of self-worth by being the more circumspect member of a fragile partnership. In the play's title scene, the sergeants drunkenly sing 'Beautiful Streamer' to the tune of Stephen Foster's 'Beautiful Dreamer', a song, explains Rooney, 'a man sings when he's going down through the air and his chute don't open'. Intended as nothing more than fatalistic gallows humour, the song produces profound discomfort in its young listeners, who understand its literal and metaphoric truth. For Cokes, it conjures a wide-eyed vision of his own approaching demise – a vision so vivid he faints at its conclusion. Once revived, Cokes speaks of his leukemia diagnosis and admits that it is probably accurate ('Rooney, my mother had it. She had it') but, abetted by Rooney's instinctual avoidance of truth and feeling, he quickly lapses into denial. Coming near the halfway mark of the film, the incident decisively invalidates Rooney and Cokes as moral guides, leaving the younger soldiers alone in their uncertainty.

Broken warriors: Sgts. Cokes (George Dzundza) and Rooney (Guy Boyd) sing their drunken death hymn, 'Beautiful Streamers'.

Conventional war films offer cathartic combat heroics that extol the military Gesellschaft of cold-blooded machismo and physical courage. *Streamers* turns the war film paradigm inside out by staying indoors and stateside as it nullifies patriarchal authority and explores the nihilistic dread that manly posturing seeks to conceal but inadvertently expresses. The angst that permeates the barracks – which is a kind of purgatorial anteroom to hell – is made manifest at the outset by Martin (Albert Macklin), a closeted gay recruit who slits one of his wrists in a half-hearted suicide attempt to get himself ejected from the army: a ploy that succeeds. Richie, also gay, but an upper-class Manhattanite who has enlisted, comes to Martin's aid by bandaging his wound. Though he empathises with Martin's plight, Richie chooses to rebel against the prevailing code of military machismo in a different way: by flaunting his homosexuality. Partial to Greek fisherman's caps, kimonos and Japanese platform sandals for his casual attire, Richie flounces around the barracks and teases Billy, with whom he's infatuated, with a constant stream of lascivious innuendo. Billy fends off Richie's provocative gibes, sometimes with threats of physical mayhem, but shows signs of increasing agitation, probably because he is uncertain about his own sexual orientation. Indeed, the attraction may be less one-sided than it appears.

Roger and Carlyle (who is an interloping 'transient' from nearby 'P' Company) initially contend over the interlocking questions of race and class identity. A desperately lonely, racially angry – 'fuckin' officers is always white, man' – but deeply frightened street tough, Carlyle is a profanity-spewing outcast who wants to befriend Roger but also suspects that Roger is too respectable, too friendly with his white barracks buddies, to find any common ground with a black brother from the lower depths. Carlyle's bitterly conflicted intensity makes Roger wary of him, ultimately forcing Carlyle to cross race, class and heteronormative boundaries to pursue a sexual liaison with Richie. But before that occurs, several scenes emphasise sexual identity conflicts as the play's latent but abiding concern. After Rooney and Cokes leave the barracks room and turn off the lights, Roger plaintively councils Richie to cure himself of homosexual tendencies by 'doing pushups'. Billy matches Roger's naiveté with a story about a putatively heterosexual friend who became 'hooked' on gay sex as if it were a highly addictive drug (but Richie comes to suspect that Billy is really referring not to 'friend' but to himself). Later Carlyle, desperately drunk and filled with hysterical self-pity, bursts into the barracks to seek comfort and ends up sprawled on the floor. Richie, always compassionate, covers him with a blanket. A day or two later, Carlyle returns to the barracks looking for Roger. Encountering Richie instead, Carlyle proceeds to deny his earlier display of extremely neediness and vulnerability – a rank violation of machismo – and begins to menacingly interrogate Richie as to whether or not he's the barracks room 'punk'. Witnessing Carlyle's sociopathic verbal assault on Richie, Billy vows 'to move myself out of here if Roger decides to adopt that son-of-a-bitch!' To Billy's chagrin, Roger *does* adopt Carlyle as a friend and even persuades Billy to join them in a visit to a brothel on a stormy night. Disaster ensues upon their return to the barracks. Carlyle, quite drunk and still wrongly convinced that Richie is the barracks sex slave, decides that he wants to satisfy his libidinal urges. Seeking to arouse jealousy in Billy, Richie begins to play along but Richie's gambit backfires – or works too well; an infuriated Billy flies into a towering homophobic rage and hurls vicious insults at Richie ('You wanna be a faggot, a goddamn swish-sucking cocksucker taking it in the ass? Be my guest!'). But when Billy turns on Carlyle, calling him 'nigger' and 'Sambo', Carlyle spontaneously reacts by fatally stabbing Billy in the stomach with Cokes' serrated trench knife. Shortly thereafter a drunken Rooney appears on the scene and attempts to disarm Carlyle but Carlyle stabs him to death as well. Summoned by Richie, MPs swarm in, remove the corpses, apprehend Carlyle, and interrogate and quarantine the survivors. Soon thereafter Cokes breaks in through a window, looking for Rooney, with whom he was playing hide and seek. Not knowing what has just transpired in the room, Cokes drunkenly regales Richie and Roger about the wild night he just had with Rooney in nearby Washington, DC. Richie begins to weep, prompting Cokes to ask why. When Richie deflects the horrible truth by simply confessing he's 'queer', he finds Cokes surprisingly sanguine about his disclosure. The play/movie ends with Cokes mournfully singing his 'Beautiful Streamers' song in some made-up approximation of an Asian language, to impersonate the Viet Cong soldier in a 'spider hole' he killed with a grenade: an expression of genuine sorrow and empathy for the dead that can only be realised by a man like Cokes, who now fully understands death and all its existential and moral implications.

Trusting the inherent power of the material, Altman kept the emphasis on the performances themselves by having Pierre Mignot film *Streamers* in ways unusually conventional for an Altman film: almost no overlapping dialogue, a relatively static camera with lots of medium- and medium-long shots, shot/reverse-shots, two-shots and the occasional close-up for dramatic emphasis. The result was a startling *tour de force* that constitutes a radical critique of military culture: a world suffused by patriarchal Gesellschaft ideology in its purest, most violent and most authoritarian incarnations. In the barracks – society writ small and intensified – sexual repression and psychic torment are so deep and lacerating that fratricidal catastrophe ensues long before there is any chance for martial glory: a scenario that predates a similar scenario in the first half of Stanley Kubrick's better-known Vietnam movie, *Full Metal Jacket* (1987). A bitter denunciation of degraded masculinity, *Streamers* was too disturbingly downbeat and gritty to ever reach a wide audience. It did however garner a remarkable and singular honour: the *entire cast* was named 'Best Actor' at the 1983 Venice Film Festival.

Secret Honor: A Political Myth (1984)

At the invitation of theatre impresario Bill Bushnell (Scotty Bushnell's ex-husband), Altman attended a performance of *Secret Honor: The Last Testament of Richard M. Nixon*, a one-man play at the tiny Los Angeles Actors' Theater in the summer of 1983. Written by activist-playwrights Donald Freed and Arnold M. Stone (an ex-national security adviser), directed by Robert Harders and starring the then-little known actor, Philip Baker Hall, *Secret Honor* strays far from historical fact to present a caustic but oddly sympathetic portrait of the nation's 37th president. The play's premise is intriguing but far-fetched; that Nixon contrived his own downfall in order to deliver himself and the country from greater corruptions being plotted by his oligarchic handlers. Fascinated by what he had seen, Altman resolved on the spot to take the play to New York as an off-Broadway production and film it thereafter, as he had done with *Come Back to the Five and Dime, Jimmy Dean, Jimmy Dean*. True to his word, Altman acted as producer for a run of the play at the Provincetown Playhouse in New York's Greenwich Village in the autumn of 1983. Though it received a respectful review from *New York Times* theatre critic Mel Gussow, *Secret Honor* lasted only forty-seven performances (8 November to 18 December 1983). A spell of rainy weather, the play's sheer length (two hours, cut down from two and a half), its disagreeable subject matter (a disgraced and widely reviled ex-president) and the lugubrious reputation of one-man shows on famous personages – all conspired against its success on the New York stage.

Undaunted, Altman took the play to the University of Michigan at Ann Arbor, where he had accepted a temporary position as Visiting Professor of Film in the Communications Department. Though he was at a low point in his fortunes, Altman put up nearly $100,000 of his own money to finance a week-long shoot, 23–30 January 1984 (see Makuch 1984). While having to pay his actor, Philip Baker Hall, his cinematographer, Pierre Mignot, his assistant director, Allan Nicholls and a few other professionals, Altman minimised production overhead by relying on the unpaid services of some two dozen graduate film students who were learning the craft – a ploy denounced by the manager of a local theatrical union as a way to avoid paying union members their standard $8.20 an hour but defended by the University of Michigan as a 'goodwill gesture' and by the students themselves as an exciting opportunity take part in professional filmmaking (see Anon. 1984: 14). The University further accommodated their famous faculty member by having its Contemporary Directions Ensemble perform George Burt's musical score. It also provided Altman with a film set, free of charge: the stately Red Room, a student lounge in the Martha Cook Building, a 1915 Tudor-style women's dormitory with leaded glass windows and elegant wood paneling. Dressed with oil paintings (portraits of Washington, Lincoln, Wilson, Eisenhower and Henry Kissinger), heavy furniture, and *objets d'art* by set designer Stephen Altman (Altman's son), the room exuded the pomp that one would associate with the residence of an ex-president.

While embellishing the set, Altman left the play unaltered. As he notes in his director's commentary to the 1992 Criterion DVD, the play Altman filmed was virtually the same play that Philip Baker Hall and Robert Harders had perfected on stage: 'I feel my creative input was getting it done. This was pretty much the piece that he did. I did not interfere with it much at all… Bob Harder was really the director of this play.' What Altman did add, to convert the play into a film, was a much more elaborate set and Mignot's extremely fluid camera work; facilitated by a custom-designed short boom, his roving camera provided the drama with more visual interest and kinetic energy. Altman also added a side-by-side bank of four black and white closed-circuit television monitors on a side table in Nixon's study: a prop that points up Nixon's paranoid obsession with security and an ingenious solution to the problem of devising cutaways that would lend some variety of perspective on his monologue. When Altman wanted to shift tone and point of view he would cut to one of the monitors, which had the additional effect of reminding viewers that they mostly knew Nixon through mediated images all the way back to his infamous 'Checkers Speech' in 1952.

Secret Honor starts slowly. During the first ten minutes Nixon enters his study, changes into a smoking jacket, pours himself a copious glass of Chivas Regal scotch whiskey, removes a fully loaded nickel-plated revolver from a wooden box (hinting at suicidal intentions), and then begins to fiddle with an expensive tape recorder he does not know how to operate. A solitary actor on stage interacting with a tape recorder will remind more erudite viewers of Samuel Beckett's play, *Krapp's Last Tape* (1958): a melancholy monologue featuring a lonely and broken old man reviewing his life and trying rationalise it, or at least make sense of the choices he has made that rendered him isolated and loveless in his twilight years. Viewers unfamiliar with Beckett will certainly be reminded that audio tapes were Nixon's *bête noire*. On a dramaturgical level, his ineptitude with the tape machine generates some mildly comical moments and is also sound characterisation; Nixon was notoriously clumsy (see Volkan and Itzkowitz 1997: 86–7).

Once he more or less masters the machine, Hall's Nixon begins to tape-record a rambling confessional monologue about his political demise that he evidently wishes to have transcribed and released after his death, as a last testament that will exculpate him. Characteristic of the lawyer he had been, Nixon frames his statement as a defence attorney's plea to a judge on behalf of his client (himself). The judge to whom Nixon appeals is his own tortured conscience but also seems to be an amalgam of transcendental signifieds: God, the People, Posterity, even his late, beloved, but emotionally detached mother, Hannah (Milhous) Nixon – his ultimate moral arbiter.

By turns angry, maudlin, self-righteous, despairing and self-pitying, an agitated and progressively more inebriated Nixon manifests personality disintegration as he gesticulates and spouts profanities, meandering from one tangent to another.[6] Declaring that 'the whole story [of Watergate] could not be told during my lifetime because the nation could not have stood the whole story', Nixon is reminded of the JFK assassination: another event whose underlying causes are allegedly too disturbing for public disclosure. Thinking of the Kennedy brothers associatively reminds Nixon of his own four brothers, two of whom (Arthur and Harold) died young from tuberculosis ('Goddamn TB up and down both sides of the family'). The lingering sorrows of a lonely and emotionally barren youth soon give way to numerous, bitter resentments: toward Eisenhower, who snubbed him because he was 'not to the manor born'; toward his Secretary of State, Henry Kissinger, whom he characterises as a 'slimy, two-faced, brown-nosed, ass-licking kraut son of a bitch'; toward the press and liberals ('they're yellow'). But Nixon reserves his deepest antipathy for the 'Committee of 100' (a group of prominent Republicans who drafted him to run for Congress in California's 12th congressional district in 1945), along with the oligarchs who congregate annually at an exclusive resort in Monte Rio, California known as the Bohemian Grove. As Nixon tells it, his backers – the powerful war profiteers who comprise America's ruling elite – wanted him to 'continue the war in Vietnam until 1976. Whatever the cost… Accept a draft in '76 for a third term [and] seal the deal with China against the Soviets and then carve up all the markets of the goddamn world'. Overcome with moral revulsion at the notion that thousands more will die in Vietnam to fill the coffers of the plutocrats, Nixon contrives his own removal from office, a gambit he describes as 'secret honor and public shame'. In the end, some time after his resignation and pardon by Gerald Ford, Nixon judges America's body politic thoroughly rotten and corrupt: a 'world [that] is nothing more than a bunch of second-generation mobsters, and the lawyers, and the PR guys, and the New Money crooks who made theirs in the war and the Old Money crooks who made theirs selling slaves and phony merchandise to both sides during the Civil War… That is what public life is all about.' Brought to the point of suicide, Nixon puts the gun to his head but angrily rejects the idea as exactly the outcome his puppeteers would prefer. 'Fuck 'em!' he shouts, as he jabs the air with a fierce uppercut: an image of heroic defiance successively repeated on the TV monitors for final emphasis.

The central conceit of *Secret Honor* – that Nixon deliberately instigated the Watergate crisis to escape an irredeemably corrupted presidency – is startling theatre but a rank falsehood, especially egregious in light of persuasive evidence that Nixon committed treason to get elected president.[7] *Secret Honor* does, however, contain deeper and more elliptical truths. Though he does not resemble Richard Nixon or sound like him, Philip Baker Hall brilliantly captures Nixon's distinctly paranoid brand of narcissism: gnawing insecurity and low self-esteem, stemming from humble origins, family trauma and a lack of parental love and nurture that drove him to overcompensate by striving for the highest levels of success, whatever the means or the cost.[8] In a more generalised way *Secret Honor* is also on target in its depiction of Nixon as a pliable and amoral front man for America's ruling class, as are all modern presidents – an unpleasant insight concerning concentrated capital's domination over American life long shared by Altman and dramatised, in various ways, in *Brewster McCloud, McCabe*

& Mrs. Miller, Nashville and *HealtH*. In his Criterion commentary, Altman observes: 'Nixon was doing a job for these people who took him and groomed him and sent him into the Congress and steered his way, all the way up to the presidency... We misconstrue what the office is; we don't elect these people, we hire them.' Though Altman abhorred Nixon's politics, he obviously identified with the plight of a once-powerful man brought low by an unforgiving, duplicitous power structure and his own eccentricities. When he describes Nixon as 'a tragic character ... trapped by the system' and 'duped by himself', Altman is perhaps unconsciously referring to his own situation as a once-esteemed filmmaker with a now tarnished reputation, reduced to tiny budgets and desperate expedients to continue working. Responding to critics who thought the film was too sympathetic to Nixon, Altman refuted the charge in an interview with Pat Aufderheide: 'They don't want to deal with the truth of the matter, which is that [Nixon] is a human being... You have to give someone their humanity in order to hold them accountable' (in Sterritt 2000: 119). Screened at a few film festivals in 1985 (Portland, Oregon; Cleveland; 3 Rivers, Pittsburgh) and exhibited at a few art cinemas (e.g., the Thalia in New York City), *Secret Honor* did not reach many viewers or recoup its very modest production costs. It did, however, garner mostly strong reviews and several film critics ranked it among the best films of 1985. Vincent Canby termed it 'one of the funniest, most unsettling, most imaginative and most surprisingly affecting movies of its very odd kind' (1985: n.p.).

The Laundromat (1985)

After *Secret Honor*, Altman and his wife, Kathryn, decamped for Paris, where they would live from 1984 to 1989. Effectively banished from Hollywood and self-exiled from Reagan's America – though Altman's work would bring him back to the United States and Canada for extended periods – he continued to work prodigiously across several media (theatre, television, opera and film), albeit on a much smaller scale, for considerably less money and with minimal fanfare. Altman's first project as an expatriate was for HBO: an hour-long film adaptation of *Third and Oak: The Laundromat*, a 1979 play by Marsha Norman (the 1983 Pulitzer Prize winner for her play *'night, Mother*). Filmed over a ten-day period at Studios Éclair in Paris, *The Laundromat* is another woman-centred Altman film that stars Carol Burnett – in her third and last Altman role – as Alberta, a starchy middle-aged teacher, Amy Madigan as Deedee, a restless and very talkative twenty-year-old housewife, and Michael Wright (Carlyle in *Streamers*) as Shooter Stevens, a swaggering black disc jockey who briefly enlivens the proceedings. Once again, Altman opted not to open up the play with exterior shots; all the action takes place within the lonely confines of the laundromat, which becomes a kind of character in its own right – and thematically significant. As Grace Epstein notes, 'the laundromat not only represents an intersection for differing social groups of women, but also, of female-associated activity with male-identified public space' (1996: 32).

Alberta and Deedee meet in the middle of a rainy night in a laundromat and begin to converse. Like the women in *Come Back to the Five and Dime, Jimmy Dean, Jimmy*

Dean, both women are in denial about their lives and the laundering of dirty clothes becomes an obvious metaphor for self-revelation and emotional cleansing. After a while Deedee discloses her angry desperation; her auto-worker husband, Bob, is a philanderer who makes her feel like she's 'a TV set and he's changed the channels'. Initially frosty toward a woman she deems inferior, Alberta comes to empathise with Deedee's plight and is moved to reveal her own loneliness and sense of desolation. She finally admits that her husband, Herb, is not away on business, as she previously claimed, but has been dead for over a year. Thus gender commonalities trump generational and social class differences and two lonely women form a bond outside of the patriarchal order. *The Laundromat* aired on HBO on 3 April 1985 and reviewers lauded the strong performances given by Burnett and Madigan.

Fool for Love (1985)

In mid-January 1984, just as Altman was preparing to shoot *Secret Honor* in Ann Arbor, he received a handwritten letter from distinguished playwright Sam Shepard, praising *Come Back to the Five and Dime, Jimmy Dean, Jimmy Dean* as 'amazing' and inquiring if Altman would be interested in filming *Fool for Love*, his new play about a fading rodeo rider and his half-sister/lover locked in a torturous on-again, off-again relationship, then in rehearsals with Ed Harris and Kathy Baker before its premiere at the Magic Theater in San Francisco on 8 February 1984. That summer Altman saw the play during its second run, at the Circle Repertory Theater in New York, and was impressed by its power. He did not, however, commit to a film version until two other projects subsequently fell through: *Biarritz*, a Robert Harders-scripted romance that was never made, and *Heat*, a Las Vegas thriller written by William Goldman, starring Burt Reynolds, ultimately directed by Dick Richards and Jerry Jameson, and released in 1986 (see Thompson 2006: 139).

Toward the end of 1984 Altman managed to secure a generous $6 million production deal with Israeli cousins Yoram Globus and Menahem Golan, owners since 1979 of the Cannon Group, a film production company known for making low-budget cinematic trash (e.g., *The Happy Hooker Goes Hollywood* (1980), *Death Wish II* (1982) and *The Delta Force* (1986)). The arrangement was mutually beneficial, inasmuch as Altman needed the money and Cannon was anxious to polish its brand name by working with a famous director. As for the crucial role of Eddie, Altman persuaded Sam Shepard himself to take it on. The idea that the author would appear as an actor in his own material Altman found 'irresistible' but initially Shepard *did* resist; he felt that Ed Harris, who was great in the play because he was not as close to the material, would also do a better job in the movie version. Rising star Kim Basinger, fresh from her steamy role opposite Mickey Rourke in Adrian Lyne's controversial *9½ Weeks* (shot in the summer of 1984 but not released until February 1986), lobbied Altman for the part of Eddie's half-sister, May, and won it after Shepard's partner, Jessica Lange, dropped out at the last moment. The other three main parts – the Old Man, Martin and the Countess – went to Harry Dean Stanton, Randy Quaid and Deborah McNaughton, respectively. Stanton's emaciated, craggy looks made him eerily believable as a spectral, lovelorn proletarian Westerner, a role similar to Travis Henderson, the lead character he played in Wim Wenders' *Paris, Texas* (1984).

Since most of the action in *Fool for Love* takes place at a fictive motel called the El Royale on the edge of the Mojave Desert, Altman and his son, Steve, scouted motels all over the Albuquerque-Santa Fe, New Mexico area but could not find one that exactly matched their requisites: a small, rundown, pastel-coloured adobe motel on an otherwise deserted highway, facing West, toward the sunset. In the end, Altman decided to do what he had done with *McCabe & Mrs. Miller* and *Popeye*; build his own set on location. Over a six-week period in the spring of 1985 construction workers built a neon-accentuated motel office-café and six cottages arranged in a semi-circle around it on Route 285 in El Dorado, just south of Santa Fe. In back of the motel Altman created a sprawling junkyard filled with derelict automobiles, all manner of refuse and scrap metal and some old house trailers.[9] The motel complex was so realistic that travellers regularly pulled in to inquire about renting rooms, much to Altman's amusement.[10]

With *Come Back to the Five and Dime*, *Streamers* and *Secret Honor* Altman adhered closely to the original playscripts and kept the action under psychological pressure by confining it to prescribed, claustrophobia-inducing interior settings. With *Fool for Love* Altman decided to open up the frame to the wider world, to make the movie markedly more 'cinematic' and to accentuate its western themes. Accordingly, the film's first ten minutes crosscut between shots of May and the Old Man at the motel with following shots of Eddie driving his pickup and horse-trailer rig on the highway toward the motel, circling it, finally stopping and then prowling the grounds on foot looking for May. While much of the subsequent action at the El Royale takes place in May's cottage – after Eddie literally dives through her locked front door – and at the motel café, there are numerous exterior scenes, including occasional crane shots of the motel and environs. These shots keep the drama immersed in a stark desert landscape that recalls *3 Women*'s depiction of the American West as a vacuous spiritual waste-land. Altman took further advantage of the superior representational capabilities of film over theatre by dramatising Eddie's, May's and the Old Man's conflicting memories, not as dialogue but as fully realised flashback scenes, shot with wide lenses to give them a distinctive look. He then added another level of complexity by having the action depicted often contradict voice-over descriptions of it. 'I can pretty much say that everybody does lie, all the time – but not maliciously,' Altman says in his director's commentary, by way of explaining why he constructed dissonance between the various accounts and between words and imagery; our memories morph and evolve over time in mysteriously self-serving ways, eliding, distorting or wholly inventing details that reconfigure or repress painful truths. Altman also employed another innovation: staging flashbacks of past moments that occurred at the El Royale in the same frame as the present action: 'I turned this thing around on itself. In other words, there are scenes at that motel where you see the Old Man drive in twenty years previous and you see May [as a child]. And I mixed them with real time... So it was kind of a thing inside of a thing. It was very incestuous, which is what the play was about.'[11] Altman's final bit of tinkering had to do with enlarging the character of the Old Man. In the play Shepard situates the Old Man in a chair on a platform to one side of the stage, commenting on the action like a Greek chorus, the stage directions indicating that he 'exists only in the minds of May and Eddie'. In Altman's opened-up film version, the Old Man is afforded physicality and movement. He emerges from his small house trailer in the junkyard to steal liquor from Eddie's truck and to challenge May and Eddie over their conflicting renditions of past events at the motel café. Until the film's closing moments there is no indication that the Old Man is anything less than a real human being.

As had been the case with *Come Back to the Five and Dime* and many other memory plays, the Freudian-Gothic principle of the Return of the Repressed determines the shape of the narrative. Riven by festering sins and secrets that always reemerge with a vengeance, psychologically damaged individuals either explode or implode, as do afflicted families and relationships. Likewise, the present collapses under the gravitational pull of an overburdened and unresolved past. (As William Faulkner puts it in *Requiem for a Nun*, 'The past is never dead. It's not even past.') Such is the case with *Fool for Love*. As is eventually revealed, Eddie and May are the victims of a cruel twist of fate that continues to govern their lives. Experiencing an irresistible sexual attraction the moment they meet, they fall in love with each other as teenagers, despite their awareness that as half-siblings – the offspring of different mothers but the same, bigamist father (the Old Man) – they are breaking a primal taboo.

In the first third of the film Eddie, always shielding himself in the stereotypical persona of the macho cowboy, attempts to reconcile with an emotionally exhausted and wary May, who is ensconced in her own stereotypical persona, as the alluring blonde bombshell. Eddie makes aggressive overtures and May parries them with acerbic banter but she soon tires of it all. After softening him up with a passionate kiss, she knees him in the groin. The backstory behind all this *Sturm und Drang* begins to unfold when Martin, a local handyman (also, the audience's surrogate), shows up at the motel to take May on a date just after Eddie's latest lover, the Countess, wheels by the motel in a black limo and shoots up the place in an evident fit of jealous rage. Anxious to sour Martin on May, Eddie reveals his actual relationship to and with her. (May and the Old Man are also present in this extended, concluding scene at the motel café and all are drinking heavily.) Eddie's version of the story is that he met May when he accompanied his father on a surreptitious visit to her mother's house on the other side of town. May dismisses Eddie's account as 'crazy' and offers her own version, i.e. that her mother tracked down her elusive husband with his other family and made a bid for his exclusive attentions, still unbeknownst to Eddie's mother. She claims the Old Man resided with May and her mother for a couple of weeks but then disappeared altogether, never to be seen again. In the meantime, recalls May, she and Eddie fell in love – an incestuous affair that deeply distressed May's mother. She begged Eddie not to see her daughter. When that failed, she went to Eddie's mother with her plea. Previously unaware that her husband had another family and that her son and his half-sister are now lovers, Eddie's mother succumbs to horror and despair and blows her brains out with the Old Man's shotgun. Hearing all this, the Old Man angrily refutes May's account, claiming to know nothing about the suicide. Trying to enlist Eddie on his side, he angrily blames May's mother for going 'out of her way' to draw him in against his best intentions: a threadbare rationalisation that is obviously transparent to Eddie and May, so much so that they come together and embrace, not as lovers but as half-brother and sister wronged by the sins of their heedless father. Long in thrall to a repetition compulsion that had him returning to May and then repeatedly abandoning her for other women – a cycle of libidinal self-indulgence and guilty self-punishment that is also an unconscious acting out of his father's duplicity and elusiveness – Eddie is finally able to let go of the Old Man's archetypal ghost. At that moment, *Deus ex machina*, the Countess returns and shoots up Eddie's truck. It explodes in flames, spreading symbolically cathartic hellfire through the motel and junkyard. Having been lured out of the Unconscious and finally repudiated, the Old Man's forlorn spectre leaves the café and enters the Armageddon of his burning trailer in the junkyard. Eddie rescues his horses, mounts one and rides off trying to lasso the Countess's car as it speeds down the highway. Evidently freed from her own repetition compulsion, May packs a suitcase, leaves the motel and begins to walk down the highway after refusing a ride proffered by Martin.

In his reminiscences concerning the film, Sam Shepard damns Altman with faint praise – 'Bob did a commendable job' – while reciting a litany of regrets, complaints and negative judgements that make it clear that he remains disappointed with the final product. Shepard begins by characterising Altman as having dragooned him into the project when it was Shepard who approached Altman. He goes on to mention his reluctance to play Eddie and offers the opinion that the film doesn't work as well as the play because its spatial diffusion waters down the play's 'intensity and the presence of the actors [so that it] comes across as kind of a quaint little western tale of two people lost in a motel room... It doesn't have the power. In the theater it was right in front of your face, it was so intense it was kind of scary' (in Zuckoff 2009: 391). (In Altman's defence, opening up the *mise-en-scène* seems the logical and appropriate choice for a film version of the play; an entire movie confined to a tiny motel room is hard to imagine.) Shepard also complains that he was told he would be involved in the editing process but that 'Altman kind of took the film and went to Paris and cut the whole thing there and that was it' (ibid.). Still, Shepard admits that he 'was spoiled to a large extent by working in the theater ... with great directors ... who know actors inside and out. Who have dialogue with them, who spend weeks in rehearsal. You don't have that luxury in film' (in Zuckoff 2009: 392). It's clear from these remarks that, even though he wrote the play and knew Eddie's character better than anyone, Shepard would have preferred an intensive collaboration with his director, i.e. the kind of hands-on acting direction that Altman always categorically refused to do. The result was an uneasy creative vacuum at the movie's centre that manifests on the screen as a slight staginess and lack of verisimilitude, despite or perhaps because of the lurid intensity of the material. Furthermore, the film's closure by literal fireworks is a resolution too grandiose and mechanical for its own good. Reviews were mixed and, after a short and very limited run, from December 1985 to February 1986 (widest release: 57 theatres), *Fool for Love* closed $1.2 million in the red – another noble Altman experiment that was a commercial flop.

Aborted Projects

What followed, in the midst of other undertakings, were two abortive projects of note. Altman was hired to do a film version of the Ernest Hemingway novel, *Across the River and Into the Trees* (1950), supposedly with Roy Scheider and Julie Christie slated for the lead roles. Altman and Robert Harders, stage director of *Secret Honor*, developed a script but the funding ultimately fell through (see McGilligan 1989: 545). Shortly thereafter *Nashville* producer Jerry Weintraub approached Altman with a proposal to make a sequel that would be titled *Nashville 12* (i.e. another Nashville film released in 1987, twelve years after the original). Altman agreed but wanted a sequel more politically incisive and darker in mood than its predecessor. After Altman and Joan Tewkesbury, the original screenwriter, could not come to agreement on the direction of the sequel, Altman brought in Harders again, who worked full-time for two years on a script and produced some two-dozen drafts. In Harders' sequel Linnea Reese (Lily Tomlin) runs for governor of Tennessee; her ex-husband (Ned Beatty) is now the local District Attorney married to the tone-deaf singer, Sueleen (Gwen Welles); country music impresario Haven Hamilton (Henry Gibson) is now a cable TV mogul; folk singer Tom (Keith Carradine) is now married to LA Joan (Shelley Duvall). Like the first *Nashville*, the sequel would also end with an onstage death – that of the elderly woman who had saved Barbara Jean from a fire and whose son, Norman (David Arkin) would later kill the singer. Eventually, Harders even resurrected Barbara Jean herself, as a Barbara Jean female impersonator! But a *Nashville* sequel was not to be. Lily Tomlin wasn't sure she could carry a picture in the lead role and contrary to Altman's usual methods Jerry Weintraub wanted a script that would be followed to the letter. He also wanted something less grim than Harders' sequel, from which no character survives undamaged. Though never officially cancelled, the project petered out and expired by 1988.

Basements (1987)

Altman and British playwright Harold Pinter – who would win the Noble Prize for Literature in 2005 – became acquaintances in 1984, after Pinter expressed his admiration for *Secret Honor*. So when Gary Pudney, vice president in charge of specials and talent for ABC Entertainment, afforded Altman the opportunity to do a TV theatre special, Altman reciprocated Pinter's admiration by choosing to do teleplays of two Pinter 'comedies of menace': *The Room* (1957) and *The Dumb Waiter* (1960).[12] Presenting dark, enigmatic dramas to American television audiences weaned on puerile fluff might seem foolhardy or deliberately perverse but Altman, true to form, never shied away from a risky endeavour. Besides, in a broad sense, Altman and Pinter were kindred spirits, i.e. artists whose principal theme is social alienation; their works examine the dehumanising forces of Gesellschaft modernity on hapless individuals caught in its crushing hierarchical structures, whether they are rich or poor, comprehending or oblivious, rebellious or conforming. How these characters react to their oppressive circumstances is what matters in terms of dramaturgy and philosophical import.

Altman's attraction to these plays likely also owed to their lonely settings, redolent of obscurity, powerlessness and quiet desperation. Except for brief exterior establishing scenes added to make them more cinematic, both plays take place in claustrophobia-inducing rooms: a broken-down bedsit in a rundown rooming house (*The Room*) and the windowless basement of a café (*The Dumb Waiter*). As one critic has noted: 'Pinter's rooms are stuffy, non-specific cubes, whose atmosphere grows steadily more stale and more tense. At the opening curtain these rooms look naturalistic, meaning no more than the eye can contain. But, by the end of each play, they become sealed containers, virtual coffins' (Cohn 1962: 56). Except for *Fool for Love*, all of Altman's play adaptations take place in similarly closed and confining spaces – conveniently cheap to stage but also, obviously, spatial metaphors for *anomie*-inducing social isolation and entrapment. Altman even enhanced the effect by showing a basement room only alluded to in the playscript of *The Room* and by locating the basement setting of *The Dumb Waiter* in an isolated, rotting and seemingly abandoned country house in winter. He further emphasised the Dostoyevskian nature of the settings (and lowly status of their occupants) by ultimately presenting the two plays together as one special entitled *Basements*.

The Room, Pinter's first play, is both naturalistic and symbolic and Altman's production preserves that duality. The room's drab furnishings, the characters' shabby clothing and their desultory speech patterns – all are clear markers of dreary British working-class life in the 1950s. The teleplay's two main characters are Rose (Linda Hunt, Mrs. Oxheart in *Popeye*) and her husband, Bert Hudd (David Hemblen), middle-aged denizens of a nondescript upstairs flat in a city rooming house. On a cold winter day near nightfall Rose serves Bert a meal and then paces around the room while carrying on a dialogue that is really a monologue because Bert is too intent on pursuing his solipsistic leisure passion – building ships in bottles – to converse or to evidently even listen (in the playscript he is reading a magazine).[13] Soon Mr. Kidd (Donald Pleasance), the landlord, calls on the Hudds and peppers Bert with questions about when and if he will leave the room – questions answered by Rose while Bert continues to remain silent. The ensuing 'dialogue' between Rose and Mr. Kidd is not really a dialogue; the subject is always elliptical and changes frequently. The two speakers are on different wavelengths, avoiding subjects and not really listening to each other, making for a bewildering exchange that is cryptic, irrational and vaguely menacing. At the end of the scene Bert, who appears to be a truck driver, leaves to drive off in his van. Thereafter, Rose's attempt to take out the garbage is interrupted by a young couple, Mr. and Mrs. Sands (Julian Sands and Annie Lennox, of Eurythmics fame) who tell her they are looking for a flat and have been told by a man in the basement that the Hudds' flat is vacant. After they leave a blind black man named Riley (Abbott Anderson), who has purportedly been waiting in the basement according to the Sands and Mr. Kidd, suddenly arrives at the Hudds' room to deliver a mysterious and disquieting message to Rose: 'Your father wants you to come home.' Bert suddenly returns and delivers a sexually-suggestive monologue about his experience driving his van – which he refers to as if it were a woman – on the icy streets and returning safely. Finally noticing Riley, Bert screams 'Lice!' while smashing one of his bottles over Riley's head, possibly killing him. Rose, now evidently blind, carefully locks the door against the outside world.

As astutely noted by Pinter critic Leonard A. Stone, *The Room* is, in the final analysis, a '(re)presentation of late-1950s [British] working-class consciousness' – a consciousness that is insular, disjointed, irrational, non-communicative and intensely privatised:

> In terms of solidarity it bears none of the hallmarks of class loyalty and by *de facto* antagonism toward the bourgeois 'higher class'. Pinter's depiction of working-class consciousness is far removed from collectivist rhetoric. His conception of working-class consciousness is one of fragmentation, of particularism. More-over, Pinter's working-class characters take this particularism to its extreme. It follows that working-class consciousness has not only been fragmented but also taken one stage further and extinguished. Pinter's working class – like D. H. Lawrence's working class – are not engaged in class conflict. They also lack any form of political consciousness. Working-class characters in Pinter's plays are oppressed. This oppression is taken a stage further with Pinter in that it now takes the acute form of mental anguish… [T]here is no longer a working-class consciousness as class consciousness. Instead, only private consciousness exists along with its petty bourgeois connotations. (2003 n.p.)

Antisocial and apolitical, Pinter's self-estranged characters exist in the absolute solitariness of their agonised private worlds. Because they lack a shared, congruent vision of life, their attempts to express themselves or communicate with each other inevitably devolve into absurd utterances. From an allegorical perspective, the Hudds' hermetic room is the embodiment of alienated working-class consciousness: a blinkered survivalist mentality unable to understand itself, form genuine human bonds, comprehend or deal with a menacing Gesellschaft, or come to terms with temporality and the consciousness of mortality – the latter allegorised by Riley's emergence. Dreaded basement-dweller from the Id, Riley's appearance is the Return of the Repressed that must be neutralised so that Rose and Bert Hudd can maintain their existential blindness (a now literal condition for Rose at play's end).

The Dumb Waiter features hit-men Gus (Tom Conti) and Ben (John Travolta) waiting in a cluttered and filthy basement room for their next assignment. Like the characters in *The Room*, Gus and Ben while away the time with off-kilter repartee that often devolves into the absurd but here the conversation acts out an implicit power struggle; Gus, the elder partner, must parry Ben's rhetorical attempts to upstage him. Meanwhile the play's title prop, a dumbwaiter, descends to retrieve occasional food orders: mysterious and puzzling occurrences because the basement is no longer a working kitchen. Ben has to explain to the people above, via the dumbwaiter's speaking tube, that there is no food – except for the provisions the two have brought with them, which they send up. Just after Gus leaves the room to get a drink of water in the bathroom, the dumbwaiter's speaking tube whistles, indicating a message. Ben listens and responds in such a way that the audience infers that their intended victim has arrived and is on his way to the basement. Ben shouts for Gus. When the door that their target is supposed to enter from opens, it is Gus who enters, minus his gun (which he has accidentally sent upstairs in the dumbwaiter). A gunshot is heard, Ben leaves alone, and a van marked 'Compleat Cleaning Service' pulls up to the house – details added by Altman to make Gus's fate obvious.

The Dumb Waiter bears resemblance to Samuel Beckett's *Waiting for Godot* (1952), another absurdist comedy about two men waiting in a universe seemingly devoid of meaning or purpose. One could argue, though, that *The Dumb Waiter* goes Beckett's essentially existentialist scenario one better by adding an illuminating political dimension to the proceedings. Gus and Ben aren't waiting for some transcendental signified that may or may not appear; they are poised to fulfill an actual task (murder) assigned to them by their real but unseen underworld bosses. As members of the criminal underclass, Gus and Ben are both 'dumb waiters', i.e. disempowered subjects relegated to Gesellschaft society's basement, receiving orders from above that they can neither fully comprehend or fulfill without succumbing to (self-)destruction. Accordingly, Pinter critic Michael Billington interprets the play as being 'about the dynamics of power and the nature of partnership. Ben and Gus are both victims of some unseen authority and a surrogate married couple quarrelling, testing, talking past each other and raking over old times…[*The Dumb Waiter* is] a strongly political play about the way a hierarchical society, in pitting the rebel against the conformist, places both at its mercy [and] a deeply personal play about the destructiveness of betrayal' (2007: 89). Both teleplays were shot in Montreal in February 1987. *The Dumb Waiter* aired on ABC on 12 May 1987 and *The Room* aired on 2 December 1987. Both films subsequently aired together under the title *Basements* on 10 February 1988.

O.C. and Stiggs (1987)

The one Reagan-era feature film Altman made that was not based on a play was *O.C. and Stiggs* (filmed in the summer of 1983 but not released until July 1987). Featuring two characters in the last of a series of stories by Ted Mann and Todd Carroll ('The Ugly, Monstrous, Mind-Roasting Summer of O.C. and Stiggs') in the October 1982 issue of *National Lampoon*, *O.C. and Stiggs* was supposed to be a teen exploitation comedy about the misadventures of two high school delinquents from Phoenix, Arizona who wreak havoc on the Schwabs, a suburban family described by Patrick McGilligan as 'bloated with all-American pretense' (1989: 528). Through the auspices of producer Peter Newman, MGM execs Freddie Fields and Frank Yablans hired Altman, who needed the work, and afforded him a $7 million budget on the promise that he would stick to the script and not badmouth the studio in the press. Altman, who hated teen exploitation films, proceeded to rewrite the script, styling it as a satire of the genre, much to the chagrin of co-screenwriters Ted Mann and Donald Cantrell, who were kept off the set during principal photography. Predictably, despite a strong supporting cast (Paul Dooley, Ray Walston, Tina Louise, Cynthia Nixon, Melvin van Peebles, Dennis Hopper, Martin Mull and Louis Nye), *O.C. and Stiggs* did poorly in test marketing with its teenage target audience; so poorly that MGM shelved it for four years after Altman refused to recut the picture. When it was finally released in 1987, it played in only eighteen theatres for a week, earning less than $30,000 against a production cost of $7 million. Reviews were likewise dismal. Altman deemed it 'a suspect project from the beginning' (in Thompson 2006: 134).

Beyond Therapy (1987)

The last of Altman's many play adaptation films was of Christopher Durang's *Beyond Therapy* (from 1981), a light-hearted comic farce that focuses on Prudence (a highly-strung neurotic) and Bruce (a somewhat prissy bisexual): two lonely Manhattanites seeking romance with the help of their psychiatrists, Stuart and Charlotte, each of whom suggests their patient place a personal ad in the newspaper. Despite a fine cast – Jeff Goldblum as Bruce, Julie Hagerty as Prudence, Glenda Jackson as Charlotte, Tom Conti as Stuart and Christopher Guest as Bruce's live-in lover, Bob – Altman reverts too often to slapstick for a cheap laugh. Consequently, *Beyond Therapy* is 'killed by whimsy', in the astute words of Roger Ebert (1987: n.p.). It is arguably Altman's worst film.

Recalling his experience of working with Altman, Christopher Durang blamed him for taking over too much and for subverting any subtlety the play allegedly possessed:

> When he doesn't make a good film [Altman] goes very far off sometimes – and this was [for me] a very unhappy experience and outcome. Altman wrote his own adaptation of the play before I even started to write mine – which certainly wasn't the agreement. Then I wrote mine, which he pretty much ignored. And he was hurt I didn't like his version. Eventually I requested that we have a shared credit (since his version still had chunks of the original play in it), and I secretly hoped that the actors would improvise a lot, as was known to happen in Altman films. However, the finished film is pretty close to what Altman wrote. His version, in my opinion, throws the psychological underpinnings out the window, and people just run around acting 'crazy'. I think the play would have made a good commercial comic film if the track-able psychology from the play had been kept. As well as more of the play's dialogue.[14]

The Rake's Progress and *Aria* (1987)

Always the restless experimenter, Altman even tried his hand at opera in the 1980s. At the invitation Paul C. Boylan, Dean of the University of Michigan's School of Music, Altman directed Igor Stravinsky's *The Rake's Progress* (1951, libretto by W. H. Auden and Chester Kallman, based on eight William Hogarth paintings and engravings, 1733–35) at Ann Arbor in the fall of 1982 and again at the Opéra du Nord in Lille, France in May 1986.[15] Altman departed from the original script in several ways. He concentrated the action by turning three acts into two. Instead of the many locations specified in the libretto, Altman decided to use just one location: London's Bedlam, a massive, phantasmagorical stage set configured by *Popeye* set designer Wolf Kroeger as combination prison, insane asylum and hell. Altman's other innovation was to split Anne Truelove, the female lead/soprano, into two roles, to signify a schizoid personality. As Paul C. Boylan later noted, Altman's interpretation of *The Rake's Progress* set off 'a firestorm of controversy'; academics condemned his revisionist re-staging 'as an inexcusable distortion of Stravinsky's intent [while] most of the professional critics, the vast majority of the public who attended performances in Ann Arbor and France, and Altman himself, of course, viewed his conception of this work as a re-animation, a unique perspective, that allowed the audience to gain new insights into an opera that many had previously considered dated and anachronistic' (1993: 55).

Altman also contributed a seven-minute segment to *Aria*, a 1987 British anthology film produced by Don Boyd consisting of ten short films of opera arias by a variety of directors (among them Ken Russell, Jean-Luc Godard, Derek Jarman, Bruce Beresford and Nicolas Roeg). For his segment Altman re-created the opening night of Jean-Philippe Rameau's *Abaris ou les Boréades* (Libretto by Louis de Cahusac) at Paris's Théâtre Le Ranelagh in 1734. Instead of showing the opera, Altman kept his camera on the audience, consisting of a few bored aristocrats in their boxes but mostly filled with a louche assortment of inmates from a local asylum – a trope that allowed Altman to recycle costumes from *The Rake's Progress*, which dates from the same period. As Gayle Sherwood Magee notes, 'By focusing on the inmates extreme, irrational, raunchy, and absurd reactions to the sophisticated and refined opera soundtrack, Altman invites viewers to experience Rameau through the lens of madness' (2014: 153).

The Caine Mutiny Court Martial (1988)

Another made-for-television movie project involved remaking Herman Wouk's celebrated and oft-staged *The Caine Mutiny Court Martial* (1953), adapted from his Pulitzer Prize-winning novel, *The Caine Mutiny* (1951). Altman initially demurred but took on the assignment after watching the Iran-Contra Hearings, televised in the spring and summer of 1987. He told an interviewer, 'If the [TV] audience liked Iranscam, they'll like this' (Hanuaer 1988: 33). His production – not a remake of the 1954 Edward Dmytryk film, *The Caine Mutiny* starring Humphrey Bogart, but of the Broadway play that focuses only on the court-martial – was shot in December 1987 in an old gym at Fort Worden, a decommissioned army base in Port Townsend, Washington: a somewhat rustic venue compared to the more august setting specified in the playscript ('the General Court-Martial Room of the Twelfth Naval District, San Francisco'). As customary in such proceedings, long tables were arranged on three sides of 'the stand', actually just a chair in the middle of a large room allotted for the deposition of witnesses, with the court martial judges sitting directly opposite the isolated chair, and the prosecution and defence attorneys facing each other at tables on either side. Running counter to his usual *modus operandi*, Altman decided to 'de-dramatise' the drama, hoping that a TV-viewer who suddenly flipped to *The Caine Mutiny Court Martial* on his TV dial would think 'he's tuned into C-SPAN by mistake'. To make what was a wordy courtroom drama visually engaging, Altman often shifted focus and altered perspectives while he had his cinematographer, Jacek Laskus, keep the camera subtly moving into, away from and across speakers and listeners. Altman also took care to cast young actors, as most of the naval officers would have been in their twenties and thirties.

Starring Brad Davis of *Midnight Express* fame as Capt. Queeg (Keith Carradine turned down the part), Jeff Daniels as Lt. Stephen Maryk, Queeg's second-in-command, performance artist/actor Eric Bogosian as Maryk's defense attorney, Lt. Barney Greenwald, Peter Gallagher as Lt. Com. John Challee, Kevin J. O'Connor as Lt. Thomas Keefer, and Altman stalwart Michael Murphy as Captain Blakely, *The Caine Mutiny Court Martial* dramatises the prosecution of Lt. Maryk, who is accused of mutiny for forcibly relieving his commanding officer, Capt. Queeg, during a typhoon. Eventually, under Barney Greenwald's expert cross-examination, Queeg disintegrates on the witness stand and Maryk is acquitted, but Greenwald is not entirely happy with the outcome. He pities Queeg, views Maryk as fundamentally decent and well-meaning, but loathes Lt. Keefer, a patrician intellectual snob who did everything he could to turn Maryk and the rest of the crew against Queeg. At a post-acquittal party, a disgusted Greenwald denounces Keefer and throws a glassful of yellow wine into his face (echoing the insulting nickname of 'Old Yellowstain' the crew members had given to Queeg), before walking out of the now ruined party. Aired as a CBS special in May 1988, *The Caine Mutiny Court Martial* garnered solid reviews as an intelligent drama, skillfully executed and featuring almost uniformly strong performances.

Notes

1   Flashbacks are further marked by period music on the jukebox – usually McGuire Sisters' songs – and often rainy weather; scenes in the present take place in the midst of a prolonged heat-wave and drought that reflects the characters' spiritual desiccation.

2   In an interview, Altman explains how he came up with the mirror idea: 'When I did readings of the play there were mirrors all around my office, and I kept watching the actresses through these mirrors. That's how that idea of crossing time through the mirror came about. And it was much easier to do when I made the film' (in Thompson 2006: 129).

3   The name 'McCarthy' evokes repression by alluding to Sen. Joseph McCarthy, the notorious red-baiter who orchestrated anti-communist paranoia in the early 1950s.

4   The only woman featured in *Streamers* has a non-speaking bit part as a soldier's girlfriend.

5   The drill is performed by Major Jim Brackenridge and the Sam Houston Rifles (aka 'Jodies'), part of the ROTC Program at the University of Texas at Austin.

6   Early on Nixon switches all four CCTV monitors to the camera that covers his study; the duplicate images of himself suggest psychic splintering.

7   The real Richard Nixon was no secret martyr to democracy. He was much the opposite: a compulsively devious and paranoid schemer who inadvertently engineered his own downfall by authorising dirty tricks when they were utterly unnecessary (he won the 1972 election in the third largest landslide in American history). Worse yet; extended versions of Nixon's papers released in 2014 conclusively show that when he was a presidential candidate in 1968, Nixon ordered Anna Chennault, his liaison to the South Vietnam government, to persuade them to refuse a cease-fire with North Vietnam being brokered by President Lyndon Johnson.

Nixon's interference with LBJ's peace negotiations violated the 1797 Logan Act, which bans private citizens from intruding into official government negotiations with a foreign nation (see Fitrakis and Wasserman 2014).

8   See Volkan and Itzkowitz's psychobiography for a highly persuasive treatment of Nixon's psychological make-up.

9   The motel rooms, shacks and trailers not used for filming were used for equipment storage and dressing rooms.

10 A flashback scene was shot at 1001 7th Street, Las Vegas, New Mexico: exteriors and interiors of a small house that served as Eddie's mother's residence.

11 *Robert Altman: Art and Soul*, a featurette that was part of the 2004 DVD release.

12 The term, 'comedy of menace' was coined by British drama critic Irving Wardle, who borrowed it from the subtitle of David Campton's play *The Lunatic View: A Comedy of Menace*, in reviewing Pinter's and Campton's plays in *Encore* in 1958. The four Pinter plays considered comedies of menace are *The Room* (1957), *The Birthday Party* (1957), *The Dumb Waiter* (1960) and *The Caretaker* (1960).

13 Bert Hudd's hobby was a feature added by Altman.

14 See http://www.christopherdurang.com/filmtv2.htm

15 Altman went on to stage *McTeague* (based on the Frank Norris novel) with William Bolcom at Lyric Opera of Chicago in 1992 and *A Wedding, The Opera*, with Bolcom and Arnold Weinstein, also at Lyric Opera of Chicago in 2004.

CHAPTER SIX

Return to Form

You can't blame the minnow for being the natural enemy of the bass. The fish are always going to eat him. The artist and the multitude are natural enemies.
— Robert Altman

Tanner '88 (1988)

After a long string of commercial and critical disappointments, near-misses, and obscure minor works covering the decade since the fiasco that was *Quintet*, Altman's luck began to turn around in 1988. Toward the end of 1987 Bridget Potter, Vice President of Original Programming at HBO, approached Pulitzer Prize-winning *Doonesbury* cartoonist Garry Trudeau to write a comedy series on a bogus presidential campaign. Trudeau agreed to write the series if Altman directed. As a longtime commentator on presidential politics (e.g. *Nashville, HealtH* and *Secret Honor*) and a *Doonesbury* fan, Altman eagerly assented and the two entered into a collaborative partnership as executive producers (see Morreale 2009: 103). The concept that Trudeau and Altman came up was both inspired and audacious: they decided to mix fact and fiction, E. L. Doctorow fashion. To parody the media circus that is a modern US presidential campaign, they created a fictive candidate, placed him in real campaign settings interacting with other real candidates, actors and the public, and shot it all in mock *cinéma vérité* fashion, in order to amplify the illusion of a real candidacy and to comment on the artificiality of the entire electoral process.

The series was scripted but Altman allowed for plenty of found moments on location, some improvisation and lots of last-minute revisions. As Trudeau recalls: 'Imagine my surprise when I found out that certain things that I had written would be shot verbatim and other things would be dropped entirely, and then everything in between' (in Zuckoff 2009: 399). Between December 1987 and the airing of the series' one-hour pilot episode ('The Dark Horse') in mid-February 1988, Altman hurriedly assembled a cast headed by Michael Murphy as Tanner; Pamela Reed as T. J. Cavanaugh, his feisty campaign manager; Cynthia Nixon as Alex Tanner, his bossy college-age daughter; Wendy Crewson as Joanna Buckley, his sexy girlfriend (and a campaign official for rival candidate, Michael Dukakis); and E. G. Marshall as his curmudgeonly father, a retired Army general. Cast and crew then traveled to New Hampshire, where Tanner was depicted as entering the all-important New Hampshire Primary, the initial vetting ground for presidential aspirants that always elicits intense media coverage. Unsure of his message and his identity as a candidate, Tanner has his first campaign commercial evaluated by a focus group: a routine commodification procedure that Tanner finds offensive. Fortunately Tanner's motel room rant to staffers about the phoniness of the focus group process is surreptitiously caught on tape. It becomes his first TV campaign ad and inspires his campaign slogan ('For Real') – fiendishly clever postmodern irony when one stops to consider that Jack Tanner is decidedly *not* for real. Indeed, a staffer initially misspells the new slogan as 'For Reel'.

On the strength of the pilot HBO contracted ten half-hour episodes, aired irregularly from March to August 1988: a timeframe that coincided with the actual run-up to and aftermath of that year's Democratic National Convention in Atlanta (18–21 July). During this crucial period Tanner travels to Nashville, gets the endorsement of Country and Western star Merle Haggard (a liberal in real life), and then has a speech interrupted by a scuffle between one of his staffers and a man with a knife who is mistakenly identified as a would-be assassin. Nonetheless, the incident garners Tanner Secret Service protection for the remainder of his campaign and provides Altman with another object of ridicule already well satirised in *Brewster McCloud* and *A Wedding*: the self-important yet unctuous cop/security official in dark suit, sunglasses, earpiece, concealed weapon and wrist microphone that epitomises an authoritarian personality type. Altman also gets to lampoon the Secret Service's penchant for code names; Tanner is absurdly dubbed 'Moonwalker' and Alex is designated 'Bookbag'.

Seeking advice on courting the black vote, Tanner calls on an old but long-neglected friend, the Rev. Billy Crier (Cleavon Little), a Baptist minister and respected Civil Rights activist. Leaving what was supposed to be a private meeting, the two men are confronted by a bevy of reporters and cameramen summoned by Stringer Kincaid (Daniel Jenkins), an overzealous Tanner operative. Thinking that Tanner has betrayed his trust by luring him into an unwanted photo op in order to exploit his reputation, Crier quietly turns away, much to Tanner's very public embarrassment. Tanner fires Stringer but the PR damage has been done and a friendship is destroyed only moments after it has been revived. A poignant commentary on the inability of the white establishment to relate to black concerns, the episode ('Night of the Twinkies', aired 12 April 1988) foregrounds America's racial divide.

Proceeding on to Washington, DC from Nashville, Tanner is tutored on campaigning pitfalls by Bruce Babbitt, actual former Democratic Secretary of the Interior and Governor of Arizona who dropped out of the race in February 1988, after losing in New Hampshire and Iowa. When Stringer tries to join the Dukakis campaign he discovers Tanner's girlfriend, Joanna, is a Dukakis staff member: a revelation later leaked to a reporter that precipitates a scandal for Tanner and angers T. J., who was kept in the dark about Tanner's relationship with Joanna. To diffuse the bad publicity, Tanner and Joanna contrive to marry while Tanner is campaigning in Detroit but decide to postpone nuptials after Tanner's disapproving father ruins the event with an obscene toast. In the same episode ('The Girlfriend Factor', aired 11 July 1988), the topic of race is revisited in the series' most poignant and politically incisive set piece when Tanner meets with 'So Sad', a real African-American community group in Detroit dedicated to lessening gun violence. Tanner listens to their stories about drugs, crime and poverty in the ghetto of a dying city and is schooled on an America he barely knew existed. Already discomfited, Tanner is deeply shaken when he and his entourage cross a vacant lot after the meeting and stumble upon a dying black boy, evidently shot during a botched drug deal, or for no reason whatever: a representative slice of urban reality seldom seen on mainstream television or discussed by 'real' presidential candidates.

Sincere and well-meaning but an awkward campaigner, Tanner makes a number of missteps. In a (fictional) televised debate with Michael Dukakis and Jesse Jackson, he endorses the legalisation of all illicit drugs: a proposal too far ahead of its time to be taken seriously. At a campaign stop in LA he lectures bemused kindergarten children on tax abatements. An encounter with a 'talking' robot in Detroit likewise goes awry. Lacking in natural charisma and the requisite glad-handing and baby-kissing skills, Tanner is eventually compelled to seek a public speaking coach to upgrade his persona and better commodify his candidacy – another reminder by Trudeau and Altman that modern presidential campaigns are really media-orchestrated beauty contests heavy on image and light on substance. In the end, though, Tanner's make-over efforts come to naught. Despite the best backroom efforts of convention delegate coordinator Billy Ridenour (Harry Anderson), Tanner, vying with Jesse Jackson, fails to secure enough state delegates to upset Dukakis's nomination. In the aftermath of the DNC Convention, while Tanner's campaign office is being dismantled and his finances audited, T. J. and other loyal staffers investigate the possibilities for Tanner running as a third party candidate. Joanna meets with (the real) Kitty Dukakis, who asks her to persuade Tanner to endorse her husband (who will run against and lose to George H. W. Bush, nominated at the GOP Convention in New Orleans four days before the last *Tanner '88* episode aired). The series ends with Tanner not answering Joanna's query about endorsing Dukakis while he dreamily ruminates on a possible third party candidacy.

Early in its first run on HBO, *Tanner '88* garnered a lukewarm review from TV critic John Corry of the *New York Times*: 'Call it imaginative; call it satire; call it a mixed result. *Tanner '88*… is too real to be funny, but it's also not real enough' (1988a: C21). A month later Corry was still sceptical about the series' merits: 'At heart … the point of view is cynical. Mr. Trudeau and Mr. Altman are satirizing politics, although we're never quite sure why. Tanner seems to be made up of leftover parts from Gary Hart and Bruce Babbitt. Maybe he has new ideas and maybe he's all decency, but somehow he recedes from sight. *Tanner '88* … also recedes. It's slick and occasionally witty, but it's still hard to tell what it's about' (1988b: C18). Though it certainly made up for the virtual non-release of *HealtH* in 1980, *Tanner '88* was not widely seen when it first aired; HBO's subscriber base was still comparatively small and sophisticated political satire will always have limited appeal. In retrospect, however, *Tanner '88* has come to be seen as a trailblazing series. For example, Dana Stevens, writing for *Slate* in 2004 when *Tanner* had its second run on HBO, praised it as slyly blending 'fiction and documentary, with real-life political and media figures – Bob Dole, Bruce Babbitt, and Linda Ellerbee among them – crossing paths with, and commenting upon, Tanner's grass-roots campaign. But *Tanner's* formal complexity – a loose, layered blend of group improvisation, scripted set pieces, and the intervention of pure chance – manages to point up not only the laziness of reality shows like *Survivor* and *The Bachelor* but their moral and political vacuity' (2004: n.p.). In his commentary for the 2004 Criterion DVD edition, Altman deemed *Tanner '88* 'the most creative work I've ever done – in all films and theatre'.

Vincent & Theo (1990)

Back on the cultural radar screen with *Tanner '88*, Altman furthered his return from obscurity with a relatively high-profile television/movie project: a biopic of Vincent van Gogh. In the fall of 1988 a Dutch television producer named Ludi Boeken approached him with an offer to direct a four-hour docudrama miniseries on Van Gogh for European television, to mark the centennial anniversary of the painter's death in 1890 (in Zuckoff 2009: 410). Altman initially balked. As he told John Tibbetts: 'I didn't want to make that kind of picture. I don't like those biographical things. I just don't believe them, for one thing' (1992: 39). Eventually he accepted the assignment, with the proviso that he be allowed to cut a feature-length film version from the mini-series for separate release.

When Altman took over the directorial reins, the shape and mood of *Vincent & Theo* was already largely determined by Julian Mitchell's screenplay: a script that Altman subjected to minimal tampering because he understood and agreed with Mitchell's refreshingly mordant slant. In modern times van Gogh has been caricatured in the popular imagination as the epitomic mad artist who cut off his own ear (actually, it was just the lobe) or idealised as a gentle, tortured visionary in such sentimental hagiographies as Vincente Minnelli's *Lust for Life* (1956), starring a blustery Kirk Douglas. It took Leonard Nimoy's *Vincent* (1981), a made-for-TV movie of Phillip Stephens' eponymous one-man play based on van Gogh's letters, and Paul Cox's *Vincent: The Life and Death of Vincent van Gogh* (1987), a documentary also based on the letters, to articulate a revisionist portrait of the artist as a sophisticated and self-aware spiritual striver struggling to achieve elusive aesthetic ideals while battling inner demons that would ultimately overwhelm him. In a somewhat different but complementary vein, Mitchell's script counters the romantic myth of Vincent van Gogh as tragic martyr to art and insanity by playing up the arduous ordinariness of his struggle to survive and paint. As Derek Malcolm observed in his review of *Vincent & Theo* for *The Guardian*, 'What the film ... attempts to show us is that masterpieces do not appear out of thin air but as a result of constant enervating struggle' (in Zuckoff 2009: 401). As Altman himself told an interviewer, 'My whole purpose [in making *Vincent & Theo*] was to demythify art ... I was trying to convey that the value of art is not in its existence, but in its doing' (in Thompson 2006: 204). By giving Theo equal billing and screen time, the film foregrounds the key role that Theo van Gogh played in sustaining his brother's life and work. The ampersand between Vincent and Theo in the film's title recalls *McCabe & Mrs. Miller*, another tragically tenuous pairing of romantic and pragmatic sensibilities. The ampersand logogram is also traditional in business titles. In both films the use of it instead of 'and' emphasises the primacy of the business partnership in keeping the personal relationship afloat; its use in *Vincent & Theo* subtly reminds viewers that art always has a material basis.

Central to Altman's demythification project is the film's characterisation of Vincent van Gogh as a real and deeply flawed human being: self-absorbed, mercurial, sometimes violently petulant, perhaps suffering what would now be termed bi-polar disorder. Frustrated that Theo cannot sell his paintings and thereby get him the recognition and financial independence he knows he deserves, Vincent nonetheless remains devoted to his brother and obsessively committed to his art. As for Theo, the film depicts him as more conventional but equally passionate and troubled – a husband and father struggling to hold down a middle-class job and support a family in the face of formidable challenges: jittery nerves, miserable bosses, a fickle art market swarmed by philistines, a needy and demanding brother competing for his attentions with his wife and young son and the syphilis infection that will eventually kill him.

Working within the confines of a tight budget, Altman shot *Vincent & Theo* at many of the original locations in Holland and France with Dutch and French actors – except for the lead roles. In keeping with Mitchell's revisionist portrait, Altman cast British actors Tim Roth as Vincent and Paul Rhys as Theo. Though of slighter build than van Gogh, Roth with hair his dyed red, closely resembles him. His established screen persona, based on roles as a white power skinhead, working-class East Ender, apprentice hitman, etc. emanated a strong punk-rebel-outlaw aura. Rhys brought his own brand of 'street cred': he had been a genuine punk rocker in his youth. Schooled in the British acting style – more technical and less emotional than Method acting – Roth and Rhys brought a dry, bracing edginess to their respective roles (especially Roth). Another key element in sustaining the film's tense and sombre mood is Gabriel Yared's mournful musical score, punctuated by jangling, crashing figures that recall Stomu Yamashta's 'sound sculptures' in *Images* and evoke a palpable sense of anguish and doom. As for the film's visual content, Altman's initial impulse was to not show any of van Gogh's paintings but he re-thought himself and had Stephen Altman, his son and production designer, commission a couple of dozen French art students to make copies of fifty van Gogh paintings that only needed to be good, not perfect, as the camera never lingered on them. Not surprisingly, the Altmans also gave careful consideration to the film's overall colour palette. In the scenes taking place in Holland, the predominant colours are earthy dark browns and rich ochres, consistent with van Gogh's work and the prevailing fashions in art at that time and place. The Paris scenes feature lots of washed-out greys and pastel blues, again reflecting van Gogh's work and the work of his contemporaries. In the scenes at Arles bolder hues of yellow, red and blue predominate. Altman also had has cinematographer, Jean Lépine, make slight and gradual increases to the film's colour saturation in order to make the movie more subtly vivid as it went along.[1]

As is often the case in Altman's work, the opening sequence foregrounds the film's central themes: Vincent's visionary passion, the brothers' close but vexed relationship, art versus commerce – art versus life itself. *Vincent & Theo* begins with stock footage of the auctioning of van Gogh's 'Still Life: Vase with 15 Sunflowers' (1888) at Christie's in London on 30 March 1987. The scene then shifts to van Gogh's squalid lodging in a miner's house in Cuesmes, Brussels in 1880. Here Vincent tells his worried brother that he's decided to become a painter (actually it was Theo who encouraged Vincent to take up painting). The two proceed to argue over art, specifically the uncompromising variety versus the kind that Theo allegedly sells, which an aroused Vincent characterises as 'crap'. Theo cites Jean-François Millet, an artist Vincent admires, as one of his clients, prompting Vincent to launch into a brief but all-consuming rant: 'Millet is art. Millet is real life! But there's real life here! And there's God here! God is in everything! Except in the church! And except in our bloody family!' Stung by Vincent's outburst, Theo storms out, only to immediately return, to inform Vincent that the money 'Pa has been sending you – well, it's not his. It's from me!' Theo storms out again. Seemingly rebuked, Vincent breaks into a broad smile; he's now committed to his life's work and knows his brother loves him and will likely continue to offer financial and moral support despite their differences. The scene cuts back to Christie's, where 'Fifteen Sunflowers' has just sold for a then-record £22.5 million ($39.9 million). Finally there is a shift back again to the past and the Dutch offices of the Parisian art dealers Goupil & Cie in The Hague, where Theo works (and Vincent also worked between 1869 and 1873). Film critic William F. van Wert astutely points out that the juxtaposition of van Gogh's extreme poverty to the astronomical value later accorded his paintings is famously ironic but not quite the irony that Altman intends:

> The irony is much more internal and structural, that there is in fact a book-ending within this false prologue, one in which the disclosure of Theo is bracketed by one kind of gallery (the auction at Christie's) at the beginning and by another kind of gallery, the art gallery in which Theo is an apprentice manager/curator. It's this second gallery that serves as the springboard into the rest of the film [and] launches the 'real time' of the rest of the film. What the irony of this false prologue also does, of course, is free the film from any fixed point of view, any first-scene fixity or identification for the spectator. By prologue's end, the film is neither from Theo's point of view nor Vincent's, but rather an alternation, the points of which are fixed by Altman but between which the characters are allowed some brilliant acting, miming, and gesturing room. (1991: 38)

Van Vert calls the opening a 'false prologue' because conventional Hollywood narrative logic would dictate that the Christie's auction scene either simply be placed at the end of the film in order to provide a triumphant *dénouement*, or split between the beginning and end, to bookend the film proper – thus transforming van Gogh's life story into a noir-style flashback that would bolster the triumphalist effect by suggesting the inevitability of his ultimate vindication. Altman refuses this tempting filmic cliché on the grounds that van Gogh experienced no happy ending; he took his own life in despair, convinced he was an abject failure. The stark reality is that posthumous fame and veneration, however great, are of no use to a man who no longer exists. Placing the final emphasis on art market big money and commodity fetishism would also obviously run counter to the meaning of van Gogh's life and of the film itself.

A two-hour redaction from a four-hour mini-series, *Vincent & Theo* has to elide the first twenty-seven years of van Gogh's life and concentrate on the artist's last decade. What is lost is a depiction of young Vincent's earnest pursuit of a religious vocation before he became an artist.[2] Also omitted from the movie version of *Vincent & Theo* is the crucially significant reason why van Gogh lost his religious faith. He hoped to marry his first cousin, Kee Vos Stricker, but Kee's father, Johannes Stricker, a prominent Dutch theologian and biblical scholar, prevented the marriage on the grounds that Vincent was unable to support himself: adherence to bourgeois pragmatism and propriety that van Gogh interpreted as rank hypocrisy for a man of the cloth. Though it is rendered in a kind of emphatic shorthand – 'God is in everything! Except in the church!' – the film makes it clear from the beginning that van Gogh's single-minded quest to become a great artist is rooted in an intense but unorthodox spirituality.

Nonetheless *Vincent & Theo* shows that the sacred (art) and the profane (life) exist in separate realms of Spirit and Matter. Despite the artist's best efforts, these spheres can never be conjoined and reconciled – an insight that Altman readily accepts but van Gogh does not. Accordingly, a long sequence of scenes that encompass the first thirty-five minutes of the film's running time establish that van Gogh's actual life and his lofty artistic aspirations will always be in conflict. Van Gogh forms an intimate relationship with a hired model, Clasina Maria 'Sien' Hoornik (Jip Wijngaarden), a pregnant prostitute with a five-year-old daughter, and soon he has Sien and her daughter come to live with him in his garret home in The Hague. To dramatise the distance between art's ethereal realm and the brute facticity of quotidian reality, the film invents a scene in which Vincent takes Sien and her daughter to the Panorama Mesdag: an impressively realistic diorama of the sea, beaches and village of Scheveningen that Sien pronounces 'so real. Very, very clever.'[3] She marvels that it was all painted by one man but Vincent corrects her, noting that Hendrik Mesdag had the help of his wife and several other artists – Altman's way of reminding us that painting huge murals is a collaborative enterprise like filmmaking (and vice versa). At this point Sien's daughter, Marie, steps onto the artificial sand dune between the observation platform and the diorama and squats and urinates – an unselfconscious fulfillment of biological need that violates bourgeois propriety and breaks the illusive aesthetic frame (though, in paradoxical way, she also confirms the power of the illusion by behaving as if she's at a real beach). As Joe McElhaney notes: 'The world of painting, of art promises a world of "forever", outside of the conventional limits of the temporal and spatial. At the same time, Altman remains a representational filmmaker and his films never fully give themselves over to abstraction. To live outside of conventional space/time relations, to float

Nature's call: Marie Hoornik (Sarah Bentham) squats to relieve herself in the liminal space between art and reality.

above the awful abyss, is situated by *Vincent & Theo* as a type of delusion or hallucination, and the urinating body of the child brings the spectator back to the reality of the biological and, within the realm of aesthetics, of figuration' (2015: 148).

Almost immediately thereafter Altman engages in cunning self-reflexive irony by taking his audience to the real beach pictured in Mesdag's diorama. Here Vincent, accompanied by Sien and Maria, runs into his cousin-in-law, Anton Mauve (Peter Tuinman), a distinguished painter of The Hague School who has been a mentor and patron but now sternly condemns Vincent's relationship with a woman of ill repute. The two men argue. An angry Vincent counters his relative's unctuous disapproval by pointing out that Mauve is with his mistress, not his wife, and then proceeds to smear and ruin the man's painting. But once again, the exigencies of real life trump art. Sien wades into the sea, not to drown herself like Roger Wade in *The Long Goodbye*, but to have her baby – an event that will exert more pressure on an already fragile domestic relationship. In the scenes that follow, poverty pushes Sien back into prostitution, the makeshift family dissolves into discord, and Sien leaves Vincent (in point of fact, it was Vincent who left Sien and her children). Intercut scenes show that Theo has contracted syphilis from a prostitute: an occurrence that establishes sexual commonality between the brothers despite their different class positions (i.e. Vincent is unashamedly while Theo continues to aspire to bourgeois respectability). Prostitution obviously carries larger thematic resonances as well. Its prominence in *Vincent & Theo* points up the sexual repression and social hypocrisy that pervades nineteenth-century European society while providing an ironic metaphor for Vincent's career; he may consort with whores but the last thing he wishes to do is to prostitute his art.

The second half-hour act of *Vincent & Theo* (covering the years 1883 to 1888) shows both men on upward but diverging life trajectories. Vincent takes painting lessons and obsessively hones his craft while Theo's love life is transformed when he meets Johanna

Bonger (Johanna ter Steege), the sister of his friend Andries (Hans Kesting). Johanna and Theo fall in love, eventually marry and have a child together – even though she knows early on that Theo has syphilis. By way of contrast, the film's pivotal third act depicts Vincent's disastrous relationship with Paul Gauguin (Wladimir Yordanoff). With Theo's encouragement and financing, Gauguin joins Vincent in Arles, in the south of France, to live and paint together but Gauguin's haughtiness crushes Vincent's fragile ego (as it evidently did in real life). As the friendship deteriorates into an acrimonious rivalry, Vincent's behaviour becomes more erratic. After just two months together he threatens Gauguin with bodily harm but directs his anger and frustration at himself, by cutting off part of his left ear with a straight razor: an infamous act of self-mutilation that lands Vincent in the hospital and stigmatises him as insane. In a brief but telling scene, shot though bed curtains, Theo visits Vincent in the hospital and takes his brother's hand but a silent Vincent only looks at him askance. The implication is that he is ashamed of himself but equally suspicious that his brother deliberately palmed him off on a dangerous acquaintance, to be rid of the bother of caring for him.

The fourth and final act of *Vincent & Theo* covers the last year-and-a-half of Vincent's life (1889–90), when he lived at Saint-Paul Asylum in Saint-Rémy-de-Provence, and then for the last few weeks of his life in Auvers-sur-Oise, to be near his physician, Dr. Paul Gachet (Jean-Pierre Cassel), and closer to Theo. Here the film takes considerable poetic license in depicting Gachet as a somewhat younger, much handsomer, and far more cheerful man than Gachet was in real life (Van Gogh's first impression was that the melancholic Gachet was 'sicker than I am, I think, or shall we say just as much'). The real Dr. Gachet was a dilettante – an avid art collector, doctor to artists, an amateur artist himself – and so is the filmic Gachet but much more so. Rightly or wrongly, he is also portrayed as a shallow, puritanical and patronising boor. Vincent's discomfort turns into alienation after Gachet admonishes his daughter, Marguerite (Bernadette Giraud) to steer clear of him after he overhears her offering her services to van Gogh as a nude model. Vincent calls on Theo with the obvious intention of asking if he can live with him but an upset and exhausted Johanna and squalling baby make it clear that Theo is in no position to take in his sick brother: a *de facto* betrayal that the film implicitly suggests leads Vincent to shoot himself in an Auvers field shortly thereafter.[4] After an elaborate wake and funeral, a heartbroken Theo arranges a memorial exhibit of Vincent's work in his gallery and angrily ejects Johanna from the gallery – and from his life – after she expresses impatience. We last see Theo naked in an asylum cell. Half-mad and dying he utters, 'Vincent, where are you? Help me.' A final shot is of the brothers' graves in the Auvers-sur-Oise Town Cemetery; appropriately they are side by side for eternity.

Though *Vincent & Theo* received generally favourable reviews, some critics were apt to see the film as a self-pitying personal statement by Altman about the sad fate of uncompromising artists like himself, scorned by critics and rejected in the market place, perhaps only really understood and appreciated long after death. In a 1990 interview with Beverly Walker, Altman was quick to dismiss this view as facile: 'I am not Vincent van Gogh – I'm the luckiest person I know... I've had my ups and downs but I'm on top of a rollercoaster and van Gogh never got off the ground. He overcame so much. He was not a gifted draftsman; he had no imagination, no ideas. But his incredible passion did come through, not to the dealers but to people, eventually, somehow. It's an astonishing phenomenon and it tells you something about art. Art is not a skill, though that's part of it. Art is a passion' (in Sterritt 2000: 128). Ever the scourge of businessmen, Altman would level his own passion at *Vincent & Theo* producer Ludi Boeken. In an interview with a London newspaper at the 1992 Cannes Film Festival, Altman called Boeken a 'thief, liar and pimp' for violating the terms of their contract – remarks that Boeken countered with an $800 million libel suit, which Altman's lawyers were able to dismiss in a Los Angeles court. Altman went on to win a $2 million counterclaim against Boeken's company, Belbo Films, which was ultimately settled 'for a few hundred thousand dollars' (see Zuckoff 2009: 401–2).

The Player (1992)

In 1988 movie producer David Brown read an excerpt from Michael Tolkin's Hollywood novel, *The Player* (Atlantic Monthly Press, 1988) in the now defunct magazine, *Manhattan Inc*. Brown felt that Tolkin captured the baleful essence of the industry but did not see at first how it could be made into a movie because the book contained lots of interior monologue that would be impossible to film without excessive amounts of voice-over narration. Some months later Brown had lunch at the Century Club in New York City with Ned Chase, a senior editor at the publishing firm bringing out a paperback edition of *The Player* in 1989. His interest rekindled, Brown read the galleys and was impressed with the book's authenticity – but he remained sceptical about its adaptability to the screen, so much so that he optioned the property from Tolkin for the nominal sum of $2,500 (a figure that so angered Tolkin's agent, he released him). Brown and Tolkin nonetheless became co-producers and Tolkin wrote a screenplay in about eight weeks. He later confessed surprise at how quickly he was able to turn his novel around: 'I thought a book so internal would be difficult to translate, but what I found was the structure of the plot was sound enough that what Griffin [Mill] is going through is enough. There was enough suspense and enough pressure on the character so it wasn't internal' (in Zuckoff 2009: 405).

Brown and Tolkin sent the script to Sidney Lumet but the deal fell through after the studio balked at his $2 million asking price to direct (see Zuckoff 2009: 407). Mark Rydell, Walter Hill and various other directors were offered the property but nothing materialised. They also sent the script to Ned Chase's son, comic actor Chevy Chase, who wanted to star in the film but Warner Bros. warned him that playing Griffin Mill, a villainous character, could cost him his audience (see Prigge 2004: 11). After Tolkin's agent fired him he went to the William Morris Agency. Altman had also switched agents, from Johnnie Planco to Stan Kamen at William Morris, so he was privy to an early draft of Tolkin's screenplay at a time he needed work. (Having returned to the United States in February 1989, Altman had completed the screenplay for *Short Cuts,* then known as *LA Short Cuts*, with co-writer Frank Barhydt and had largely finalised casting but the project stalled for lack of financing.) In one interview,

Altman recalled thinking *The Player* script was 'dreadful' – which he said about every script – and that he only reluctantly took it on (in Thompson 2006: 150). Conversely, in his commentary to the 1997 DVD edition, Altman spoke of having *The Player* offered to him 'as a picture they were going to make. I was a director for hire. I needed the job – I saw it as an easy shoot. I kinda liked the idea of it, so I did it'. David Brown's recollection differs; he remembers Altman calling him and saying, 'You own a property I was born to direct, *The Player*' (in Zuckoff 2009: 406). Whatever the exact impetus, Altman was hired as director (for a $500,000 fee) after he and Scotty Bushnell met with co-producers Brown, Tolkin and Nick Wechsler in March 1991. Tolkin thought Altman, who had just turned 66, looked rheumy-eyed and ill. Tolkin also got a distinctly negative impression of Bushnell, whom he characterised as 'a thin, depressed chain-smoker, distractedly hostile [who] slouched like an embarrassed teenager'. David Brown convinced his colleagues to 'ignore Altman's health, that Altman was a brilliant director who hadn't had a hit for a few years and was due for one' (Altman and Vallan 2014: 225). With Altman on board, Avenue Pictures CEO Cary Brokaw agreed to provide development financing but the money soon ran out; in the long run it was Dawai Bank of Tokyo that completed production underwriting (see Priggé 2004: 11)

As it turned out, David Brown's intuition about Altman would prove correct. The timing of *The Player* also proved to be highly fortuitous. During Altman's Paris years an American independent film movement – abetted by the Independent Feature Project, Robert Redford's Sundance Film Festival, rising markets for home video and cable television, etc – had been gathering momentum as a reaction to the increasingly commercial nature of mainstream Hollywood cinema with its pre-packaged 'high concept' (i.e. simple formula) blockbusters and juvenile pablum. Indeed, the indie movement achieved a major breakthrough in 1989 when Steven Soderbergh's low-budget feature, *sex, lies, and videotape* won critical acclaim, the Palme d'Or at the Cannes Film Festival and an Academy Award nomination. It also earned an impressive $25 million at the box office, proving that feature films developed outside the major studios were, once more, a force to be reckoned with. A number of other independent producer-directors (e.g. Richard Linklater, David Lynch, the Coen brothers, John Sayles, Jim Jarmusch, Spike Lee) were also enjoying considerable success by the early 1990s – so much so that conglomerate Hollywood began to co-opt the indie movement by buying the smaller, independent studios and starting their own: a phenomenon dubbed 'Indiewood'. In a sense, then, Altman's return to Hollywood with *The Player* would echo his initial breakthrough with *M*A*S*H* twenty-two years earlier; his insistence on artistic autonomy and some degree of psychological realism and social critique were Hollywood Renaissance values back in vogue among many of his peers and appreciated by a sizeable audience segment.

Equipped with a moderate budget of $8 million, Altman started shooting the film in Los Angeles on 7 June 1991. Having already cast Tim Robbins in *Short Cuts*, Altman settled on Robbins for *The Player*'s lead role as Griffin Mill, a slick, unscrupulous Hollywood studio executive who kills an aspiring screenwriter in a fit of pique and gets away with it, and even prospers. Despite pressure from his producers to hire a better known actor, Altman kept Robbins in the picture (in Zuckoff 2009: 408). As was usually the case, Altman's casting instincts were impeccable. A gifted actor with the requisite physical attributes – tall, trim and wholesome looking – Robbins exuded the elegant self-assurance one would associate with a 'golden boy' studio executive. Some of Altman's other casting choices were typically more quirky and innovative, lending the film an aura of the messy incongruence of real life. Michael Tolkin's script called for the slain writer's girlfriend, June Mercator, to be an art director at Wells Fargo: a smart and strong young professional woman, decidedly American. Finding such a character too ordinary, Altman cast a foreigner – Greta Scacchi, an Italian-Australian actress (and then-wife of Vincent D'Onofrio who plays David Kahane, the murdered writer) – and maximised her otherness by fashioning June as a self-absorbed, amoral and dubiously talented artist who never finishes a painting and is utterly uninterested in movies. To emphasise her icy remoteness, Altman also makes June Icelandic (accordingly changing her last name to Gudmundsdottir). She is always dressed in white, as is the interior of her little Hollywood bungalow, which is also festooned with lots of transparent plastic sheeting, suggestive of ice falls. A smitten Griffin Mill calls her a 'pragmatic anarchist'. June's polar opposite in the film is Detective Susan Avery, the Pasadena cop investigating Kahane's murder. The script designates her as a blonde woman with 'an athletic haircut' but Altman goes Tolkin one better by casting wise-cracking African-American comic actress Whoopi Goldberg as Avery, who comes across as sardonic, warm and earthy – in marked contrast to June's sterile narcissism. The script describes Avery's partner, Detective DeLongpre as a man with a 'mustache and shaggy hair, like a ballplayer'. Casting against type, Altman hired country/folk singer-songwriter Lyle Lovett (also cast in *Short Cuts*) to play DeLongpre. Tall, gaunt and soft-spoken, with a craggy face and towering pompadour, Lovett looked and sounded nothing like the stereotypical homicide detective. As for extras, Altman managed to populate *The Player* with sixty-four Hollywood actors, many of them celebrities, playing themselves, e.g. Harry Belafonte, Karen Black, Gary Busey, Cher, James Coburn, John Cusack, Peter Falk, Teri Garr, Jeff Goldblum, Elliott Gould, Joel Grey, Anjelica Huston, Sally Kellerman, Sally Kirkland, Jack Lemmon, Marlee Matlin, Andie MacDowell, Malcolm McDowell, Nick Nolte, Burt Reynolds, Mimi Rogers, Susan Sarandon, Rod Steiger, Robert Wagner, etc. The idea was not new – Altman had done the same in *Nashville*, with Julie Christie and Elliot Gould, and had blended a few real politicians and celebrities with his actors in *Tanner '88* – but the sheer number of movie star cameos in *The Player* vastly augmented the film's sense of authenticity and satiric bite, made it more fun to watch, and implicitly attested to Altman's Olympian prestige among Hollywood's thespian community; no other director could have mustered such a display of talent, gratis. For his part, Altman saw his colleagues' unpaid involvement as akin to a mass protest against rapacious Gesellschaft corporatism and its deleterious effects on art and human values: 'It was like signing a petition. I think we were making a political statement about Western civilization and greed and people who take, take, and take, and give nothing back' (in Sterritt 2000: 153).

True to form, Altman overhauled Tolkin's script, only retaining the basic plot as an armature on which to mold corresponding scenes of his own invention. Most of

Tolkin's original dialogue was revised for comic effect, or to sharpen the narrative import of individual scenes and amplify the film's main purpose: to satirise the Hollywood film industry (and, by extension, the accelerating rapaciousness of the post-Reagan corporate order). Unable to see the method in Altman's madness, Tolkin fretted and grumbled. He later admitted to being 'out of my mind a few times on the set, at one point taking Altman outside to rant at him in a way that was primitive, stupid, and rude' (Altman and Vallan 2014: 225). Tolkin thinks that had he not been a producer, he would have been banned from the set (see Zuckoff 2009: 411). A comparison of the script to the film shows that Tolkin's fears were unfounded; Altman's revamped dialogue and visually compelling choices of setting and cinematographic technique resulted in a movie more sharply etched, richly textured and witty, also one that was markedly more *political*. As Geoff Andrew put it, 'the film uses Tolkin's basic plot as the starting motor for a far funnier, all-embracing satire on the greed, philistinism, and rampant egotism of contemporary Hollywood, a town where relationships, morality, and even the movies themselves are all subservient to the pursuit of power for power's sake' (in Sterritt 2000: 184).

The Player begins on a note of self-reflexive irony. A studio alarm bell sounds, there's the standard call for 'quiet on the set' then 'Scene 1, Take 10, marker' is spoken while a clapperboard (inscribed with *The Player*, Altman, cinematographer Jean Lépine, and the date) is held in front of a large mural of Charles Bragg's 'The Screen Goddess', a slightly satiric lithograph depicting silent-era filmmaking featuring a director (who looks like Erich von Stroheim), a cameraman, violinist and various technicians, all facing a movie queen making her glamorous entrance. 'Action!' is called, a modern phone rings, and a young administrative assistant in 1990s garb answers, as the camera pulls back slightly to show that the mural is located behind her desk at the office of studio head Joel Levison (Brion James). Hence the mural comes alive as the movie itself, and the past becomes present, contrasting the two eras but also suggesting an essential continuity between them.

The first four scenes in Tolkin's script depict a series of writers pitching their movie ideas to Griffin Mill in his office. Altman takes Tolkin's rather bland and static opening and transforms it into a minor cinematic masterpiece. Except for the opening interior shot, Altman's title sequence, incorporating the four writers' pitches, is composed of a single, elaborately choreographed following shot from a 25ft crane in the studio parking lot. Jean Lepine's camera fluidly follows eleven 'miked-up' actors in motion and dialogue, following two or three for a moment, then intercepting other actors on opposing trajectories, or dwelling outside windows to listen in on the movie pitches made to Griffin Mill. The shot, nearly nine minutes in duration (i.e. one complete 800ft reel of 35mm film), is comprised of fourteen distinct phases: the young admin rushes across the lot to retrieve the morning mail on orders from Levison's imperious secretary, Celia (Dina Merrill); Mill pulls up in his black Range Rover and is importuned with a sci-fi movie pitch by screenwriter/director Adam Simon (playing himself); Walter Stuckel (Fred Ward), head of studio security, conversing with mail clerk Jimmy Chase (Paul Hewitt), recalls the famous four-minute following shot that opens Orson Welles' *Touch of Evil* (1958); Buck Henry (as himself) pitches a movie idea – a sequel to *The Graduate* – to

Mill (shot from outside Mill's office window but with sound fully audible); outside the studio, Adam Simon continues to pitch his movie idea, now to story editor (and Mill's girlfriend) Bonnie Sherow (Cynthia Stevenson); Jimmy Chase's golf cart crashes in the parking lot and Bonnie Sherow shows her compassion by coming to his aid; he's shaken but uninjured; Reggie Goldman (Randall Batinkoff), the privileged son of a studio banker, drives up in his Porsche and mistakes a starlet for Rebecca de Mornay (the joke is that she really is Rebecca de Mornay); a group of Japanese business people are led through on a studio tour; Joel Levison arrives in his black Mercedes; Marty Grossman (Mike Kaplan) and two other studio execs discuss rumours of a management shake-up that might oust Griffin Mill; seen from outside his office, Mill takes a pitch from Patricia Resnick and Joan Tewksbury (two veteran Altman screenwriters playing themselves); Alan Rudolph (an Altman protégé playing himself) arrives at Mill's office; Stuckel and Buck Henry discuss famous 'tracking' shots (they really mean *following* shots); Bonnie Sherow warns her young assistant not to date Alan Rudolph; photographed through Mill's office window Rudolph, pitches a movie idea to Mill – during which Mill receives a nasty postcard ('I hate your guts, Asshole!').

Altman's single-shot expository prologue accomplishes much more than Tolkin was able to imagine in the abstract; it sets the film's bustling tone and pace, introduces many of the major players, and broaches key themes and plot points while managing to be highly entertaining. Walter Stuckel's mention of the opening shot of *Touch of Evil* alerts movie *cognoscenti* that they are watching a parody rendition of the same device – a protracted following shot – though twice as long in duration and many times the complexity of what Orson Welles accomplished. Altman later claimed, though, that he was not showing off: 'Really I was making fun of myself and all those pretentious people who think these things are important. The shot itself was a conceit; it becomes story-telling in itself rather than an element with it' (in Thompson 2006: 156).

As for themes, the opening shot sketches the corporate hierarchy that is the Hollywood studio, from mail clerk up to CEO, a rigid pecking order denoted by demeanour, dress and make of vehicle (e.g. the mail clerk's golf cart versus Levison's Mercedes). Another theme, conveyed by the writers' pitches, is the strictly formulaic nature of commercial Hollywood cinema, which relies on well-worn genre forms and familiar, audience-tested narrative devices to insure a reasonable expectation of return on investment in an otherwise highly fickle business that can never guarantee the success of any given project, no matter how promising it may appear. Screenwriters know that the name of the game is to pander to low- and middle-brow tastes by trotting out slightly different permutations of recognisable storylines that have proven successful in the past. They also know that their chances of having a script bought and actually produced are infinitesimally small. The pitches presented in Altman's prologue, improvised by his actors (who happen to be real screenwriters), are uniformly hilarious because they parody the lengths that desperate writers go to in order to sell their wares to equally desperate producers. The best of these pitches, by Patricia Reznick and Joan Tewkesbury, reaches sublime absurdity:

PATRICIA: It's a TV star and she goes on safari in Africa.

GRIFFIN: You're talking about a TV star in a motion picture?

PATRICIA: Not a real TV star. It would be played by a movie star.

GRIFFIN: A movie star playing a television star.

PATRICIA: Goldie [Hawn], Julia [Roberts], Michelle [Pfeiffer]... Bette [Midler], Lily [Tomlin].

GRIFFIN: Dolly Parton.

PATRICIA: Dolly.

JOAN: She would be very good.

GRIFFIN: I like Goldie.

JOAN: Goldie Goes to Africa.

GRIFFIN: Great. We have a relationship. That would be great. Goldie Goes to Africa. Goldie Goes to Africa.

JOAN: She becomes worshiped.

GRIFFIN: Worshiped?

JOAN: Well, she's found by this tribe...

GRIFFIN: Yes?

JOAN: Of small people. But then she has to... She's found by this tribe and they worship her. But then...

GRIFFIN: I see. It's like a *Gods Must Be Crazy* ... except the Coke bottle's now a television actress.

JOAN: Yeah, exactly right. It's *Out of Africa* meets *Pretty Woman*. And she has to decide ... whether to stay with the TV show or save this entire African tribe.

With millions of dollars staked on educated guesswork, Hollywood is always struggling to find the winning balance between novelty and familiarity without offending dominant sensibilities. A manufactured product carefully contrived and calibrated to fill a pre-existing market niche, the typical Hollywood movie is therefore the antithesis of real art, i.e. self-expressive creativity for its own sake.

Altman's nine-minute opening sequence introduces three interrelated plot strands that structure the rest of the movie. The primary plotline concerns Mill's safety and well-being (he has been receiving threatening postcards from a disgruntled screenwriter to whom he evidently gave short shrift). A subplot concerns his job status (which apparently is in jeopardy with the hiring of Larry Levy, another hotshot producer played by Peter Gallagher). Another subplot concerns Mill's love life (Bonnie Sherow is Mill's girlfriend but he has a roving eye).

The stalking writer subplot propels the movie's first, forty-minute act. After thinking he has identified the writer as David Kahane, Mill drives out to Kahane's bungalow at night, stands outside and telephones by cell phone. Kahane's girlfriend, June Gudmundsdottir answers, and the two carry on a flirtatious conversation while Mill, an unobserved Peeping Tom, directs his male gaze at her while she talks to him on the phone – an Altman flourish not in the script that makes Mill a scopophilic voyeur, i.e. a typical moviegoer, and provides foreshadowing and unconscious motivation for what Mill will soon do to Kahane. Before hanging up June informs Mill that Kahane has gone to the Rialto Theater in Pasadena to see Vittorio De Sica's Italian neorealist classic, *The Bicycle Thief* (1948). Mill drives there, introduces himself after the screening, and the two go to a nearby Japanese restaurant, listen to karaoke and drink while Mill tries his best to be conciliatory. Kahane angrily rejects Mill's overtures, the two men quarrel in the parking lot behind the Rialto, a scuffle ensues and Mill ends up killing Kahane by drowning him in a pool of standing water – an impulsive act of violence somewhere between manslaughter and second-degree murder. Mill takes Kahane's watch and wallet and smashes one of his car windows to make the crime look like a botched robbery but he's left behind a trail of circumstantial evidence that ties him to the victim: the phone conversation with June and lots of eyewitnesses who can place him with Kahane at the theatre and the restaurant shortly before Kahane's death.

Soon after the murder another threatening postcard arrives. Faced with the crushing realisation that he has killed the wrong man, Mill must now fend off a determined police investigation, escalating harassment from his unknown stalker and Joel Levison's bid to replace him with Larry Levy. Despite the enormous pressures he's under Mill, an excellent actor in 'real life', is able to maintain a façade of innocence, cool detachment and executive competence – perhaps not a façade at all because Mill is most likely a fully-fledged sociopath. Much to the chagrin of Bonnie, Mill also distracts himself by pursuing and eventually winning June; taking the woman of the man he's vanquished is the natural impulse of the Alpha male. Mill also survives something like an attempt on his life by the postcard stalker, who puts a rattlesnake in a cooler in Mill's car.[5] Out of curiosity Mill opens the lid and is nearly bitten but manages to extract the snake from his car and kill it with his umbrella. Just as crucially Mill enjoys astonishing good luck with the Pasadena police; the murder indictment hanging over his head suddenly disappears when a befuddled eyewitness fails to identify him in a lineup.

Still, the key plot element that drives the film's seventy-minute second act is the development of a movie project that will make or break Griffin Mill. When Mill goes to an arranged nocturnal meeting with the postcard writer at a Hollywood restaurant he is accosted by a jumpy talent agent named Andy Civella (Dean Stockwell) and his client, an earnestly pompous English screenwriter named Tom Oakley (Richard E. Grant). The men pitch Mill 'Habeas Corpus', a crime thriller about a California DA who convicts the wife of a rich man of the first degree murder of her husband, even though the body is never found. In Tolkin's script the DA discovers that the husband is still alive, having faked his own death. He rushes to San Quentin's gas chamber, blasts open one of its windows with a shotgun, and rescues the woman in the nick of time. Altman's version of Civella and Oakley's pitch is markedly different in three ways: (i) the DA falls in love with the wife for added dramatic impact; (ii) there is no 'Hollywood ending' (the DA learns the truth too late to save the girl because, as Oakley puts it, 'that's the reality – the innocent die'); (iii) Oakley insists that the movie use unknown actors in the lead roles 'because this story is too damn important to risk being overwhelmed by personality'. Mill thinks the idea is a sure loser but a property that can be turned to his personal advantage. As he tells his secretary, Jan (Angela Hall): 'They have a completely fucked-up idea that has no second act. If I hadn't heard it myself I never would have believed it. Larry Levy liked the idea because he's a dick brain. Levy will sell the idea to Levison and I will let Levison have the brilliant idea of letting Larry take over the project from me. See, Levison can't wait to get in bed with Levy. This piece of shit idea will blow up in both their faces. Then I will step in and save the day.'

The film's brief (twelve-minute) final act, set a year later, shows that Mill's cunning scheme has worked to perfection. It begins with a film within a film: a print of *Habeas Corpus* being screened for Civella, Oakley, Levy, Bonnie and other studio personnel for final vetting before the film is released. We see the movie's melodramatic finale, in which Bruce Willis rescues Julia Roberts from the gas chamber just after the cyanide pellets drop: a cliché Hollywood happy ending with big name stars that Oakley was adamant to avoid. When Bonnie rightly accuses Oakley of selling out – 'What about truth? What about reality?' – he irritably replies, 'What about the way the ending tested in Canoga Park? Everybody hated it. We reshot it. Now everybody loves it. *That's reality!*' To add injury to insult Levy, doing Mill's dirty work, fires Bonnie after she threatens to go over his head to preserve the film's artistic integrity. A desperate Bonnie tries to make her plea to Mill directly but he – who has replaced Levison as head of the studio – refuses to talk to her, except to offer cold comfort: 'Bonnie, you'll land on your feet. I know it. You're a survivor.' Bonnie, the film's good-hearted moral exemplar, collapses in tears on Mill's office steps as he walks past her, puts on his sunglasses, and gets into his brand-new black Rolls-Royce Corniche convertible (an upgrade from the Land Rover) to drive home.

Altman might have ended the film at this point but he and Robbins concocted another dialectical twist inspired by the explicitly self-reflexive ending of *M*A*S*H*. On the way home Griffin Mill receives a cell phone call from Larry Levy relaying another writer's pitch. This one, though, is not really a pitch but actually a thinly veiled shakedown from his postcard-writing stalker – the only one beside Mill (and his office confidante, Jan) who knows about the postcards, i.e. a compelling motive for slaying David Kahane that has to be kept under wraps (when Mill realises what the caller is actually saying, he instructs Levy to get off the line). In making his 'pitch' – ironically yet another instance of naked greed trumping artistic integrity – the vengeful writer turned blackmailer inevitably describes the movie we've been watching, which he calls 'The Player', of course: a self-deconstructive rupture of the film's illusory world that is a perfect example of Brecht's alienation effect, a device designed to prevent viewers from losing themselves in the narrative and making them consciously critical observers instead. As Altman stated: 'It's saying that this movie is about itself. I want the audience to see that many of the scenes, the ways the actors acted it, the way the sets were, the way it was shot was *movies*, not life. The melodrama was movie melodrama, not real life melodrama' (in Sterritt 2000: 209). Mill agrees to pay some undisclosed sum of blackmail money to keep the writer quiet, i.e. to prevent the 'movie' we've just seen from ever being 'made'. On a non-metaphoric level this constitutes a logical impossibility that wittily demonstrates the ontological promiscuousness of art, a liberating force from the iron laws of necessity that govern real life. The film closes with Mill pulling up to his resplendent home with its white picket fence and exquisite rose garden, where a very pregnant and glowing June lovingly greets him. In the end,

Evil rewarded: in the end, homicidal movie mogul Griffin Mill (Tim Robbins) gets to have it all.

Griffin Mill's abominably anti-social behaviour has netted him the American Dream: a perfect home and trophy wife, family in the offing and considerable wealth and power. As Tom Oakley would say, 'That's reality!' On the other hand, Griffin Mill has gained the world but lost his soul. As Altman put it in an interview, 'he's become nothing' (in Sterritt 2000: 161). That, too, is reality.

Funny, well-acted and expertly paced, *The Player* succeeds on its own hybrid terms, as an ostensive suspense/crime film that is essentially a satire of Hollywood and, by extension, corporate capitalism. Entered at Cannes in 1992 *The Player* was a smash hit with the audience and was nominated for the Palme d'Or while Altman won for Best Director and Tim Robbins won for Best Actor. Altman, Michael Tolkin and the film's editor, Geraldine Peroni, were subsequently nominated for Academy Awards. Many other awards, including BAFTAs and Golden Globes, were forthcoming and critical response was likewise overwhelmingly positive. The movie earned $21.7 million at the box office: Altman's most commercially successful film in over a decade and his third highest grossing after *M*A*S*H* and *Popeye* – though he felt that 'it could have made a lot [more] money, if [Fine Line Features] had spent more on marketing' (in Thompson 2006: 159). In sum, *The Player*'s critical acclaim and popularity fully restored Altman's reputation in Hollywood and allowed him to secure financing for *Short Cuts* with Cary Brokaw of Avenue Pictures at Cannes, the project he was planning before *The Player* came along. Though obviously gratified that the movie had been well-received, Altman bristled at talk of a 'comeback'; he pointed out to critics that he had never stopped working. He also countered facile assessments of the movie as a 'scathing indictment' of the movie business. For his part, Altman found *The Player* 'a very, very soft indict-ment of Hollywood, an unrealistic look at that arena. It's really more of a farce, because although we did lift up a few rocks, Hollywood is much crueler and uglier and more calculating than you see in the film. It's all about greed, really, the biggest malady of our civilization, and it was Hollywood as a metaphor for society' (in Thompson 2006: 151).

Short Cuts (1993)

Altman discovered the short fiction of Raymond Carver on a ten-hour flight from Rome to New York in February 1990, after a planned film on Italian opera composer Gioachino Rossini fell though. Supplied by his secretary with a collection of Carver stories, Altman read a couple of them on the plane. As he later told interviewer Robert Stewart, 'You have to understand that I was in a fragile state. I was coming from an aborted picture and a big defeat. I got off the plane, and I remember walking down the ramp and thinking, "There's a movie here"' (1993: 3). When Altman sought to obtain screen rights to some of Carver's stories, he discovered that an independent filmmaker named Jill Godmilow had already optioned many of them and was well underway with her own Carver movie. Indeed, Godmilow had discovered Carver under almost exactly the same circumstances as Altman had, but four years earlier. On a flight from Paris to New York in 1986, Godmilow was given a copy of Carver's short-story collection, *What We Talk About When We Talk About Love* (Knopf, 1981). Like Altman, she immediately recognised the potential for filmic adaptation. As she told Scott Foundas, 'I figured out that even though the stories were about different characters, they were all stories from his life and that you could string them back like pearls, with blackouts in between. That way, the Carver would be preserved' (2007: n.p.). Godmilow developed a script with Martha Gies that she says Carver 'loved'. Sadly, Carver died of lung cancer at the age of fifty in August 1988 while Godmilow and her producers, James Schamus and Ted Hope, were still raising money toward a projected $2 million budget. They were half a million dollars short when Altman began fundraising for his own Carver film. Godmilow recalls Altman telephoning her and saying things like, 'Look, just give me the rights. You're never going to make this film.' Godmilow, who had optioned a good number of Carver's more recent stories, held her ground, so Altman had to choose from what remained. In the summer of 1990 he optioned nine Carver stories and a poem, all written between 1964 and 1981. The deal, funded by Cary Brokaw, was struck with the poet Tess Gallagher, Carver's widow and literary executor, for $195,000: a princely sum for Gallagher, who sorely needed the money. Godmilow has remained bitter over Altman's usurpation of her cherished project, admitting 'I've never seen *Short Cuts*, and I never will' (ibid.).

Altman's fascination with Carver's fiction seems a bit unlikely at first glance. The two artists were from markedly different backgrounds, possessed utterly dissimilar sensibilities, and created work describing social worlds that might well have taken place on different planets. A confident scion of Midwestern affluence, Altman was in many ways a Whitmanesque visionary: ebullient, risk-taking, prone to making sweeping statements about American life often rendered in expansive, near-operatic terms. Conversely, Raymond Carver – dubbed 'the American Chekhov' by poet Donald Justice – was of working-class pedigree from the Pacific Northwest who specialised in terse, minimalist short fiction exploring the moral and emotional travails of white, rural blue-collar people, mostly inarticulate and many of them alcoholic (as was Carver himself, until he achieved sobriety in June 1977 and maintained it for the last eleven years of his life). In Carver's hardscrabble world – 'Carver Country', as it has come to be known – mere survival passes for triumph enough in life. What Altman saw and appreciated in Carver's work was its quiet but evocative realism and perceptiveness, also its existentialist emphasis on the workings of chance in shaping individual destinies. In his Introduction to *Short Cuts: Selected Stories*, the literary companion to the film, Altman praises Carver for making 'poetry out of the prosaic', capturing 'the wonderful idiosyncrasies that exist amid the randomness of life's experiences. And human behavior, filled with all its mystery and inspiration, has always fascinated me' (in Carver 1993: 7). Recurrent themes in Carver's stories – mortality, sexual and family dysfunction, a general sense of social malaise and discontent – obviously resonated with Altman; the same concerns animate his own work. Carver's stature, as one of the most revered American fiction writers of the late twentieth century, was another powerful lure for Altman; prestigious source material is always a strong selling point, especially for a filmmaker with Altman's counterculture cachet. Sketchy and self-contained, the stories themselves presented tantalising creative challenges and opportunities. There was the interesting problem of how to transform a grouping of unlinked short narratives into a cohesive feature-length film. By the same token, Carver's decidedly non-descriptive style allowed Altman to flesh out characters and fill in the visual content any way he pleased.

Altman and his co-writer, Frank Barhydt, characteristically avoided the straight-forward approach that Godmilow had followed, i.e. presenting some Carver stories anthology fashion, one after another, with demarcating fadeouts in between. Altman and Barhydt started with the premise that Carver's work exhibits overall thematic coherence, that 'all of Carver's work [is] just one story', as Altman puts it: sufficient rationale for a radical form of filmic adaptation that extracts isolated elements – vignettes, plot points and characters (dubbed 'Carver soup' by Altman) – from selected Carver stories and then combines and reconfigures and them (through expansion, contraction or alteration) into the sprawling movie mosaic that is *Short Cuts*. As Altman noted in his Introduction to *Short Cuts: Selected Stories*: 'We've taken liberties with Carver's work: characters have crossed over from one story to another; they connect by various linking devices; names have been changed... The film is made of little pieces of his work that form sections of scenes and characters out of the most basic elements of Carver's creations – new but *not* new' (in Carver 1993: 8). Altman and Barhydt also invented a couple of characters out of whole cloth: Tess Trainer (Annie Ross) and Zoe (Lori Singer), a jazz-singing mother and her cello-playing daughter, who provide the musical bridges in the film. Another major liberty taken was with locale. Altman and Barhydt transposed the settings from the Pacific Northwest countryside to populous Southern California because, as Altman put it, 'we wanted to place the action in a vast suburban setting so that it would be fortuitous for the characters to meet. There were logistical considerations as well, but we wanted the linkages to be accidental. The setting is untapped Los Angeles, which is also Carver Country, not Hollywood or Beverly Hills – but Downey, Watts, Compton, Pomona, Glendale – American suburbia, the names you hear about on freeway reports' (in Carver 1993: 9). What Altman doesn't acknowledge is that he also upgraded the social status of a number of Carver's characters: dubious poetic licence, perhaps, but meant to make them more interesting and a more credible fit as denizens of the LA suburbs.

A complex film, with an unusually large number of characters and locations, *Short Cuts* presented daunting logistical challenges. To film it, Altman and his production team devised a ten-week shooting schedule, divided into weekly units for each of the nine Carver stories and the poem that make up the movie. Each set of actors were available for just one week (or less) so a multi-coloured chart was created, detailing how the twenty-two principals would be juggled between the various locations: a regimen that prevented Altman from shooting in sequence, his preferred *métier*. Shooting started on 27 July 1992 and wrapped on 1 October.

The film opens with a small fleet of helicopters spraying Malathion for medflies: a visually compelling device invented by Altman and Barhydt to implicitly tie together the lives of some two dozen major characters (nine families) below their flight path over the greater Los Angeles area. The choppers noisily evoke Altman's 1950s *Whirlybirds* TV series, the opening of *M*A*S*H*, even Francis Ford Coppola's surreal Vietnam allegory, *Apocalypse Now* (1979). These aircraft spewing toxic chemicals over the city also suggest that something is fundamentally out of joint in the modern American megalopolis and that the cure might even be worse than the disease.

The first twenty minutes consists of a rapid-fire series of opening vignettes that introduce all the principal players. The characters who populate the film's main story are the first to be introduced: local TV news commentator Howard Finnigan (Bruce Davison), who lives with his wife, Anne (Andie MacDowell) and their young son, Casey (Zane Cassidy) next door to Zoe and her mother, cabaret singer Tess. The Finnigans are characters pulled from Carver's 'A Small, Good Thing'. Their story, which concerns Casey's accidental death, is basically the same as Carver's but in his version Ann and Howard's last name is Weiss, their son's name is Scotty, and Howard's profession is unspecified. In the movie the Finnigans are the ideal bourgeois American family living the American Dream, a family that takes every precaution to secure its health, prosperity and safety – all the more to amplify the devastating impact when a chance occurrence disrupts normality.

Another vignette introduces Dr. Ralph Wyman (Matthew Modine) and his wife, Marian (Julianne Moore) and another couple – Stuart (Fred Ward) and Claire Kane (Anne Archer) – attending Zoe's cello concert, already having met and made a spontaneous Sunday dinner date. The Wymans have been extracted from Carver's 'Will You Please Be Quiet, Please?' but their story has been truncated. In Carver's story they have two children. In the film, they are childless. In the story Ralph goes to a bar after learning that his wife has had an affair. He loses all the money he's carrying in a poker game and subsequent mugging. The film reveals the affair but elides the aftermath: a condensation that allows Ralph and Marian more screen time to play supporting roles to the Finnigans' story (Ralph is Casey's doctor). The Kanes are characters lifted from 'So Much Water So Close to Home' but their story is altered for the movie. In Carver's story Stuart and Claire have a son named Dean, who was dropped from the film. So is Mel Dorn, one of Stuart's fishing companions in Carver's story. The film also elides an unnerving encounter between Claire and a pickup truck driver when she is driving to the funeral of a woman whose corpse was discovered by Stuart and his fishing buddies. Of the many *Nashville*-like character intersections in *Short Cuts* (that never occur in Carver's writings) the conjoining of the Wymans and the Kanes ranks as perhaps the least convincing. The Wymans are upper-middle-class in the movie while Kanes remain working-class, like their literary antecedents (Stuart is an unemployed machinist and Claire – Catherine in Carver's story, occupation unspecified – is a self-employed clown in the movie who works children's parties and hospital wards). In real life, inter-class social mixing is extremely rare and the Kanes would not likely attend a cello recital in the first place.

Another vignette introduces Marian's sister Sherri (Madeleine Stowe), ensconced in a troubled marriage to philandering, petulant motorcycle cop Gene Shepard (Tim Robbins). Another installment in Altman's unflattering portraits of police officers, Shepard concocts amusingly preposterous cover stories to hide his affair with Betty (Frances McDormand): a scenario loosely based on Carver's story, 'Jerry and Molly and Sam'. Betty, in turn, is in the midst of divorcing one of the helicopter pilots, Stormy Weathers (Peter Gallagher). Doreen (Lily Tomlin), a diner waitress, is married to an alcoholic limo driver named Earl Piggot (Tom Waits). Both characters derive from Carver's 'They're Not Your Husband', but in the story Earl is Earl Ober, an unemployed salesman. The Finnigans' pool cleaner is Jerry Kaiser (Chris Penn), whose wife, Lois (Jennifer Jason-Leigh) supplements the family income as a phone-sex operator, tending to the children (and saving on child care expenses) while she deftly arouses anonymous male callers – a practice that perplexes and humiliates her husband.[6] As characters the Kaisers originate in the Carver story entitled 'Vitamins'. In the story Lois is called Patti, her husband is the story's unnamed narrator, profession unspecified, while Patti's vocation isn't phone-sex but something innocuous: selling multiple vitamins door to door. Giving Lois a risqué profession in the film might seem like gratuitous sensationalism but one could argue the opposite; the rather grotesque spectacle of Lois providing paid phone-sex while caring for her children and doing domestic chores constitutes a searing indictment of American cultural decadence, a parody of the absurdities of male desire, and an example, albeit a far-fetched one, of the routine indignities of working-class life. Altman once again breaks down barriers between stories by making Jerry and Lois friends with Doreen's daughter, Honey Piggot Bush (Lily Taylor) and her husband Bill Bush (Robert Downey Jr.), who is in training to be a makeup artist. Honey and Bill derive from Arlene and Bill Miller, the protagonists of the Carver story titled 'Neighbors' but in the source story the nature of Bill's work is unspecified.

Once the movie's omnibus introduction concludes, the main plotline begins. The day before Casey Finnigan's eighth birthday Doreen Piggot accidentally hits Casey with her car as he's crossing the street on the way to school. Appearing unhurt, Casey refuses Doreen's offer of a ride home because he's been instructed never to take rides from strangers. His mother comes home from ordering his birthday cake from baker Andy Bitkower (Lyle Lovett) to find Casey slumped, semi-conscious, on a sofa in the den. He soon falls into a deep sleep from which he cannot be awoken. An alarmed Ann calls her husband Howard at the TV station, who advises her to immediately take Casey to the hospital, where he remains unconscious. Bitkower, the baker, calls the next day to inform Ann that her cake is ready, but Howard, wanting to keep the line free, abruptly ends the call. Bitkower immediately calls back, angered at being hung up on, provoking another angry hang-up by Howard. While the Finnigans maintain their vigil, the baker continues to call and harass them at all hours. Howard's long-estranged father, Paul Finnigan (Jack Lemmon) turns up at the hospital and recalls that Casey's hospitalisation is reminiscent of the day that Howard had an accident as a boy – a plot point derived from the Carver poem, 'Lemonade'. (When Howard's mother went to her sister's house, she found her in bed with her husband. That led to divorce and the long-standing estrangement between father and son.)

Stuart Kane and his two friends, Gordon Johnson (Buck Henry) and Vern Miller (Huey Lewis), sexually harass Doreen at the diner before they depart on a three-day fishing trip – an unsavoury incident witnessed by Doreen's husband, Earl. Instead of coming to his wife's defense, Earl blames the victim by suggesting that she lose weight: misogynist bigotry that marks Earl as yet another unregenerate Neanderthal. (The kernel of the incident is based on the Carver story, 'They're Not Your Husband'.) But the misogyny gets worse. On the first day of their fishing expedition, the three men find a young woman's body submerged in the stream near some rocks. After some discussion, they decide to tie the corpse to the rocks, continue fishing, and report it when they are done with their holiday. When Stuart comes home, he recounts the incident to Claire. She is horrified that they could fish for days within sight of the woman's body. The corpse is identified as a 23-year-old woman who was raped and murdered (in Carver's story she has a name: Susan Miller). Claire attends her funeral out of a sense of compassion and guilt over her husband's bizarre indifference. This movie version, though truncated, quite closely follows Carver's 'So Much Water So Close to Home'. It also preserves Claire's moral anguish (the original story is told from her point of view).

The theme of violence against women continues but takes a sublimated form when Stormy Weathers visits his former home, ostensibly to pick up his mother's heirloom floor-standing clock. Instead, a vengeful Stormy spends the day destroying Betty's clothing with scissors and bleach and cutting the furniture to pieces with electric saws – a fracas interrupted by a vacuum cleaner salesman (Dirk Blocker) who calmly proceeds to wash and shampoo the carpets in an otherwise destroyed house. The carpet-cleaning motif is derived from Carver's story 'Collectors' but is shorn of its original meaning, which had to do with a sense of lonely paralysis experienced by a man named Slater, who is confined to a small space as the cleaning proceeds. In the film, the carpet-cleaning functions mostly as a sight gag. Home violation and misogynistic violence continues in a different vein as Bill and Honey Bush entertain themselves in a neigh-bours' apartment that they are watching while its owners are on vacation (the basic plotline of 'Neighbors'). Bill takes photos of Honey, whom Bill has made up to look like she has been brutally beaten. Subversion of domestic tranquility takes on another configuration when Gene Shepard abandons the family dog on a distant suburban street because he cannot endure its constant barking. After listening to his family's complaints for several days, Gene returns to the neighborhood and retrieves the dog. (Shepard's infidelity and the unwanted dog motif come from Carver's story, 'Jerry and Molly and Sam'.) Elsewhere in suburbia, the Wymans get into a heated argument just

A parent's worst nightmare: Howard (Bruce Davison) and Ann Finnigan (Andie MacDowell) witness the death of their young son, Casey (Zane Cassidy).

before their Sunday dinner party with the Kanes. In the movie's most notorious scene, Marian – nude from the waist down after removing her dress to clean it of spilled wine – admits to having had sex with another man after a drunken party: the basic scenario of Carver's 'Will You Please Be Quiet, Please?' Once Stuart and Claire Kane arrive both couples alleviate their anguish through heavy drinking all night long.

The movie's climactic sequence commences at the hospital when Casey's eyes suddenly begin to flutter. His parents are elated but just as he appears to be waking, the brain-injured boy expires. Witnessing the crisis, Howard's father – a cowardly, avoidant personality – quietly leaves the hospital. The heartbroken couple returns home and informs a stunned Zoe of Casey's death. Early the next morning Ann Finnigan, starting from sleep, suddenly realises who has been making the harassment calls. She and her husband go to the bakery to confront the baker over his abusive calls while they were in deep distress. Ann slaps and curses Andy Bitkower, displacing all her sorrow and rage at the death of her son. When Bitkower learns why the Finnigans never picked up the cake, he apologises profusely, asks them to stay, and gives them coffee and freshly baked goods (hence Carver's title, 'A Small, Good Thing'). As a rare instance of deep empathy and poignant human consolation in a world of selfish narcissists, the scene might well have served as the movie's closing moment – but Altman abruptly truncates the moment and then ill-advisedly continues on for another fifteen minutes running time with contrasting episodes depicting suicide, murder and natural catastrophe.

Zoe Trainer, evidently distraught by her mother's alcoholism, her own isolation and Casey's senselessly tragic death, commits suicide by starting a car engine inside her garage, playing her mournful cello as she succumbs to carbon monoxide: an event that viewers might find gratuitously bleak but one that Altman defends as thought-provoking: 'the reasons why someone commits suicide are so complex, and yet so simple – it's luck. If I have a message, it's not any profound truth, it's this: "I am going to expose an event to you that you yourself will get a hunch that will tell you about other things in your life experience"' (in Sterritt 2000: 202). Later that morning,

Zoe's mother returns from the nightclub and discovers that her talented and beautiful daughter is dead – a devastating revelation she is unable to fathom. On a lighter but still macabre note, Honey Bush picks up her photos from the developer and discovers that they have been switched with the set belonging to the next person in line: Gordon Johnson. Gordon is shocked to see the pictures of Honey evidently beaten so badly, while she is horrified by the pictures he took of the body in the water. They hastily exchange photos and walk away from each other memorising the other person's license plates. Images of misogynistic violence usher in the film's final sequence, which features Honey and Bill on a picnic with Jerry and Lois and their children. In the park, Jerry and Bill make excuses to go off on their own, to try to seduce two young women bicyclists they encountered earlier. Personable and outgoing, Bill quickly partners with one of the women. As they walk away from Jerry and the other woman, they hear her scream. They turn around to see Jerry hitting her in the head with a rock, just as a major earthquake strikes (the earthquake is an Altman invention but the killing derives from Carver's chilling story, 'Tell the Women We're Going'). In the aftermath of the quake, Jerry's murder of the woman is attributed to a falling rock during the earthquake; evidently Bill and Jerry silence the victim's friend with threats on her life.

A narratively intricate, caustic and generally downbeat movie-mosaic some three hours long (the rough cut clocked in at six hours), *Short Cuts* did not enjoy the popularity that *The Player* had seen; it cost $12 million to make but returned only $6.1 million in domestic box office receipts. The film won its share of honours – the Golden Lion and other awards at the 1993 Venice Film Festival, a special Golden Globe ('Best Ensemble Cast'), an Academy Award nomination for Altman for Best Director and a raft of other awards from film critics' societies and festivals – but the critical response tended to be mixed at best. Altman's perennial champion, Roger Ebert, awarded the film a perfect score (four stars out of four) and commended Altman on his fidelity to Carver's existentialist vision, albeit transplanted to Southern California: 'Los Angeles always seems to be waiting for something. Permanence seems out of reach; some great apocalyptic event is on the horizon, and people view the future tentatively. Robert Altman's *Short Cuts* captures that uneasiness perfectly in its interlocking stories about people who seem trapped in the present, always juggling' (1993: n.p.). While *Variety*'s Todd McCarthy praised Altman's narrative virtuosity – 'Most films have trouble enough telling one story, but Altman makes juggling a trunk load of them seem easy' – he nonetheless observed that 'there are ways in which the film comes up short. Some uncomfortable traces of condescension toward the characters creep in, and the film may not be as funny as it sometimes strives to be' (1993: n.p.). *Washington Post* senior film critic Desson Howe also mixed condemnation with praise: 'Altman does such an impressive directorial job, it cloaks the thematic (and often mean-spirited) emptiness in the film [yet] *Short Cuts* [remains] head and shoulders above most of the competition' (1993: 50). Rita Kempley, Howe's colleague at *The Washington Post*, published a rejoinder review the same day. Kempley detested the film and blasted it as 'a cynical, sexist and shallow work from cinema's premier misanthrope, Robert Altman, who here shows neither compassion for – nor insight into – the human condition' (1993: C1). Equally damning was Robert Coles' *New York Times* review. Long an admirer and teacher of Carver's work, the esteemed Harvard-based child psychologist dismissed *Short Cuts* as 'a movie full of male swagger, with women always at the edge of things; a movie that lacks Carver's gentle humor and prompts laughter at people; a movie stripped bare of human ambiguity; a movie relentless in its cynical, sardonic assault on anyone and everyone, as if America itself is beyond the pale morally and psychologically; a movie in which gruff, smug detachment keeps clubbing empathy over the head. Alas, that last attitude (to be cool, cool, cool) has been noted by some reviewers with no great alarm' (1993: 25).

While critics tended to respond to *Short Cuts* in impressionistic and visceral ways, the most penetrating and systematic analyses of the film's weaknesses (or at least debatable aesthetic strategies) belong to film scholars Daniel O'Brien, Kasia Boddy and Pamela Demory. O'Brien's critique of *Short Cuts* is essentially stylistic. He rightly notes that Altman 'overplays his camera technique at times, as when he zooms in on the injured Casey's untouched glass of milk, then cuts and zooms out from the image of a spilled glass of milk playing on the Piggot's television (part of a safety commercial)' (1995: 124). He cites Altman's heavy-handedness in other scenes while also arguing that many of the film's set pieces suffer from a 'lack of development or resolution (or even a point of view)' (1995: 125).

Kasia Boddy's critique is both aesthetic and ideological in character. She calls into question Altman's first premise: the notion that Carver's writings are 'just one story', i.e. a cohesive body of work susceptible to homogenising adaptation strategies: 'Altman's making "soup" from Carver's discrete and diverse short stories denies the importance the fragmentary form plays in Carver's work, and so inevitably results in a distortion of that work. This disturbance, moreover, is not simply formal. The change in medium is bound up with highly significant shifts in location, class, and sexual politics' (2000: 9). As regards setting, Boddy acknowledges that Carver himself invited geographic transposition of his work when he affirmed that his stories could 'take place anywhere' because human behaviour, at least the modern American variety, is predictably uniform. What Carver's work doesn't allow for, argues Boddy, is Altman's shift from the countryside to the metropolis: a shift that radically alters the nature of spatial and social relations. Boddy also notes that Los Angeles is a city uniquely mediated, noisy, competitive and socially self-conscious: a far cry from 'Carver Country [which] is not frenetic like LA – in fact no one talks much at all' (2000: 13). Changes in setting would seem to necessitate some changes in social status as rural working-class folk morph into middle- and upper-middle-class suburbanites but Boddy sees these changes as a matter of differing sensibilities. She rightly notes that 'Altman is not interested in the tediously anxious life of the unemployed and poor'; accordingly Carver's characters are given 'more glamorous, more "idiosyncratic" lives' (2000: 15). Stormy Weathers is unemployed in the Carver story but a helicopter pilot in the film. Bill, a machine parts salesman in 'Neighbors', becomes a make-up artist in the movie. Ralph and Marian Wyman are high-school teachers in Carver's world but a physician and an artist in Altman's. In fairness to Altman, though, at seven or eight of the movie's main characters remain more or less blue collar: the Kanes, the Piggots and the Kaisers, the vacuum cleaner salesman, even Andy Bitkower, the baker who is self-employed but working 'sixteen hours a day to make ends meet'. Boddy also doesn't account for changes in temporal setting; America in 1992–93 was a considerably more prosperous and hedonistic culture than it had been in the 1970s, when Carver wrote most of the source stories. Boddy is on firmer ground when she takes Altman to task for his foregrounding sexual violence, a concern which usually remains 'a latent tension' in Carver's stories (2000: 17).

Feminist film scholar Pamela Demory supplements Boddy's critique of Altman's sexual politics by arguing, à la Laura Mulvey, that Short Cuts 'contains a pervasive pattern of female nudity and a preoccupation with the activity of looking' at women's bodies with an objectifying gaze (1999: 96). Demory goes on to observe that the 'film's nudity – and its self-conscious treatment of that nudity – does contribute to several thematic strains that originate in Carver's stories – voyeurism, gender-role stereotypes, marital and sexual conflicts of various sorts. But nudity itself (except for the dead woman in the river) does not' (1999: 102). Recalling the sexual humiliations that Altman heaped upon 'Hot Lips' Houlihan in M*A*S*H as evidence of his longstanding misogyny, Demory, Rita Kempley and other feminist critics were apt to find Short Cuts a textbook example of white male heterosexual cinematic entitlement run amok: a view that is difficult to refute prima facie but one that needs to be put into perspective by noting that the film's more pervasive focus is on men behaving badly. Ironically, the it's bitterest detractor, Rita Kempley, offered an important critical insight by noting that the central preoccupation of Short Cuts isn't misogynistic sex and violence per se but the pervasiveness of narcissism in American society: 'Short Cuts is about not noticing the important things in life – the wife, kids, family pets and the occasional corpse. Essentially, it blames self-absorption for the collapse of Western civilization' (1993: C4).

For critics like Robert Coles and Rita Kempley, Short Cuts was bombastic and mean-spirited, a cynical and sexist distortion of its source material, but this debatable perspective unnecessarily forecloses the movie's strengths as social critique. In 1993 perhaps only admirers of the work of Christopher Lasch were willing to see that America's pandemic of self-centredness had grown appreciably worse since Lasch's ground-breaking analysis (Culture of Narcissism) in 1979 and that Short Cuts was offering a valid depiction of that phenomenon. Now, decades later, Altman's unforgiving view of postmodern America as intensively privatised and fragmented Gesellschaft breeding high levels of social indifference and casual violence looks both tame and prophetic. At any rate, Altman himself was unfazed by the controversy. In an interview with Cathy Horyn for the Washington Post shortly after the film's release, he responded to Coles' critique by rightly noting that Coles was 'someone who doesn't have a knowledge of the difference between literature and film'. He continued:

I'm not doing a literal translation of Carver, nor did I ever say I was going to. If anything, the film is a reflection not just of my interpretation, but of those of a hundred other people who worked on it. We were all responding to the material… The suggestion has been made that we – my collaborator Frank Barhydt and myself – could have drawn more conclusions. Well, many of Carver's pieces are more like news stories. He tells what happened and he makes no comment. We tried to do the same thing. But you know, so what? We're not saying this film is anything other than what it is. So, maybe all I can say in response to Coles is, "Tsk, tsk, I wish he had got it". (1993: G-1)

Altman found his staunchest ally in Raymond Carver's widow, Tess Gallagher, who collaborated with him on script revisions and repeatedly defended him and the film in public against charges of cynicism or aesthetic malfeasance.

Notes

1   See *Film as Fine Art* [special feature of the MGM DVD edition].
2   After failed attempts to study theology and become a pastor, van Gogh took a temporary post as a missionary in the village of Petit Wasmes in the coal-mining district of Borinage in Belgium. His identification with his flock, expressed in self-imposed poverty of the harshest sort, scandalised his superiors and led to his dismissal.
3   Van Gogh visited Mesdag's Panorama in August 1881 with friend and fellow artist Théophile de Bock, just as it opened to the public and six months before he met Sien Hoornik; see http://www.vangoghletters.org/vg/letters/let171/letter.html
4   Once again Altman takes poetic license. Biographical accounts indicate that after he shot himself van Gogh returned home after dark, unnoticed. To maximise dramatic effect, Altman has a bevy of startled crows fly away when van Gogh shoots himself and then has him walk back to Auvers, bleeding profusely, in broad daylight.
5   In the script, the stalker, in another car, shoots at Mill while he's driving. Altman's rattlesnake in a cooler ploy is more eerily believable and also nicely self-reflexive, referring to his 1982 production of Frank South's eponymous play.
6   Jennifer Jason Leigh diligently researched her role by visiting five different phone-sex operators in the Los Angeles area, observing them while they worked and taking notes on their dialogues. She also discovered that phone-sex operators were able to multitask, doing routine chores while pretending to be intimately engaged with their callers.

CHAPTER SEVEN

Final Phase: More Large Canvases and Minor Works

The only ending I know of is death.

– Robert Altman

By the time *Short Cuts* was released in October 1993, Altman was 68 years old and in perilously frail health. He had had a stroke in 1992 and was experiencing fatigue, shortness of breath, chest pains and abnormal heart rhythms due to an enlarged left heart ventricle.[1] In sum, Altman was dying from cardiovascular disease brought on by chronic obesity, years of heavy drinking and overwork. Most filmmakers would have opted to retire under such circumstances but Robert Altman was not like most filmmakers. He lived to make movies and would make eight more of them in the remaining thirteen years of his life: a slowing down from his usual film-a-year pace but still a remarkable feat of stubborn will, courage and sheer endurance. Altman's health was dramatically improved by a successful heart transplant in early December 1995 but he was seriously ailing when he made *Prêt-à-Porter* in the spring of 1994 and was gravely ill when he made *Kansas City* a year later: a factor that needs to be entered into the critical calculus when evaluating these films.

Prêt-à-Porter (1994)

In 1956 Altman directed a Calvin Company production of *The Model's Handbook*, a thirteen-minute promotional film that featured Dorian Leigh, a top Ford model, providing beauty and workout tips for aspiring models. The film also offered behind-the-scenes glimpses of the Ford Modeling Agency, for whom it was made (the screenplay was by agency founders Eileen and Jerry Ford who also appear on screen). Altman returned to the subject of fashion twenty-eight years later, with his thirty-first feature film, *Prêt-à-Porter*. The movie had its genesis in September 1984, almost a decade before it was made. Altman and his wife, Kathryn, were in Paris to promote *Streamers* when she dragged him to a fashion show put on by designer Sonia Rykiel. Altman later recalled, 'I really had no interest in going at all, but then the lights went out, the music began, and I thought, "So that's it, it's a circus. I've got to make a film about this!"' (in Thompson 2006: 170). Altman invented characters and situations and hired several writers to develop treatments and scripts but wasn't satisfied with any of them. The property lay fallow until the success of *The Player* in 1992 prompted producer Harvey Weinstein (co-founder of Miramax Films with his brother, Bob) to green-light a development deal, script unseen. Altman asked Barbara Shulgasser, a film critic for the *San Francisco Examiner* whom he met in 1990, to write a fashion show screenplay 'on spec' (i.e. unpaid). In March 1992 Altman and Shulgasser flew to Paris to attend the spring fashion shows. They worked on the script on the plane, discarding the main plot and devising a substitute (see Shulgasser 1994: 175). Though he hadn't read the screenplay himself, Altman sent it to Miramax on the assumption that the Weinstein brothers would cancel the project once they read it. A year later (May 1993) Miramax informed Altman that they loved the script, so he decided to go ahead. His son Stephen recalls Altman saying, 'Let's just do it. We'll make it up as we go along' – which is exactly what they did (in Zuckoff 2009: 442). Pre-production activities – location scouting, casting and script revisions – began in earnest in October 1993 and continued until shooting began the following March, during the spring iteration of Paris Fashion Week, so that Altman could incorporate genuine *haute couture* runway shows, fashion designers and top models into the film, to lend his movie authenticity and provide glamour and star-gazing appeal, as he had done in the Hollywood context with *The Player*. Altman finally read Shulgasser's revised script a year-and-a-half after Shulgasser first sent it to him.

Conceived as another large scale, multi-protagonist mosaic – a half-dozen storylines involving thirty-two cast members, with five real fashion designers, ten real supermodels and fourteen celebrity cameos (mostly other designers) also featured – *Prêt-à-Porter* echoes the celebrity-studded carnival of *The Player* but actually bears closer resemblance to *Nashville* in its more diffuse depiction of the interpersonal and careerist machinations driving a popular culture industry that is all business behind the show business spectacle. While Paris Fashion Week provides the requisite spatial-temporal unities that lend Altman's many-ringed 'circus' an overall sense of coherence, he adds (actually feigns) an overarching intrigue plot involving a putative murder, to infuse some mild sense of suspense and ersatz gravitas into the proceedings. Altman also supplies a kind of tour guide (termed a 'commentator' by Helene Keyssar), a character defined by Maria del Mar Azcona as 'usually a newcomer or outsider to the group or the professional sector under scrutiny who shares the viewer's initial feeling of disorientation as in the case of Opal (Geraldine Chaplin), the inquisitive BBC reporter in *Nashville*' (2011: 145). The 'tour guide' for *Prêt-à-Porter* is Kitty Potter (Kim Basinger), a drawling, dim-witted reporter for FAD-TV (a mythical entertainment programme) who bears a more than passing resemblance to Mary Hart, the host of the syndicated gossip and entertainment round-up programme, *Entertainment Tonight*.

Prêt-à-Porter's 23-minute opening sequence is a multi-character arrival montage that echoes similar opening arrival montages in *Nashville* and *HealtH* but this one also features a red herring: Altman's perennial warning to viewers that conventions will not be followed and things are not what they seem. Sergei (aka Sergio) (Marcello Mastroianni), an Italian tailor, is shown buying two identical neckties at what viewers assume to be a Paris outlet of Christian Dior. When he leaves the store and walks along a city street, the following shot reveals the 'actual' locale: Moscow's Red Square. The film's title and Altman's name are superimposed on the screen in indecipherable Cyrillic script and disoriented viewers wonder for a moment if they're watching the wrong film. Just as suddenly, though, screen credits in English list the expected cast members, the camera whirls around and around 360 degrees, and the setting changes to Paris. The implicit suggestion here, just two years after the dissolution of the Soviet Union, is that decadent consumer capitalism epitomised by *haute couture* now reigns supreme, even in Russia – though in point of fact Christian Dior did not open a boutique in Moscow until 1998 (see Anon. 1998: n.p.). Olivier de la Fontaine (Jean-Pierre Cassel), president of the Fédération Française de la Couture (French Fashion Council), receives a package at home containing one of the ties Sergei purchased in Moscow and a letter with rendezvous instructions. After being cursed by his wife, Isabella (Sophia Loren), evidently for infidelity, he puts on the tie, but not before stepping in excrement left by Isabella's Bichon Frisé – the first of a number of similar (and increasingly tired) sight gags spoofing Paris's infamous dog waste problem. A television set in Olivier's dressing room shows Kitty Potter, on camera at the Carrousel de Louvre (an underground shopping mall), introducing a behind-the-scenes episode of Paris Fashion Week for her FAD TV show, *On the Scene*. Potter's vapid, cliché-ridden commentary ('The only rule is that there are no rules!') skewers the celebrity-fawning inanities of *Entertainment Tonight*. When she questions real fashion designer Thierry Mugler about the sexism implicit in the overt sexuality of his designs, he disarmingly replies, 'Well, it's all about looking good, helping the silhouette. And it's all about getting a great fuck, honey!' – a moment of subversive candour that would, of course, never get on American television. A brief scene spoofs Fashion Week from another angle as it shows Isabella de la Fontaine entering her pampered pet dog in a *prêt-à-porter* fashion show for canines. Olivier visits his mistress, designer Simone Lowenthal (Anouk Aimée), before meeting Sergei, arriving from Moscow at Charles de Gaulle Airport. The airport is also where Kitty Potter greets and interviews Olivier, per chance, and arriving fashion magazine editors dubbed 'the Paris Troika': Sissy Wanamaker (Sally Kellerman) of *Harper's Bizarre*, Nina Scant (Tracey Ullman) of British *Vogue* and Regina Krumm (Linda Hunt) of *Elle* – allegedly based on fashion editors Liz Tiberis, Alexandra Schulman and Suzy Menkes (see Thompson 2006: 171). Other arrivals include Slim Chrysler (Lauren Bacall), an aging, colour-blind fashionista (supposedly based on Diana Vreeland); Clint Lammeraux (Lyle Lovett), Texas high-fashion cowboy boot entrepreneur; Anne Eisenhower (Julia Roberts), a reporter with the *Houston Chronicle, sans* her suitcase (inadvertently left behind at the airport bar in Houston); Milo O'Brannigan (Stephen Rea), a 'hot' but arrogant Irish fashion photographer always wearing sunglasses, even at night, supposedly based on photographer Steven Meisel (ibid.). Brief cross-cut scenes featuring rival gay fashion designers Cy Bianco (Forest Whitaker) and Cort Romney (Richard E. Grant) give way to Olivier de la Fontaine and Sergei sitting out a traffic jam – an allusion to the airport exit traffic jam scene in *Nashville* – in the back seat of Olivier's limo on the Champs-Élysées as they return to Paris. Suddenly, Olivier dies while eating a ham sandwich. A bewildered Sergei flees the limo, vaults over idling vehicles, and then jumps off the Pont Alexandre III into the Seine, to evade arrest and interrogation – but not before being photographed, long distance, by Fiona Ulrich (Lily Taylor): another red herring because the photographs do not lead to an identification. Sergei/Sergio will haunt subsequent events as an anonymous fugitive, just as Olivier's demise – conspicuously unmourned by his widow and everyone else who knew him, except his mistress – will subtly taint Paris Fashion Week with a scent of disease in much the same way that Nettie Sloan's death stigmatises subsequent nuptial festivities in *A Wedding*.

The next sequence, ten minutes in length, takes place at Paris's Le Grand Hotel, where many of the out-of-town participants in Paris Fashion Week are staying. What might be termed the check-in mix-up montage involves three sets of couples, one accidental, one covert and one platonic. Joe Flynn (Tim Robbins), an American sports reporter for the *Washington Post*, is checking out when he receives a phone call from the home office instructing him to stay on and report developments related to the death of Olivier de la Fontaine. Anne Eisenhower checks into the room that Flynn has supposedly just vacated but he refuses to check out. While they vie for the same room, a lurking Sergei – the movie's mysterious wild card figure – steals Flynn's suitcase, putting him in the same, vulnerable position as Anne Eisenhower: without spare clothes at a festival that is the ultimate celebration of clothing. Both refuse to relinquish the room, so they both stay in it: an awkward situation that soon develops into a cloistered, nonstop sexual fling – a scenario somewhat reminiscent of Frank Capra's screwball comedy, *It Happened One Night* (1934) but without the wholesome romance of that bygone era. In another vignette, Marshall Fields fashion buyer Major Hamilton (Danny Aiello) discovers that his wife, Louise Hamilton (Terri Garr), has left a pair of her panties in his suitcase. He calls her at the Hotel Splendid to tell her to be more careful or she'll blow his cover (he is later revealed to be a transvestite who wants to conceal the fact that he is married). In yet another vignette, Nina Scant and Regina Krumm are accidentally assigned each other's adjacent suites (the 'Faust Suite' and the 'Salomé Suite') but soon rectify the mistake. Robert T. Self discerns deep symbolic significance in the allusion to Faust and Salomé, ancient tales that embrace 'two cultural codes, two mythic paradigms, whose generic force identifies key ideological issues in the film. On the one hand, the Faustian exchange of one's soul for knowledge reflects a sense of identity as a power transaction that involves short-term gain and long-term loss. On the other, the feminine dance of multilayered fashion and sensuality aims to procure the head and silence the voice of male prophecy' (2002: 228). An alternate reading might note that the movie *conflates* the devil's bargain motif evoked by Faust with the feminine mystique motif evoked by Salomé, insofar as Scant and Krumm (Beckettian names that suggest impoverished identities) are two fashionistas essentially interchangeable. Indeed, they allude to the fact that the same hotel room mix-up has happened to them before. Thus the vignette constructs a kind of allegorical axiom: high fashion's Salomé business – narcissistic preening for purposes of social status posturing and sexual seduction – is a soul-nullifying pact with the devil but one that involves no Faustian aspirations toward higher knowledge. Indeed, the solemnity of the suite names mocks the paltry nature of their occupants.

The long (ninety minutes) middle part of the film tracks various intrigues among the fashion moguls, designers, editors, photographers and models and the theme that predominates over all other themes (competition, display, deception) is *betrayal*: the human tendency most naturally arising from Gesellschaft, where, as Ferdinand Tönnies points out, 'everybody is by himself and isolated, and there exists a condition of tension against all others' (2001: 65). While the dizzying proliferation of short scenes rapidly crosscut between the various fictional storylines, actual runway shows and Kitty Potter's interviews with real designers may have looked sloppy and chaotic to many viewers and critics, the sheer welter Altman creates formally enacts the fragmentary and frenetic character of postmodern Gesellschaft's war of all against all. Here, once again, is the picture of a fast-paced, hyper-competitive society dedicated to conspicuous consumption and bereft of real community. Accordingly, British designer Cort Romney and his wife, Violetta (Anne Canovas) compete head-to-head with Cy Bianco and Reggie (Tom Novembre), his assistant and lover. In the end, the success both designers achieve is spoiled when their clandestine affair with each other is accidentally revealed to their partners, as is the affair their partners are having with each other: betrayal squared. The three fashion editors compete with each other to secure the exclusive services of Milo O'Brannigan but he betrays all three in turn by photographing them in humiliating circumstances. In the end, though, Sissy Wanamaker betrays Milo by stealing his valuable photo negatives. Jack Lowenthal (Rupert Everett), Simone's son, is scheming to betray his mother by selling the business to Clint Lammeraux. He is also betraying his wife, supermodel Dane Simpson (Georgianna Robertson), by having an affair with her sister, Kiki (Tara Leon). A comical form of betrayal occurs when it finally becomes clear why Sergei/Sergio came to Paris – to win back Isabella de la Fontaine, the love of his life he abandoned forty-two years earlier to pursue the life of a communist in Moscow. When Sergei and Isabella finally get together in a hotel room to consummate their long-lost love, Isabella begins to perform a striptease to arouse him but Sergei 'betrays' her by promptly falling asleep – spoofing a similar moment portrayed by both actors in Vittorio de Sica's *Ieri, oggi, domain* (*Yesterday, Today, and Tomorrow*, 1963) when they were thirty years younger. Altman mildly betrays audience expectations when an autopsy reveals that Olivier de la Fontaine was not 'murdered' at all but merely choked to death on his ham sandwich. Finally, in the film's *dénouement*, Simone Lowenthal betrays the pretentious world of high fashion to the wider world when she stages her climactic show: a bevy of models strutting around the runway completely nude – an 'emperor's new clothes' spectacle met at first with respectful silence by the show's puzzled audience, then with a thunderous standing ovation. The only one who doesn't get the joke is Kitty Potter, who tries to put the best face on Simone Lo's stunt but finally concedes defeat: 'What the hell am I talking about? I mean, crissakes, what's going on? Can you tell me what's going on? This is fucking fruitcake time! I mean, is that fashion? I mean, is there a message out there? You got a lot of naked people wandering around here. I mean, I've been forever trying to find what this bullshit is all about. You know what? I have had it! I have had it! Goodbye. Au revoir.' Kitty hands over her microphone to her European assistant, Sophie Choiset (Chiara Mastroianni) and quits the scene.

The film concludes with an allegorical scene that emphasises the biological-existential reality of the human body – which is born, lives, ages and dies in contradistinction to its inert, idealised representations in fashion advertising. Thus, Olivier de la Fontaine's funeral procession is shown proceeding past Sergio waking from a hard night's sleep on a Paris park bench (and gazing wistfully at Isabella as she passes by). Also occurring in the same park is a Milo O'Brannigan fashion photo shoot involving naked babies placed in front of a Trussardi billboard advertisement that depicts a pair of post-coital lovers, naked but demurely shot from the waist up. The ad's pretentious caption – 'Get real!' – is an admonition that the scene ironically actualises.

Released just before Christmas in 1994 in the US, *Prêt-à-Porter* did poorly at the box office despite an expensive promotional campaign; it cost more than $17 million to make but brought in only $11.3 million in ticket receipts. It also fared poorly with most reviewers. Janet Maslin, film critic for *The New York Times*, expressed the general critical consensus when she observed that Altman's 'laissez-faire satirical style prove[d] ineffectual for shooting fish in this barrel. Fashion is too self-conscious to be skewered so casually. It's more willfully absurd than the worlds of film (*The Player*), country music (*Nashville*) or campaign politics (*Tanner '88*), and it calls for a sharp scalpel. Yet this time Mr. Altman, such a stunningly intuitive portraitist when he truly plumbs the mysteries that guide his characters, works without inventiveness and with glaring nonchalance' (1994: C1). Maslin went on to note that *Prêt-à-Porter* has 'no narrative. There are only several dozen characters who cross paths or echo one another's amusing actions' (1994: C10). Maslin's criticisms are valid; though it contains some stunning visual imagery, a pulsating pop music soundtrack, and a number of amusing set pieces, *Prêt-à-Porter* suffers from excessive narrative diffusion that reduces characterisation to caricature – disintegrative dissemination not present in *Nashville* because that film managed a more defined narrative arc and thematic focus. Much like *A Wedding*, *Prêt-à-Porter*'s earnest striving for easy laughs – too many of which are tasteless sexual jibes – dilutes its satiric bite, making for an inconsequential farce that ultimately neither celebrates nor critiques its subject.

Kansas City (1996)

In his director's commentary to the DVD edition of *Kansas City*, Altman recalls telling Frank Barhydt, fellow Kansas City native and frequent collaborator with whom he was working on *Tanner '88*, that he wanted 'to do a story about Kansas City, the jazz period, the Thirties, gangsters, that kind of culture'. Though Altman didn't admit it, a nostalgic return to the world of his youth was obviously a kind of swan song; not the end exactly – he would recover his health and make many more films – but the beginning of the end. The opportunity to actually make such a picture presented itself at the Cannes Film Festival in 1992. While Altman was basking in the success of *The Player*, he was approached by Ciby 2000, a French art-house production/distribution company founded in 1990 by Francis Bouygues that had Jane Campion's *The Piano* (1993) in development and offered to make anything Altman had in mind. Altman mentioned his Kansas City movie idea and a $16 million production deal was forged, *sans* screenplay, which Altman and Barhydt proceeded to write after *Prêt-à-Porter* wrapped on 18 May 1994.

Barhydt and Altman obviously researched the era they were writing about. Their script (originally entitled 'Blondie'), which concerns a rather far-fetched kidnapping caper, is set against the backdrop of Kansas City's 1934 mayoral election. On 27 March of that year, Bryce B. Smith – the candidate sponsored by Tom Pendergast, the county's powerful and unutterably corrupt Democratic machine boss – would be reelected to a second term in a contest that proved to be the most crooked and violent in the city's history, one marked by massive, overt vote fraud. Vagrants were trucked in from out of town and paid to vote repeatedly, using names culled from local cemeteries, while Pendergast's hired thugs intimidated or assaulted scores of election officials, reporters and voters. They also murdered four election workers on the city's east side. Albert Ross Hill, the reformist candidate running for mayor against Smith, warned Governor Guy Park (another Pendergast crony) that election violence was inevitable. Hill called for National Guard intervention but Park predictably did nothing. The resulting chaos at the polls scandalised the nation and marked the gradual decline of machine politics in Kansas City (Pendergast was finally toppled from power in 1939 and spent two years in prison for income tax evasion).

While it lasted, Boss Pendergast's rule over municipal politics spilled over into daily life, making Kansas City one of the most corrupt and lawless cities in America in the 1930s. Organised crime, particularly prostitution and gambling, was rampant but the prosperous, wide-open nature of life in KC also had its salutary consequences. Payoffs and kickbacks to Pendergast's political machine kept the city's countless brothels, nightclubs and gambling halls open all night and an already lively jazz scene thrived. Musicians, black and white, flocked to Kansas City – a major regional railway hub – where decent jobs were plentiful in an otherwise barren economic landscape. In their wake followed dancers, whores, revelers, gamblers, grifters and jazz aficionados. Business legal and otherwise boomed, making Kansas City largely immune from the effects of the Great Depression. This was the city that Altman, born in 1925, knew as a schoolboy. He heard stories of crime and decadence but it was Kansas City's African-American jazz music scene that had the greatest impact on him. By the late 1930s, Altman was going to 'a whole lot of jazz clubs just up and down Twelfth Street' (in Zuckoff 2009: 447). As he told David Thompson, 'Though we were white kids in a black venue, we were treated well. I felt very accepted by the black community' (2006: 177).

In sum, the constellation of the four elements just enumerated – politics, crime, race and music – made Kansas City a uniquely vibrant microcosm of Depression-era America in all its contradictory glory. These are the elements that Altman and Barhydt attempted to fuse together in order to ground their script in the appropriate period ambience. As was always the case with Altman, the musical element was of particular importance. Indeed, Altman later spoke of envisioning '*Kansas City* like a musical piece, a fugue, with each character represented by an instrument. Harry Belafonte was the trumpet, Dermot Mulroney was the trombone, Jennifer Jason Leigh and Miranda Richardson were tenor saxophones doing a duet, and in a way their dialogue was like variations on a theme that didn't have too much to do with advancing the plot' (in Thompson 2006: 178). For actual music, the movie features top musicians in period garb re-creating Count Basie's orchestra and guest artists during Basie's Kansas City years, when he fronted his own band or performed with Bennie Moten: saxophonists Lester Young (Joshua Redman), Coleman Hawkins (Craig Handy), Herschel Evans (David Murray) and Ben Webster (James Carter); pianists Basie (Cyrus Chestnut) and Mary Lou Williams (Geri Allen); guitarist Freddie Green (Mark Whitfield) and bassist Walter Page (Ron Carter). As Morris Holbrook puts it, 'an exceedingly impressive roster of major jazz talent plays full time 'round-the-clock jazz on a 24/7/365 basis in a kind of perpetual musical nirvana, more or less oblivious to the vile corruption that surrounds them on all sides' (2011: 162). If this were not enough, an extended scene midway through the film depicts tenor sax players Lester Young and Coleman Hawkins engaging in a 'cutting contest', testing each other's improvisatory skills – a legendary battle of titans that evidently occurred in Kansas City in December 1933 (see Gabbard 2000: 148). In the movie all of this takes place at the Hey Hey Club on 18th Street, owned and operated by Seldom Seen (Harry Belafonte), the city's premier black gangster, a character based on a real person: Ivory Johnson, aka Seldom Seen (1893–1985), a dapper Kansas City gangster who ran gambling houses and bordellos (see Rice and Schofield 1995). The club is named after an actual Kansas City jazz venue – a former feed barn on 4th and Cherry Streets called the Hey Hay Club – but according to Krin Gabbard, the establishment in the movie is 'probably a composite of the city's better known clubs, especially the Reno' [at 602 E. 12th Street, between Cherry and Holmes, and known as the 'Queen' of Kansas City nightclubs] (2000: 144). Altman also inserts Charlie Parker, aka 'Bird' (Albert J. Burnes) into the picture, the legendary saxophonist who was a Kansas City native. As depicted in the film, Parker was thirteen years old in the spring of 1934, playing horn in the city's Lincoln High School Marching Band, and learning his craft by listening to jazz musicians at various clubs in the city. Parker's mother, Addie (Jeff Feringa) is also given a prominent place in the plot. A night-shift cleaning lady at Western Union at Union Station in the movie (as she was in real life), Addie is therefore acquainted with the film's protagonist, Blondie O'Hara (Jennifer Jason Leigh), who works as a telegrapher at the same office. Blondie enlists Addie in her machinations, so some of the action takes place at the Parkers' boardinghouse, filmed at a house near the actual one at 1516 Olive Street, which was no longer extant when the film was made. The movie also provides young Charlie Parker with a love interest, Pearl Cummings (Ajia Mignon Johnson). A pregnant teenage girl who has come to Kansas City to have her baby at a home for unwed mothers, Pearl is loosely based on Rebecca Ruffin, a 17-year-old in 1934 who was not pregnant but boarding with the Parkers with her divorced mother and siblings and would become Charlie's first wife in 1936 (see Woideck 1998: 5).

As for the kidnapping plot, Altman and Barhydt adapted it from an actual incident. On 27 May 1933 four amateur kidnappers, masked and armed with a shotgun,
abducted Mary McElroy, the 25-year-old opium-addicted daughter of Henry McElroy,
Kansas City's City Manager, from her father's home. When a $30,000 ransom was
paid, Mary McElroy was released unharmed after twenty-nine hours in captivity. Her
kidnappers were later caught, tried and sentenced to life in prison amidst frenzied
media coverage. In the film, Mary McElroy becomes Carolyn Stilton (Miranda Richardson), the unloved, laudanum-addicted wife of Henry Stilton (Michael Murphy),
an advisor to President Roosevelt.[2] The four male kidnappers are transformed into one
female kidnapper in the movie: Blondie O'Hara, who resorts to abduction when her
husband, a dim-witted hoodlum named Johnny 'Guts' O'Hara (Dermot Mulroney)
is captured and threatened with death by Seldom Seen and his henchmen. O'Hara's
offence: in collusion with a black cab driver named 'Blue' Green (Martin Martin), he
has posed in blackface to rob one of Seldom's out-of-town clients, Sheepshan Red (A.
C. Smith) of a cash-stuffed money belt. On pre-election night (i.e. 26 March 1934,
though no specific date is designated until later in the film), Blondie goes to the Hey
Hey Club to appeal to Seldom Seen to release her husband. He refuses and has her
bodily ejected from the building, kicking and screaming. Left with little recourse,
Blondie decides to kidnap Carolyn Stilton at gunpoint in order to force her powerful
husband to intervene and win Johnny O'Hara's release. Blondie's plan encounters a
snag, though, when she learns that Henry Stilton is on a train headed for Washington,
DC. She takes Carolyn Stilton to Kansas City's Union Station, momentarily leaves
her with Addie Parker in an adjoining office and proceeds to send a Western Union
telegram to Henry Stilton on the train with instructions to contact her.

Blondie's hare-brained scheme is obviously derived from the movies, which is also
the source of her entire persona. As Altman points out in his director's commentary:
'This poor little girl was acting like [the starlets] she had seen in the movies and she
was behaving in that manner. She "was" Jean Harlow [a Kansas City native]. So she
was in her own life trying to be that character, finally dyed her hair so she looked like
[Harlow].' As he had done in his other Depression-era crime film, *Thieves Like Us*,
Altman dramatises the interpellative power of the mass culture industry in shaping the
identities and dispositions of ordinary Americans. In *Kansas City* these indoctrinated
structures of feeling also manifest as white racist attitudes and assumptions – ideology
deftly skewered by Harry Belafonte, who wrote all his own dialogue as Seldom Seen.
In a scene in the backroom of the Hey Hey Club, Seldom berates 'Blue' Green for
degrading himself by conspiring with a white man against his own people. Seldom
then turns on Johnny O'Hara, castigating him for assuming that black people are
simpletons who could be easily fooled by the blackface disguise that O'Hara donned
to commit the robbery: 'You come swinging in here like Tarzan right in the middle
of a sea of niggers, like you're in a picture show.' Seldom then asks Johnny if he likes
picture shows. When Johnny replies that he 'can take 'em or leave 'em', Seldom says, 'I
recommend you leave 'em after what they done to your ass with all that Hambone and
Stepin Fetchit shit.' Seldom then goes on to denounce radio as well, citing the wildly
popular *Amos 'n' Andy* programme (featuring two white actors portraying drawling,

dim-witted black men for laughs) as another major purveyor of racist stereotypes that have nothing to do with reality. He concludes: 'Movies and radio: white people just sittin' around all day, thinkin' up that shit – and then they believe it!'

Appropriately, the movie segues to Blondie taking Carolyn to a Jean Harlow/Clark Gable picture while she waits for her wire to catch up with Henry Stilton. The picture, which Blondie has seen repeatedly, is *Hold Your Man* (1933), an absurdly contrived crime melodrama that romanticises an otherwise cynical woman's undying love for a small-time criminal: a plot close to her own story and just the kind of pseudo-righteous romance pablum that Blondie feeds upon to justify her misplaced loyalty to Johnny O'Hara. Blondie reluctantly leaves the movie, Carolyn in tow, to phone Henry from a payphone in the theatre lobby. She explains the situation, makes her demands, and puts Carolyn on the phone as evidence of her veracity. A stunned Henry agrees to cooperate, then phones Gov. Guy Park (Cal Pritner) in Jefferson City, Missouri for assistance. Park suggests mobilising the state police but Stilton, fearing the publicity will adversely affect his own political ambitions, insists that countermeasures be pursued surreptitiously, through Italian gangster boss John Lazia (Joe Digirolamo), another Boss Pendergast crony. Thus, Altman neatly ties corrupted government to its negative mirror image in the underworld.

The next sequence details the early morning hours of pre-election night. After arguing about Jean Harlow, whom Blondie idolises but Carolyn considers 'cheap' – a difference of opinion accentuating the social class divide that initially separates them – Blondie runs out of gas. She and Carolyn witness men in careening cars exchanging machinegun fire near the gas station where they go to fill up a gas can: a shootout between Lazia's men and law enforcement, we later learn. Thereafter Blondie takes Carolyn back to Union Station, to spend the night sleeping on a wooden bench in the station's massive Waiting Hall. Adrian Danks observes that the train station stands as 'a symbol of modernity and the vast interlocking networks of transportation lines that enmesh the country and are channeled through Kansas City' (2015: 333): part of a power matrix that dwarfs Blondie and her desperate efforts to affect control over her life. These scenes are crosscut with an extended musical interlude at the Hey Hey Club that features the cutting contest between Lester Young and Coleman Hawkins and a brutal scene in a dark alley, where Seldom Seen and his goons take 'Blue' Green to be executed for his treachery. Seldom's lieutenants surround Green and stab him to death: a ritualised assassination obviously reminiscent of the Roman senators' murder of Julius Caesar – Altman's way of suggesting that gangland slayings have a political dimension; they're about keeping the rabble in line while maintaining reputation with rivals, the same concerns that animate 'legitimate' politics. During the killing, Seldom Seen stands in the foreground of a deep focus shot and nonchalantly tells his driver a tasteless joke about a 'kike', a 'nigger' and a 'cracker' who find a genie's bottle and make a wish. The first two men wish for the repatriation of all 'kikes' and 'niggers' to the Holy Land and Africa respectively, a development the 'cracker' celebrates with *his* wish, for a martini. Seldom's joke, inspired by Marcus Garvey's 'Back to Africa' movement, demonstrates his psychopathic indifference to the murder in progress and reminds viewers of the brutal inter-tribal hostilities that have always been an integral part of American history, shaping Seldom's nihilistic pragmatism and dictating 'Blue' Green's fate.

The next morning – Election Day – Henry Stilton is shown returning to Kansas City from Fort Hamilton, Iowa while machine boss Tom Pendergast is shown voting: a visual juxtaposition that implicitly puts Stilton on the same dubious ethical level as Pendergast. Stilton is, of course, a more refined and respectable species of gangster but is avid to deny the fact, as evidenced by his extreme discomfort when he returns home to find two of Lazia's men already there to offer assistance. He throws them out and phones Lazia to complain. Cut to Blondie taking Carolyn to The Ship (a real bar that was in Kansas City's Bowery district, opened in 1935, razed in 1996, and known for cheap drinks and a rowdy clientele). In the film The Ship is owned by Blondie's mean-spirited brother-in-law, Johnny Flynn (Steve Buscemi), a Pendergast associate who has assembled a platoon of out-of-town derelicts, each of whom will vote 'ten, twelve times' for the candidate they're told to vote for. While Blondie and Carolyn are parked outside, Carolyn naively observes that Flynn has 'got a lot of customers'. Blondie corrects her misapprehension – 'Those aren't customers; those are voters!' – and explains the mechanics of wholesale voter fraud. Surprised, Carolyn asks, 'Democrats do that?' Blondie sagely replies, 'Democrats? They're whatever they're paid to be. This is America, lady': a barely audible throwaway line that constitutes a concise and devastating judgement on the corruption that plagues American 'democracy'. As if the point were not abundantly clear, a moment later Blondie and Carolyn witness Johnny Flynn mercilessly assault one of his unruly 'voters' with a baseball bat. Summoned to The Ship by Flynn who recognises Carolyn, Blondie's sister, Babe Flynn (Brooke Smith) tries to persuade Blondie to abort her kidnapping scheme. Failing that, Babe attempts to call the police but Blondie fires her gun in her sister's direction, curses her, and departs with Carolyn – a glaring example of white family dysfunction, in marked contrast to the Gemeinschaft solidarity we see displayed at the Hey Hey Club and at Addie Parker's house. A series of crosscuts ensue, showing Flynn trucking his voters to a polling place and the jazz musicians at the Hey Hey Club in full swing. When a voting official tries to stop all the illegal voting, he is seized, taken around the corner and shot to death by John Lazia's mafia thugs: a more or less accurate rendition of the historical reality that day. Crosscuts back to the musicians playing their sumptuous jazz suggest that, as artists, they are immune from the political corruption going on all around them – either superior to it or merely oblivious, depending upon one's point of view.

To achieve dramatic focus the final act of the film narrows its attention to its two principal pairings – Blondie and Carolyn; Johnny O'Hara and Seldom Seen – by cross-cutting between them. On Election Day Blondie and Carolyn repair to Addie Parker's boardinghouse – a subaltern counterculture enclave not unlike Mrs. Miller's bordello in *McCabe & Mrs. Miller* – where they can safely hide and get some sleep. As they lie on a bed together in an upstairs bedroom, Blondie trusts Carolyn enough to speak of her love for Johnny: a moment of shared intimacy that signals a growing bond between the two women. In another small but telling vignette, Blondie awakens to find Carolyn already downstairs, asking Addie: 'Are you familiar with the works of

Annie Fellows Johnston? Well, the South that I saw is not at all as she depicted in her novels.' This allusion will fly past most viewers but Johnston (1863–1931) was the prolific author of children's fiction who wrote the popular 'Little Colonel' series, the basis for the Shirley Temple film *The Little Colonel* (1935): another egregious example of the sort of racist propaganda that Seldom Seen denounced earlier in the film. Carolyn's recognition of Johnston's speciousness shows that she is not merely a drug addict but a woman of some intelligence and progressive instinct, i.e. a neglected wife whose opium dependency has more to do with her husband's misogynistic narcissism than with some innate character flaw. Likewise, Altman allows us to see Blondie as more than simply a tough-talking moll who has derived her sense of self from Hollywood gangster movies. When Blondie and Carolyn drive Pearl Cummings to the unwed mothers' home to have her baby, Blondie offers encouragement to Pearl ('I don't know what your story is but you'll do all right'): an expression of genuine empathy and female solidarity that transcend the dominant racist discourse of her day, also a moment of unintentional self-revelation not lost on Carolyn.

On Election Day afternoon Blondie and Carolyn settle in at Blondie's apartment, after Henry Stilton has disingenuously assured Blondie by phone that Johnny will be released unharmed when the polls close that evening. Meanwhile, at the Hey Hey Club, Johnny attempts to persuade Seldom Seen to let him live, arrogantly invoking white privilege by warning Seldom that killing a white man may come back to haunt him. Johnny also tries the opposite tack by offering to be Seldom's 'slave' for life – an inversion of America's racist legacy that Seldom finds grimly amusing, though he remains noncommittal as to Johnny's fate. At Blondie's home Carolyn continues to bond with her captor by helping Blondie dye her hair platinum to better resemble her screen idol Jean Harlow, as she endeavours to turn Johnny's homecoming into the ideal Hollywood ending of her fantasy life. Finally, a car pulls up and Johnny walks through the door but almost immediately collapses. It's an entrance that echoes another sort of Hollywood ending, the fate of Tom Powers (James Cagney) in William A. Wellman's classic gangster movie, *The Public Enemy* (1931), but one, post-Hays Code, that is considerably more graphic and brutal; Johnny's suit jacket falls open to reveal that he's been eviscerated. A hysterical Blondie tries to stop the massive haemorrhaging but Johnny is already dead. When she calls out to Carolyn for help, Carolyn calmly obliges by taking up Blondie's pistol and putting a bullet into the back of her head – a mercy killing, not an act of vengeance, as Carolyn understands that Blondie is broken by Johnny's death and will face the death penalty for kidnapping.

As was the case in *Thieves Like Us* and almost all gangster/crime films, when lumpen individuals turn to crime to try and circumvent the crushing imperatives of the dominant order, they are inevitably annihilated – a 'crime doesn't pay' reaffirmation of the capitalist hegemon that marks the genre as resolutely conservative. Yet Altman problematises the standard ideology with a concluding scene that refuses to fully restore or affirm order to the bourgeois world. Leaving the carnage at the O'Hara home, evidently clear-headed for the first time since her kidnapping began, Carolyn discards her laudanum bottle on the street before she climbs into her husband's waiting limousine. Tellingly, Henry Stilton evinces no joy that his wife has been returned to

No Hollywood ending: Blondie (Jennifer Jason Leigh) realizes that her husband, Johnny 'Guts' O'Hara (Dermot Mulroney) is dead.

him unharmed. The indifference is mutual; Carolyn only stolidly confesses to him that she didn't vote: an anti-climactic utterance considering all she has been through but also tacit notice that she's been politicised by her ordeal, has in effect become the anti-Constance Miller, not succumbing to opium's oblivion but waking up from it. The audience's surrogate, she now knows how the System really works and how the other half really lives – and dies.

Ostensibly an example of a period crime drama with neo-noir overtones, *Kansas City* demolishes the default 'tough guy' race and gender prerequisites of the noir style by featuring a feisty female protagonist battling a powerful African-American gangster and having the latter easily win the contest: a decidedly atypical storyline that makes a clearly progressive ideological statement. Furthermore, the movie's richly textured evocation of 1934 Kansas City culture allows for a degree of semiotic complexity that is the cinematic equivalent of Clifford Geertz's 'thick description', i.e. 'intensive, small-scale, dense descriptions of social life from observation, through which broader cultural interpretations and generalisations can be made' (Scott and Marshall 1998: 761). While other historically grounded fiction films feature the appropriate cars, clothing and hair styles etc, as the backdrop for a generic male hero-protagonist plot, *Kansas City* attempts the far more difficult task of presenting a subversive plotline while re-creating characteristic ideological structures and practices of the place/era and critiquing them, implicitly and explicitly, within the film's diegesis – cultural work never attempted by more conventional neo-noirs. Altman was also aware that he was taking additional risks by foregrounding the music as much as he does: a gambit that further destabilises audience-friendly genre protocols. As he admitted to David Thompson, 'But I think there was a dichotomy in the film: there was too much music for the people who wanted action-melodrama, and too much melodrama for the music fans' (2006: 178).

For all they knew most moviegoers who saw *Kansas City* probably registered its music as vaguely authentic but perhaps too intrusive. Jazz aficionado Morris Holbrook lauds the movie's 'ambi-diegetic cinemusical performances' because they were 'filmed in real time – that is, we see the jazz musicians captured on film *as they are actually playing*, a stupendously worthwhile innovation in jazz filmology that harks back to the work of Bernard Tavernier in *'Round Midnight'* (2011: 164). On the other hand, as Gayle Sherwood Magee notes, jazz purists tended to fault the music as an 'anachronistic hybrid resulting from 1930s standards played by jazz-actors impersonating earlier, famous musicians but in a 1990s style' (2015: 185). As emblematic of this view, Magee quotes a *New York Times* article by Peter Walrous that she characterises as 'perhaps the highest-profile attack on the film's music'; therein Walrous chastises trumpeter Steve Bernstein and music producer Hal Willner for imagining a Kansas City style 'overloaded with riffs and shouting and honking, as if rock-and-roll predated it, not the other way around' (ibid.). However one gauges its degree of stylistic authenticity – and whether or not that's even an important issue is debatable – the jazz music that animates the Hey Hey Club defines the best aspects of Gemeinschaft: a harmonious community dedicated to the life-affirming power of art, but one that also allows for individual exhibitions of innovative ingenuity. As already noted, the music functions as an implicit rebuke to the alienation, corruption and violence that mark the racist American Gesellschaft in which it is embedded and remains the only valuable and enduring legacy of Depression-era Kansas City.

The Gingerbread Man (1998)

In 1991, just before his second novel, *The Firm*, became a runaway bestseller, criminal lawyer-turned-author John Grisham signed a contract with producer Jeremy Tannenbaum's Enchanter Entertainment for an original film script entitled 'The Gingerbread Man', based on an early story he had written. Tannenbaum shopped various iterations of the script around Hollywood for a number of years while Grisham churned out formulaic bestselling legal thrillers that were quickly adapted into a series of blockbuster movies: *The Firm* (Sydney Pollack, 1993), *The Pelican Brief* (Alan J. Pakula, 1993), *The Client* (Joel Schumacher, 1994), *A Time to Kill* (Joel Schumacher, 1996), *The Chamber* (James Foley, 1996) and *The Rainmaker* (Francis Ford Coppola, 1997). In 1996, at the height of Grisham's popularity, Polygram Filmed Entertainment (PFE) purchased 'The Gingerbread Man' as a star vehicle for Shakespearian actor-director-writer-producer Kenneth Branagh, also at the height of his popularity. Paid $4 million and given control over the screenplay and choice of director, Branagh chose Altman, who expressed his usual reservations about the quality of the script which he called 'dreadful' but he wanted to work with Branagh and also 'naughtily hoped [there] might [a] creative collision between him and John Grisham', as Branagh later put it (in Zuckoff 2009: 457). Altman signed on for $4 million after securing an agreement from Branagh that he 'be willing to become a flawed character ... a [Bill] Clinton-like figure who couldn't keep his dick out of trouble' (in Thompson 2006: 181, 182). Altman's collaboration with Branagh would prove to be mutually gratifying but a collaboration with John Grisham did not materialise; Grisham detached himself from the project and, as Altman put it, 'didn't want anything to do with what we made' (in Thompson 2006: 181).

Before and during principal photography (which occurred in the early months of 1997), Altman, Branagh and actor-screenwriter-producer Clyde Hayes (under the pseudonym Al Hayes), re-wrote Grisham's script, which crossed Lawrence Kasdan's *Body Heat* (1981) with J. Lee Thompson's *Cape Fear* (1962), remade by Martin Scorsese in 1991 – a display of the sort of well-worn combinatory logic that Altman satirises in *The Player*. *Body Heat* is an erotic thriller about a libidinous bachelor-lawyer who falls for a beautiful married damsel in distress, in reality a sociopathic *femme fatale* who enlists him as the unwitting fall guy in a scheme to murder her husband for a hefty life insurance payout – a plot borrowed, in turn, from Billy Wilder's noir classic, *Double Indemnity* (1944). Grisham's story differentiates itself from *Body Heat* and *Double Indemnity* by making its lawyer-protagonist a divorced father of two young children who becomes involved with a married woman (falsely claiming to be divorced) who schemes to trick him into killing her father so she and her husband can inherit his estate, valued at $10–15 million. *Cape Fear* concerns a southern lawyer and his family being stalked and terrorised by a vengeful, psychopathic former client. Grisham expropriates the menacing stalker plot from *Cape Fear* and melds it with *Body Heat*'s duped lover plot. In *The Gingerbread Man* the *femme fatale* falsely characterises her harmlessly eccentric father as her demented stalker in order to cast herself as a helpless victim and to set him up for elimination.

Altman retains the general contours of Grisham's derivative scenario but effects his usual changes in characterisation, visual content and tone in order to put an entirely different spin on the grinding plot machinery, one that problematises Grisham's all-too-obvious bourgeois-liberal moralism and moves the film toward very dark neo-noir territory, inflected with horror film stylings. As Branagh later observed, 'I think he was trying to create happenings in the film, to try and capture life in an unexpected way that at the same time worked inside familiar genres ... and subvert those genres. He was not a man who talked about the first act or third act or the story-arc stuff. He didn't want knowable, tangible coherence' (in Zuckoff 2009: 458). Besides making Branagh's character, Rick Magruder, likeable but flawed, Altman subverts the *femme fatale* cliché by making Mallory Doss (Embeth Davidtz) inscrutably neurotic rather than conventionally sexy. Otherwise wan, thin and glum, Mallory is attractive to Rick as an alleged victim who projects an aura of mystery. Evidently striving for a kind of doubling effect, Altman casts Famke Janssen, an Embeth Davidtz lookalike, as Magruder's ex-wife, Leeanne, and turns her into an embittered alcoholic. As for the 'gingerbread man' (i.e. the boogeyman) of the title, Altman casts Robert Duvall as Mallory's semi-feral father, Dixon Doss – a role well suited to an actor famous for playing monomaniacal oddballs (e.g. 'Boo' Radley in *To Kill a Mockingbird* (1962), Lt. Col. Bill Kilgore in *Apocalypse Now*, Mac Sledge in *Tender Mercies* (1983), Euliss 'Sonny' Dewey in *The Apostle* (1997)). Tom Berenger as Mallory Doss's husband, Pete Randle, is another solid bit of casting; his tough guy screen persona, mostly based on his best-known role as Sgt. Barnes in Oliver Stone's *Platoon* (1986), lends him the requisite brawny menace. Robert Downey Jr.'s role, as drunken private detective Clyde Pell, is Altman's only dubious casting choice; though a highly talented actor, Downey exudes a boyish insouciance that seems out of sync with the film's grim ambience – an overall atmosphere that owes much to Scorsese's Grand Guignol version of *Cape Fear*, from which Altman obviously derived inspiration. In *Cape Fear* a full-bore tropical storm on the coast of North Carolina accompanies and magnifies the mortal danger that Sam Bowden (Nick Nolte) and his family face at the hands of their crazed stalker, Max Cady (Robert De Niro) in the film's culminating showdown. Bookended by storms, *The Gingerbread Man* goes *Cape Fear* one better. The movie opens on a night that erupts in heavy rain: graveyard weather that harkens the approach of 'Hurricane Geraldo', a storm not in Grisham's original script that eventually lashes usually sunny Savannah with howling winds and torrential rain, creating a wild aura of darkness and impending doom in keeping with the film's violent climax. By Altman's own admission another and more muted inspiration for him was the fairy tale/nightmare ambience of Charles Laughton's offbeat *The Night of the Hunter* (1955), a southern gothic noir-horror film starring Robert Mitchum as a psychopathic monster menacing a widow and two young children, shot in a distinctively shadowy expressionistic style. Seeking to achieve a similar effect, Altman brought in a foreign cinematographer to interpret the southern milieu with fresh eyes, as he had done with Jean Boffety for *Thieves Like Us* twenty-three years earlier. For *The Gingerbread Man* Altman hired Changwei Gu, the Chinese cameraman who had filmed Chen Kaige's critically acclaimed *Farewell My Concubine* (1993). As Altman told David Thompson, 'I was anxious to get a look that was different, very dark, with little accents of red here and there – [Rick Magruder's] car, his umbrella, his bathroom' (2006: 183). As Tom Dorey notes, 'Altman continues to play with bold reds throughout the film to demarcate deceitfulness' (2015: 408), and he cites Magruder's red vest, the red sheets on Mallory's bed, Magruder's red life vest when he visits Pete Randle on his barge, Mallory's red silk nightgown and numerous other examples. Altman also sought to enhance the general weirdness of mood with a soundtrack that would complement the blustery rain and wind sound effects. But after finding that the synthesised sounds designed by Andrew Allen-King 'would be a little tough on the audience' (in Thompson 2006: 183), Altman used a subtler soundtrack by film composer Mark Isham.

Altman wastes no time defamiliarising the conventional, plot-driven thriller. During the opening title sequence aerial shots of Savannah's convoluted tidal flats form abstract patterns disorientingly difficult to interpret until familiar features hove into view, e.g. trees, a river, finally a highway. A distant aerial following shot picks up Rick's flashy red Mercedes convertible on the highway, traversing this barren landscape – a latter-day Red Cross Knight venturing across the American Wasteland – as he returns to Savannah after a winning a high-profile police misconduct case in Jacksonville, Florida. The win has evidently been an especially big one; Rick's loyal secretary, Lois Harlan (Daryl Hannah) has thrown a surprise party in his honour attended by law firm colleagues, friends and well-wishers. But Rick's world is far from perfect; he exchanges snide remarks with his ex-wife, Leanne, and her boyfriend, ironically also her divorce lawyer, Carl Alden (played by Altman's co-writer, Clyde Hayes). In a celebratory mood but unattached and lonely, Rick drinks too much and comes on to Lois, who gently refuses him. Leaving the party alone at the end of the evening, Rick encounters Mallory Doss, a barely noticed waitress off-duty from Rick's party who has just had her car allegedly stolen. In heavy rain, Rick offers Mallory a ride home and the die is cast. As Altman told David Thompson: 'In the Grisham script, it had the classic beginning with the girl coming into the lawyer's office and saying she's in trouble. We wanted to do something different and show him being sucked into the plot' (2006: 182).

When they arrive at her house on the outskirts of town, aptly described by Steve Vineberg as 'a kind of post-hippie gothic cottage with beaded doorways and creeping patches of refracted light' (2012: n.p.), her car is safely parked outside. Though her car was likely 'stolen' and driven there by Mallory's collusive husband to bait Rick, she blames its brief disappearance on her father, Dixon Doss, whom she describes as a terrifying monster: a version of the archetypal 'Gingerbread Man' not from American folklore (whose Gingerbread Man is just runaway food eventually eaten by a fox). It's Doss's use of the story to frighten his young daughter ('My daddy used to warn me it was just as easy for little children to disappear as it was for Gingerbread Men') that makes him a threatening figure.[3]

Mallory's self-professed victimhood interpellates Rick Magruder as her rescuer: always a tantalising role for the modern knight errant between quests, a role sweetened by Mallory's seductive sexual wiles. The two make love that very night and Rick, egotistically oblivious to the danger signs, gets to have his cake and eat it too; he can savour his moral rectitude as Mallory's supposed rescuer while he savours her body. Though he is unaware of it, Rick has already become deeply entangled in a triangle involving himself, Mallory and Dixon Doss: a cinematic rendition of the sort of 'drama triangle' posited by Transactional Analysis (TA) theorist Stephen Karpman, who uses triangles to model conflicted relationship transactions defined by three roles: Persecutor, Rescuer (the one up position) and Victim (one down position), all of which offer different sorts of psychological 'pay-offs' for their role-players. Karpman, a former member of the Screen Actors Guild, chose the term 'drama triangle' rather the term 'conflict triangle' inasmuch as the Victim in his model is not intended to represent an actual victim, but rather someone feeling or acting like a victim (see Johnson n.d.). In the film, Mallory deploys the usual *modus operandi* of the *femme fatale* by feigning the victim role to bring Rick under her sway and to disguise her real role, as persecutor (of her father). Ricks thinks he's a rescuer but he's actually being positioned as a victim. As Steve Vineberg points out, Altman and Embeth Davidtz make sure that that viewers are conscious of the dangers she poses to Rick: 'When Mallory pulls off her shirt, the strange blue tattoo on her arm suggests either a totem or a warning; we can't be sure which' (n.p.).[4] Vineberg also observes that 'the cat meandering through Mallory's house is likely an intended visual link to that earlier noir, where Elliott Gould's cat disturbs his sleep and finally takes off on him. Gould's Philip Marlowe, clinging to a code of ethics that is as anachronistic in 1970s L.A. as a suit of armor, is one or two steps behind throughout most of the film. Rick Magruder, thinking with his soft heart as well as with his hard-on, misreads every piece of information that comes his way. That is, he reads only the side that's presented to him' (ibid.).

In real life, roles within the Karpman drama triangle shift constantly, to keep the interpersonal turmoil at full boil, *in lieu* of authentic self-confrontation and problem-solving. In the thriller genre, role shifting is in service to a suspense plot designed to maintain and heighten anxious viewer engagement. Taking Mallory's bait hook, line and sinker, Rick goes to court with her to have her father committed to a mental institution, presumably so that Mallory can attain Power of Attorney over him to expropriate his estate. In what Vineberg calls 'an interplanetary episode, darkly comic and very unsettling' (ibid.), Rick and Mallory (and the judge) become persecutors while Dixon Doss is thrust into the victim role – a role that Robert Duvall's long-haired, sullen, menacingly disheveled Doss rejects with angry defiance, as do his derelict apostles in the back of the courtroom – but to no avail; commitment is duly ordered. Enraged by the verdict, Doss momentarily assumes the role of persecutor when he tries to physically attack his daughter and has to be carried from the courtroom. Soon thereafter Doss's cultic friends collectively take on the rescuer role by springing him from the asylum on a dark and stormy night while Altman crosscuts to Mallory in bed with Rick, awaking from a nightmare of her father as the dreaded Gingerbread Man that has haunted her childhood. Once Dixon Doss is at large again, he seems to pursue the persecutor role with a vengeance. Someone, presumably Doss, sends Mallory a photo of herself with the eyes burned out with a cigarette and immediately thereafter her car is torched. Rick tries to enlist the help of the Savannah Police but, feeling persecuted by a high-profile prosecuting attorney who wins police misconduct cases against their kind, they refuse the rescuer role. Rick redoubles that role himself by having Mallory stay with Lois for safety's sake but then, midway through the film, he encounters his own turn at explicit victimhood. A photograph of his two children arrives at his office, their eyes burned out. Filled with mortal terror, Rick assumes another version of the rescuer role by extracting his kids from school – a hasty and ill-advised move that transforms him into a wanted felon because he fails to secure his ex-wife's permission – and, for good measure, strike down a custodian who tries to intervene (making Rick a persecutor on two counts). Now outside the law that once defined his personal and professional identity, Rick drives his children to a remote location to hide them and summons Mallory to join him by bus but while he's on the phone his children disappear from the motel room where he left them. Pitched from would-be rescuer to victim once again, Rick, who is in possession of Mallory's handgun, goes into full panic mode. He picks Mallory up at the bus station and instructs her to direct him to her father's 'old hunting place' in the woods, where he is sure his children are supposedly being held. Prowling the property, Rick is confronted by Doss, who levels a shotgun at him for trespassing. Both men fire their weapons simultaneously but only Doss is hit – a mortal wound to the throat. Some of Doss's associates speed off in a car, presumably with Rick's kids, and Rick jumps in his car to give chase but the police soon cut off both vehicles and Rick learns that his children were not in the car he was chasing but are safe, having been dropped off at the police station by an unidentified co-conspirator. The police take Rick back to Doss's hunting compound, which Mallory has set on fire, and it finally begins to dawn on him that he might be the victim of an elaborate deception – a moment Altman marks with a slow zoom. Rick's suspicions are soon confirmed when he learns the true value of Dixon Doss's land holdings and his hired private detective, Clyde Pell, informs him that Mallory and Pete Randle were never officially divorced.

The closing moments of the film devolve into the standard chase and showdown scenario indispensable to the thriller genre. As Hurricane Geraldo envelops Savannah in dark chaos, Rick follows leads to Pete Randle's barge on the river, discovers Clyde Pell's body, wrapped and weighted for surreptitious burial at sea, and ends up in a life-or-death struggle with Randle when Mallory fires a flare pistol at them. Hit in the back by the projectile, Randle falls dead into the roiling water. Mallory tries to kill Rick too but he manages to lock her in the barge wheelhouse; she is subsequently arrested, convicted of kidnapping and murder, and sent away – after learning from Rick that she was wrong about her father's malevolence; he left her everything in his will but now she'll never be able to enjoy those riches. In the end, Rick's shooting of Dixon Doss is chalked up to self-defence. He takes a plea bargain to avoid prison time, gets five years' probation, community service, and loses his license to practice law: an outcome a chastened Rick accepts as just. In the end, Rick Magruder the aspiring rescuer has rescued no one; his essential identity is as his own persecutor and victim.

An otherwise routine thriller markedly improved by Altman's gothic flourishes, *The Gingerbread Man* did not do well when it was screened for test audiences in Woodland Hills and Los Angeles on three successive occasions in the summer of 1997. Altman made changes after each test screening but the low scores remained unchanged. Frustrated PolyGram executives complained that, even after tweaking, Altman's final cut was too long, didn't build sufficient tension, and had a musical score that was too minimalist and electronic (see Puig 1997). They took the film away from him, replaced his editor, Geraldine Peroni, and re-cut it their way but the test results were even worse: "'They tested it. And it tested a little more poorly than ours had,' recalls Altman. "So they then gave it back to me with – they said, 'Now [here are] some things we think you should do.' And I said, 'No. You either give this film back to me, or you don't.' I said, 'I've gone through that, I've gone through all this collaboration process.' And they gave it back to me, and I finished the film and delivered it to them'" (Bay 1998: n.p.). In January 1998 Altman's version was released at just eight screens in Los Angeles and New York. The movie garnered good reviews and took in $118,000 at the box office on opening weekend: respectable results that boded well for a much wider release. Unfortunately, PFE's founder and CEO Michael Kuhn, doubtful about the film's commercial potential and resentful that Altman had publicly complained about having the film temporarily taken away from him, squelched the movie. At its widest release, *The Gingerbread Man* was shown in only thirty US theatres and received virtually no promotion. Consequently the movie earned less than $1.7 million at the box office while costing $25 million to make. In the wake of this fiasco, Altman became depressed and ill and was hospitalised. Producer David Levy recalls Altman was lifted from his funk after he and Altman's son, Steve, equipped with a map and video footage, presented 'a dog and pony show' to Altman in his hospital room about possible Mississippi shooting locations for his next film, already contracted: *Cookie's Fortune*: 'He got really excited about making a movie again … It's a cliché, but the work seemed literally like lifeblood in that instance' (in Zuckoff 2009: 458, 459).

Cookie's Fortune (1999)

The location Altman ultimately chose was Holly Springs, Mississippi. A town of slightly less than 8,000 people (75 per cent African-American) in the northernmost part of the state, Holly Springs is a former cotton plantation market town rich in Civil War and African-American history (e.g. the birthplace of Mississippi Delta blues artists Ida B. Wells, R. L. Burnside, Junior Kimbrough, Syl Johnson and Robert Belfour). As Altman later told David Thompson, 'We shot the whole film there, and it was as if we were living on the set. Everyone there helped out on the film. The locale was a large part of the story' (2006: 187). As for the script, Altman engaged the services of neophyte screenwriter Anne Rapp, the wife of Ned Dowd, an assistant director on *Fool for Love* whose passion for racetrack gambling brought the couple into regular contact with Altman. In 1994, after Rapp and Dowd separated, she left her script supervisor job in Hollywood to enroll in a short-story writing course taught by Barry Hannah at the University of Mississippi. Altman asked Rapp to send him some of her stories, thought they were 'terrific', and put her under exclusive contract to write for him. Altman and Rapp turned one of her short stories ('All the President's Women') into an episode of *Gun*, a short-lived television anthology mini-series for which Altman acted as executive producer in 1997. At the time Altman hired her, Rapp was writing a story about an elderly woman who commits suicide to be with her deceased husband 'in heaven'. When the woman's estranged nieces try to cover up the suicide their scheme backfires. After Altman told her how to make it 'cinematic', Rapp developed the story into the script for *Cookie's Fortune* (see Thompson 2006: 186).

Longing to be reunited in the afterlife with her late husband Buck, wealthy dowager Jewel Mae 'Cookie' Orcutt (Patricia Neal) takes one of Buck's pistols from the downstairs hall gun cabinet up to her bedroom and shoots herself – the movie's key plot point, which doesn't occur until thirty-three minutes into the film: a violation of standard expository practice that Altman explains as quite deliberate: 'I didn't want it to be a suspense film. We took a long time to set up the characters and give the audience a feeling for them before Cookie kills herself. We played against the melodrama of the situation, using bright Easter colours throughout, to emphasise it was more of a character piece than anything else, just ordinary people living their lives' (ibid.). Prior to Cookie's death the film follows the meanderings of her genial African-American factotum and confidante, Willis Richland (Charles S. Dutton), who evinces a certain eccentric moral integrity by 'borrowing' pints of Wild Turkey from the town liquor store and replacing them the next day. In contrasting cross-cuts Cookie's pompous niece, Camille Dixon (Glenn Close), is shown bossily directing rehearsals for an amateur Easter production of Oscar Wilde's 1891 play, *Salomé*.[5] Also depicted in cross-cuts is Cookie's grand-niece, Emma Duvall (Liv Tyler). The feisty daughter of Camille's passive and dim-witted younger sister, Cora (Julianne Moore), Emma has returned to town from a stay in Biloxi after being ejected from her mother's house. She lives in a broken-down Econoline van and takes a job gutting catfish for Manny Hood (Lyle Lovett), the local fishmonger – a *déclassé* lifestyle frowned upon by status-conscious Cora and Camille but one that implicitly associates her with Cookie, another staunch individualist who smokes pipes and dresses in manly clothing in defiance of class and gender norms governing southern bourgeois femininity.

Upon discovering Cookie's body and a suicide note addressed to Willis, Camille is not horrified by her aunt's death but by the thought that the manner of it will bring scandal upon the family name. Also motivated by the notion that she'll likely inherit Cookie's mansion, Camille literally eats Cookie's final note to Willis and she and Cora proceed to stage the entire house to make it look as though Cookie was murdered by robbers during a home invasion – theatrical set dressing applied to the 'real world'. They then notify the sheriff's department, who conduct an officious but inept investigation; no one heeds the ubiquitous crime scene tape and evidence is trampled upon wholesale. Nonetheless, law enforcement soon has a suspect. Because he cleaned all her guns just before her suicide, ample fingerprint evidence points to Willis Richland as the culprit in her 'murder'. He is arrested and jailed, conjuring a long and brutal history of racial injustice involving black men in the South prosecuted for crimes against whites they didn't commit. But Altman keeps the mood light in accordance with his comic aims. As Michael Haas notes, 'a sign shown in passing – 'In 1897 nothing happened here' – seems to suggest that the Supreme Court's decision legalising segregation, Plessy versus Ferguson, was never implemented in Holly Springs' (n.d.: n.p.). A hospitable Gemeinschaft mostly populated by easy-going oddballs reminiscent of *The Andy Griffith Show* (though Griffith's Mayberry was almost entirely white), Altman's Holly Springs is a utopian place, not the real town of its setting, the one actually embedded in the South's lugubrious history of slavery, lynchings and Jim Crow. Consequently, no one seems to consider Willis's predicament particularly dire, least of all Willis, who enjoys the support of a number of white allies. Sheriff Lester Boyle (Ned Beatty) is convinced Willis is innocent because 'We've fished together.' The town's amicable attorney, Jack Palmer (Donald Moffat) is also on his side, but Willis's most vociferous advocate is Emma, who knows that Willis loved Cookie (and vice versa) and that he is by nature a thoroughly non-violent man. She even insists on staying with Willis in his always unlocked and convivial jail cell. Murder suspicions notwithstanding, Willis and Emma share a sumptuous Easter dinner there. In another jail cell scene Willis plays a vigorous game of Scrabble with Lester, Jack and Emma. To further leaven the mood, one comic bit of business (borrowed from a similar moment in Bill Forsyth's *Local Hero* (1983)) celebrates sexual exuberance by having Emma and her boyfriend, a young sheriff's deputy named Jason Brown (Chris O'Donnell), sneak off to make love every chance they get. In short, Camille's cruel ruse complicates life in Holly Springs but doesn't really alter the tenor of prevailing social relations, which remain unhurried and amicable.

Inevitably, Camille's hastily contrived hoax falls apart. Police investigators discover blood of a rare type at the alleged crime scene, a type that does not belong to Cookie or Willis but does belong to Camille (from a cut she sustained when she dropped a glass fruit salad bowl upon discovering Cookie's corpse). A neighbour boy comes forward to testify that he saw Camille drop Cookie's gun in her backyard for the sheriffs to find. During the Easter night performance of *Salomé* at the First Presbyterian Church, a suspicious Lester searches Camille's purse and finds Cookie's missing jewelry. Camille is arrested and jailed on suspicion of murder but before Willis is released, Jack Palmer comes to the jail to read Cookie's will, which leaves her entire estate to Buck's 'closest living relative: his nephew, Willis Richland'. The son of Buck's brother and a black mother, Willis has concealed the fact that he's part of the racially mixed Orcutt clan so as to spare Cookie any hint of scandal – a self-abnegating personal sacrifice not unlike Luigi Corelli's in *A Wedding* who concealed his humble class origins to protect the dignity of family matriarch, Nettie Sloan. The surprising revelation of Willis's true lineage delights Emma when she realises she and Willis are, in fact, cousins. Emma is further surprised to learn that her biological mother is not Cora but Camille. Impregnated by Cora's ne'er do well husband, Donny, when the three were living together right after Cora and Donny married, hypocritical Camille conceals her indiscretion by giving the baby to Cora to raise and mother. Their identities finally resolved, Willis and Emma agree to share Cookie's house as *de facto* brother and sister. As for Camille, she is hoisted on her own petard when Cora renders her best acting performance by refusing to admit to authorities that Camille disguised Cookie's suicide as murder: an exhilarating parody of her former subservience that liberates her from her sister's lifelong dominance. Jailed for a murder that never happened a hysterical Camille writhes on her jail cell bed as she more or less loses her mind. Altman ends the film on an appropriately bucolic note, with Jack, Willis, Emma and Lester sitting on a dock happily fishing.

A movie that structures its action around Easter, *Cookie's Fortune* inevitably invites interpretation as a Christian parable about death and resurrection. Though she is no Christ figure who rises from the dead on the third day, Cookie Orcutt is most certainly a benevolent matriarch. She bestows ample posthumous blessings on her worthy family members, Willis and Emma, who are able to finally come into their own in the wake of her death: a renewal that counts as a kind of resurrection. In the preternaturally just world of the movie the avatars of kindness, loyalty and genuineness of character are rewarded and Camille, who embodies pretention, egotism and greed, is punished. Altman's casting choices subtly bolster this ethical paradigm. Patricia Neal, the actress who plays Cookie, was famous as a courageously resilient individual who overcame multiple devastating life challenges: the near-death of her infant son, Theo; the death of her seven-year-old daughter, Olivia, from encephalitis; her own battle to recover from a stroke at the age of thirty-nine; a bitter divorce from writer Roald Dahl. Charles S. Dutton, the actor who plays Willis, was a middle school drop-out from the East Baltimore slums who served ten years in prison on manslaughter and weapons convictions. While incarcerated Dutton became interested in drama and acting, eventually earned a master's degree in acting from the Yale School of Drama, and has since built an impressive resumé in television and film: a remarkable story of self-transformation that both ironises and deepens his role as a mild-mannered handyman. Glenn Close, the actress who plays Camille, is a six-time Academy Award nominee perhaps best known for playing mentally disturbed or malevolent women, e.g. Alex in Adrian Lyne's *Fatal*

Attraction (1986) and Cruella de Vil in *101 Dalmatians*, the 1996 animated Disney hit. Her casting as Camille Dixon was almost a foregone conclusion.

As usual, Altman carefully bolsters astute casting choices through equally effective uses of setting. In the world of the film, the church (tellingly used as a theatrical space), the jail and an alleged crime scene are places of amusement, punishment and deception that serve as the centres of activity for the white denizens of Holly Springs. While Robert T. Self reads deep symbolic significance in Altman's play-within-a-movie use of Wilde's *Salomé* as implicit commentary on the film's overall meaning, its function can be seen is more modest terms, as a synecdoche for Camille's destructive theatricality (2002: 167–72). Cora plays Salomé in Camille's play, but Camille plays Salomé in Altman's movie; her murder hoax is her own dance of the seven veils, an elaborate but thinly disguised exhibition meant to please the authorities so that she can conceal Cookie's suicide and acquire her fortune – and figuratively have the head of Willis (literally the head of John the Baptist in the Salomé story), though the latter consequence is unintended. Instead, Camille is in effect handed her own head. While the principal white spaces in Holly Springs are largely sites of archaic spectacle, fraud, misapprehension and mischief, the town's main black space, the Theo Club, resembles the Hey Hey Club in *Kansas City* as another African-American Gemeinschaft enclave, this one specialising in the blues: an indigenous Mississippi Delta art form that transmutes humdrum life under an oppressive social order into joyful, cathartic aesthetic expression.

While it turns the South's hegemonic landscape topsy-turvy, *Cookie's Fortune* also destabilises gender and race categories as fixed identity markers of inherent worthiness. Emma, a short-haired tomboy in overhauls – subliminally a grown-up and sexualised version of Scout in *To Kill a Mockingbird* – enjoys a vibrant love life, as did mannish Cookie evidently, whereas Camille, the most stereotypically feminine character in the film, is largely asexual. In similarly subversive fashion, the revelation that Willis is a blood relation of the Orcutt family airs the historical reality of southern miscegenation, an irrefutable truth that nullifies white supremacist notions of racial purity, of the very concept of race itself, therefore a phenomenon the white power structure has always sought to efface. Underdog products of illicit unions that transgressed racial and sexual taboos, Emma and Willis also happen to be the most likable and righteous inhabitants of Holly Springs by virtue of their unselfconscious genuineness and instinctively compassionate dispositions: a triumph of nature over circumstance that affirms Rousseauesque notions of innate goodness. Furthermore, the sibling-like pairing of Emma and Willis at film's end cancels out traditional gender and race divides, auguring a New South liberated from long-standing repressions and injustices – wishful utopianism further enhanced by the fact that Cookie's inherited wealth will now make their lives carefree. A pleasing, good-natured movie, well-scripted – Anne Rapp's screenplay earned her 1999 Independent Spirit Award and Edgar nominations – and well-acted, *Cookie's Fortune* made a modest profit at the box office and met with mostly friendly critical notices. Though considered a minor part of Altman's oeuvre, it stands as one of his most accomplished and satisfying films: a comic vision not of the American South as it is, but as it should be, if the usual tyrannies were cast aside.

Dr. T & the Women (2000)

After the success of *Cookie's Fortune* Altman worked with Anne Rapp on a follow-up movie: *Dr. T & the Women*, another contemporary comedy-drama but of a very different sort. Based on another one of Rapp's short stories, the film follows the increasingly tangled fortunes of Dr. Sullivan 'Sully' Travis (Richard Gere), a fifty-something Dallas society gynecologist in the throes of a mid-life crisis that comes to resemble the Old Testament story of Job. Dr. T's mounting troubles stem from the fact that he is an incurable romantic who views women as 'sacred and should be treated that way'. As Rapp puts it: 'Dr. T's religion is women: not in a bad way, not in a sexual way, but in the way of being a complete savior of women. He takes care of them, he loves them, he understands them; he's a faithful servant to his wife, daughters and patients' (in Sragow 2000; n.p.). Convinced that he needed a major movie star 'to make the character work ... so the audience would have a preconception of him', Altman sent Rapp's script to Gere, who accepted the role and partnered with Altman to produce the film (see Thompson 2006: 189). In casting Gere, Altman was subversively casting against his well-known screen persona, epitomised in Garry Marshall's mega-hit romantic comedy, *Pretty Woman* (1990), as an unbearably handsome rake possessed of an unshakable faith in his own sex appeal. Based on Gere's public image (*People* magazine's 'sexiest man alive' in 1999) and the film's gynecological slant, viewers had every right to expect a leering, comedic sex romp. What they got instead was the story of a prominent women's doctor surrounded by female sexuality – a man who should be living the ultimate masculinist dream – but one who is actually lonely, overworked and increasingly confused as his world begins to crumble around him.

Dr. T's troubles begin when his wife, Kate (Farrah Fawcett) decides to strip naked and cavort in a shopping mall fountain pool in full view of dozens of onlookers: a spectacular mental breakdown that gets her committed to a private asylum and will keep her incommunicado from her family for extended periods of time. Kate's psychiatrist, Dr. Harper (Lee Grant) subsequently diagnoses Kate with a case of 'the Hestia Complex', a syndrome invented by Rapp whereby affluent, middle-aged women mysteriously regress into a state of sexless infantile narcissism. To further complicate matters, Dr. T's alcoholic sister-in-law, Peggy (Laura Dern) moves into the Travis household with her three young daughters in tow. Meanwhile Dr. T's youngest daughter, Dee Dee (Kate Hudson), an aspiring cheerleader, is preparing for her upcoming wedding, all the while concealing the fact that she's a lesbian who is still in love with her former college roommate, Marilyn (Liv Tyler). Dr. T's other daughter, Connie (Tara Reid), a quirky JFK conspiracy theorist, competes for her father's attention by repeatedly reminding him that he doesn't need to worry about her. Needless to say, Dr. T finds no refuge from troubled females at his office. There he is under daily siege by a clamoring horde of demanding Dallas socialites with every manner of sexual malady, real and imagined. To escape this women's world that threatens to engulf him, Dr. T goes hunting on weekends with friends Harlan (Robert Hays), Bill (Matt Malloy) and Eli (Andy Richter) but these excursions get rained out, fail to find game, or are otherwise spoiled, invalidating the world of male comradery as a viable alternative. Dr. T has better luck at his country club when meets Bree Davis (Helen Hunt), a self-assured golf pro who displays none of the neediness or instability of the other women in his life. (Bree is a character likely inspired by Jordan Baker, the aloof, somewhat androgynist, and slightly unethical amateur golfer who is Nick Carraway's girlfriend in F. Scott Fitzgerald's *The Great Gatsby*.) Immediately infatuated, Dr. T asks Bree out on a dinner date but she controls the terms of the seduction by inviting him to her condo, cooking him dinner and summoning him to bed when the time comes – another instance of women controlling his life.

One day at work all of Dr. T's impending crises seem to converge. His two daughters and his sister-in-law and her brood all invade his office on an impromptu visit. Connie lingers after the others leave, tells her father the truth about her sister's sexuality, and begs him to intervene and call off the wedding. Bree shows up as well, to find out why Dr. T reneged on a lunch date. When he tries to tell her what Connie told him about Dee Dee in order to solicit her opinion and get her support, Bree can only offer empty platitudes ('Dee Dee is Dee Dee!'). After Bree leaves, a phone call from his lawyer informs Dr. T that his wife wants a divorce. Ironically, Dr. T's next patient is Marilyn, Dee Dee's lover and Maid of Honour, who seems to have contracted a yeast infection. Dr. T becomes flustered as he examines her genitalia, knowing full well that Dee Dee has been there before him. To make matters worse, Dr. T's office waiting room erupts into chaos when one of his patients – Eli's hypochondriacal wife, Dorothy Chambliss (Janine Turner) – is tripped by another patient, hits her head on a table edge and is knocked unconscious, necessitating transport to the hospital by ambulance. After hours, at the end of a hellish day, Dr. T's trusty head nurse, Carolyn (Shelley Long) subjects him to further embarrassment when she reveals her crush on him by partially disrobing.

In the end, Dee Dee's wedding devolves into a chaotic fiasco: an outcome not dissimilar to the derailed matrimonials depicted in *A Wedding* and the aborted marriage episode of *Tanner '88*. Taking place outdoors, at the Dallas Arboretum & Botanical Garden, the elaborately grandiose ceremony is wrecked by an incoming storm that rivals the hurricane in *The Gingerbread Man* and by Dee Dee's impulsive but wise decision to defy heteronormative protocols and flee the scene with Marilyn, leaving her bridegroom in the lurch. Laughing at the cosmic joke that his life has become, Dr. T decides to follow Dee Dee's lead by acting on sheer impulse: a favoured motif in the romcom genre because it affirms carefree spontaneity as the ultimate self-liberating gesture. Accordingly, Dr. T drives to Bree's condo in his Cadillac convertible (which was supposed to serve as his daughter's honeymoon vehicle) and gets soaked in the process when the car's top fails to deploy, a drenching that echoes a similar scene in *A Perfect Couple*. Surprisingly, though, Dr. T remains 'all wet' when Bree flatly refuses his gleeful offer to run away with him – because she's already become involved with one of his hunting buddies on the sly. Thus Altman sets up the generic Prince Charming proposal-and-acceptance climax that makes for the perfect Hollywood ending in *Pretty Woman* and countless other romantic comedies, only to offer a jarring parody of it instead. Commenting on the revisionist meaning of the scene, Altman told David Thompson that Dr. T 'made the assumption that because [Bree] went to bed with him, she loved him. That shows the tight, socially opinionated, egocentric man he is – he believes he loves women but he's been looking at them from the wrong end all his life!' (2006: 190–1). Instead of the standard romance ending tacitly affirming male agency and female objectification, Altman presents a culminating sequence borrowed in part from *The Wizard of Oz*. After Bree rejects him, Dr. T takes to the road out of town on a solo adventure but the raging storm's tornadic winds seize his car and sends it spinning around and around in an apparent death spiral like Dorothy's Kansas farmhouse. In the final scene, the morning after the storm, Dr. T miraculously awakens near his wrecked automobile in a desert landscape – allegorically a new and alien world – and is summoned by Mexican women to a nearby house where a young woman is giving birth. They speak only Spanish, a language that Dr. T does not understand, so in a sense the scene plays out for him in the pre-verbal realm of the Real, free of all the complaining, demanding chatter of privileged white women that has heretofore been the soundtrack of his life. Dr. T delivers a boy in the first medically explicit scene of a baby being born in a Hollywood movie: graphic realism that runs counter to all the displays of frivolous extravagance that have preceded it. In the end, Dr. T's core identity as a skilled physician is affirmed and the gender and social class imbalances that have distorted his life are finally redressed – an ending diametrically opposed to the thoroughly gynocentric conclusion of *3 Women*, another film whose ending smacks of implausible contrivance rather than the natural outgrowth of the action that precedes it.

In his interview with Altman David Thompson remarked that 'the film received quite a bit of criticism for its portrayal of the Dallas ladies with their perfect hair and obsession with clothes and accessories' (2006: 191). Altman's rejoinder was that the movie was satiric by default, i.e. by being anthropologically realistic in its depiction of Dallas socialites: 'You'll see them down there dressed to the nines. Rich women don't have anything else to do down there. And the women in the picture playing those women *were* those women. I had big sessions with them – twenty a day would come in – and they told me that's all they did, they tried to get their names in the paper, so they get invited to more parties. It's kind of a contest and everybody behaves like that' (ibid.). What some critics mistook for misogyny was really parody of a particularly ostentatious social formation. Anne Rapp testified that she 'never had any sense that Bob was a misogynist in life or in his work. I know Bob loved women and wanted to be around women. He was more comfortable in the world of women than in the world of men' (in Zuckoff 2009: 463). In his review, Andrew Sarris echoed Rapp's assessment: 'Mr. Altman is never condescending to the women, only somewhat fearful of their amazing power and persistence' (ibid.). Roger Ebert voices a similar view: 'Robert Altman would never admit this, but I believe Dr. T, the gynecologist in his latest film, is an autobiographical character. Played by Richard Gere with tact, sweetness and a certain weary bemusement in the face of female complexity, Dr. T works for and with women, and sometimes dares to love them. So it is with Altman, who is more interested in women than any other great director, with the exception of Ingmar Bergman' (2000: n.p.). María del Mar Azcona supports a reading of the film as both anti-generic and women-friendly when she details how the movie's female ensemble consistently decentres Dr. T as individual male hero-protagonist: 'Amidst the tornado of women that surrounds him, Dr. T's role becomes that of an "empty hub": his privileged narrative position in the wealthy Dallas world of the film is increasingly subverted in both narrative and visual terms by the centrifugal pull of the chaotic and unruly power of the female ensemble' (2015: 450).

Gosford Park (2001)

Actor and filmmaker Bob Balaban met Altman at the Sherry-Netherland Hotel in New York City when he was casting for *Brewster McCloud* in 1970 (see Zuckoff 2009: 468). The part went to Bud Cort but Balaban and Altman became friends over the ensuing years. Sometime in 1999 Balaban approached Altman with the proposal that they work on a film project together. Altman, who admitted to being something of an anglophile, suggested an Agatha Christie-type whodunit murder mystery, as he had never made that sort of film. Balaban agreed, but developing a suitable storyline proved difficult; they found Agatha Christie mysteries not yet made into movies predictably formulaic. Altman and Balaban hired Eileen Atkins and Jean March, co-creators (with John Hawkesworth and John Whitney) of the *Upstairs, Downstairs* TV series (1971–75) to write an outline, but what they wrote was in Altman's words, 'the exact opposite of what I wanted it to do – it was rather sentimental' (in Thompson 2006: 195). In January 2000, at Balaban's suggestion, Altman phoned British actor-screenwriter Julian Fellowes – a to-the-manor-born son of a diplomat well suited to write a movie about Britain's upper classes – and gave him a brief synopsis of the film i.e. that it was to be 'set in a country house in the '30s and to have a murder in there somewhere, but for it to really be an examination of class'. As Fellowes noted in his Afterword to the published shooting script: 'From the start, it was not Altman's intention that the murder plot should ever dominate the movie – either before or after it has taken place. "This isn't a Who-Dunnit", he declared, "It's a Who-Cares-Who-Dunnit"' (2002: 164). Anxious to work with a director of Altman's calibre, Fellowes took on the assignment. To better ascertain what Altman wanted, he watched all the director's films he could find and discovered that Altman 'was happiest in the genre of multi-arc, multi-strand storytelling' (Altman and Vallan 2014: 283). What Fellowes subsequently formulated in about six or seven weeks of intensive work was, in his words, 'not an homage to Agatha Christie, but a reworking of that genre'.[6] Pleased by Fellowes' work, Altman invited him to California and over a period of several days the two rearranged elements and a viable script began to take shape (see Thompson 2006: 195). Altman's own contribution, which Fellowes considered 'brilliant', was to introduce a real figure, Ivor Novello (1893–1951), a Welsh composer and actor who became one of the most popular British entertainers in the early decades of the twentieth century. Played by Jeremy Northam, Novello plays piano and sings his own songs, supplying 'some practical [i.e. diegetic] music instead of just having a score' (Altman and Vallan 2014: 284). Altman also found Fellowes' proposed movie title – 'The Other Side of the Tapestry' – unwieldy; he changed it to *Gosford Park*, a more mnemonic title that also better expressed the notion that the movie treated British class society as a whole. Once the project began to cohere, Altman 'wanted the behavior and manners to be right [inasmuch as] I knew I would be under scrutiny' (in Thompson 2006: 196) as an American intervening in English cultural history. He commissioned script doctor Ezna Sands to vet the screenplay and hired Arthur Inch, a retired butler, Ruth Mott, a retired cook and Violet Liddle, a retired parlour maid, to stay on set and serve as consultants to verify that depictions of servant manners were authentic. All three had started working at English country estates in the 1930s and knew procedures and protocols to the letter. (Besides writing the script Julian Fellowes also served as on-set consultant from the 'upstairs' perspective.) As for casting, the script provided for only two American roles: a gay, Jewish film director specialising in Charlie Chan movies named Morris Weissman, played by Bob Balaban, and his young lover, Henry Denton, played by Ryan Phillippe after Jude Law dropped out just before shooting began. British casting director Mary Selway hired the forty-one other cast members, all from the UK, among them seven British knights and dames of the theatre: Alan Bates, Derek Jacobi, Michael Gambon, Eileen Atkins, Helen Mirren, Kristin Scott Thomas and Maggie Smith. Following Altman's directions, costume designer Jenny Beavan (*The Remains of the Day* (1993)) and hair designer Jan Archibald (*The Shooting Party* (1995)) took fastidious care to ensure that the clothing and hair styles were appropriate to the era (November 1932), without any hint of theatrical ostentation or contrivance (see Fellowes 2002: 170). As Fellowes notes, Altman was 'especially keen, when dealing with a period subject, that one should never lose the sense that these were real people leading real lives' (ibid.).

To ensure authenticity of setting, Altman mixed location shooting with studio work. The exteriors, staircase, dining room and drawing room of Wrotham Park (pronounced 'Rootam'), a neo-Palladian English country house in Hertsmere, Hertfordshire, designed by Isaac Ware in 1754, stood in for William McCordle's fictional Gosford Park. Filming in the upstairs bedrooms occurred at Syon House, the Duke of Northumberland's 400-year-old home in West London. Altman shot the opening sequence outside Lady Trentham's home at Hall Barn, near Beaconsfield, Buckinghamshire. Its landscape park and woodlands were used as the setting for the lunch scene after the pheasant shoot. The servants' quarters below stairs were designed by Altman's son, Stephen, and built on sound stages at Shepperton Studios in London. As Stephen explains: 'We set our sights on building our own below stairs set because we were unable to find anything intact and convenient for filming. The set was based on a composite of pretty much everything that we'd seen, whether from research or actual places that we visited. In compiling it, I tried to get the scale and geography right with our above stairs location house. We duplicated a couple of staircases that connected above and below stairs, but otherwise it's the best bits of many places.'[7] To heighten realism and 'take the preciousness out of the period drama', Altman had his British cinematographer, Andrew Dunn, shoot many scenes with two roving cameras, which would slowly track around different sections of the action, ensuring that the cast members in a scene were always potentially in the shot: cinematographic technique designed 'to take the formality out of it' (in Thompson 2006: 197). In large ensemble drawing room scenes static cameras cover the entire room, prompting viewers to visually scan the scene however they choose, as they would if they were watching a stage play. As Altman had done so often in ensemble scenes since *California Split* in 1974, he eschewed boom mics in favour of equipping actors with hidden radio microphones and had them mostly improvise dialogue without knowing if their words would be made audible in the final sound mix: a technique that minimises an actor's self-consciousness and helps foster a more naturalistic performance. As was also his usual *modus operandi*, Altman required that the actors commit to staying with the production throughout the ten weeks of principal photography (mid-March to early May 2001) in order to create the harmonious artists' Gemeinschaft so vital to the success of his film projects.

All of Altman's painstaking efforts to create an authentic representation of English class society in the inter-war period would have been for naught, however, without a script that captured the essence of that era's social order, i.e. a sclerotic caste system at the end of its imperialist tether, hanging onto the old customs, prejudices and injustices even after the senseless carnage of the First World War, wholesale corruption of the 1920s and economic devastation of the Great Depression had rendered that order morally and fiscally bankrupt. As F. Scott Fitzgerald so eloquently put it in *Tender is the Night*, 'England was like a rich man after a disastrous orgy who makes up to the household by chatting with them individually, when it is obvious to them that he is only trying to get back his self-respect in order to usurp his former power' (1934: 288). Julian Fellowes grasped the ideological precariousness of that historical moment and so built a storyline centred on privilege redolent of abuse and neglect, one he admits was partly inspired by the life of William Whiteley (1831–1907), a multi-millionaire London department store owner who was shot dead on 24 January 1907 by Horace George Raynor, aged 29, a man who claimed to be Whiteley's illegitimate son (2002: 164–5). Accordingly, the main plot of *Gosford Park* revolves around the sexual depredations of a latter-day Whiteley figure named Sir William McCordle (Michael Gambon). The master of Gosford Park, Sir William is 'a hard-hearted randy old sod' who has indulged in a long string of exploitative liaisons with his female factory workers and house servants: common practice among the amoral English upper-crust for hundreds of years (though McCordle is, in fact, a *nouveau riche arriviste* who has acquired his title by marrying into an impoverished family of aristocrats). When one of McCordle's forced sex objects becomes pregnant, he presents her with an ultimatum: give up the baby or lose your job. The girls are told that their babies have been adopted by good families when in reality McCordle dumps them in an orphanage. In short, the essentially corrupt nature of Gosford Park is embodied in William McCordle, an arrogant brute who has used his wealth to expropriate the meritocratic trappings of aristocracy so he can enjoy high social status and satisfy his baser urges while insulating himself from the destructive consequences. McCordle's usurpation of an aristocratic title points up the triumph of modern industrial capitalism over a residual social formation that was equally exploitative and brutal but based its elitist imperatives on family lineage, not solely on capital accumulation. In this regard McCordle, a much nastier version of Snooks Brenner in *A Wedding*, augurs the beginning of the end of the gentrified life, a way of life that will virtually cease to exist less than seven years later, with the outbreak of World War II.

Another inspiration for *Gosford Park* was the aforementioned *The Shooting Party*, a well-regarded British film based on an eponymous novel by Isabel Colegate (1980) and directed by Alan Bridges. Set on the eve of the Great War, *The Shooting Party* contrasts dissolute British aristocrats gathered for pheasant shooting at a country estate with the austere lives of the rural poor. Still another major influence (for Altman more than Fellowes) was Jean Renoir's masterpiece, *La règle du jeu* (*The Rules of the Game*, 1939), a large-canvas comedy of manners that depicts members of France's decadent and morally callous aristocracy just before the outbreak of World War II. Altman admits he became 'more interested' in having *Gosford Park* resemble *La Règle du jeu* than *Gosford Park*'s ostensive precursor, George Pollock's *Ten Little Indians* (1965), the film version of Agatha Christie's drawing room murder mystery, *And Then There Were None* (1939); the film's murder mystery plot became little more than a structuring device. For Altman the complicated class antagonism that marked relations between the aristocracy and its servant cadre was his true subject: 'It was like having the Iraqis and Americans living in the same house. It was these two totally different societies, who had totally different opinions of each other. To me, that became the drama, what the film was about' (in Thompson 2006: 202). Altman was also very keen to show deeper complexities and contradictions within this perverse symbiosis; that the upstairs people were wholly dependent upon their downstairs subordinates in order to function; that fraternisation between the classes was deeper and more pervasive than anyone cared to admit; that the servant class lived vicariously through their 'betters' and internalised the dominant master/servant ethos by observing rigid hierarchies within their own ranks; that the best servants were the ones who most thoroughly effaced their own identities – a terrible price to pay, to excel at one's job.

While *Gosford Park* seeks to paint a picture of Britain's class society, it consistently does so through the point of view of the servant class. As Altman told interviewer David Gritten: 'The camera can't be on the posh people unless a servant is present. You may hear an argument inside a room, but if a servant enters, it'll stop. If a servant leaves a room, so does the camera. This may not be that evident. The audience may not perceive it. But the story is transmitted through downstairs gossip, through what the servants know' (2000: n.p.). More than just taking their perspective as a distancing device, the movie implicitly identifies with the servants as an oppressed class. It subtly establishes its partisan credentials in the opening sequence, which depicts Lady McCordle's insufferably snobbish Aunt Constance, the Countess of Trentham (Maggie Smith), departing from her estate to Gosford Park by chauffeured limousine. She is accompanied by her young and inexperienced maid, Mary MacEachern (Kelly Macdonald), who has to wait outside in the pouring rain while the Countess, shielded by a butler's umbrella, gets takes her time getting into her car. On the road the Countess needs help opening her thermos, necessitating that the car stop and Mary get out and assist, getting soaked in the process. Mary gets even more drenched when a car carrying matinée idol Ivor Novello, Hollywood producer Morris Weissman, and Weissman's valet (and clandestine lover) Henry Denton, also on the way to Gosford Park, stops to enquire if everything is, in American parlance, 'okay'. The two parties linger over introductions with no thought for Mary's discomfort. Once they arrive at Gosford

A servant's life: Mary MacEachern (Kelly Macdonald) waits in the rain while her 'betters' exchange idle chit-chat.

Park, Mary gets out of the car in naïve anticipation of accompanying the Countess into the house but a butler brusquely directs Mary to trudge around to the rear of the building on the muddy pavement: she is, after all, a non-entity.

Unfortunately, the only people that matter at Gosford Park are the least worthy: William McCordle, his wife, Lady Sylvia (Kristin Scott Thomas), Isobel McCordle (Camilla Rutherford) and Sylvia's two sisters: Louisa, Lady Stockbridge (Geraldine Somerville) and Lady Lavinia Meredith (Natasha Wightman). Lady Trentham and a few other relatives, in-laws, friends and aforementioned guests fill out the rest of the company, all of whom are on hand for an autumn weekend shooting party. Despite their elite social status, most of the individuals who comprise McCordle's coterie are inauthentic human beings: selfish, unhappy, duplicitous snobs and social-climbers hiding sexual transgressions and other sins while some of them desperately scheme to avail themselves of a share of Sir William's wealth. While the rot starts at the top with petulant, priapic William McCordle, the mistress of the manor, Lady Sylvia, epitomises the existentialist notion of *mauvaise foi* (bad faith), *avant la lettre*, which afflicts most of her social set to greater or lesser degrees. Succumbing to societal pressure to exchange her title for money, she has traded cheap expediency for her innate freedom: self-alienation that leads to a life of aimlessness and ressentiment. Arbitrarily chosen (by a higher cut of cards) over her sister, Louisa, to wed the loathsome McCordle for purely mercenary ends, Sylvia stays in her loveless marriage to reap the material rewards. To assuage her conscience she pantomimes rebellion against her compromised circumstances by becoming a mean-spirited virago who loathes her husband, is ashamed of her graceless daughter and takes malicious delight in mocking Louisa's husband, Raymond, Lord Stockbridge (Charles Dance), with whom she has had an affair – though her usual choice of paramour is a visiting servant. (Indeed, Lady Sylvia's predilection for handsome male servants results in her humiliation when she discovers that Henry Denton, supposedly Morris Weismann's valet, is actually a Hollywood actor posing as a servant to research a movie role.) Sylvia's daughter, Isobel McCordle, is also living a lie. Blackmailed by Freddie Nesbitt (James Wilby) after having aborted

Freddie's illegitimate child, Isobel loves penniless Lord Rupert Standish (Laurence Fox) but feels she cannot marry him because her mother disapproves. Isobel could obtain freedom and emotional authenticity if she gave herself to Rupert but that would entail rebelling against her parents and sacrificing the luxuries of Gosford Park for a life of uncertain prospects and probable hardships – a gamble she is not prepared to take, so like her mother, she chooses to dwell in an existential limbo instead. Dowager Aunt Constance's bad faith manifests in her extreme, almost theatrical snobbery: superciliousness that belies her total economic dependency on Sir William, whom she despises (the feeling is mutual). Lady Sylvia's younger sister Louisa is likely in love with Sir William and decidedly not in love with her own husband but cannot act on her true feelings because social proprieties dictate otherwise.

Tellingly, the further the distance from the money/power nexus, the more authentic are the emotional ties between spouses. Lady Sylvia's youngest sister, Lady Lavinia Meredith, genuinely loves her somewhat hapless husband, Lieutenant Commander Anthony Meredith (Tom Hollander), but her affection is complicated by Anthony's dire financial straits: a condition he hopes to rectify by persuading Sir William to continue to invest in a scheme to supply boots to soldiers in the Sudan. Toward the bottom of the pecking order Rupert's 'friend', Jeremy Blond (Trent Ford), is using Rupert as his entrée into society: another example of self-serving dishonesty trumping genuineness of character and feeling. Somewhat removed from the British caste system is singer/actor/composer Ivor Novello, who typifies the popular artist figure in modern society, enjoying creative freedom and celebrity but nonetheless still dependent upon the patronage of the aristocracy for his livelihood; at Gosford Park he must literally sing for his supper. Finally, the American film producer Morris Weissman is, to a certain extent, an Altman surrogate, i.e. an outsider figure exempt from the rigid social strictures that rule Gosford Park and free to observe them with an unjaundiced eye – though he seems to spend most of his time on phone calls to Hollywood, trying to resolve casting issues for his upcoming film, *Charlie Chan in London* (a real movie, released in 1934 but produced by John Stone). Weissman's Jewishness also raises the spectre of anti-Semitic sentiment among the 1930s British aristocracy, which was in fact pronounced. Except for Constance's noticeable wincing when she hears the name Weissman, the film downplays this issue.

Long, complex and covering numerous upstairs/downstairs subplots (143 scenes over a running time of 137 minutes), *Gosford Park* defies concise summary. Suffice to say that one of the main plots begins to coalesce at an outdoor luncheon after a morning pheasant shoot when Commander Meredith pleads with Sir William not to renege on his investment in the military supply deal. When Sir William refuses to change his mind, the Commander, now desperate, violates decorum by grabbing Sir William's arm, causing him to shatter his Bloody Mary cocktail glass on the ground – a harbinger of worse things to come. That night at dinner, Meredith reveals that he is leaving in the morning to start bankruptcy proceedings ('When you're ruined there's so much to do!'), a caustically bitter announcement that elicits cold indifference from Sir William ('Yes, there is, isn't there?'). Ensuing attempts by diners to steer the conversation into neutral territory founder when an exasperated Lady Sylvia verbally attacks her husband as narrow-minded and venal: an insult that causes the head housemaid, Elsie (Emily Watson), to impetuously come to Sir William's defence – a shocking breach of the class barrier that reveals her affair with 'Billy' to everyone at the table. Mortified and knowing that she will be sacked for her indiscretion, Elsie flees from the room. Later that evening, when Sir William is found dead in his study – evidently murdered *twice*, by poison and a knife to the chest – there is no shortage of suspects. As is the case with one subset of whodunits, the subsequent police investigation is earnest but incompetent. Tall and stately, Inspector Thompson (Stephen Fry) projects serene confidence but is in fact one more installment in a long line of foolish, bumbling Altman cops (e.g. he misses obvious clues and continually contaminates the crime scene with his own fingerprints). On the other hand, Thompson's uniformed subordinate, Constable Dexter (Ron Webster) is alert and efficient: another example of the film's sly deconstruction of the stereotypical notion that meritocratic virtue correlates to social status. Incidentally, in the wake of the killing, Henry Denton has to admit that he is not Weissman's Scottish valet but an American actor playing one – a revelation that fills the downstairs staff with disgust; the idea that a free man of privilege would attempt to pass as a servant strikes them all as both disrespectful of their plight as lifelong domestics and the worst sort of class apostasy.

In keeping with the film's proletarian sympathies, the person who ultimately solves the mystery of Sir William's double murder is Gosford's lowliest servant, Mary MacEachern. Privy to snippets of conversations upstairs and downstairs, Mary deduces that Raymond's valet Robert Parks (Clive Owen) is Sir William's shunned bastard son by Jane Parks, a cook in his factories in Isleworth and Twickenham thirty years ago – now known as Mrs. Wilson (Helen Mirren), the head housekeeper at Gosford Park. When Parks discovered Sir William was the father who had forsaken him, he entered service to gain employment with someone in McCordle's circle so he'd be in a position to exact revenge. Mary goes to Parks's room and tells him that she knows he is the murderer. When Parks tells Mary that he did not poison Sir William, Mary is relieved, knowing Parks only stabbed a corpse. The real murderer is of course Mrs. Wilson, ironically the heretofore perfect servant who freely admits that 'I have no life'. Recognising Parks as her long lost son when he arrives at Gosford Park as Raymond's valet and surmising that he is there to kill Sir William, she strikes first in order to spare him the fatal consequences of a murder conviction. Another secret revealed is that Mrs. Wilson and Mrs. Croft (Eileen Atkins), the irascible head cook at Gosford Park, are in fact sisters – a key script change only made toward the end of the shoot when Altman saw Helen Mirren and Eileen Atkins in the lunch hall together in costume for the first time and realised how alike they looked (in Thompson 2006: 203). As rewritten, the script reveals that Mrs. Croft was also impregnated by William McCordle but kept the baby (though it soon died of scarlet fever) and has never forgiven her sister for making the choice to keep her job rather than keep her infant child; hence the icy relations between them. The two finally reconcile in a private scene fraught with intense emotion. The usually stoical Mrs. Wilson breaks down sobbing for all the loss she's endured but Mrs. Croft reminds her that 'At least your boy is alive. That's all that matters.' As for Mary, she learns that Mrs. Wilson has no intention of confessing to her crime lest it somehow implicate her son. Inspired by Mrs. Wilson's suffering and courage, Mary opts to remain silent as well: an act of rebellion against capitalist patriarchy that is also a compassionate expression of gender and class solidarity. In sum, Mary's eventful weekend at Gosford Park has rendered her wise to the rapacious ways of the aristocracy – an inverse mirror image of the enlightening cross-class experience that Carolyn Stilton had as Blondie O'Hara's captive in *Kansas City*.

Two months after it premiered at the London Film Festival (7 November 2001), *Gosford Park* went into wide release, eventually earning $41.3 million in the US and $36.4 million in foreign markets for an impressive total of $87.7 million in worldwide box office receipts against a production cost of $19.8 million: Altman's second most commercially successful film after *M*A*S*H*. *Gosford Park* also garnered mostly excellent reviews and was nominated for 63 awards (including six Academy Awards, eight BAFTA and four Golden Globe nominations). Altman won the AFI's Director of the Year award for 2002, the Golden Globe for Best Director, and the National Society of Film Critics for Best Director but the Academy Award for Best Director eluded him for the fifth time (it went to Ron Howard for *A Beautiful Mind* (2001), a good movie but inferior to *Gosford Park*). Julian Fellowes (who won *Gosford Park*'s only Academy Award, for Best Original Screenplay) attributed Altman's loss to a smear campaign mounted against him by the Hollywood establishment for his outspokenness about the 9/11 terrorist attacks. In an 18 October 2001 interview widely circulated by the Associated Press, Altman blamed Hollywood for inspiring, perhaps even teaching terrorists how to commit large-scale atrocities by continually showing mass destruction in movies: a debatable claim but one not totally lacking in merit (in Zuckoff 2009: 477). Indeed, widespread reaction to video footage of the World Trade Center attacks was that the real images of destruction – especially the second hijacked airliner crashing into the South Tower – closely resembled a Hollywood disaster film. Julian Fellowes believes 'that if 9/11 had not happened, the following March [Altman] would have won the Oscar' (in Zuckoff 2009: 478). Though he was once again repudiated by Hollywood officialdom, Altman knew he had made a great movie and was sanguine, even 'giddy' on Oscar night, according to Bob Balaban (ibid.).

The Company (2003)

Altman's next project after the phenomenal success of *Gosford Park* was supposed to be 'Voltage', an Alan Rudolph adaptation of Robert Grossbach's satiric novel about the high-tech industry, *A Shortage of Engineers* (St. Martin's, 2001). Having lined up a stellar ensemble cast that included Joaquin Phoenix, Philip Seymour Hoffman, Steve Buscemi, Bob Balaban, Harry Belafonte, William H. Macy, Tony Shaloub, Elliott Gould and Liv Tyler, Altman started prepping the film in New York and Long Island in October 2001, but could not raise the $21 million needed before the shoot's scheduled start date (15 May 2002) so the project had to be aborted (see Magee 2014: 222). Altman next took on *An Unfinished Life*, a Miramax production slated to star Altman's friend, Paul Newman. Pressured by Miramax CEO Harvey Weinstein to fire Naomi Watts whom he had just hired as the film's female lead, Altman quit the film, as did

Newman eventually. Robert Redford took Newman's part, Lasse Hallström replaced Altman as director and a decidedly mediocre Jennifer Lopez filled the role initially given to Watts (see Thompson 2006: 204–5). Ultimately released in 2005, *An Unfinished Life* was a solid but predictable melodrama that tanked at the box office – which it may well have done under Altman's direction but his version would likely have been quirkier and far more interesting.

After quitting the Miramax project Altman opted to direct *The Company*, a neo-realist pseudo-documentary dance film conceived by Neve Campbell, a hot property after starring in the popular TV teen drama series *Party of Five* (1994–2000) and Wes Craven's horror franchise *Scream* films in 1996, 1997 and 2000. A dancer long before she became an actor, Campbell had always wanted to make a realistic film about the world of dance. To develop a dance film script she teamed up with Barbara Turner (ex-wife of the late Vic Morrow, mother of Jennifer Jason Leigh, and screenwriter of *Georgia* (1995) and *Pollock* (2000)). Campbell and Turner did their research by visiting Chicago's Joffrey Ballet – America's premier company – over two successive seasons. They interviewed the dancers at length and, in Campbell's words, 'basically ended up with hundreds of pages of conversations' (in Zuckoff 2009: 480). When Campbell and Turner had a screenplay completed in August 2001, they sent it to Altman via a small production company founded by Christine Vachon and Pamela Koffler called Killer Films. Having known Altman for decades, Turner felt that 'he would be the only person who would understand it' (ibid.). Altman read the script as a favour to Turner but told her 'I'm never going to do this, as I know nothing about dance and there's no point in me thinking about it' (in Thompson 2006: 204). Undaunted, Campbell and Turner met with Altman repeatedly in New York. His curiosity piqued, Altman quizzed Campbell about dance. She later recalled him asking her 'why this film could be important and what it was like to be a dancer. I think the more I talked about the dance world and what sacrifices dancers make, the more he identified with it' (in Zuckoff 2006: 480). Furthermore, an ensemble movie about the creative inner workings of an obsessively dedicated artistic Gemeinschaft doubtless resonated with Altman; this was, after all, an alternate version of his own world (indeed the Joffrey, a maverick dance company that had always struggled to stay afloat financially, was the dance world's equivalent to Lion's Gate Films). Eventually Altman reconsidered and signed on in the summer of 2002, just after withdrawing from *An Unfinished Life*. As he told David Thompson, he thought, 'Why not jump into the abyss? I didn't know anything about country music, but I made *Nashville*' (2006: 205). Shortly thereafter, an agreement was reached to film at the Joffrey (though it is not named in the film). With the project suddenly fast-tracked, Campbell and Turner did two complete revisions of the script in July and August and Campbell began an intensive five-month regimen at the Joffrey to reacquire her dance skills and learn a raft of individual ballet numbers before the shoot began in late October 2002 (see Magee 2014: 224).

Upon assuming the helm Altman politely informed Barbara Turner that her script was 'wonderful' but it was his movie and he would shape it according to his own dictates, as was always the case (see Zuckoff 2009: 480). Accordingly, Altman shot *The Company* the same way he shot *Gosford Park* – without a shooting script at hand. He might consult notecards that offered basic synopses of each scene's purpose or not even bother. Always open to technical innovations, Altman opted to forego traditional celluloid in favour of High Definition Video, having his cinematographer, Andrew Dunn (who also shot *Gosford Park*) shoot *The Company* using four hi-def video cameras to cover all the dance sequences from different angles simultaneously and two or three for other scenes (see Altman and Vallan 2014: 286). To counter the flatness typical of video, *The Company* was the first film processed using DarbeeVision, a digital lab process that achieves image dimensionality by 'pre-emphasiz[ing] those parts of the image that tell the brain how round objects are, how they are separated in depth, what their details are, and which objects are worthy of attention', according to its inventor, the late Paul Darbee.[8] As for casting, Altman's first move was to hire Malcolm McDowell to play the company's flamboyant, demanding artistic director, Alberto Antonelli (aka 'Mr. A'); a character loosely based on Gerald ('Jerry') Arpino (1923–2008), co-founder of the Joffrey Ballet with Robert Joffrey and its artistic director after Joffrey's death in 1988. (Mr. A is, of course, also a version of Altman himself.) Altman also hired James Franco to play Josh, a sous chef who becomes the love interest of Neve Campbell's character, Loretta 'Ry' Ryan, a promising young dancer poised to become a star of the company. Barbara Robertson was cast as Harriet, a veteran dancer near the end of her career. There was discussion about hiring actors to play the dancers but Altman ultimately chose to have Joffrey's forty-four dancers play themselves: another instance of him 'mixing the faux and the real, but blurring the distinction even further', as David Thompson puts it (2006: 206). Altman spent months with the dancers before the shoot began, spoke to each of them privately, and came to admire and respect them as artists of enormous self-discipline fanatically devoted to their art, a dedication that involves sacrificing the comforts of life that most people take for granted. In his 'Director's Statement' for the movie press kit, Altman praised them in extravagant terms:

> Dancers do the impossible. And yet we all want to be them. They are that beautiful, that vulnerable, and that expressive. They are the essence of what we mean by ethereal… On a daily basis, and in the most impossible and dramatic terms, dancers face what we all face: biological clocks and the force of gravity telling us NO. Yet for some part of their working lives dancers literally prevail over those forces. The fact that they (like the rest of us) will all ultimately be trumped by time doesn't diminish or compromise their efforts. It only enriches them … and us.[9]

The admiration appears to have been mutual. Barbara Turner reports that, 'To the dancers, [Altman] was already a god when he walked on the set. He treated them with respect, just the way he treats actors… They could feel the love pouring all over them' (in Zuckoff 2009: 481).

Even more so than most Altman films, *The Company* deliberately lacks a recognisable dramatic arc, or even a central narrative thread, insofar as the movie foregrounds the dances themselves: ten short ballets (or excerpts thereof), expertly performed, stunningly lit and evocatively shot, thanks to camera coverage from four different points of view, fully exploited by Geraldine Peroni in the editing process – in the words of film critic David Edelstein, 'some of the most gorgeously fluid ballet sequences ever committed to film' (2004: n.p.). Several of these numbers are by Gerald Arpino but the most prominent among them is Lar Lubovitch's 'My Funny Valentine', a *pas de deux* early in the film, danced by Ry and her male dance partner, Domingo Rubio, supposedly at the Ravinia Summer Festival at Chicago's Highland Park on Lake Michigan while a fierce summer storm moves in that infuses the number with a sense of wild urgency and danger and confers a kind of heroic stature to the dancers for completing the piece in the teeth of Nature's fury – a scene based on an actual incident with the Joffrey that also recalls the disruptive rain storms in *A Perfect Couple, The Gingerbread Man* and *Dr. T. and The Women*.[10] Altman went on to use various renditions of 'My Funny Valentine' as a leitmotif throughout the film, to represent the relationship between Ry and Josh: a musical trope used more insistently and to different effect in *The Long Goodbye*. The other major ballet that closes the film is *The Blue Snake* by French-Canadian choreographer Robert Desrosiers: a surreal postmodern work whose inception and development Neve Campbell witnessed and was inspired by when she was an eleven-year-old ballet student at the National Ballet of Canada in Toronto in 1985. When Desrosiers proposes 'The Blue Snake' for the company's season finale, Antonelli finds it too costly, admonishing the choreographer to always remember 'Budget! Budget! Budget!' – but he also declares Desrosiers a 'genius' and proceeds to develop the work anyway. Interspersed among all these performance pieces are numerous rehearsal segments, backstage vignettes and after-hours incidents that illustrate the physical and emotional arduousness of ballet and the financial precariousness of the enterprise, e.g. Antonelli argues with a dancer over improvisatory tactics whose merits seem arbitrary; a rivalry ensues between Ry and another dancer; Ry's mother meddles in her life; Ry's relationship to Josh never fully flourishes because both lovers are too busy with their frenetic work lives; a dancer snaps an Achilles tendon during rehearsal, effectively ending her career; Ry also suffers an injury that removes her from Desrosiers' climatic dance piece, etc. The net effect of all this is to show that seemingly effortless dance performances are the result of endless of hours of grueling work and that the day-to-day life of the aspiring artist is an exhausting grind to perfect one's craft combined with the usual struggle for survival – a theme Altman had already treated in-depth in *Vincent & Theo*.

Visually and aurally lush but narratively amorphous, even evanescent, *The Company* feels exhaustively immersive, naturalistic and strangely dreamlike at the same time: a complexity of tone and content that elicited an unusually wide range of critical opinion. *Entertainment Weekly*'s Owen Gleiberman captured the film's unsettling weirdness when he described it as a 'fiction that feels like a Zen documentary, and it's unique in the Altman canon. Watching it, I felt by turns engrossed, detached, dazzled, bored, curious, enlightened, and moved' (2004: n.p.). *Salon*'s David Edelstein pronounced *The Company* 'an absolutely miraculous movie'; Charles Taylor, also writing for *Salon* found the film a 'surpassingly beautiful ballet movie [that] feels lighter than air – but in fact it's the great director's most tender and memorable film in years; *Slant*'s Ed Gonzalez was equally effusive: 'It's a shame that people may not connect with *The Company*. Unlike most films, Altman's latest masterpiece is a picture worth a thousand movements.'[11] Many other critics found *The Company* merely dull and uninvolving. Members of the dance community were likewise unimpressed. *The Guardian*'s Judith Mackrell asked a number of British dancers their opinion of the film; Mark Baldwin, artistic director of London's Rambert Dance Company, opined that the 'real problem [with the film] was that the choreography was so bad – and it wasn't very well filmed. The dancing was never allowed to build to any significance, so it was hard to believe in the significance of the dancers' world'; Christina Arestis, Royal Ballet soloist, told Mackrell, 'I didn't like the feeling of martyrdom the film projects – the image of dancers working so hard and making such sacrifices. We do, but only because we love the job; what the film doesn't show is the exhilaration. Even though some the choreography is beautifully shot it doesn't make you feel as if you're actually there. I got bored.'[12] On the other hand, dance historian Leland Windreich, writing for *Ballet Dance* magazine, praised *The Company*'s visual lyricism: 'With few exceptions, all of the dancing scenes are translated magically into the film medium, and the eye is continually enchanted by the erotic imagery and kinetic flow in each episode. Altman delivers … a documentary mosaic of the participants in the rarefied milieu of a working ballet company. And he does this with style and a deep acknowledgment of the power that dancing can have on us all' (2004: n.p.). Offering no judgement as to the film's verisimilitude or its entertainment value, Roger Ebert made the most astute observation of all when he noted that '*The Company* is the closest that Robert Altman has come to making an autobiographical film… As for Altman, I imagine some of the most heartfelt scenes in the movie for him are the ones involving Mr. A's attempt to create art while always having to think about money. Altman has rarely had big box-office hits (his most popular film was one of his earliest, *M*A*S*H*), and yet he has found a way to work steadily, to be prolific, despite almost always choosing projects he wants to work on. How does he do it? *The Company* offers some clues' (2003: n.p.). Released on Christmas Day 2003, the movie earned only $6.4 million in worldwide box office receipts versus a production budget of $15 million – another in a long line of artistically courageous Altman flops.

A Prairie Home Companion (2006)

Except for a hiatus in the late 1980s *A Prairie Home Companion*, Garrison Keillor's popular two-hour Saturday night live radio variety show has been broadcast continuously on National Public Radio from St. Paul, Minnesota since 1974. Keillor describes the show as 'a knock-off of *The Grand Ole Opry* in Nashville … since transmogrified into a loose amalgam of the *Opry*, *Fred Allen*, *Lux Mystery Theater*, *Let's Pretend*, and Bobby Benson and the B-Bar-B Gang' (2006: ii). A film version of *A Prairie Home Companion* would take four attempts over a twenty-year period to be realised. When Keillor's *Lake Wobegon Days* (Viking Press, 1985), a comic novel based on characters and materials from the radio show, achieved international success, director Sydney Pollock invited Keillor to write a screenplay based on the book but a year of effort produced nothing that could be turned into a film. In 1990 director-choreographer

Patricia Birch asked Keillor to write a screenplay based on a comic monologue from the radio show: a project that went into development at Disney and later at Miramax but finally fizzled out. Some years later, prolific British director Michael Winterbottom commissioned Keillor to write a screenplay based on his novel, *Wobegon Boy* (Viking Press, 1997) but that too failed to cohere into a movie. As Keillor put it, 'Three movie projects, zero movies' (ibid.).

In the early part of 2003, while *The Company* was in post-production, Altman began to explore the possibility of making a *Prairie Home Companion* 'backstage drama' (at the urging of his wife, Katherine, an ardent *PHC* devotee). He attended *PHC* road shows in New York and Ocean Grove, New Jersey and another show at Keillor's home base, the Fitzgerald Theater in St. Paul, before coming to the conclusion that, in Keillor's words, 'there absolutely was a movie here' (ibid.). Tasked by Altman to write a script, Keillor produced several drafts between July 2003 and June 2005. One draft concerned a blackout at the theatre that plunges the show into darkness: a trope Altman found uncinematic. Another draft featured 'a singer who has gone on to become a big star writing cheesy patriotic anthems [who] returns to the show and whom the stagehands consider a jerk and try to sabotage' (ibid.) – perhaps rejected because of too close a resemblance to Henry Gibson's unctuous Haven Hamilton character in *Nashville*. In yet another draft Keillor posited the Johnson Girls, 'the remnant of a larger sister act … who have survived a series of mishaps in the music business' (2006: iv). Altman liked this idea and recruited Meryl Streep to play Yolanda Johnson and Lily Tomlin to play Rhonda Johnson. Lindsay Lohan, who lobbied hard for a part, was cast as Meryl's somewhat morbid daughter, Lola. Kevin Kline took on the role of Guy Noir, a stock comical private eye character in *PHC* played by Keillor himself, but turned into the show's security man for the film version. Keillor also invented a pair of wisecracking singing cowboys (Woody Harrelson as Dusty and John C. Reilly as Lefty), perhaps an oblique, satiric reference to Townes van Zandt's maudlin ballad, 'Pancho and Lefty' (1972). Making further script revisions in the autumn and winter of 2004, Keillor added a singer named 'Chuck Akers', actually a pseudonym used by country guitarist Chet Atkins to check into hotels anonymously. (Played by 78-year-old western character actor, L. Q. Jones, Akers dies in a backstage dressing room while awaiting a tryst with the show's 'Lunch Lady', played by Marylouise Burke – a death that naturally rattles *PHC*'s cast but is kept quiet; like Nettie Sloan's death in *A Wedding*, it is not allowed to interrupt the proceedings.) Keillor amplified the death theme with a character he called 'Dangerous Woman', played by Virginia Madsen. Initially conceived of as 'a crazy listener who thought the announcer was in love with her and turned into an addled songwriter auditioning for a spot on the show', Dangerous Woman later morphed into Asphodel, a beautiful, blonde Angel of Death clad in a white raincoat who haunts the backstage areas of the Fitzgerald Theater on the final night of the show before it is closed down forever (see Keillor 2006: iv–v). Madsen's Asphodel (a flower associated in Greek mythology with death and the Underworld) recalls Angelique, Jessica Lange's nubile Angel of Death in Bob Fosse's semi-autobiographical musical fantasy, *All That Jazz* (1979) – though Keillor's Asphodel is depicted as gentle and wise, more like one of Wim Wenders' empathic angels in *Der Himmel über Berlin* (aka

Beneficent death: 'Dangerous Woman' (Virginia Madsen), the film's Angel of Death, is kind, wise and gentle-spirited.

Wings of Desire, 1987), whereas Fosse's sexy Angelique simmers with erotic seductiveness. Keillor also added 'The Axeman', a no-nonsense corporate honcho from Texas played by Tommy Lee Jones who arrives at the Fitzgerald to close down the show for financial reasons: another twist on the death theme, as in the death of old time live radio and all the folksy, Gemeinschaft values it represents (though ironically the Axeman is himself killed when his chauffeured limo crashes on the way to the airport after the show). To counter its aura of impending doom, the film features lots of vibrant musical numbers and comic bits and also includes Molly, the show's stage manager played by Maya Rudolph, who was coincidentally very much pregnant with her first child with director Paul Thomas Anderson during the shoot in June and early July 2005. At the insistence of the movie's insurers, Anderson, a friend and admirer of Altman, was on stand-by throughout the production to replace Altman – an eighty-year-old stroke survivor and heart transplant recipient undergoing radiation treatments for cancer – if Altman became incapacitated or died. A tangible affirmation of life's insistent resiliency, Rudolph's pregnancy is also an extradiegetic allusion to Anderson's youth and vitality, one of a new generation of filmmakers poised to build on Altman's unconventional legacy after his demise, which was obviously imminent. As Gayle Sherwood Magee notes in her discussion of the film, Garrison Keillor made his script much darker and more elegiac in successive drafts (2014: 236–7); tacit recognition on Keillor's part that his movie's implicit subject was Robert Altman's life and work, both of which were coming to a close. Altman did nothing to alter or sugar-coat Keillor's elegiac tone; he, too, knew it was likely to be his last project, though in the spring of 2006 Altman did go on to direct the Arthur Miller play, *Resurrection Blues*, at London's Old Vic theatre, albeit with disastrous results; lambasted by critics and poorly attended, the play closed early – a fiasco that producer Scott Griffin blames on Old Vic director Kevin Spacey, whom he characterises as a mercurial hypocrite 'who was arrogant and cruel' to Altman and his wife, Katherine (in Zuckoff 2009: 496). Altman's final triumph came just before his rueful Old Vic experience. At the 78th annual Academy Awards in March 2006, Altman was awarded an honorary Lifetime

Achievement Academy Award to a standing ovation from Hollywood's *crème de la crème*. Released in June 2006 (after an early premiere at the Berlin Film Festival), *A Prairie Home Companion* made a healthy $16 million profit for New Line Cinema and received mostly favourable critical notices, even though as Roger Ebert noted, the movie 'is not about anything in particular' (2006: n.p.). On 20 November 2006 Robert Altman died in Los Angeles at the age of eighty-one while planning another movie: 'Hands on a Hard Body', a fictionalised version of S. R. Bindler's 1997 documentary about an endurance/sleep deprivation contest at a Texas car dealership to win a Nissan Hardbody pick-up truck (the last person to remain standing with his or her hand on the truck wins it). The film would have starred Billy Bob Thornton, Hilary Swank and Dwayne Johnson.

Notes

1   Altman's 'History and Physical Examination' dated 27 February 1991, from Altman Archives, University of Michigan.
2   Originally Kim Basinger was slated to play the role of Carolyn Stilton but had to drop out when she became pregnant (Magee, 2014, 181).
3   Other versions of the Gingerbread Man derived from Hungarian and Russian folktales make him a distinctly sinister figure. In the Hungarian version of the tale known as 'The Little Dumpling' ('A kis gömböc') the *gömböc* (a dumpling made from a stuffed pig's stomach) first consumes the family that made it, then it rolls on the road eating others, the last of whom is a swineherd, whose knife opens the *gömböc* from the inside, and the people run home. In another variation the *gömböc* bursts after eating too many people. A similar Russian tale titled 'The Clay Man' features an old childless couple who make themselves a clay child, who grows up, eats all their food, then eats them, then a number of other people, until he meets a goat who offers to jump right into his mouth, but instead the goat rams the clay man, shattering him and freeing everyone. Like all folktales, there are many variations of the Gingerbread Man story but the point here is that it bifurcates into two opposing types of narrative of Desire: one that makes the title character a victim of the gluttony of others and another that makes him the rapacious monster of bottomless appetite. Mallory applies the latter characterisation to her father but events will show Dixon Doss to be the victim of cupidity, not the perpetrator.
4   Vineberg characterises Davidtz's performance as 'ambiguous (and, I think, superb) … she's simultaneously seductive and retreating, [hinting] at a damaged core that can't be healed, as with other memorable women in Altman movies: Shelley Duvall in *Thieves Like Us*, Sandy Dennis in *Come Back to the Five and Dime, Jimmy Dean Jimmy Dean*, and especially Nina Van Pallandt in *The Long Goodbye*, which the Gingerbread Man harks back to in a number of ways' (n.p.).
5   The surname Dixon invokes Thomas Frederick Dixon Jr. (1864–1946), a Southern Baptist minister, playwright, lecturer, North Carolina state legislator, lawyer and author, best known for writing *The Clansman* (1905), the book that inspired D. W. Griffith's white supremacist film, *The Birth of a Nation* (1915).

6   Pete Hammond (Moderator), 8 March 2002. Cast and Filmmaker's Q&A Session (DVD), USA Films.

7   See 'Dressing Gosford Park', Land of Might-Have-Been: A Gosford Park Fan Site: http://www.loony-archivist.com/gosford/notes_dressing.htm

8   See http://www.sonyclassics.com/thecompany/theCompany.pdf

9   Ibid.

10   According to Gayle Sherwood Magee, the scene was actually shot at the Petrillo Band Shell in Chicago's Grant Park in October (2014: 228).

11   See http://www.slantmagazine.com/film/review/the-company

12   See http://www.theguardian.com/stage/2004/may/05/dance

Coda

Robert Altman summed up his philosophy of filmmaking better than anyone else could have when he received his honorary Academy Award in 2006:

> I equate it more with painting than with theatre or literature. Stories don't interest me. Basically I'm more interested in behaviour. I don't direct. I watch. I have to be thrilled if I expect the audience to be thrilled. Because what I really want to see from an actor is something I've never seen before, so I can't tell them what that is… [Filmmaking] is just such a joyous, collaborative art. When you start looking back, the real reward is the process of doing it and the people that you do it with… To me, I just made one, long film. I've always said that making a film is like making a sandcastle at the beach. You invite your friends and you get them down there and, say, you build this beautiful structure, several of you, and you sit back and have a drink, watch the tide come in, and the ocean just takes it away. And that sandcastle remains in your mind.

The sandcastle analogy doesn't entirely work, insofar as the films palpably survive and presumably will endure and be watched, enjoyed, sometimes reviled but studied and pondered as long as there are cinephiles. What comes through from these remarks, though, is Altman's abiding interest in capturing the poignant, beautiful and spontaneous reality of experience rather than constructing a filmic commodity along the lines specified by industry and commerce – a healthy-minded impulse that always automatically placed him on the side of art, life and humanity and opposed to the authoritarian structures that continue to crush the human spirit.

FILMOGRAPHY

Countdown (1967)
Production Company: William Conrad
  Productions for Warner Bros.-Seven
  Arts
Producers: William Conrad, Jimmy
  Lydon
Director: Robert Altman
Screenplay: Loring Mandel
Cinematography: William W. Spencer
Editor: Gene Milford
Main Cast: James Caan (Lee Stegler),
  Joanna Moore (Mickey Stegler),
  Robert Duvall (Chiz), Barbara Baxley
  (Jean), Steve Ihnat (Ross Duellan),
  Michael Murphy (Rick), Ted Knight
  (Walter Larson), Stephen Coit
  (Ehrman)

That Cold Day in the Park (1969)
Production Company: Factor-Altman-
  Merrill Films Ltd./Commonwealth
  International
Producers: Robert Eggenweiler, Donald
  Factor, Leon Mirell
Screenplay: Gillian Freeman
Cinematography: László Kovács
Editor: Danford B. Greene
Original Music: Johnny Mandel

Main Cast: Sandy Dennis (Frances
  Austen), Michael Burns (the boy),
  Susanne Benton (Nina), David
  Garfield (billed as John Garfield
  Jr.) (Nick), Luana Anders (Sylvie),
  Michael Murphy (the Rounder),
  Edward Greenhalgh (the doctor)

M*A*S*H (1970)
Production Company: Aspen/20th
  Century Fox
Producers: Ingo Preminger, Leon
  Ericksen
Director: Robert Altman
Screenplay: Ring Lardner Jr.
Cinematography: Harold E. Stine
Editor: Danford B. Greene
Original Music: Johnny Mandel
Main Cast: Donald Sutherland (Capt.
  Benjamin Franklin 'Hawkeye' Pierce),
  Elliott Gould (Capt. John Francis
  Xavier 'Trapper John' McIntyre),
  Tom Skerritt (Capt. Augustus
  Bedford 'Duke' Forrest), Sally
  Kellerman (Major Margaret 'Hot Lips'
  Houlihan), Robert Duvall (Major
  Frank Burns), Roger Bowen (Lt.
  Col. Henry Braymore Blake), René
  Auberjonois (Father John Patrick

'Dago Red' Mulcahy), David Arkin (SSgt. Wade 'Lee' Douglas Vollmer), Jo Ann Pflug (Lt. Maria 'Dish' Schneider), Gary Burghoff (Cpl. 'Radar' O'Reilly), Fred Williamson (Capt. Oliver Harmon 'Spearchucker' Jones), Michael Murphy (Capt. Ezekiel Bradbury 'Me Lay' Marston IV), John Schuck (Capt. Walter Koskiusko 'The Painless Pole' Waldowski, DDS), G. Wood (Brig. Gen. Charlie Hammond), Bud Cort (Pvt. Lorenzo Boone)

Brewster McCloud (1970)
Production Company: An Adler-Phillips/Lion's Gate Production for MGM
Producers: Lou Adler, Robert Eggenweiler, James Margellos, John Phillips
Director: Robert Altman
Screenplay: Doran William Canon
Cinematography: Lamar Boren, Jordan Cronenweth
Editor: Lou Lombardo
Original Music: John Phillips
Main Cast: Bud Cort (Brewster McCloud), Sally Kellerman (Louise), Michael Murphy (Detective Frank Shaft), William Windom (Weeks), Shelley Duvall (Suzanne), René Auberjonois (The Lecturer), Stacy Keach (Abraham Wright), John Schuck (Officer Johnson), Margaret Hamilton (Daphne Heap), Jennifer Salt (Hope), Corey Fischer (Officer Hines), G. Wood (Det. Capt. Crandall), Bert Remsen (Officer Breen)

McCabe & Mrs. Miller (1971)
Production Company: An Altman-Foster Production for Warner Bros.

Producers: David Foster, Mitchell Brower, Robert Eggenweiler
Director: Robert Altman
Screenplay: Robert Altman, Brian McKay
Cinematography: Vilmos Zsigmond
Editor: Lou Lombardo
Original Music: Leonard Cohen
Main Cast: Warren Beatty (John McCabe), Julie Christie (Mrs. Constance Miller), René Auberjonois (Sheehan), William Devane (Clement Samuels, Esq.) John Schuck (Smalley), Corey Fischer (Rev. Elliot), Bert Remsen (Bart Coyle), Shelley Duvall (Ida Coyle), Keith Carradine (Cowboy), Michael Murphy (Eugene Sears), Antony Holland (Ernest Hollander), Hugh Millais (Butler), Manfred Schulz (Kid), Jace Van Der Veen (Breed)

Images (1972)
Production Company: Lion's Gate Productions (Dublin) for the Hemdale Group
Producer: Tommy Thompson
Director: Robert Altman
Screenplay: Robert Altman
Cinematography: Vilmos Zsigmond
Editor: Graeme Clifford
Original Music: Stomu Yamashta; John Williams
Main Cast: Susannah York (Cathryn), René Auberjonois (Hugh), Marcel Bozzuffi (René), Hugh Millais (Marcel), Cathryn Harrison (Susannah), John Morley (Old Man)

The Long Goodbye (1973)
Production Company: Lion's Gate Films for United Artists
Producers: Elliott Kastner, Jerry Bick
Director: Robert Altman

Screenplay: Leigh Brackett
Cinematography: Vilmos Zsigmond
Editor: Lou Lombardo
Original Music: John Williams
Main Cast: Elliott Gould (Philip
  Marlowe), Nina van Pallandt
  (Eileen Wade), Sterling Hayden
  (Roger Wade), Mark Rydell (Marty
  Augustine), Henry Gibson (Dr.
  Verringer), David Arkin (Harry),
  Jim Bouton (Terry Lennox), Warren
  Berlinger (Morgan), Jo Ann Brody
  (Jo Ann Eggenweiler), Stephen Coit
  (Detective Farmer)

Thieves Like Us (1974)
Production Company: A Jerry Beck-
  George Litto Production for United
  Artists
Producer: Robert Altman
Director: Robert Altman
Screenplay: Joan Tewkesbury, Calder
  Willingham, Robert Altman
Cinematography: Jean Boffety
Editor: Lou Lombardo
Main Cast: Keith Carradine (Bowie
  Bowers), Shelley Duvall (Keechie),
  John Schuck (Elmo 'Chicamaw'
  Mobley) Bert Remsen (T.W. 'T-Dub'
  Masefield), Louise Fletcher (Mattie),
  Ann Latham (Lula), Tom Skerritt
  (Dee Mobley)

California Split (1974)
Production Company: Won World for
  Columbia Pictures
Producers: Joseph Walsh, Robert Altman
Director: Robert Altman
Screenplay: Joseph Walsh
Cinematography: Paul Lohmann
Editor: O. Nicholas Brown, Lou
  Lombardo
Main Cast: George Segal (Bill Denny),
  Elliott Gould (Charlie Waters), Ann

Prentiss (Barbara Miller), Gwen Welles
  (Susan Peters), Edward Walsh (Lew),
  Joseph Walsh (Sparkie), Bert Remsen
  ('Helen Brown'), Jeff Goldblum
  (Lloyd Harris)

Nashville (1975)
Production Company: American
  Broadcasting Corporation (ABC) for
  Paramount Pictures
Producers: Robert Altman; Scott
  Bushnell; Robert Eggenweiler; Martin
  Starger; Jerry Weintraub
Director: Robert Altman
Screenplay: Joan Tewkesbury
Cinematography: Paul Lohmann
Editors: Tony Lombardo, Tom Walls,
  Mark Eggenweiler, Maysie Hoy
Original Music: Arlene Barnett, Jonnie
  Barnett, Karen Black, Ronee Blakley,
  Gary Busey, Juan Grizzle, Allan
  Nicholls, Dave Peel, Joe Raposo
Main Cast: David Arkin (Norman),
  Barbara Baxley (Lady Pearl), Ned
  Beatty (Delbert Reese), Karen
  Black (Connie White), Ronee
  Blakley (Barbara Jean), Timothy
  Brown (Tommy Brown), Keith
  Carradine (Tom Frank), Geraldine
  Chaplin (Opal), Robert DoQui
  (Wade), Shelley Duvall (L.A. Joan
  [Martha]), Allen Garfield (Barnett),
  Henry Gibson (Haven Hamilton),
  Scott Glenn (Pfc Glenn Kelly), Jeff
  Goldblum (Tricycle Man), Barbara
  Harris (Albuquerque), David Hayward
  (Kenny Fraiser), Michael Murphy
  (John Triplette), Allan Nicholls (Bill),
  Dave Peel (Brad Hamilton), Cristina
  Raines (Mary), Bert Remsen (Star),
  Lily Tomlin (Linnea Reese), Gwen
  Welles (Sueleen Gay); Keenan Wynn
  (Mr. Green), Richard Baskin (Frog)

Buffalo Bill and the Indians, or Sitting Bull's History Lesson (1976)
Production Companies: United Artists (USA); Dino De Laurentiis Productions (overseas)
Producer: Dino De Laurentis
Director: Robert Altman
Screenplay: Alan Rudolph, Robert Altman
Cinematography: Paul Lohmann
Editors: Peter Appleton, Dennis M. Hill
Original Music: Richard Baskin
Main Cast: Paul Newman (William F. 'Buffalo Bill' Cody), Joel Grey (Nate Salisbury), Burt Lancaster (Ned Buntline), Kevin McCarthy (Major John Burke), Harvey Keitel (Ed Goodman), Allan Nicholls (Colonel Prentiss Ingraham), Geraldine Chaplin (Annie Oakley), John Considine (Frank Butler), Robert DoQui (Oswald Dart), Bert Remsen (Crutch), Denver Pyle (McLaughlin),
Evelyn Lear (Nina Cavalini), Frank Kaquitts (Chief Sitting Bull), Will Sampson (William Halsey), Pat McCormick (Pres. Grover Cleveland), Shelley Duvall (Frances Folsom)

3 Women (1977)
Production Company: Lion's Gate Films for 20th Century Fox
Producers: Robert Altman, Scott Bushnell, Robert Eggenweiler
Director: Robert Altman
Screenplay: Robert Altman, Patricia Resnick
Cinematography: Charles Rosher Jr.
Editor: Dennis M. Hill
Original Music: Gerald Busby
Main Cast: Shelley Duvall (Millie Lammoreaux), Sissy Spacek (Pinky Rose), Janice Rule (Willie Hart, Robert Fortier (Edgar Hart), Ruth

Nelson (Mrs. Rose), John Cromwell (Mr. Rose)

A Wedding (1978)
Production Company: Lion's Gate Films for 20th Century Fox
Producer: Robert Altman
Director: Robert Altman
Screenplay: John Considine; Allan F. Nicholls; Patricia Resnick; Robert Altman
Cinematography: Charles Rosher Jr.
Editor: Tony Lombardo
Main Cast: Carol Burnett (Tulip Brenner), Paul Dooley (Snooks Brenner), Amy Stryker (Muffin Brenner), Mia Farrow (Buffy Brenner), Dennis Christopher (Hughie Brenner), Gerald Busby (Rev. David Ruteledge), Peggy Ann Garner (Candice Ruteledge), Marta Heflin (Shelby Munker), Lillian Gish (Nettie Sloan), Nina van Pallandt (Regina Corelli), Vittorio Gassman (Luigi Corelli), Desi Arnaz Jr. (Dino Corelli), Dina Merrill (Antoinette Godard), pat McCormick (Mackenzie Goddard), Howard Duff (James Meecham), Ruth Nelson (Beatrice Sloan), John Cromwell (Bishop Martin), Geraldine Chaplin (Rita Billingsley), John Considine (Jeff Kuykendall), Lauren Hutton (Florence Farmer), Dennis Franz (Koons), Pam Dawber (Tracey Farrell), Gavan O'Herlihy (Wilson Briggs), Bert Remsen (William Williamson)

Quintet (1979)
Production Company: Lion's Gate Films for 20th Century Fox
Producers: Robert Altman, Allan F. Nicholls, Tommy Thompson
Director: Robert Altman

Screenplay: Robert Altman; Lionel
Chetwynd, Patricia Resnick, Frank
Barhydt Jr.
Cinematography: Jean Boffety
Editor: Dennis M. Hill
Original Music: Tom Pierson
Main Cast: Paul Newman (Essex),
Vittorio Gassman (St. Christopher),
Fernando Rey (Grigor), Bibi
Andersson (Ambrosia), Brigitte
Fossey (Viva), Nina van Pallandt
(Deuca), David Langton (Goldstar),
Thomas Hill (Francha), Craig Richard
(Redstone)

A Perfect Couple (1979)
Production Company: Lion's Gate Films
for 20th Century Fox
Producer: Robert Altman
Director: Robert Altman
Screenplay: Robert Altman, Allan
Nicholls
Cinematography: Edward L. Koons
Editor: Tony Lombardo
Original Music: Tom Pierson, Tony
Berg, Allan Nicholls
Main Cast: Paul Dooley (Alex
Theodopoulos), Marta Heflin
(Sheila Shea), Titos Vandis (Panos
Theodopoulos, Belita Moreno
(Eleousa Theodopoulos), Tony Berg,
Craig Doerge, Jeff Eyrich, David
Luell, Butch Sandford, Art Wood,
Renn Woods (Keepin' 'Em Off the
Streets)

HealtH (1980)
Production Company: Lion's Gate Films
for 20th Century Fox
Producer: Robert Altman
Director: Robert Altman
Screenplay: Frank Barhydt, Robert
Altman, Paul Dooley
Cinematography: Edmond L. Koons

Editors: Tony Lombardo, Dennis M.
Hill, Tom Benko
Original Music: Joseph Byrd, Allan
Nicholls
Main Cast: Glenda Jackson (Isabella
Garnell), Lauren Bacall (Esther Brill),
Carol Burnett (Gloria Burbank),
James Garner (Harry Wolff), Dick
Cavett (Himself), Paul Dooley
(Harold Gainey), Donald Moffat
(Colonel Cody), Henry Gibson
(Bobby Hammer), Alfre Woodard
(Sally Benbow)

Popeye (1980)
Production Company: Paramount/Walt
Disney
Producers: Robert Evans
Director: Robert Altman
Screenplay: Jules Feiffer
Cinematography: Giuseppe Rotunno
Editors: Tony Lombardo, John W.
Holmes, David Simmons
Original Music: Harry Nilsson, Van
Dyke Parks, Tom Pierson
Main Cast: Robin Williams (Popeye),
Shelley Duvall (Olive Oyl), Ray
Walston (Poopdeck Pappy), Paul
Dooley (Wimpy), Paul L. Smith
(Bluto), Richard Libertini (Geezil),
Donald Moffat (Taxman), Allan
Nicholls (Roughhouse), Robert Fortier
(Bill Barnacle), Dennis Franz (Spike),
David Arkin (Mailman/Policeman)

*Come Back to the Five & Dime, Jimmy
Dean, Jimmy Dean (1982)*
Production Company: Sandcastle 5/
Mark Goodson/Viacom
Producer: Scott Bushnell
Director: Robert Altman
Screenplay: Ed Graczyk, based on his
own play
Cinematography: Pierre Mignot

Editor: Jason Rosenfield
Production design: David Gropman
Main Cast: Sandy Dennis (Mona), Cher (Sissy), Karen Black (Joanne), Sudie Bond (Juanita), Kathy Bates (Stella Mae), Marta Heflin (Edna Louise), Gena Ramsel (Sue Ellen), Ann Risley (Phyllis Marie), Dianne Turley Travis (Alice Ann)

Streamers (1983)
Production Company: Streamers International Distributors
Producers: Robert Altman, Nick J. Mileti
Director: Robert Altman
Screenplay: David Rabe, based on his own play
Cinematography: Pierre Mignot
Editor: Norman Smith
Production design: Wolf Kroeger
Main Cast: Matthew Modine (William 'Billy' Wilson), Michael Wright (Carlyle), Mitchell Lichtenstein (Richard 'Richie' Douglas), David Alan Grier (Roger Hicks), Guy Boyd (Sergeant Rooney), George Dzundza (Sergeant Cokes), Albert Macklin (Martin), B. J. Cleveland (Pfc Bush), Bill Allen (Lieutenant Townsend), Paul Lazar (MP Lieutenant), Phil Ward (MP Sergeant Kilick), Terry McIlvain (Orderly), Todd Savell (MP Sergeant Savio), Mark Fickert (Dr. Barnes), Dustye Winniford (Staff Sergeant), Robert S. Reed (MP)

Secret Honor (1984)
Production Company: Sandcastle 5/University of Michigan (Communications Dept.)/Los Angeles Actors' Theater
Producer: Robert Altman
Director: Robert Altman

Screenplay: Donald Freed, Arthur M. Stone, based on their own play
Cinematography: Pierre Mignot
Editor: Juliet Weber
Original Music: George Burt
Production design: Stephan Altman
Main Cast: Philip Baker Hall (Richard Milhous Nixon)

Fool for Love (1985)
Production Company: The Cannon Company
Producers: Menahem Golan, Yoram Globus
Director: Robert Altman
Screenplay: Sam Shepard, based on his own play
Cinematography: Pierre Mignot
Editors: Luce Gruenwaldt, Steve Dunn
Original Music: George Burt
Production Design: Stephen Altman
Main Cast: Sam Sheppard (Eddie), Kim Basinger (May), Harry Dean Stanton (Old Man), Randy Quaid (Martin), Martha Crawford (May's mother), Louise Egolf (Eddie's mother), Sura Cox (Teenage May), Jonathan Skinner (Young Eddie), April Russell (Young May), Deborah McNaughton (The Countess), Lon Hill (Mr. Valdes)

O.C. & Stiggs (1987)
Production Company: Sand River Productions for MGM/UA
Producers: Robert Altman, Peter Newman
Director: Robert Altman
Screenplay: Donald Cantrell, Ted Mann, based on a story by Tod Carroll, Ted Mann
Cinematography: Pierre Mignot
Editor: Elizabeth Kling
Music: King Sunny Ade and his African Beats

Production Design: Scotty Bushnell
Main Cast: Daniel H. Jenkins (Oliver
Cromwell 'O.C.' Ogilvy), Neill
Barry (Mark Stiggs), Jane Curtin
(Elinore Schwab), Paul Dooley
(Randall Schwab), Jon Cryer (Randall
Schwab Jr.), Laura Urstein (Lenore
Schwab), Victor Ho (Frankie Tang),
Ray Walston (Gramps), Tina Louise
(Florence Beaugereaux), Cynthia
Nixon (Michelle), Dennis Hopper
(Sponson), Louis Nye (Garin Sloan),
Martin Mull (Pat Coletti), Melvin
van Peebles (Wino Bob), Bob Uecker
(himself), Nina van Pallandt (Clare
Dejavue), Thomas Hal Phillips (Hal
Phillip Walker)

Beyond Therapy (1988)
Production Company: New World
Pictures/Sand Castle 5
Producers: Roger Berlind, Steven Haft
Director: Robert Altman
Screenplay: Christopher Durang,
Robert Altman, based on a play by
Christopher Durang
Cinematography: Pierre Mignot
Editors: Steve Dunn, Jennifer Ague
Production Design: Stephen Altman
Main Cast: Julie Haggerty (Prudence),
Jeff Goldblum (Bruce), Glenda
Jackson (Charlotte), Tom Conti
(Stuart), Christopher Guest (Bob),
Geneviève Page (Zizi), Chris Campion
(Andrew)

Vincent & Theo (1990)
Production Company: Belbo Films
(Paris), Central Films (London)
Producers: Ludi Boeken, David Conroy,
Emma Hayter
Director: Robert Altman
Screenplay: Julian Mitchell
Cinematography: Jean Lépine

Editors: Françoise Coispeau, Geraldine
Peroni
Music: Gabriel Yared
Production Design: Stephen Altman
Main Cast: Tim Roth (Vincent van
Gogh), Paul Rhys (Theo van Gogh),
Johanna ter Steege (Jo Bonger),
Wladimir Yordanoff (Paul Gaugin),
Jean-Pierre Cassel (Dr. Paul Gachet),
Bernadette Giraud (Marguerite
Gachet), Mogna Mehlem (M.
Ravoux), Thérèse Crémieux (Mme
Ravoux)

The Player (1992)
Production Company: Avenue
Entertainment
Producers: David Brown, Michael
Tolkin, Nick Wechsler
Director: Robert Altman
Screenplay: Michael Tolkin, based on his
own novel
Cinematography: Jean Lépine
Editor: Geraldine Peroni
Music: Thomas Newman
Main Cast: Tim Robbins (Griffin
Mill), Greta Scacchi (June
Gudmundsdottir), Fred Ward (Walter
Stuckel), Whoopi Goldberg (Detective
Susan Avery), Peter Gallagher (Larry
Levy), Brion James (Joel Levison),
Cynthia Stevenson (Bonnie Sherow),
Vincent D'Onofrio (David Kahane),
Dean Stockwell (Andy Civella),
Sydney Pollack (Dick Mellon), Lyle
Lovett (Detective DeLongpre),
Dina Merrill (Celia), Frank Barhydt
(Frank Murphy), Michael Tolkin
(Eric Schecter), Stephen Tolkin (Carl
Schecter), Angela Hall (Jan), Brian
Brophy (Phil), Michael Tolkin (Eric
Schecter), Stephen Tolkin (Carl
Schecter)

Short Cuts (1993)
Production Company: Spelling Films
 International, Fine Line Pictures,
 Avenue Pictures
Producers: Cary Brokaw
Director: Robert Altman
Screenplay: Robert Altman, Frank
 Barhydt, based on the writings of
 Raymond Carver
Cinematography: Walt Lloyd
Editor: Geraldine Peroni
Original Music: Mark Isham
Main Cast: Andie MacDowell (Ann
 Finnigan), Bruce Davison (Howard
 Finnigan), Jack Lemmon (Paul
 Finnigan), Zane Cassidy (Casey
 Finnigan), Julianne Moore (Marian
 Wyman), Matthew Modine (Dr.
 Ralph Wyman), Anne Archer (Claire
 Kane), Fred War (Stuart Kane),
 Jennifer Jason Leigh (Lois Kaiser),
 Chris Penn (Jerry Kaiser), Lili Tyler
 (Honey Bush), Robert Downey
 Jr. (Bill Bush), Madeleine Stowe
 (Sherri Shepard), Tim Robbins
 (Gene Shepard), Lily Tomlin
 (Doreen Piggot), Tom Waits (Earl
 Piggot), Frances McDormand (Betty
 Weathers), Peter Gallagher (Stormy
 Weathers), Annie Ross (Tess Trainer),
 Lori Singer (Zoe Trainer), Lyle
 Lovett (Andy Bitkower), Buck Henry
 (Gordon Johnson), Huey Lewis (Vern
 Miller), Robert DoQui (Knute Willis)

Prêt-à-Porter (1994)
Production Company: Miramax Film
 International
Producer: Robert Altman
Director: Robert Altman
Screenplay: Robert Altman, Barbara
 Shulgasser
Cinematography: Pierre Mignot, Jean
 Lépine

Editor: Geraldine Peroni
Original Music: Michel Legrand
Main Cast: Danny Aiello (Major
 Hamilton), Anouk Aimée (Simone
 Lowenthal), Lauren Bacall (Slim
 Chrysler), Kim Basinger (Kitty
 Potter), Jean-Pierre Cassel (Olivier
 de la Fontaine), Rupert Everett
 (Jack Lowenthal), Teri Garr (Louise
 Hamilton), Richard E. Grant (Cort
 Romney), Linda Hunt (Regina
 Krumm), Sally Kellerman (Regina
 Wanamaker), Ute Lemper (Albertine),
 Tara Leon (Kiki Simpson), Sophia
 Loren (Isabella de la Fontaine), Lyle
 Lovett (Clint Lammeraux), Chiara
 Mastroianni (Sophie Choiset),
 Marcello Mastroianni (Sergei/Sergio),
 Tom Novembre (Reggie), Stephen Rea
 (Milo O'Brannigan), Tim Robbins
 (Joe Flynn), Georgianna Robertson
 (Dane Simpson), Julia Roberts (Anne
 Eisenhower), Lili Taylor (Fiona
 Ulrich), Tracey Ullman (Nina Scant),
 Forest Whitaker (Cy Bianco)

Kansas City (1996)
Production Company: Ciby 2000/
 Sandcastle 5
Producer: Robert Altman
Director: Robert Altman
Screenplay: Robert Altman, Frank
 Barhydt
Cinematography: Oliver Stapleton
Editor: Geraldine Peroni
Music: Hal Willner, Steven Bernstein
Main Cast: Jennifer Jason Leigh
 (Blondie O'Hara), Miranda
 Richardson (Carolyn Stilton), Harry
 Belafonte (Seldom Seen), Michael
 Murphy (Henry Stilton), Dermot
 Mulroney (Johnny O'Hara), Steve
 Buscemi (Johnny Flynn), Brooke
 Smith (Babe Flynn), Albert J. Burnes

(Charlie Parker), Tawanna Benbow
(Rose), Joe Dirgirolamo (John Lazia)

The Gingerbread Man (1998)
Production Company: Polygram Filmed
Entertainment, Island Pictures/
Enchanter Entertainment
Producers: Jeremy Tannenbaum
Director: Robert Altman
Screenplay: Al Hayes, Robert Altman,
based on an original story by John
Grisham
Cinematography: Changwe Gu
Editor: Geraldine Peroni
Original Music: Mark Isham
Production Design: Stephen Altman
Main Cast: Kenneth Branagh (Rick
Magruder), Embeth Davidtz (Mallory
Doss), Robert Downey Jr. (Clyde
Pell), Daryl Hannah (Lois Harlan),
Robert Duval (Dixon Doss), Tom
Berenger (Pete Randle), Famke Janssen
(Leeanne)

Cookie's Fortune (1999)
Production Company: October Films
presents a Sandcastle 5 and Elysian
Dreams production
Producers: Robert Altman, Etchie Stroh
Director: Robert Altman
Screenplay: Anne Rapp
Cinematography: Toyomichi Kurita
Editor: Mark Weingarten
Original Music: David A. Stewart
Main Cast: Glenn Close (Camille
Dixon), Julianne Moore (Cora
Duvall), Liv Tyler (Emma Duvall),
Chris O'Donnell (Jason Brown),
Charles S. Dutton (Willis Richland),
Patricia Neal (Jewel Mae 'Cookie'
Orcutt), Ned Beatty (Lester Boyle),
Donald Moffat (Jack Palmer), Lyle
Lovett (Manny Hood)

Dr. T & The Women (2000)
Production Company: Initial
Entertainment Group presents a
Sandcastle 5 production
Producers: Robert Altman, James
McLindon
Director: Robert Altman
Screenplay: Anne Rapp
Cinematography: Jan Kiesser
Editor: Geraldine Peroni
Production design: Stephen Altman
Main Cast: Richard Gere (Dr. Sullivan
Travis, aka 'Dr. T'), Helen Hunt (Bree
Davis), Farrah Fawcett (Kate Travis),
Laura Dern (Peggy), Shelley Long
(Carolyn), Tara Reid (Connie Travis),
Kate Hudson (Dee Dee Travis), Liv
Tyler (Marilyn), Robert hays (Harlan),
Matt Malloy (Bill), Andy Richter
(Eli), Lee Grant (Dr. Harper), Janine
Turner (Dorothy Chambliss), Holly
Pelham-Davis (Joanne), Ramsey
Williams (Menopausal patient)

Gosford Park (2001)
Production Company: Capitol Films and
The Film Council in association with
USA Films, a Sandcastle 5 production
in association with Chicagofilms and
Medusa Film
Producers: Robert Altman, Bob Balaban,
David Levy
Director: Robert Altman
Screenplay: Julian Fellowes, based on
an idea by Robert Altman and Bob
Balaban
Cinematography: Andrew Dunn
Editor: Tim Squyres
Original Music: Patrick Doyle
Production design: Stephen Altman
Main Cast: Above Stairs: Maggie Smith
(Constance Trentham), Michael
Gambon (William McCordle), Kristin
Scott Thomas (Sylvia McCordle),

Camilla Rutherford (Isobel McCordle), Charles Dance (Raymond Stockbridge), Geraldine Somerville (Louisa Stockbridge), Tom Hollander (Lt. Commander Anthony Meredith), Jeremy Northam (Ivor Novello), Bob Balaban (Morris Weisman), James Wilby (Freddie Nesbitt), Lawrence Fox (Rupert Standish), Trent Ford (Jeremy Bond), Ryan Phillippe (Henry Denton); Visitors: Stephen Fry (Inspector Thompson), Ron Webster (Constable Dexter); Below Stairs: Kelley Macdonald (Mary Maceachran), Clive Owen (Robert Parks), Helen Mirren (Mrs. Wilson), Eileen Atkins (Mrs. Croft), Emily Watson (Elsie), Alan Bates (Jennings), Derek Jacobi (Probert), Richard E. Grant (George), Jeremy Swift (Arthur), Sophie Thompson (Dorothy), Meg Wynn Owen (Lewis), Adrian Scarborough (Barnes), Frances Low (Sarah), Joanna Maude (Renee), Teresa Churcher (Bertha), Sarah Flind (Ellen), Finty Williams (Janet), Emma Buckley (May), Lucy Cohu (Lottie), Laura Harling (Ethel), Tilly Gerard (Maud), Will Beer (Albert), Leo Bill (Jim), Gregor Henderson Begg (Fred), John Atterbury (Merriman), Frank Thornton (Mr. Burkett), Ron Puttock (Strutt)

The Company (2003)
Production Company: Capitol Films in association with CP Medien, a Killer Films/John Wells Production in association with First Snow Productions and Sand Castle 5
Producers: David Levy, Joshua Astrachan, Neve Campbell, Robert Altman, Christine Vachon, Pamela Koffer

Director: Robert Altman
Screenplay: Barbara Turner
Cinematography: Andrew Dunn
Editor: Geraldine Peroni
Original Music: Van Dyke Parks
Production design: Gary Baugh
Main Cast: Neve Campbell (Ry), Malcolm McDowell (Alberto Antonelli), James Franco (Josh), Barbara Robertson (Harriet), William Dick (Edouard), Susie Cusack (Susie), Marilyn Dodds Frank (Ry's mother), John Lordan (Ry's father), Mariann Mayberry (Stepmother), Roderick Peeples (Stepfather), Yasen Peyankov (Justin's Mentor), The Joffrey Dancers: David Robertson (Alec), Deborah Dawn (Deborah), John Gluckman (John), David Gombert (Justin), Suzanne L. Prisco (Suzanne), Domingo Rubio (Domingo), Emily Patterson (Noel), Maia Wilkins (Maia), Sam Franke (Frankie), Trinity Hamilton (Trinity), Julianne Kepley (Julianne), Valerie Robin (Veronica), Deanne Brown (Dana), Michael Smith (Michael), Michael Roy Prescott, Lar Lubovitch, Robert Desrosiers (The Choreographers), Charthel Arthur, Cameron Basden (The ballet mistresses), Mark Goldweber, Peter Lockett, Adam Sklute (The Ballet Masters)

A Prairie Home Companion (2006)
Production Company:
Producers: Robert Altman, Fisher Stevens
Director: Robert Altman
Screenplay: Garrison Keillor, based on a story by Garrison Keillor and Ken LaZebnik
Cinematography: Edward Lachman
Editor: Jacob Craycroft

Main Cast: Garrison Keillor (himself), Woody Harrelson (Dusty), John C. Reilly (Lefty), L. Q. Jones (Chuck Akers), Tommy Lee Jones (Axeman), Kevin Kline (Guy Noir), Lindsay Lohan (Lola Johnson), Virginia Madsen ('Asphodel', aka, Dangerous Woman), Marylouise Burke (Lunch lady), Tim Russell (stage manager), Maya Rudolph (assistant stage manager), Meryl Streep (Yolanda Johnson), Lily Tomlin (Rhonda Johnson), Robin and Linda Williams (themselves), Tom Keith (Sound effects guy), Sue Scott (Make-up artist)

BIBLIOGRAPHY

Allsop, Christopher D. (2013) 'Turn Off the Lights as You Leave: Altman and his *Short Cuts* with Carver', *Journal of Film and Video*, 65:1/2, 62–75.

Altman. Director: Ron Mann. Sphinx Productions, 2014.

Altman, Kathryn Reed and Giulia D'Agnolo Vallan (2014) *Altman*. New York: Harry N. Abrams.

Altman, Robert, Frank Barhydt and Raymond Carver (1993) *Short Cuts: The Screenplay*. New York: Capra Press.

Anon. (1980) *New York Magazine*, November, 84.

____ (1984) *The Cavalier Daily*, 30 March, 14.

____ (1998) 'Christian Dior Opens', *Moscow Times*, 19 December; http://www.themoscow-times.com/sitemap/free/1998/12/article/christian-dior-opens/282039.html

Arnold, Gary (1974) 'Robert Altman's "Thieves Like Us"', *The Washington Post* March 14, C13.

Arthur, Paul (2003) 'How the West was Spun: *McCabe and Mrs. Miller* and Genre Revisionism', *Cineaste*, 28:3, 18–21.

Aufderheide, Patricia (1985) '*Secret Honor*: Interviews with Donald Freed and Robert Altman', *Cineaste*, 14:2, 13–14.

Azcona, María del Mar (2011) 'A Cinema of Plenty: Robert Altman and the Multi-Protagonist Film', in Rick Armstrong (ed.) *Robert Altman: Critical Essays*. Jefferson, NC: McFarland, 139–55.

____ 'Making Sense of a Multi-Protagonist Film: Audience Response Research and Robert Altman's *Short Cuts* (1993)', *Miscelánea: A Journal of English and American Studies* 32 (2005), 11–22.

____ (2015) '*Dr. T & the Women* and Altman's Multi-Protagonist Narratives', in Adrian Danks (ed.) *A Companion to Robert Altman*. Oxford: Wiley Blackwell, 448–64.

Bachman, Gregg (1997) '*McCabe & Mrs. Miller*: Altman's Showdown with the Western', *Genre Creative Screenwriting*, 4:3, 97–111.

Bay, Willow (1998) 'Test audiences have profound effect on movies', *CNN Newsstand*, 28 September; http://www.cnn.com/SHOWBIZ/Movies/9809/28/screen.test/

Billington, Michael (2007) *Harold Pinter*. 2nd edition. London: Faber & Faber.

Billman, Carol W. (1978) 'Illusions of Grandeur: Altman, Kopit, and the Legends of the Wild West', *Literature Film Quarterly*, 6:3, 253–61.

Biskind, Peter (1998) *Easy Riders, Raging Bulls: How the Sex-Drugs-and-Rock 'n' Roll Generation Saved Hollywood*. New York: Simon & Schuster.

Boddy, Kasia (2000) '*Short Cuts* and Long Shots: Raymond Carver's Stories and Robert Altman's Film', *Journal of American Studies*, 34:1, 1–23.

Boozer, Jack (2013) 'Novelist-screenwriter Versus Auteur Desire: *The Player*', *Journal of Film and Video*, 65:1/2, 75–87.

Boylan, Paul C. (1993) 'Artists in the Academy', *Presidential Lecture Series on Academic Values*. Ann Arbor: University of Michigan, 49–60.

Breskin, David (1992) 'The *Rolling Stone* Interview: Robert Altman', *Rolling Stone*, 628, 16 April, 72.

Brussat, Frederic and Mary Ann Brussat (n.d.) Review of *Buffalo Bill and the Indians*, *Spirituality&Practice:ResourcesforSpiritualJourneys*;http://www.spiritualityandpractice. com/films/reviews/view/2778/buffalo-bill-and-the-indians

Cagin, Seth and Philip Dray (1994) *Born to be Wild: Hollywood and the Sixties Generation*. 2nd edition. Boca Raton, FL: Coyote.

Canby, Vincent (1995) 'Film: Nixon Tale, 'Secret Honor' *New York Times*, 7 June; http:// www.nytimes.com/movie/review?res=9F0DE2DA1539F934A35755C0A963948260

Cardullo, Robert J. (1976) 'The Space in the Distance: A Study of Altman's *Nashville*', *Literature Film Quarterly*, 76:4, 313.

Carson, Tom (2002) 'McCabe and Mrs. Kael: Robert Altman's New *Gosford Park* Sends our Reviewer on a Trek through the 1970s "Golden Age." But how golden was it?' *Esquire*, 137:1, 38–41.

Carver, Raymond (1993) *Short Cuts: Selected Stories*. Introduction by Robert Altman. New York: Vintage Contemporaries.

Cohn, Ruby (1962) 'The World of Harold Pinter', *Tulane Drama Review*, 6, 55–7.

Coles, Robert (1993) 'Compassion from Carver, Swagger from Altman', *New York Times*, 17 October, H1, 25.

Combow, Robert C. (1979) 'Quintet', *Movietone News*, 62/3, 29 December, 47.

Combs, Richard (1997) 'Kansas City, Kansas City', *Film Comment*, 33:2, 68–71.

____ (2007) 'Robert Altman: Death and the Maidens', *Sight & Sound*, 17:2, 14–17.

Comolli, Jean Louis and Jean Narboni (1976) 'Cinema/Ideology/Criticism', trans. Susan Bennett, in Bill Nichols (ed.) *Movies and Methods: An Anthology*. Berkeley, CA: University of California Press, 22–30.

Corry, John (1988a) 'Tanner '88: A Satire on Presidential Campaigns', *The New York Times*, 15 February, C20.

____ (1988b) 'Tanner '88: For Real', A Campaign', *The New York Times*, 15 March, C18.

Cribbs, John (n.d.) '*A Perfect Couple*', *The Pink Smoke*; http://www.thepinksmoke.com/ perfectcouple.htm

Danks, Adrian (2000) 'Just Some Jesus Looking for a Manger: *McCabe & Mrs. Miller*', *Senses of Cinema*, September; http://sensesofcinema.com/2000/cteq/mccabe/

____ (2010) '*Hell's Highway, The Elusive Pimpernel* and *Brewster McCloud*', *Quarterly Review of Film and Video*, 27:5, 355–8.

____ (ed.) (2015) *A Companion to Robert Altman*. Oxford: Wiley-Blackwell.

Debord, Guy (2000) *Society of the Spectacle*. Detroit, MI: Black & Red.

Decker, Christof (2007) '"Irony is a Cheap Shot": Robert Altman, Luis Buñuel, and the Maneuvers of Comic Deconstruction', *American Studies*, 5:1, 63–79.

Delson, James (1979) '*Quintet*: the Altman Interview', *Fantastic Films*, June 24–30.

Demory, Pamela (1999) "'It's about Seeing…": Representations of the Female Body in Robert Altman's *Short Cuts* and Raymond Carver's Stories', *Pacific Coast Philology*, 34:1, 96–105.

Denby, David (1979) 'Glamorous Shadows', *New York Magazine*, 12, 19 February, 80–1.

Di Piero, W. S. (1978) 'Wish and Power: Recent Altman', *Chicago Review*, 3:1, 34–51.

Dorey, Tom (2015) 'Lawful Lawyer, Vigilante Father: Atman, Masculinity and "The Gingerbread Man"', in Adrian Danks (ed.) *A Companion to Robert Altman*. Oxford: Wiley Blackwell, 401–21.

Dunkle, Robert J. (1987) *The Long Goodbye: Raymond Chandler's Novel and Robert Altman's Film*. [Doctoral dissertation] Ann Arbor, MI: UMI.

Durham, Chris Louis (2010) "'We Must be Doing Something Right to Last Two Hundred Years": *Nashville*, or America's Bicentennial as Viewed by Robert Altman', *Wide Screen*, 1:2, 1–16.

Ebert, Roger (1971) Review of *McCabe & Mrs. Miller*; http://www.rogerebert.com/reviews/mccabe-and-mrs-miller

_____ (1974) Review of *Thieves Like Us*; http://www.rogerebert.com/reviews/thieves-like-us

_____ (1987) Review of *Beyond Therapy*; http://www.rogerebert.com/reviews/beyond-therapy

_____ (1993) Review of *Short Cuts*; http://www.rogerebert.com/reviews/short-cuts

_____ (2000) Review of *Dr. T and the Women*; http://www.rogerebert.com/reviews/dr-t-and-the-women

_____ (2003) Review of *The Company*; http://www.rogerebert.com/reviews/the-company

_____ (2006) Review of *A Prairie Home Companion*; http://www.rogerebert.com/interviews/eberts-altman-home-companion

Edelstein, David (2004) Review of *The Company*, *Slate*; http://www.slate.com/articles/arts/movies/2004/01/good_company.html

Edmundson, Mark (2008) 'Alone at the Movies: My days in the dark with Robert Altman and Woody Allen', *American Scholar*, 77:1, 63–73.

Epstein, Grace (1996) 'At the Intersection: Configuring Women's Differences through Narrative in Norman's *Third and Oak: The Laundromat*', in Linda Ginter-Brown (ed.) *Marsha Norman: A Casebook*. London: Routledge, 27–46.

Farber, Stephen (1977) 'California Dreaming: Altman's *3 Women*', *New West*, 9 May, 83–4.

Feineman, Neil (1978) *Persistence of Vision: The Films of Robert Altman*. New York: Arno Press.

Fellowes, Julian (2002) *Gosford Park: The Shooting Script*. Screenplay and Afterword by Julian Fellowes; Introduction by Robert Altman. New York: Newmarket Press.

Ferncase, Richard K. (1991) 'Robert Altman's *The Long Goodbye*: Marlowe in the Me Decade', *Journal of Popular Culture*, 25:2, 87–90.

Fitrakis, Bob and Harvey Wasserman (2014) 'George Will Confirms Nixon's Vietnam Treason', *Common Dreams*; http://www.commondreams.org/views/2014/08/12/george-will-confirms-nixons-vietnam-treason

Fitzgerald, F. Scott (1934) *Tender is the Night*. New Yiork: Scribner's.

Foundas, Scott (2007) 'The Sundance Kids', *Miami New Times*, 1 February; http://www.miaminewtimes.com/film/the-sundance-kids-6334856

Funderburg, Christopher (n.d.) '*A Wedding*', *The Pink Smoke*; http://www.thepinksmoke.com/wedding.htm

Funke, Lewis (1969) 'Origin of "Indians" Recalled by Kopit', *New York Times*, 15 October, 37.

Gabbard, Krin (1980) 'Altman's *3 Women*', *Literature Film Quarterly*, 8:4, 258–63.

_____ (2000) 'Kansas City Dreamin': Robert Altman's Jazz History Lesson', in James Buhler (ed.) *Music and Cinema*. Hanover, NH: University Press of New England, 142–57.

Gates, Philippa (2004) 'Always a Partner in Crime: Black Masculinity in the Hollywood Detective Film', *Journal of Popular Film and Television*, 32:1, 20–9.

Gilbey, Ryan (2003) *It Don't Worry Me: Nashville, Jaws, Star Wars, and Beyond*. London: Faber & Faber.

Giles, Paul (1991) 'The Cinema of Catholicism: John Ford and Robert Altman', in Lester D. Friedman (ed.) *Unspeakable Images: Ethnicity and the American Cinema*. Urbana, IL: University of Illinois Press, 140–66.

Giroux, Henry A. (2011) *Zombie Politics and Culture in the Age of Casino Capitalism*. New York: Peter Lang.

Gleiberman, Owen (2004) Review of *The Company*, *Entertainment Weekly*; http://www.ew.com/article/2004/01/08/company

Graham, Peter W. (2002) 'From Mansfield Park to Gosford Park: The English Country House from Austen to Altman', *Persuasions: Journal of the Jane Austen Society of North America*, 24, 211–25.

Griffiths, Mark (n.d.) 'Acting Up: Do Gambling Films Accurately Portray Pathological Gambling?; http://drmarkgriffiths.wordpress.com/2012/03/23/acting-up-do-gambling-films-accurately-portray-pathological-gambling/

Gritten, David (2001) 'You Rang, Mr. Altman?', *The Telegraph*, 1 September; http://www.telegraph.co.uk/culture/4725388/You-Rang-Mr-Altman.html

Gussow, Mel (1983) 'Stage: 'Secret Honor: Nixon after the Pardon', *New York Times*, 11 November; http://www.nytimes.com/1983/11/11/theater/stage-secret-honor-nixon-after-the-pardon.html

Haas, Michael (n.d) 'Cookie's Fortune', *Political Film Society*; http://www.polfilms.com/cookie.html

Haney, Jeff (2008) 'Nobody writes gambling as well', *Las Vegas Sun*, 8 July.

Hanuaer, Joan (1988) 'Miniseries Madness!', *Boston Herald*, 7 May, 33.

Haskell, Molly (1974) 'Bankrobbers Set Adrift', *Village Voice*, 21 February, 63.

Henry, Buck (1993) 'Back Road to Short Cuts', *Film Comment*, 29:5, 34–35, 37–38, 40.

Hoberman, J. (2004) '*Nashville* contra *Jaws*, or "The Imagination of Disaster Revisited"', in Alexander Horwath, Thomas Elsaesser and Noel King (eds) *The Last Great American Picture Show: New Hollywood Cinema in the 1970s*. Amsterdam: Amsterdam University Press, 195–222.

Hohenadel, Kristin (2003) 'In Good Company: Legendary Director Robert Altman's *The Company* shows the Sweat, Tears, and Bloody Feet that Turn Dance into Art at the Joffrey Ballet', *Dance Magazine*, 77:12, 52–5.

Holbrook, Morris (2011) *Music, Movies, Meanings, and Markets: Cinemajazzamatazz*. New York: Routledge.

Holtzclaw, Robert Paul (1992) 'A New Stage: Neoformalist Analysis of Robert Altman's Theater-to-Film Adaptations of the 1980s', *Dissertation Abstracts International*, 52 (12): 4123A.

Horyn, Cathy (1993) 'Rober Altman Confronts His Critics; "Short Cuts" Has Been Called Misogynistic and Callous. The Director Replies, "So What?"', *Washington Post*, 31 October, G-1.

Howe, Desson (1993) '*Short Cuts*', *Washington Post*, 22 October; 50.

Johnson, R. Skip (n.d.) 'Escaping Conflict and the Drama Triangle', BPDFamily.com

Jones, Kent (2006) 'It Don't Worry Me: With *A Prairie Home Companion* Robert Altman Relinquishes his Firebrand Iconoclasm and Embraces the Serene Grace of an Old Master', *Film Comment* ,42.3: 30–34.

Jung, Carl Gustav (1953) *Two Essays on Analytical Psychology*, trans. R. F. C. Hull. Princeton NJ: Princeton University Press.

Kael, Pauline (1979) 'The Altman Bunker', *New Yorker*, 55, 26 February, 100–1.

_____ (1982) *5001 Nights at the Movies*. New York: Henry Holt.

Kagan, Norman (1982) *American Skeptic: Robert Altman's Genre-Commentary Films*. Ann Arbor, MI: Pierian Press.

Karp, Alan (1981) *Films of Robert Altman*. Metuchen, NJ: Scarecrow Press.

Kass, Judith M. (1978) *Robert Altman: American Innovator*. New York: Popular Library.

Kauffmann, Stanley (1979) 'Conspicuous Presumption', *New Republic*, 180, 24 February, 24.

Keane, Marian (2003) 'Robert Altman's Films and Tom Hopkins' Criticism of Them', *Film International*, 1:6, 34–49.

Keillor, Garrison (2006) *A Prairie Home Companion: The Screenplay*. New York: Penguin.

Kempley, Rita (1993) 'Short Cuts: Back Road to Hell', *Washington Post*, 22 October, C1, C4.

Kent, Leticia (1981) 'Robert Altman Turns to the Stage', *The New York Times*, 11 October, A.3.

Keyssar, Helene (1991) *Robert Altman's America*. New York: Oxford University Press.

Kirshner, Jonathan (2012) *Hollywood's Last Golden Age: Politics, Society, and the Seventies in America*. Ithaca, NY: Cornell University Press.

Kloman, Harry and Lloyd Michaels (1983) '"A Foolish Optimist": Interview with Robert Altman', *Film Criticism*, 7:3, 20–8.

Kolker, Robert (2011) *A Cinema of Loneliness*. 4th edition. Oxford: Oxford University Press.

Kuwabara, Yoshihiro (2010) 'The Ensemble Films of Robert Altman: Originated from a Consideration of Subliminal Reality', *Bigaku: The Japanese Journal of Aesthetics*, 61:1, 133–44.

Ladd, Margaret (1977) 'The Making of Robert Altman's *A Wedding*: An Actress's Point of View', unpublished manuscript (Robert Altman Archive, University of Michigan).

Landon, Paul (2013) 'Mapping a Modern Diegesis: Terre des Hommes and Robert Altman's *Quintet*', *Journal for Artistic Research*, 4; http://www.researchcatalogue.net/view/17834/52616/4700/1230

Lasch, Christopher (1977) *Haven in a Heartless World: The Family Besieged*. New York: W. W. Norton.

Lewis, Jon (ed.) (1998) *The New American Cinema*. Durham, NC: Duke University Press.

Luck, Trust and Ketchup: Robert Altman in Carver Country. Directors John Door and Mike E. Kaplan. EZTV Productions, 1993.

Magee, Gayle Sherwood (2008) 'Song, Genre, and Transatlantic Dialogue in *Gosford Park*', *Journal of the Society for American Music*, 2:4, 477–505.

_____ (2010) 'Marketing the Voice: Opera, Film, and the Case of Robert Altman', *Theatre Survey*, 51:2, 191–224.

_____ (2012) 'Songwriting, Advertising, and Mythmaking in the New Hollywood: the Case of *Nashville* (1975)', *Music and the Moving Image*, 5:3, 28–46.

_____ (2014) *Robert Altman's Soundtracks: Film, Music, and Sound from M*A*S*H to A Prairie Home Companion*. New York: Oxford University Press.

Mahar, Ted (1974) 'Radio Plays Talking Role in Altman Film', *Oregonian*, 30 June, 83.

Makuch, Susan (1984) 'Altman's Film Rolls on Martha Cook', *Michigan Daily*, 29 January, 1–2.

Man, Glenn (2008) '*Short Cuts* to *Gosford Park*: The Family in Robert Altman', in Murray Pomerance (ed.) *A Family Affair: Cinema Calls Home*. London and New York: Wallflower Press, 161–73.

Maslin, Janet (1994) 'Altman's Swipe At Fashion', *New York Times*, 23 December, C1, C10.

Masson, Alain (1979) '*Reguiler et Impair* (Quintet)', *Positif*, 216, 2–6.

McCarthy, Todd (1993) Review: *Short Cuts*; http://variety.com/1993/film/reviews/short-cuts-2-1200433451/

McClelland, C. Kirk (1971) *On Making a Movie: 'Brewster McCloud' – A Day-by-day Journal of the On-location Shooting of the Film in Houston*. New York: New American Library.

McElhaney, Joe (2015) '3 Women: Floating About the Awful Abyss', in Adrian Danks (ed.) *A Companion to Robert Altman*. Oxford: Wiley Blackwell, 146–65.

McGilligan, Patrick (1989) *Robert Altman: Jumping Off the Cliff – A Biography of the Great American Director*. New York: St. Martin's.

Melehy, Hassan (2009) 'Narratives of Politics and History in the Spectacle of Culture: Robert Altman's *Nashville*', *Scope: An Online Journal of Film Studies*, 13; http://xy4uu4wv3h.search. serialssolutions.com/?ctx_ver=Z39.88-2004&ctx_enc=info%3Aofi%2Fenc%3AUTF-8&rfr_id=info:sid/summon.serialssolutions.com&rft_val_fmt=info:ofi/fmt: kev:mtx:journal&rft.genre=article&rft.atitle=Narratives+of+Politics+and+History+in+th e+Spectacle+of+Culture%3A+Robert+Altman%27s+Nashville&rft.jtitle=Scope%3A+A n+Online+Journal+of+Film+Studies&rft.au=Melehy%2C+Hassan&rft.date=2009&rft. issn=1465-9166&rft.eissn=1465-9166&rft.volume=13&rft.externalDocID=R04206900

Menaker, Dan (1971) 'Letter to the Editor', *New York Times*, 15 August, D12.

Merrill, Robert (1990) 'Altman's *McCabe and [sic] Mrs. Miller* as a Classic Western', *The New Orleans Review*, 17:2, 80–6.

Milne, Tom (1981) 'Robert Altman: Backgammon and Spinach', *Sight & Sound* , 50:2, 182–6.

Mobilio, Albert (1999) 'Robert Altman', *BOMB*, 68, 24–30.

Morreale, Joanne (2009) '*Tanner '88* ', in Gary Edgerton and Jeffrey P. Jones (eds) *The Essential HBO Reader*. Lexington, KY: University Press of Kentucky, 103–15.

Muir, John Kenneth (n.d.) '*Quintet*: The Thoughtful Essay I Wish I'd Written'; http:// seedyroad.com/diversions/quintet.htm

Murphy, Kathleen (1994) 'A Lion's Gate: The Cinema According to Robert Altman', *Film Comment*, 30:2, 20.

Murphy, Mary (1977) 'Crisis of a Cult Figure', *New West*, 23 May, 36–42.

Newman, Kim (2014) 'Street Legal', *Sight & Sound*, 24:2, 34–7.

O'Brien, Adam (2013) 'Regarding Things in *Nashville* and *The Exterminating Angel*: Another Path for Eco-Film Criticism', *ISLE: Interdisciplinary Studies in Literature & Environment*, 20:2, 258–73.

O'Brien, Daniel (1995) *Robert Altman: Hollywood Survivor*. New York: Continuum.

Olderman, Murray (1976) 'Buffalo Bill Production Shoots Holes in Heroes', *Naples [FL] Daily News*, 18 July, 36.

Oliver, Bill (1975) '*The Long Goodbye* and *Chinatown*: Debunking the Private Eye Tradition', *Literature Film Quarterly*, 3:3, 240–8.

O'Neill, Michael C. (1982) 'History as Dramatic Present: Arthur L. Kopit's *Indians*', *Theatre Journal*, 34:4, 493–504.

Parshall, Peter F. (2012) *Altman and After: Multiple Narratives in Film*. Lanham, MD: Scarecrow Press.

Panek, LeRoy Lad (1990) *Probable Cause: Crime Fiction in America*. Bowling Green, OH: Bowling Green State University Popular Press.

The Pervert's Guide to Ideology. Director: Sophie Fiennes. Performer: Slavoj Žižek. P Guide Productions/Zeitgeist Films, 2012.

Plecki, Gerard (1985) *Robert Altman*. Boston, MA: Twayne.

Plumb, Catherine (1974) '*Thieves Like Us*: Mississippi Dreamin'', *Jump Cut*, 2, 5–6.

Priggé, Steven (ed.) (2004) *Movie Moguls Speak: Interviews with Top Film Producers*. Jefferson, NC: McFarland.

Puig, Claudia (1997) 'Altman May Take His Name off Film; Movies: The director is in another dispute with a studio – this time with Polygram Pictures over a re-edit of his latest, 'The Gingerbread Man',' *Los Angeles Times*, 9 August, F, 1:5.

Raab, Josef (2002) 'De-/Constructing Screen Identities: Robert Altman's *The Player*', in Marietta Messmer and Josef Raab (eds) *American Vistas and Beyond*. Trier: Wissenschaftlicher, 179–96.

Raab, Scott (2004) 'Robert Altman', *Esquire*, 141:2, 110–11.

Reid, Max (1974) 'The Making of *California Split*: An Interview with Robert Altman', *Filmmakers Newsletter*, 7:12, 24–17.

Rice, Glenn E. and Matthew Schofield (1995) 'Movie Recalls Gangster "Seldom Seen"', *Bangor Daily News*, 17 July, C6–7.

Rich, Frank (1982) 'Robert Altman Directs Cher', *New York Times*, 19 February, C3.

Richolson, Janice (1992) 'The Player: An Interview with Robert Altman', *Cineaste*, 19:2/3, 61.

Rickey, Carrie (1977) 'Fassbinder and Altman: Approaches to Filmmaking', *Performing Arts Journal*, 2:2, 1 October, 33–48.

_____ (1992) 'Tarnishing the Gilded Age: Robert Altman Directs *McTeague*', *Opera News*, 57, 18–20.

Ridley, Jim (2015) 'Major Robert Altman Retrospective: *Nashville* at 40, Belcourt at 90', *Nashville Scene*, 13 May; http://www.nashvillescene.com/countrylife/archives/2015/05/13/major-robert-altman-retrospective-nashville-at-40-belcourt-at-90

Roddick, Nick (2007) 'Driving with Robert Altman', *Sight & Sound*, 17:1, 4–5.

Rollin, Roger B. (1977) 'Robert Altman's *Nashville*: Popular Film and the American Character', *South Atlantic Bulletin*, 4:4, 41–50.

Rosenbaum, Jonathan (n.d.) 'California Split Reunited', *Stop Smiling*, 35 (The Gambling Issue); http://www.stopsmilingonline.com/story_detail.php?id=1099

_____ (1975) 'Improvisations and Interactions in Altmanville', *Sight & Sound*, 44:1, 90–5.

Ruppersburg, Hugh (2011) 'American Dreams and Country Music: *Nashville* and *Payday*', in Andrew B. Leiter (ed.) *Southerners on Film: Essays on Hollywood Portrayals since the 1970s*. Jefferson, NC: McFarland, 76–88.

Ryan, Michael and Douglas Kellner (1988) *Camera Politica: The Politics and Ideology of Contemporary Hollywood Film*. Bloomington, IN: Indiana University Press.

Sanjek, David (1991) 'A Case for Robert Altman', *Literature Film Quarterly*, 19:1, 66–9.

Sarris, Andrew (1977) 'Robert Altman Dreams a Movie…', *Village Voice*, 11 April, 40, 42.

_____ (1996) *The American Cinema: Directors and Directions 1929–1968*. New York: Da Capo Press.

Sawyer, David (1996) '"Yet Why Not Say What Happened?": Boundaries of the Self in Raymond Carver's Fiction and Robert Altman's *Short Cuts*', in Klaus H. Schmidt and David Sawyer (eds) *Blurred Boundaries: Critical Essays on American Literature, Language, and Culture.* Frankfurt: Peter Lang, 195–219.

Schrader, Paul (1972) 'Notes on Film Noir', *Film Comment*, 8:1, 8–13.

Schroeder, Alan (1997) '*Thieves Like Us*: Altman and Tewkesbury's Faulkner', *Creative Screenwriting*, 4:3, 24–32.

Schuyler, Michael T. (2005) '"Traffic Was a Bitch": Gender, Race and Spectatorship in Robert Altman's *The Player*', *Journal of Narrative Theory*, 35:2, 218–47.

Schweizer, Harold (1999) 'Robert Altman's *Short Cuts*: A Phenomenology of Reading', *Q/W/E/R/T/Y: Arts, Littératures & Civilisations du Monde Anglophone* 9, 169–75.

Scofield, Martin (1996) 'Closer to Home: Carver versus Altman', *Studies in Short Fiction*, 33:3, 387–99.

Scott, John and Gordon Marshall (1998) *A Dictionary of Sociology.* New York: Oxford University Press.

Self, Robert T. (1983) 'The Perfect Couple: "Two Are Halves of One"' in the Films of Robert Altman', *Wide Angle: A Film Quarterly of Theory, Criticism, and Practice*, 5:4, 30–7.

_____ (1985) 'Robert Altman and the Theory of Authorship', *Cinema Journal*, 2:1, 3–11.

_____ (2002) *Robert Altman's Subliminal Reality.* Minneapolis, MN: University of Minnesota Press.

_____ (2004) 'Resisting Reality: Acting by Design in Robert Altman's *Nashville*', in Cynthia Baron, Diane Carson and Frank P. Tomasulo (eds) *More Than a Method: Trends and Traditions in Contemporary Film Performance.* Detroit, MI: Wayne State University Press, 126–50.

_____ (2005) 'The Modernist Art Cinema of Robert Altman', *Senses of Cinema*, 34; http://sensesofcinema.com/2005/great-directors/altman/

_____ (2007) *Robert Altman's McCabe & Mrs. Miller: Reframing the American West.* Lawrence, KS: University Press of Kansas.

Self, Robert T. and Terry F. Robinson (2000) 'Troubled Masculinity and Abusive Fathers: Duality and Duplicity in *The Gingerbread Man*', *Journal of Film and Video*, 52:2, 41–55.

Shor, Francis (1984) 'Biographical Moments in the Written and Cinematic Text: Deconstructing the Legends of Joe Hill and Buffalo Bill', *Film & History: An Interdisciplinary Journal of Film and Television Studies*, 14:3, 61–8.

Shulgasser, Barbara (1994) 'House of Altman', *Vanity Fair*, 37:11, 174–84.

Smith, Gavin and Richard T. Jameson (1992) '"The Movie You Saw is the Movie we're Going to Make"', *Film Comment*, 28:3, 22–31.

Slotkin, Richard (1998) *Gunfighter Nation: The Myth of the Frontier in Twentieth-Century America.* Norman: OK: University of Oklahoma Press.

_____ (2000) *Regeneration through Violence: The Mythology of the American Frontier, 1600–1860.* Norman: OK: University of Oklahoma Press.

Soares, Marcos (2007) 'A Note on the Regressive Side of Modernization in Relation to Two Films by Robert Altman', *Colloquy: Text Theory Critique*, 14, 74–80.

Sragow, Michael (2000) 'The Sad and Hilarious Tale of Dr. T. and the Big D', *Salon*, 12 October; http://www.salon.com/2000/10/12/altman_2/

Sterritt, David (ed.) (2000) *Robert Altman: Interviews.* Jackson, MS: University Press of Mississippi.

Stevens, Dana (2004) 'Primary Colours: Robert Altman's Tanner '88 Exposes the Fiction of Democracy', *Slate*, 4 February; http://www.slate.com/articles/arts/television/2004/02/primary_colours.html

Stevens Jr., George (ed.) (2012) *Conversations at the American Film Institute with the Great Moviemakers: The Next Generation from the 1950s to Hollywood Today*. New York: Random House.

Stewart, Robert (1993) 'Reimagining Raymond Carver on Film: A Talk with Robert Altman and Tess Gallagher', *New York Times Book Review*, 12 September, 3, 31–2.

Stone, Leonard A. (2003) 'Harold Pinter and the Fragmentation of Working-Class Consciousness', *Cultural Logic: An Electronic Journal of Marxist Theory & Practice*, 6; http://clogic.eserver.org/2003/stone.html

Stuart, Jan (2000) *The Nashville Chronicles: The Making of Robert Altman's Masterpiece*. New York: Simon & Schuster.

Sugg, Richard P. (2001) 'William R. Robinson's Philosophy of Image-Freedom and Robert Altman's *The Player* and *Short Cuts*', in Richard P. Sugg (ed.) *Seeing Beyond: Movies, Visions, and Values*. New York: Golden String, 319–30.

Sundquist, Eric (1982) 'The Country of the Blue', in *American Realism: New Essays*. John Hopkins University Press.

Sutpen, Tom (2005) 'The Nixon of Our Dreams? On Robert Altman's *Secret Honor*', *Bright Lights Film Journal*; http://brightlightsfilm.com/nixon-dreams-robert-altmans-secret-honor/#.VV-pI_m-0us

Thompson, David (ed.) (2006) *Altman on Altman*. London: Faber & Faber.

Thomson, David (2000) 'Robert Altman's Decade of Astonishments', *New York Times*, 11 June, 2, 13.

Tibbetts, John C. (1992) 'Robert Altman: After 35 years, still the "Action Painter" of American Cinema', *Literature Film Quarterly* 20:1, 36–42.

Tobias, Scott (2014) 'How Robert Altman Turned *Popeye* into an Altman movie', *The Dissolve*, 9 April; https://thedissolve.com/features/departures/503-how-robert-altman-turned-popeye-into-an-altman-movie/

Tönnies, Ferdinand ([1887] 2001) *Gemeinschaft und Gesellschaft*, 8th edition. Leipzig: Buske.

Turner, Michael (2006) 'Robert Altman's Vancouver', *Pacific Cinematque*. http://web.archive.org/web/20061010093513/http://www.cinematheque.bc.ca/sept_oct_06/turner.html

Volkan, Vamik D. and Norman Itzkowit (1997) *Richard Nixon: A Psychobiography*. New York: Columbia University Press.

Van Vert, William F. (1974) 'Philip Marlowe: Hardboiled to Softboiled to Poached', *Jump Cut*, 3, 10–13.

_____ (1991) '*Vincent and Theo* [Review essay]', *Film Quarterly*, 45:1, 37–41.

Vineberg, Steve (2012) 'Neglected Gem #24: *The Gingerbread Man* (1998)', *Critics At Large*, 21 September; http://www.criticsatlarge.ca/2012/09/neglected-gem-24-ginger-bread-man.html

Walsh, David (2001) 'Class Analysis and Feeling Mean a Great Deal: *Gosford Park*, directed by Robert Altman', *World Socialist Web Site*, 28 December; http://www.wsws.org/en/articles/2001/12/gosf-d28.html

Walsh, Joseph (2008) 'Online Exclusive: JOSEPH WALSH, Screenwriter of *California Split*', *Stop Smiling* 35, 15 June; http://stopsmilingonline.com/story_detail.php?id=1093&page=1

Warren, Charles (2006) 'Cavell, Altman and Cassavetes', *Film International*, 4:22, 14–20.

Warren, Steve (1977) '*3 Women* and Many Men', *The Advocate*, 27 July, 29.

Werrett, June (2003) 'Making the Old New Again: Robert Altman's *Prêt-à-Porter*', *Film Journal*, 7, http://www.thefilmjournal.com/issue7/altman.html

Wexman, Virginia Wright and Gretchen Bisplinghoff (1984) *Robert Altman: A Guide to References and Resources*. Boston, MA: G. K. Hall.

Wilmington, Michael (1995) 'Robert Altman and *The Long Goodbye*', in Jerry Roberts (ed.) *Movie Talk from the Front Lines: Filmmakers Discuss Their Works with the Los Angeles Film Critics Association*. Jefferson, NC: McFarland, 253–73.

Wilson, R. L. (1998) *Buffalo Bill's Wild West: An American Legend*. New York: Random House.

Windreich, Leland (2004) Review of *The Company*, *Ballet Dance*; http://www.ballet-dance.com/200402/articles/companymovie2.html

Woideck, Carl (1998) *Charlie Parker: His Music and Life*. Ann Arbor, MI: University of Michigan Press.

Wood, Robin (1986) *Hollywood from Vietnam to Reagan*. New York: Columbia University Press.

_____ (2009) 'Ideology, Genre, Auteur', in Leo Braudy and Marshall Cohen (eds) *Film Theory and Criticism*. 7th edition. New York: Oxford University Press, 592–601.

Wyatt, Justin (1996) 'Economic Constraints/Economic Opportunities: Robert Altman as Auteur', *Velvet Light Trap*, Fall, 51–68.

_____ (1998) 'The Formation of the "Major Independent": Miramax, New Line and the New Hollywood', in Steve Neale and Murray Smith (eds) *Contemporary Hollywood Cinema*. New York: Routledge, 74–90.

Yacowar, Maurice (1980) 'Actors as Conventions in the Films of Robert Altman', *Cinema Journal*, 2:1, 14–28.

Zuckoff, Mitchell (2009) *Robert Altman: The Oral Biography*. New York: Knopf.

INDEX

Los Angeles   17, 19, 24, 28, 46, 59, 94, 99,
   101, 105n.3, 106, 115, 140–1, 150–1,
   155–6, 158n.6, 177, 199; postmodern
   landscape 47
Los Angeles Actors' Theater (aka Los Angeles
   Theater Center)   106, 115
Lucas, George   4, 89
Lust for Life   134

Majors, Glendora ('Glen')   2
Malcolm, Derek   134
Malick, Terrence   4, 55
Mandel, Johnny   25
Man Who Shot Liberty Valance   41
Marxism   2, 8, 21
masculinity: agency 184; Alpha male
   146; degraded 115; desire 152;
   guilty male 3; hero 38, 171, 184;
   heterosexual 157; ideology 27;
   machismo 12; male-centred 19;
   male-dominated 77; male drama
   111; male-oriented 12, 34; manhood
   26, 42, 59; masculinity-affirming
   potential 26, 27; mid-century
   style 49; misogynistic males 80;
   psychosexual identity 111; as a refusal
   3; remasculinising 27
M*A*S*H   3, 10, 12, 17, 24–9, 29, 34, 36,
   45, 53, 75, 141, 147–8, 151, 157, 192,
   196
M*A*S*H (tv series)   29
MASH: A Novel About Three Army Doctors
   (novel)   24
Maslin, Janet   164
masochism   60
mass celebrity culture   77
mass consumer society   54
Mayflower campus   65–7, 96
McCabe (novel)   34
McCabe & Mrs. Miller   3, 10, 17, 34–45,
   46, 51, 52–3, 62, 69, 72n.34, 93, 102,
   105n.5, 120, 135, 169
McCarthy, Todd   155
McGilligan, Patrick   2–3, 7, 14, 17, 30–1,
   36, 44–5, 52–3, 58, 61, 73, 83, 85, 88,
   93, 100–1, 123, 126
Mercer, Johnny   47
MGM   30–1, 33, 57–8, 104
Midnight Cowboy   23, 61, 100

Miles, Richard (aka Peter)   14
Mileti, Nick J.   111
military culture   111, 114
Miramax Films   160, 192–3, 197
mirror images   107, 168, 192
mise-en-scène   6, 53, 91, 97, 107, 122
misogyny   27, 153, 157, 184
Model's Handbook, The   159
mosaics   10, 63, 97, 150, 155, 160, 196
MPAA   23
Mr. Roberts   25
myth/mythology   63, 65–6, 69, 95, 107,
   135; bourgeois 6, 65; crime 55;
   deconstruct the 9; demythification
   135; Greek 29–30, 197; monomyth
   70n.5; myth-making 65; old folk 54;
   paradigms 162; romantic 39, 40, 57,
   134

narcissism   29, 17, 142, 170, 182; in
   American society 157
narrative   1, 5–6, 29, 47–9, 51, 54, 57, 61,
   78, 93, 121, 143, 147, 155, 185, 194,
   195; American 76; audience-tested
   144; cinematic 6, 14, 33; classical 21;
   of Desire 199n.3; Hollywood 136;
   ideological 83; no narrative 164;
   romance 95; sub-narrative 78
Nashville   6, 10, 62, 73–83, 85, 87–8,
   88n.n.3,4, 94, 96, 102, 105n.8, 118,
   123, 131, 142, 151, 160–2, 164, 193,
   197
Nashville 12   123
Native Americans   63, 65
Naughton, Edmund   34, 37, 43,
   71n.n.20,26, 72n.30
Neal, Patricia   178, 180
Network   98
New American Cinema   4, 12–13, 24, 89,
   105n.2
Newman, Paul   62, 64, 69, 91, 192–3
New York   4, 30, 41, 63, 66, 100, 106, 107,
   111, 115, 118–19, 140, 149, 177, 185,
   192–93, 197
New York Times (newspaper)   62, 107, 115,
   133, 155, 164, 172
Nicholls, Allan   66, 85, 88n.2, 91, 94–5,
   100, 115
Night of the Hunter, The   174